Study Guide

UNDERSTANDING ABNORMAL BEHAVIOR

Study Guide

Arthur G. Olguin
Santa Barbara City College

UNDERSTANDING ABNORMAL BEHAVIOR

Sixth Edition

David Sue
Western Washington University

Derald Sue
California School of Professional Psychology, Alameda
California State University, Hayward

Stanley Sue
University of California, Los Angeles

HOUGHTON MIFFLIN COMPANY BOSTON NEW YORK

Editor-in-Chief: Kathi Prancan
Senior Sponsoring Editor: Kerry Baruth
Associate Editor: Marianne Stepanian
Manufacturing Manager: Florence Cadran
Senior Marketing Manager: Pamela J. Laskey

Printed in the U.S.A.

ISBN: 0–395–959446

3456789– CRS–03 02 01

CONTENTS

TO THE STUDENT

This *Study Guide* was designed to help you master the material in the Sixth Edition of *Understanding Abnormal Behavior* by Sue/Sue/Sue. The *Study Guide* supplements the text but does not replace it. If used properly, it should help you to understand and master key facts, concepts, and issues discussed in the text.

Organization of the *Study Guide*

Each *Study Guide* chapter corresponds to a text chapter and is divided into the following sections: Learning Objectives, Chapter Outline, Key Terms Review, and Multiple-Choice Questions.

- ***Learning Objectives*** The learning objectives guide your mastery of the material by focusing your attention on the key ideas and concepts in each chapter. Page numbers corresponding to the objectives have been identified to encourage you to use the text and Study Guide interactively for maximum benefit.

- ***Chapter Outlines*** The outlines present the major ideas and topics in each chapter. Key terms are defined and page numbers corresponding to the outline material are provided. The outlines are condensed overviews of chapter material and are excellent review mechanisms. But they cannot and should not be used as substitutes for reading the chapter.

- ***Key Terms Review*** Key terms appearing at the end of each chapter in the text are also defined in the chapter outlines. To further reinforce your mastery of these terms, we provide fill-in-the-blank quizzes. This three-pronged approach to learning should strengthen your command of the terminology common to abnormal psychology.

- ***Multiple-Choice Questions*** Once you have read the text and worked your way through the first three sections of the Study Guide, you will be ready to test your knowledge of the material covered. Three sets of multiple-choice questions are provided. First, *Factual Multiple-Choice Questions* quiz your basic recall of key points in the chapter. *Conceptual Multiple-Choice Questions* add a degree of challenge by assessing your understanding of abnormal psychology concepts. These questions typically involve comparisons and contrasts, and the use of cognitive skills at a level somewhat higher than simple factual recall. Last, *Application Multiple-Choice Questions* present situations in which you will assess, diagnose, or treat the problem at hand. These application questions pose situations faced by practitioners or researchers, and challenge you to reason like a psychologist. In order to improve your understanding of the material, answers to the questions are provided with corresponding textbook page numbers referenced. In addition, a justification is provided for the incorrect answers. Don't be a passive learner. Study the reasons why you made an incorrect response. The feedback will help you sharpen your analytical skills in this class and also in other classes where similar assessment methods are used.

Study Skills

Although each student may have his or her preferred way to study a subject, research shows that many students use ineffective learning methods. Educational psychologists have studied various techniques that result in improved academic performance. Check with your professor to see whether or not your college has a learning assistance center. Typically, these centers have services to help students improve their academic success. In addition to workshops that may be offered by your college learning assistance center, an excellent printed resource is Pauk and Fiore's (1989) *Succeed in College!* Although targeted toward psychology courses, this book is recommended for all college students in any discipline and has excellent material on time management, note taking, learning from textbooks, and test-taking strategies, as well as a section on psychology and careers. One method discussed in the book is *SQ3R*, a method designed to help students read and study textbooks effectively.

The SQ3R method was developed by Francis P. Robinson, a psychologist at Ohio State University. Professor Robinson's research demonstrated that students' understanding and performance in academic courses increased by using the SQ3R method. SQ3R stands for: Survey, Question, Read, Recite, Review, and the method is outlined below.

- *Survey*. Page through the chapter, looking at the main headings and the organization of the chapter. Read the final summary of the chapter. Try to get a *gestalt* of the chapter—an overall picture of how the chapter is organized and what's to come. Why is this important? Scanning a chapter helps you develop a cognitive schema of the chapter. When you begin to read the chapter, you will have a better idea of how ideas are linked to one another, and you will organize the information you encounter more efficiently.

- *Question*. Based on your survey of the chapter, formulate some questions about the material. One way to develop questions is to turn the chapter headings into questions. Another strategy is to read the Learning Objectives in the *Study Guide* prior to reading the text material. Why is this important? When we have a question in mind, we seek to resolve the question. Presumably, this strategy makes us more active readers.

- *Read*. Actively read the chapter. Have your *Study Guide* nearby so that you can look periodically at the Chapter Outline. Break your reading into smaller segments. Don't read the entire chapter in one sitting, since there is too much material to absorb. While reading, take small breaks in between major sections of the chapter. During your break (e.g., while jogging) actively reflect on what you've read. See if you can answer the question(s) you formulated. After you have read several sections, and certainly before you quit your studying, review the Chapter Outline.

- *Recite*. Looking away from the book, briefly recite out loud the main points of the section you've read. Try to create an original example that would illustrate the concept under discussion. If a research study is discussed, summarize the main points of the research study. Another recitation strategy is to use the Key Terms Review in the *Study Guide.*

- *Review*. The Chapter Outlines in the *Study Guide* serve as a useful tool for review prior to an examination. Again, be active in your review. Look at the major headings but try to actively recite the subpoints under the heading.

You are about to embark on a fascinating journey into the world of abnormal behavior. I hope you find this *Study Guide* a helpful resource as you commence your study.

Art Olguin, Ph.D.
Santa Barbara, California

References

Pauk, W., & Fiore, J. P. (2000). *Succeed in College!* Boston: Houghton Mifflin Company (ISBN–0–395–96290–0).
Robinson, F. P. (1970). *Effective study* (4th ed.). New York: Harper & Row.

CHAPTER 1
Abnormal Behavior

LEARNING OBJECTIVES

1. Describe the primary objectives of abnormal psychology, including description, explanation, prediction, and control of abnormal behavior. (pp. 3–5)
2. Identify and distinguish between the various kinds of mental health professionals. (p. 6)
3. Identify four definitions psychologists use to define abnormal behavior and their assumptions, strengths, and limitations. (pp. 5–13)
4. Describe the multicultural perspectives in defining abnormal behavior including definitions of the terms *cultural universality* and *cultural relativism.* (pp. 7–10)
5. Distinguish between Szasz's views on mental illness and Wakefield's (1992) views of abnormal behavior, the textbook authors' definition of *abnormal behavior*, and that of the DSM-IV. (pp. 11–13)
6. Discuss how researchers determine the scope of mental disorders in the United States. (pp. 13–15)
7. Describe the most prevalent disorders and how mental disorders are influenced by age and gender. (pp. 11–12)
8. Discuss common myths concerning the mentally disturbed and the facts that refute them. (pp. 16–17)
9. Summarize the various explanations of abnormal behavior from prehistoric times through the Middle Ages. (pp. 17–20)
10. Describe the changes that occurred in the conceptualization and treatment of abnormal behavior after the era of witchcraft, including the rise of humanism and the reform movement of the eighteenth and nineteenth centuries until the present. (pp. 20–22)
11. Discuss the main assumptions of the biological and psychological viewpoints on perceptions of abnormal behavior. (pp. 22–23)
12. Discuss the contributions of mesmerism and hypnosis to the psychodynamic viewpoint. (pp. 23–24)
13. Describe the impact of the drug revolution and managed care on the mental health profession. (pp. 24–26)
14. Discuss the rise of *multicultural psychology*, and explain how social conditioning, cultural values, and sociopolitical influences may account for apparent differences in abnormality in minority groups. (pp. 26–28)
15. Explain the term *biopsychosocial approach* and its use in conceptualizing the multiple factors underlying abnormal behavior. (p. 29)

CHAPTER OUTLINE

1. **The concerns of abnormal psychology** (pp. 3–5) *Abnormal psychology* seeks to describe, explain, predict, and control those behaviors that are considered strange. In describing disorders, psychologists develop a *psychodiagnosis.* Diagnosis is a useful first step in treatment but, because of labeling, may sometimes have harmful consequences. Explanations about the causes of abnormal behavior differ depending on the psychologist's theoretical orientation. The prediction of future behavior is difficult; for instance, psychologists tend to overpredict future violent behavior. *Therapy* is the method by which psychologists try to control behavior. A growing number of individuals have entered clinical psychology and related mental health professions since 1945.

2. **The mental health professions** (pp. 5–6; Table 1.1) There are an increasing number of mental health professionals in the United States. Clinical psychologists have Ph.D. or Psy.D. degrees and are trained to assess and treat people with serious disorders. Counseling psychologists are trained in much the same way as clinical psychologists, but they traditionally treat less serious problems. School psychologists work with children and adolescents in school settings, assisting them with cognitive, social, and behavioral interventions. Psychiatrists have medical degrees and can prescribe medication. Psychoanalysts are trained in psychoanalytic institutes and engage in personal analysis. Psychiatric social workers usually get a master's degree and often work in family or community agencies. Marriage and family counseling is a new field with a wide range of training and work-setting options, but most counselors have a master's degree and many hours of supervised clinical experience.

3. **Defining abnormal behavior** (pp. 5–13) The statistical criterion defines abnormality as those behaviors that are infrequent. One problem with this standard is that it provides no consistent means for deciding what is rare and what is undesirable. For example, although high IQs are rare we do not generally consider individuals with high IQ as abnormal.

   Deviation from ideal mental health is another way to define abnormality, but there is little agreement on the positive characteristics and behaviors psychologists should choose as ideal. Further, such criteria would exclude too many people who may not meet the ideal.

   Multicultural perspectives strive for a middle ground between two opposite views. One approach is *cultural universality,* the traditional viewpoint on abnormality, which states that there are universal symptoms and disorders. The opposite is *cultural relativism,* which says that deviance designations reflect cultural values. Both approaches have merit. A central theme is what behaviors are widely considered to be abnormal given the culture and how does the culture influence the identification and treatment of abnormal behavior.

   Practical definitions for abnormality include discomfort, deviance, and dysfunction. Discomfort involves both physical and psychological pain. Deviance refers to odd behaviors, such as *hallucinations* (false sensory impressions) and *delusions* (false beliefs). *Dysfunction* is exhibited when a person's performance falls well short of his or her potential.

4. **Integrated definitions** (pp. 11–13) Since all criteria have some shortcomings, a combination of criteria may be most effective. Strupp and Hadley (1977) suggest that judgments concerning abnormality use three vantage points: the individual, the mental health professional, and society. Wakefield (1992) proposes that mental disorder be defined as a harmful dysfunction, where "harmful" is defined by societal norms and "dysfunction" is based on faulty biological processes.

5. **Two definitions of abnormal behavior** (p. 13) The authors define *abnormal behavior* as "behavior that departs from some norm and that harms the affected individual or others." The *Diagnostic and Statistical Manual of Mental Disorders (DSM-IV)* definition is similar, stressing the distress, functional impairment, risk, or loss of freedom caused by patterns of behavior.

6. **The frequency of abnormal behavior** (pp. 13–15) The goals of psychiatric epidemiology are to determine how frequent disorders are in the population, how such factors as age and gender affect their prevalence, and whether trends are changing. About 29 to 38 percent of the U.S. population have experienced at least one mental disorder. Overall, men and women are equally likely to suffer from disorders; however, men are more likely to have alcohol problems and women are more likely to become depressed or anxious. Older people are vulnerable to cognitive impairments. Fewer than one-third of people with disorders receive mental health services.

7. **Stereotypes about the mentally disturbed** (pp. 15–17) One myth is that mentally disturbed people can be readily spotted. This is not true because there are no sharp dividing lines between normality and abnormality and because some forms of deviance can be hidden. Another myth is that mental disorder is always inherited. Genetics can play a role in some disorders, but even in the few disorders where genes are thought to play a role, environmental stress is a crucial influence. Other myths are that people with mental disorders cannot be cured, that their problems stem from a lack of willpower, that those who suffer disorders contribute nothing to society, and that they are more dangerous than other people.

8. **Historical perspectives on abnormal behavior** (pp. 17–22) How people view mental disorders is related to the beliefs of their culture and time. During prehistoric times, people believed in *demonology*. Treatments included *trephining* (chipping open the skull) and *exorcism* (prayers, noisemaking, and even starvation to drive out spirits). During the Greco-Roman era, disorders were seen as being due to organic factors such as brain pathology.

   During the Dark Ages, the Catholic Church dominated all thought and explained mental disorder in supernatural terms. In the thirteenth century, whole populations were sometimes affected by such forms of mass madness as tarantism (a dance mania) and lycanthropy (in which people believe themselves to be wolves).

   Witchcraft became a common explanation for abnormal behavior during the 1500s and 1600s, when the Catholic Church was under attack. Some mentally ill people were considered witches and received brutal punishment, but most accused witches were probably sane.

   In the mid-1500s, *humanism* stressed human welfare and rejected the supernatural aspects of witchcraft. Johann Weyer asserted that people who had been thought to be witches were actually mentally disturbed. Around 1800, a reform movement called the *moral treatment movement* began in France (Philippe Pinel) and England (William Tuke). In America (Benjamin Rush), mental patients were also treated more humanely. Dorothea Dix pushed for the improvement of care for individuals with mental disorders and for the building of mental hospitals. Clifford Beers exposed the cruel treatment he and other patients experienced in mental institutions. Generally, treatment for the mentally ill has improved in this century.

9. **Causes: Early viewpoints** (pp. 22–24) Fom Hippocrates' day to our own, organic explanations of abnormality have existed. During the late 1800s, there was a strong increase in this biological *(biogenic) view*. The discovery that general paresis had an organic cause supported this idea. When certain symptoms occur in clusters, they are called *syndromes*. It was believed that each syndrome had a unique cause.

   The *psychogenic view* (that emotions can cause disorder) is an alternative view. Anton Mesmer used trances (mesmerism) to treat people with hysteria, sometimes successfully. Although he was declared a fraud, these treatments underscored the power of suggestion for curing disorder. *Hypnotism* was studied and used by several French physicians (Liebeault, Bernheim, and Charcot) to treat hysteria during the late 1800s. Breuer found that reliving past experiences (the *cathartic method*) removed symptoms, too. Sigmund Freud built upon this foundation.

10. **Contemporary trends in abnormal psychology** (pp. 24–28) Twentieth-century views of abnormality have been influenced by the introduction of psychiatric drugs in the 1950s, which led to a great reduction in patients residing in mental institutions *(deinstitutionalization)*. Psychologists have initiated legislative efforts in order to gain prescription privileges to treat individuals with mental disorders. Medical providers (psychiatrists) are opposed to non-

medical personnel having prescription privileges, and not all psychologists support psychologists' expansion into the psychopharmacological realm, fearing that psychologists will lose their own professional identity. *Managed health care*, which attempts to contain costs by increasing the oversight of treatment by outside reviewers and by requiring treatment professionals to justify their therapies, may alter the types of care provided. Professionals in abnormal psychology value research on both the biological and psychological bases of behavior. Changes in the racial and ethnic diversity of the United States have helped create a new field called *multicultural psychology*. Racial, cultural, age, and gender differences in apparent mental disorders may be explained in terms of social conditioning (stereotyping), cultural values that are taught, and sociopolitical factors such as prejudice, which prompt healthy coping mechanisms that may be seen as symptoms. Bias in diagnosis is another explanation for differences in minority mental health.

11. **Some closing thoughts** (pp. 28–30) Increasingly, professionals value a *biopsychosocial approach*, which acknowledges that biological, psychological, and social factors combine to explain most disorders. Readers may experience "medical student syndrome"—the tendency to think one has a disorder described in the text. Discussing such concerns with friends or the professor teaching the course is advised.

KEY TERMS REVIEW

1. The therapeutic use of verbal expression to release pent-up unconscious conflicts is called the ____________________.

2. The belief that mental disorders are caused by psychological or emotional factors is called the ____________________.

3. The ancient surgical technique in which part of the skull was chipped away to provide an escape for evil spirits is called ____________________.

4. The industrialization of health care, whereby organizations in the private sector control the delivery of services is called ____________________.

5. Begun by Philippe Pinel, this movement was a shift toward more humane treatment for mentally disturbed patients. It was called the ____________________.

6. A cluster of symptoms that tend to occur together, believed to be indicative of a particular disorder, is called a(n) ____________________.

7. A program of systematic intervention whose purpose is to modify a client's behavior, emotions, or thoughts is called ____________________.

8. The scientific discipline that seeks to describe, explain, predict, and control behaviors that are considered unusual is called ____________________.

9. The philosophical movement that emphasizes human welfare and the worth of the individual, and that challenged supernatural explanations of deviant behavior, is called ____________________.

10. The belief that mental disorders have a physical or physiological basis is called the ____________________.

11. The belief that the origin and manifestation of disorders are equally applicable across all cultures is called ____________________.

12. The belief that lifestyles, cultural values, and world views affect the expression and determination of deviant behavior is called ________________.

13. An attempt to describe, assess, and systematically draw inferences about an individual's psychological disorder is called a(n) ________________.

14. The contemporary approach that sees the cause of most disorders as a combination of biological, psychological, and social factors is called the ________________.

15. Behavior that departs from some norm and harms the affected individual or others is called ________________.

16. The ritual in which prayer, noise, and extreme measures such as starvation were used to cast evil spirits out of an afflicted person's body is called ________________.

17. Group hysteria in which large numbers of people exhibit similar symptoms that have no apparent physical cause is called ________________.

18. The field of psychology that stresses the importance of race, ethnicity, gender, and culture in understanding abnormal behavior is called ________________.

19. A dysfunction or disease of the brain is called a ________________.

20. The percent of individuals in a population who suffer from a mental disorder at a given point in time is called the ________________.

21. The rate of occurrence of a disorder over a period of time is referred to as ________________.

22. The total proportion of people in the population who have ever had a disorder in their life is the ________________.

FACTUAL MULTIPLE–CHOICE QUESTIONS

1. Psychologists attempt to change or control abnormal behavior through the process of
   a. psychodiagnosis.
   b. therapy.
   c. research.
   d. clinical assessment.

2. According to the practical criterion for defining abnormality, when a person complains of an extended period of anxiety, fatigue, and other physical or mental symptoms but is able to fulfill his or her expected social roles, this is evidence of
   a. dysfunction.
   b. discomfort.
   c. deviance.
   d. delusions.

3. False sensory impressions are called ________________; false beliefs that are held despite contradictory evidence are called ________________.
   a. dysfunctions; delusions
   b. hallucinations; delusions
   c. sensorimotor deviation; dementia
   d. delusions; hallucinations

4. Based on the National Institute of Mental Health epidemiological study of mental disorders in three major cities,
   a. the rate of mental disorders has steadily decreased over the past twenty years.
   b. approximately one in fifty Americans suffers from an emotional disorder.
   c. depression is among the least common disorders in the United States.
   d. alcohol problems are more common in men than in women.

5. Tarantism and lycanthropy are examples of ____________________, which occurred during the ____________________.
   a. mesmerism; 1200s
   b. mass madness; 1200s
   c. exorcism; 1800s
   d. mass madness; time of ancient Greece and Rome

6. Clifford Beers, Dorothea Dix, and Benjamin Rush were all
   a. Americans who supported Freud's psychoanalytic theory.
   b. researchers on hypnosis and hysteria.
   c. involved in improving the treatment offered in mental institutions.
   d. supporters of the idea that mental disorder stems from organic causes.

7. The technique of mesmerism was a forerunner of
   a. hypnotism.
   b. drug therapy.
   c. exorcism.
   d. trephining.

8. Most psychologists believe that mental disorders are caused by
   a. psychological factors only.
   b. heredity and brain deficits.
   c. cultural factors only.
   d. a combination of biological, psychological, and societal influences.

9. A clinical psychologist's education includes
   a. required training in psychoanalysis.
   b. four years of medical school.
   c. getting a Ph.D. or Psy.D. degree.
   d. no training in assessment or prevention of abnormal behavior.

10. Among all the mental health professionals, only the ____________________ can prescribe medication.
    a. psychiatrist
    b. clinical psychologist
    c. psychiatric social worker
    d. counseling psychologist

CONCEPTUAL MULTIPLE–CHOICE QUESTIONS

1. One limitation in using the statistical criterion for defining abnormal behavior is the inability to
   a. distinguish rare behaviors that are desirable from those that are undesirable.
   b. consider how frequently a behavior occurs in the population.
   c. show a relationship between prediction and control of behavior.
   d. use objective, empirical information about deviant behavior.

2. Dr. Chiu argues that in defining abnormal behavior, psychologists should use the ideal mental health criterion because this criterion
   a. is based on whether the individual's behavior is bizarre and inefficient and causes personal discomfort.
   b. is the most comprehensive and has the fewest drawbacks.
   c. considers deviations from positive goals assumed to be important for the individual.
   d. is based on the frequency of deviant actions.

3. In contrast to traditional views of abnormality, cultural relativism
   a. rejects the idea that behaviors defined as abnormal in western culture are abnormal everywhere else.
   b. emphasizes the idea that abnormality is best defined in terms of deviation from some ideal of mental health.
   c. argues that there is no such thing as mental illness.
   d. supports the idea that abnormality is based primarily on biological differences.

4. Wakefield (1992) suggests that mental disorder be seen as
   a. a biologically caused phenomenon that is unaffected by society.
   b. having three components: rarity, deviation from ideal, and cultural norms.
   c. a functional deficiency caused by biological factors that is seen as harmful by society.
   d. the result of poor parenting, inadequate social resources, and unavailable treatment.

5. Which of the following statements is *accurate* concerning heredity and mental disorder?
   a. Heredity plays a powerful causal influence on the occurrence of most every mental disorder and environmental factors play almost no role.
   b. Heredity has been found to play almost no role in even the most serious mental disorders.
   c. Because most mental disorders are inherited, they cannot be cured.
   d. Although heredity plays an important role in some disorders, the environment plays a major role in all of them.

6. Which of the following treatments for abnormal behavior is correctly paired with its period in history?
   a. Exorcism—Middle Ages
   b. Trephining—Renaissance
   c. Exorcism—moral treatment era
   d. Cathartic method—moral treatment era

7. Modern interpretations of witchcraft suggest that
   a. people who were seen as voluntary witches were treated with sympathy and kindness.
   b. witches were often not insane.
   c. the church actually tried to stop the hunting of witches.
   d. the church believed that witches were suffering from brain pathology.

8. A person who discusses mental disorders in terms of syndromes and believes that they are caused solely by brain disease, heredity, or metabolic disturbances supports the
   a. psychogenic viewpoint.
   b. idea of demonology.
   c. biological viewpoint.
   d. biopsychosocial orientation.

9. One explanation for differences in rates of mental disorder among ethnic and racial groups is
   a. cultural universality.
   b. social conditioning.
   c. the absence of bias in diagnosis.
   d. some groups are not susceptible to psychological distress.

10. Which of the following statements about managed health care is *accurate*?
    a. Managed-care organizations are exerting increasing control over the type and number of treatment sessions psychologists can offer.
    b. Managed care has led to a great increase in the cost of health care.
    c. Managed care is favored by psychologists because it gives them greater control over the treatment they give their patients.
    d. Over the past thirty years managed care has decreased the number of clinical psychologists in the United States.

APPLICATION MULTIPLE–CHOICE QUESTIONS

1. Dr. Eberhardt has already collected information on a client through observations and psychological tests, and is now formulating a psychodiagnosis. Dr. Eberhardt is involved in which objective of abnormal psychology?
    a. Prediction
    b. Control
    c. Research
    d. Description

2. Dr. Smith says, "Abnormality is simply based on how infrequent a particular behavior is." Dr. Wright says, "Abnormality is defined by the values of the society in which it takes place." Dr. Smith's ideas reflect the ____________________ criteria; Dr. Wright's ideas reflect the ____________________ criteria.
    a. practical; traditional
    b. ideal mental health; cultural relativist
    c. ideal mental health; traditional
    d. statistical; cultural relativist

3. Although no one is present, Martin hears voices, and he firmly believes that Martians are poisoning his oatmeal. Martin's behavior illustrates the ____________________ component of the practical criteria for defining abnormality.
    a. dysfunction
    b. deviance
    c. multicultural
    d. discomfort

4. Dr. Chavez says, "Abnormality occurs when there is a biological dysfunction that produces socially defined harm to the individual." With whom would Dr. Chavez be in agreement?
    a. A cultural relativist
    b. A cultural universalist
    c. Wakefield
    d. Szasz

5. Imagine that you work in the admissions office of a mental health center that specializes in treating alcohol dependence. Your clients would most likely be
    a. people over age sixty-five.
    b. males between twenty-five and forty-four.
    c. young children.
    d. females.

6. Karen says that people with mental illness can never contribute to society until they are cured. Karen's viewpoint
   a. reflects a myth about mentally disturbed people: artists and writers have produced some of their greatest work while seriously disturbed.
   b. reflects the cultural relativism perspective: society determines what is illness and what is a contribution to society.
   c. is supported by epidemiological research.
   d. is mistaken because most mentally disturbed people are rarely cured.

7. Strabismus lives in ancient Greece. He goes to see his physician, Hippocrates, about his problem with sadness and fatigue. What is Hippocrates likely to say to Strabismus?
   a. "You need to have a portion of your skull removed; let me get my trephining gear."
   b. "Satan has possessed you; you need to have an exorcism."
   c. "Your body fluids, and perhaps your brain, are disturbed; you need rest and good food."
   d. "Emotionally charged events from your past are affecting you; you need the cathartic method."

8. Johann Weyer and Philippe Pinel would have probably agreed that
   a. witches need to be starved and burned in order to save their souls.
   b. abnormal behavior is best treated with hypnosis.
   c. most people with behavior disorders have a form of brain pathology.
   d. witchcraft is not an acceptable explanation for mental disturbance.

9. Suzanne undergoes a process whereby, in a trance, she relives forgotten, emotionally charged events. Suzanne's treatment is called
   a. the cathartic method.
   b. mesmerism.
   c. exorcism.
   d. moral treatment.

10. Julie says, "Every time I read about a psychological disorder, I think I'm reading about myself." What is this reaction called?
    a. Catharsis
    b. Medical student syndrome
    c. Cultural relativism
    d. A biopsychosocial approach

ANSWER KEY: KEY TERMS REVIEW

1. cathartic method (24)
2. psychological view (23)
3. trephining (17)
4. managed health care (25)
5. moral treatment movement (21)
6. syndrome (22)
7. therapy (4)
8. abnormal psychology (3)
9. humanism (20)
10. biological (biogenic) view (22)
11. cultural universality (9)
12. cultural relativism (9)
13. psychodiagnosis (3)
14. biopsychosocial approach (29)
15. abnormal behavior (13)
16. exorcism (17)
17. mass madness (19)
18. multicultural psychology (26)
19. brain pathology (18)
20. prevalence (13)
21. incidence (13)
22. lifetime prevalence (13)

ANSWER KEY: FACTUAL MULTIPLE–CHOICE QUESTIONS

1. a. Psychodiagnosis identifies and labels a person's abnormality.
   *b. Therapy is a means of controlling maladaptive behavior and helping people change. (p. 4)
   c. Research increases knowledge but does not exercise control over people.
   d. Clinical assessment is a collection of procedures used to determine whether or not a person's behavior is normal or abnormal.

2. a. Dysfunction involves a failure to perform actions that are expected for one's age and social situation.
   *b. Discomfort includes such physical reactions as asthma, fatigue, and nausea. (p. 10)
   c. Deviance takes the form of delusions, hallucinations, or other rare behaviors.
   d. Delusions are mistaken beliefs that are not influenced by factual information.

3. a. Dysfunctions are impairments in performing expected role-related behaviors.
   *b. Hallucinations are false perceptions involving the senses; delusions are beliefs held by people despite contradictory evidence. (p. 10)
   c. Sensorimotor is part of Piaget's theory of cognitive development; dementia is a cognitive disorder.
   d. The terms are reversed here.

4. a. The rate of disorders has seemed to stay fairly constant over the past twenty years.
   b. Between 29 and 38 percent of the people in the three samples reported a disorder.
   c. In some studies, depressive symptoms are estimated to occur in 44 million Americans; it is a common emotional disorder.
   *d. Alcohol abuse and dependence occur in 24 percent of men but only 4 percent of women. (p. 15)

5. a. Mesmerism occurred in the late 1700s and was not a form of mass madness.
   *b. Tarantism and lycanthropy are examples of mass madness that occurred in the 1200s. (p. 19)
   c. Tarantism and lycanthropy involved disorder on a mass scale; exorcism is a form of treatment for individuals.
   d. Tarantism and lycanthropy were reported during the Middle Ages (the 1200s).

6. a. Beers, Dix, and Rush all lived before Freud's ideas were known in the United States.
   b. Charcot, Liebeault, and Bernheim were researchers who looked at hypnosis and its relation to hysteria.
   *c. Beers, Dix, and Rush worked to humanize the treatment of the mentally ill in the United States. (p. 21)
   d. Dix and Beers took no distinct stand on whether mental disorder was biogenic or not.

7. *a. Mesmerism involved a trance-like state, much like hypnotism, during which the subject was highly suggestible. (p. 23)
   b. Mesmerism made no use of drugs.
   c. Mesmerism was not a religiously oriented treatment, as exorcism is.
   d. Mesmerism did not involve the kind of skull surgery seen in trephining.

8. a. Most contemporary psychologists do not hold a purely psychogenic viewpoint.
   b. Most contemporary psychologists do not hold a purely biological (biogenic) viewpoint.
   c. Most contemporary psychologists do not hold a purely sociocultural viewpoint.
   *d. Most contemporary psychologists endorse a biopsychosocial perspective owing to evidence from psychopharmacology, as well as research on how family upbringing and social forces affect mental health. (p. 29)

9. a. Psychoanalysts require training in psychoanalysis and can be psychologists or psychiatrists; such training is not required in clinical psychology.
   b. Psychiatrists are trained in medical schools.
   *c. Clinical psychologists obtain one of two doctoral degrees, the Ph.D. or the Psy.D. (p. 26)
   d. Clinical psychologists are trained in the assessment and treatment of disturbed people. They also do original research work, which is the reason they are awarded the Ph.D. degree.

10. *a. Psychiatrists are trained in medicine and, as M.D.s, may prescribe medication. No other type of mental health professional is always trained in medicine. (p. 26)
   b. Clinical psychologists are not trained in medicine. It is against the law for them to prescribe medication, although there has recently been legislative activity to permit them to do so under certain conditions.
   c. Psychiatric social workers are not trained in medicine. It is against the law for them to prescribe medication.
   d. Counseling psychologists have the same type of training as clinical psychologists; they cannot prescribe medication.

ANSWER KEY: CONCEPTUAL MULTIPLE-CHOICE QUESTIONS

1. *a. The statistical criteria do not decide whether a rare behavior is desirable or not; they equate rare with abnormal. (p. 5)
   b. The statistical criterion emphasizes frequency.
   c. The statistical criterion concept is relevant to defining abnormality, not predicting or controlling behavior.
   d. Statistics are considered to be objective and empirical.

2. a. Discomfort, deviance, and dysfunction reflect the practical criterion for defining abnormal behavior.
   b. There are several drawbacks to the ideal mental health criterion, such as disagreement over what are ideal characteristics and traits, and uncertainty over what the goals of treatment should be.
   *c. The ideal mental health criteria require setting a positive goal (an ideal) and judging how far from that goal an individual is. (p. 7)
   d. Frequency of deviant actions reflects the statistical criterion of abnormal behavior.

3. *a. Cultural relativism focuses on the diversity of symptoms as they relate to social values. Proponents of cultural relativism do not believe that symptoms are universal across cultures. (p. 9)
   b. Cultural relativism does not use the ideal mental health criteria.
   c. Cultural relativism does not reject the possibility of mental illness; Thomas Szasz has questioned this idea.
   d. Cultural relativism emphasizes social values, not biological differences.

4. a. Wakefield does not take a pure biogenic view and accepts the importance of cultural factors.
   b. These are separate criteria for defining "abnormal" and are unrelated to Wakefield's argument.
   *c. Wakefield sees mental disorder as a "harmful dysfunction," where *harmful* is defined by society and *dysfunction* is defined by the biological sciences. (p. 12)
   d. Wakefield's view stresses biological factors as the cause of mental disorders.

5. a. Environmental factors are influential in all forms of disorder.
   b. Heredity plays a critical role in schizophrenia, bipolar disorder, and alcoholism.
   c. Most mental disorders are *not* inherited, and most people can be cured.
   *d. In some cases heredity gives a person a predisposition toward a disorder but in all cases, the environment determines whether any predisposition is expressed in behavior. (p. 16)

6. *a. During the Middle Ages, abnormality was explained in terms of demonic possession. The treatment for possession was exorcism. (p. 19)
   b. Trephining was principally used during prehistoric times.
   c. Eighteenth-century moral treatment included discussions with a physician, work, and rest; exorcism in the Middle Ages was done by a clergyman.
   d. The cathartic method was developed around the turn of the twentieth century, fifty to seventy-five years after the moral treatment era.

7. a. Voluntary witches were treated with brutality.
   *b. A comprehensive review of the period by Spanos shows that many witches were not insane. (p. 20)
   c. The church led the fight to hunt down and kill witches.
   d. The church explained abnormal behavior in terms of the supernatural, not the biological.

8. a. A psychogenic approach argues that disorders are caused by parenting, environmental factors, and other forces outside the body.
   b. Demonology involves a belief that individuals are possessed by agents of the devil.
   *c. The biological (organic or biogenic) viewpoint sees disorders in terms of clusters of symptoms (syndromes) and believes that the causes are biological. (p. 22)
   d. The biopsychosocial approach accepts the importance of biology, but also argues that psychological and social forces outside the person influence the development and course of disorders.

9. a. Cultural universality gives no emphasis to cultural influences and assumes disorders are the same in different cultural groups.
   *b. Social conditioning in the form of learned, stereotyped behavior is one explanation for apparent differences in rates of mental disorders in different groups. (p. 27)
   c. It is the presence of bias in diagnosis that helps explain gender and cultural differences.
   d. One of the few principles researchers agree upon is that all groups are susceptible to psychological distress.

10. *a. Managed health care represents an industrialization of the helping professions. These organizations have greater control over the services that professionals can provide, in order to cut health care costs. (p. 25)
    b. Managed health care aims to reduce the cost of care and has had some success in doing so.
    c. Many psychologists are fearful of managed care because it puts control of the type and duration of treatment in the hands of large organizations such as insurance companies.
    d. Over the past thirty years, the number of clinical psychologists in the United States has grown from 12,000 to more than 40,000.

ANSWER KEY: APPLICATION MULTIPLE–CHOICE QUESTIONS

1. a. Prediction involves anticipation of future events; psychodiagnosis refers to current description.
   b. Control implies treatment, not description.
   c. Research can be done on any of the objectives of abnormal psychology.
   *d. Psychodiagnosis involves description and definition of just what a person is experiencing. (p. 3)

2. a. Infrequent behavior is the main component of the statistical criteria, not of the practical criteria.
   b. The ideal mental health criteria do not base judgments on the rarity of behavior.
   c. The ideal mental health criteria do not base judgments on the rarity of behavior.
   *d. The statistical criteria are based on the rarity of behavior; cultural relativism assumes that social values determine what is abnormal. (pp. 5, 9)

3. a. There is no explicit information indicating that Martin cannot perform tasks he is expected to perform—the definition of dysfunction.
   *b. Martin is exhibiting auditory hallucinations and delusions (about Martians), which are forms of deviance. (p. 10)
   c. There is no information indicating that Martin's behavior is related to his gender, ethnic background, or race, some of the issues important in the multicultural perspective.
   d. If Martin complained about physical or psychological pain, that would be an indication of discomfort.

4. a. Cultural relativism emphasizes social values not biological dysfunction.
   b. Cultural universality would suggest that, regardless of culture, all disorders are the same in presentation, origin, and treatment.
   *c. Wakefield argues that abnormality has a biological component of dysfunction and a social component of harm to the individual defined by the culture. (pp. 12–13)
   d. Szasz's position is that mental illness is a myth and that "problems in living" are reflections of social problems only.

5. a. Older people are more likely to suffer from cognitive impairments, not alcohol dependence.
   *b. Alcohol problems are most common in men and in people between twenty-five and forty-four years old. (p. 15)
   c. It is very rare for children to develop alcohol dependence.
   d. Men are more likely to have alcohol abuse and dependence disorders than women.

6. *a. It is a myth that people with mental illness make no contributions. Picasso, Poe, and Hemingway all suffered from disorders when they created their artwork or books. (p. 16)
   b. Cultural relativism makes no statement on the potential for mentally ill individuals to contribute to society.
   c. Epidemiological research examines the number and distribution of disorders in a population, not the contributions of individuals who have them.
   d. It is also a myth to suggest that mentally disturbed people cannot be successfully treated.

7. a. Trephining was most common in prehistoric times, not in ancient Greece.
   b. What made ancient Greece and Rome unique was that their physicians did *not* believe that demons caused disorder.
   *c. Hippocrates' theory of abnormality assumed that the body's fluids were out of balance and that there may be brain pathology. (p. 18)
   d. Ideas about catharsis and emotional memories were developed around the turn of the twentieth century.

8. a. Neither Weyer nor Pinel believed that witchcraft existed.
   b. Both Weyer and Pinel lived before hypnosis was first used.
   c. Neither Weyer nor Pinel took a biogenic view of abnormal behavior.
   *d. Weyer was the first to challenge witchcraft; Pinel lived more than 100 years after witchcraft faded as a common explanation. (pp. 20–21)

9. *a. The cathartic method, hypnosis, and other techniques seek to bring to consciousness painful, forgotten memories. Breuer, and later Freud, used the method to cure patients. (p. 24)
   b. Mesmerism involved trances, but there was no goal of reviving memories.
   c. Exorcism was a religious practice with the goal of driving out demons.
   d. Moral treatment relied on work, rest, and prayer for cures.

10. a. Catharsis is the painful reliving of past memories. This is usually induced by therapy.
   *b. Medical students often see themselves described as they read about each disorder; something similar is probably happening to Julie. (p. 30)
   c. Cultural relativism means that abnormality is defined by the social values that have influenced a person.
   d. The biopsychosocial approach asserts that biological, psychological, and social factors explain most disorders.

CHAPTER 2
Models of Abnormal Behavior

LEARNING OBJECTIVES

1. Define *psychopathology* and describe what a model is. Discuss how models are used in describing psychopathology and how a clinician's choice of a model influences thought and action toward abnormal behavior. (pp. 33–34)
2. Describe the biogenic model, including the major structures of the human brain, neurons, and the role of neurotransmitters, and how knowledge of biochemistry can be used in the treatment of mental disorders. (pp. 34–37; Table 2.1)
3. Discuss the relationship between genetics and psychopathology, including the differences between genotype and phenotype. (pp. 37–38)
4. List the criticisms of the biological model and describe how the diathesis-stress approach has tried to address some of these criticisms. (pp. 38–40)
5. Describe the basic concepts of psychodynamic theory, including the components of personality structure, the concepts of psychosexual stages and defense mechanisms, and the role anxiety plays in the development of psychopathology. (pp. 40–43)
6. Briefly describe psychoanalytic therapy and how the psychoanalysis of the neo-Freudians differed from traditional Freudian psychoanalysts. (pp. 43–44)
7. Discuss the criticisms of the psychodynamic model. (p. 44)
8. Discuss the concerns of the behavioral models of psychopathology. Describe the components of the classical conditioning model and relate those components to psychopathology. (pp. 44–46)
9. Discuss how operant conditioning can be applied to understanding psychopathology. Specify the assumptions of the operant conditioning model and compare them with classical conditioning. (pp. 46–48)
10. Describe the observational learning model and its relevance to psychopathology. Evaluate the behavioral models. (pp. 48–50)
11. Describe the assumptions of the cognitive models and how unproductive schemas, irrational and maladaptive thoughts, and distortions of thought processes contribute to psychopathology. Describe the elements of cognitive therapy. (pp. 50–51)
12. Evaluate the cognitive models. (pp. 51–53)
13. Describe the contributions of the humanistic and existential approaches including the notions of the concept of the self and the actualizing tendency. Discuss the development of abnormal behavior and its treatment according to Carl Rogers. (pp. 53–55)
14. Discuss the criticisms of the humanistic and existential approaches. (p. 56)
15. Identify the three distinct assumptions of the family systems approach, including the development of personality and identity within the family, the relationship between family dynamics and psychopathology, and treatment approaches. (pp. 56–58)

16. Evaluate the strengths and limitations of the family systems model. (pp. 58–59)
17. Discuss the assumptions of the multicultural models of psychopathology, including the inferiority and deprivations/deficit models, and relate these ideas to psychopathology. Evaluate the strengths and limitations of the multicultural model. (pp. 59–62; Focus On)
18. Using Table 2.5, compare and contrast the biological, psychodynamic, humanistic/existential, behavioral, cognitive, family systems, and multicultural models of psychopathology. Discuss the utility of integrating models into an eclectic approach such as that found in the "tripartite framework." (pp. 62–65; Table 2.5)
19. Discuss the case of Steven V. from various etiological models and how each model would treat Steven V. (pp. 34, 62–65)

CHAPTER OUTLINE

1. **Models in the study of *psychopathology*** (pp. 33–34) *Models* are analogies that scientists use to describe things they cannot directly observe. To aid in analyzing the various models in abnormal psychology, the case of Steven V. is presented, describing a college student who suffers from depression and violent fantasies.

2. **Biological models** (pp. 34–40) The biological model suggests that abnormal behavior is caused by biological factors, especially involving the brain. The brain is composed of billions of *neurons* (nerve cells) that receive and transmit information. The brain is divided into two hemispheres, each controlling the opposite side of the body. The brain structures most relevant to abnormal behavior include the thalamus, hypothalamus, reticular activating system, limbic system, and cerebrum. Other structures, in the midbrain and hindbrain, manufacture chemicals that are correlated with mental disorders.

   Neurons are composed of *dendrites,* which receive signals from other neurons, and *axons,* which send the signals to other neurons. At the end of the axon is a gap called the *synapse,* into which chemicals called *neurotransmitters* are released. Imbalances in neurotransmitters are associated with many mental disorders. Certain medications can reduce symptoms of abnormal behavior by blocking or facilitating neurotransmitter activity.

   Genetics also plays an important part in explaining the development of disorders. A person's *genotype* (genetic makeup) interacts with the environment to produce physical or behavioral characteristics (the person's *phenotype*).

   The biological model is not without limitations. The biological model overemphasizes internal causes, equates organic dysfunction with mental dysfunction, and assumes that biochemical differences are the *cause* of disorder when they may be the *result. Diathesis-stress theory* argues that people can inherit a vulnerability to developing an illness, but this tendency must be activated by environmental forces for the disorder to occur.

3. **Psychodynamic models** (pp. 40–44; Tables 2.2, 2.3) Sigmund Freud's *psychodynamic model* emphasizes early childhood experiences. Anxiety results from unconscious conflicts and threatens us; in dealing with those threats, we develop symptoms. Personality is a dynamic process resulting from three interacting components: the id, the ego, and the superego. The id operates on the *pleasure principle*—a need for immediate gratification. The ego is influenced by the *reality principle.* The superego is composed of the conscience and the ego ideal.

   Personality develops through five psychosexual stages (oral, anal, phallic, latency, and genital). Fixation at any of the stages affects emotional development. Anxiety is at the root of psychoanalytic thinking and takes three forms: realistic, moralistic, and neurotic. Defense mechanisms protect the individual from anxiety and include repression, reaction formation, projection, rationalization, displacement, undoing, and regression.

   In *psychoanalysis,* therapists induce ego weakness so that unconscious material can be brought to the surface. These insights help patients understand their inner motives.

Neo-Freudians took Freud's ideas in new directions. They emphasized freedom of choice and future goals, ego autonomy, social forces, object relations, and treatment of seriously disturbed people.

Psychoanalysis has been criticized for basing its evidence on case studies, which are subject to distortion. Psychodynamic theory is biased against women and cannot be applied to a wide range of disturbed people.

4. **Humanistic and existential approaches** (pp. 53–56) The *humanistic* and the *existential approaches* emphasize the need to appreciate the world from the individual's vantage point. They also highlight freedom of choice and the wholeness of the individual. Humanistic psychologists Carl Rogers and Abraham Maslow suggested that people are motivated by the actualizing tendency to enhance the self *(self-actualization).* When society imposes conditions of worth on people, their *self-concept* and actualizing tendency can become incongruent. This incongruence produces behavior disorders. In Rogers's person-centered therapy, people are free to grow toward their potential. The therapist uses reflection of feelings and acceptance rather than advice to help the client actively evaluate his or her experience.

   The existential perspective is not a systematized school of thought but a set of attitudes that is less optimistic than humanism, views the individual within the human condition, and focuses more on responsibility to others. Both approaches lack scientific grounding, are vague, and apply therapies that are ineffective with severely disturbed clients.

5. **Behavioral models** (pp. 44–50) The *behavioral models* emphasize learning. The *classical conditioning model* involves the pairing of a neutral *(conditioned) stimulus* with an *unconditioned stimulus* that automatically produces certain responses, called the *unconditioned response.* After repeated pairing, the conditioned stimulus alone can produce a weakened version of the response, called the *conditioned response.* These concepts can be used to explain the development of phobias and deviant sexual behavior. However, the passive nature of associative learning makes it a limited explanatory tool.

   The *operant conditioning model* stresses the consequences of voluntary and controllable behaviors called *operant behaviors.* According to Thorndike's *law of effect,* these behaviors are more likely when they produce positive consequences and less likely when they produce negative consequences. Operant conditioning principles help explain such forms of psychopathology as self-injurious behavior. As in classical conditioning, operant concepts can be applied to treatment as well.

   The *observational learning model* assumes that exposure to disturbed models helps produce disturbed behavior.

   Behavioral models have made significant contributions to both the understanding and treatment of disorders. However, they are criticized for diminishing the importance of inner determinants of behavior.

6. **Cognitive models** (pp. 50–53; Table 2.4) The cognitive models assume that thoughts modify our emotional states and behavior. Our *schemas* (how we interpret events) influence our experiences. Cognitive theorists focus on irrational beliefs (Ellis) or distortions in the thought processes (Beck). Ellis describes an "A-B-C theory of personality" in which A is an event, B is a belief, and C is a consequent behavior or emotion. Beck's work on depression helped him identify six types of faulty thinking: arbitrary inference, selective abstraction, overgeneralization, magnification and exaggeration, personalization, and polarized thinking. Cognitive approaches to therapy have clients monitor their thoughts; recognize the connections between thoughts, emotions, and behaviors; examine the evidence for their assumptions; and substitute more reality-oriented interpretations. Some behaviorists warn that cognitions cannot be observed and therefore are not the stuff of science. Humanistically oriented psychologists object to reducing human beings to the sum of their cognitions. Others object to confrontative cognitive therapy methods.

7. **Family systems model** (pp. 56–59) Unlike the biological, psychodynamic, and behavioral models, which stress the individual, the *family systems model* emphasizes the influence of the family on individual behavior. The work of Harry Stack Sullivan and Erik Erikson contributed

to this viewpoint. Abnormality is seen as a symptom of unhealthy *family dynamics,* including communication problems. Three family therapy approaches emphasize communications, power, and relationship involvement among family members. Criticisms of the family systems model include difficulty defining it from different cultural viewpoints and its confusion of cause and effect over the issue of family abuse.

8. **Models of diversity and psychopathology** (pp. 59–62; Focus On) As European Americans become a numerical minority in the United States, there is a growing awareness of cultural issues in psychopathology. Early models viewed cultural minorities as genetically inferior or culturally deprived relative to white middle-class culture. The *multicultural model* argues that culture is central to all theories of pathology, that European-American concepts must be balanced by non-Western perspectives and that human development includes cultural context. The DSM-IV includes cultural considerations. Bias may help explain apparent cultural differences in psychopathology; Europeans emphasize individuality in ways other cultures do not. The multicultural perspective has been criticized for lacking empirical validation.

9. **An integrative approach to models of psychopathology** (pp. 62–68) It is useful to compare and contrast the different models of psychopathology. However, few practicing clinicians use them rigidly and most see value in an eclectic approach: we are all biological, psychological, and cultural beings.

KEY TERMS REVIEW

1. The optimistic viewpoint that people are born with self-direction and the ability to fulfill their potential is called the ____________________.

2. In psychoanalytic theory, the ego-protection strategies that operate unconsciously to shelter the person from anxiety are called ____________________.

3. The therapy based on Freud's view that unconscious conflicts must be aired and understood by the patient is called ____________________.

4. The theory that a predisposition to mental illness is inherited and that this predisposition is activated by environmental factors is called the ____________________.

5. A clinical term for abnormal behavior is ____________________.

6. The set of attitudes that agrees with humanism but that is less optimistic and that highlights alienation and responsibility to others is called the ____________________.

7. An analogy used by scientists to describe something that cannot be directly observed is called a(n) ____________________.

8. Psychologists who were strongly influenced by Freud's psychoanalytic model but who modified that model in various ways are called ____________________.

9. The view that adult disorders arise from the unconscious operation of repressed anxieties originally experienced in childhood is called the ____________________.

10. A person's genetic makeup is called his or her ____________________.

11. The observable result of the interaction of the genotype and the environment is called the ____________________.

12. The impulsive, pleasure-seeking aspect of our being, usually associated with the id, that seeks immediate gratification is called the ____________________.

13. Usually associated with the ego, the awareness of environmental demands and adjustments made to meet these demands are called the ____________________.

14. An inherent tendency for people to strive toward the realization of their full potential is called ____________________.

15. An individual's assessment of his or her own value and worth is called the ____________________.

16. In psychoanalytic theory, human beings develop through a sequence of stages (oral, anal, phallic, latency, and genital), which collectively are called ____________________.

17. The space between a sending neuron and a receiving neuron is called the ____________________.

18. The rootlike structures of a neuron that receive information are called the ____________________.

19. The long extension of the neuron that transmits a signal to the end of that neuron is called the ____________________.

20. Nerve cells are also called ____________________.

21. Chemicals that are released into the synapse so that neural messages are facilitated or blocked are called ____________________.

22. A model that assumes conscious thoughts affect an individual's emotions and response to a stimulus is called the ____________________.

23. The theory that assumes individuals learn new behaviors by watching other people and imitating them is called ____________________.

24. The theory of learning in which involuntary responses to new stimuli are learned through association is called ____________________.

25. The model of psychopathology that emphasizes the influence of the family on individual behavior is called the ____________________.

26. A theory of learning, applying primarily to voluntary behaviors, that assumes these behaviors are controlled by the consequences that follow them is called ____________________.

27. Theories of psychopathology that are concerned with the role of learning are called ____________________.

28. In classical conditioning, the learned response made to a previously neutral stimulus is called the ____________________.

29. In classical conditioning, a previously neutral stimulus that, after conditioning, acquires the ability to produce a conditioned response is called a(n) ____________________.

30. The idea that increases in behavior are associated with positive consequences and that reductions in behavior are associated with unpleasant ones is called the ____________________.

31. The underlying assumptions held by a person that influence how he or she interprets events are called ____________________.

32. In classical conditioning, the unlearned response made to the unconditioned stimulus is called the ____________________.

33. In classical conditioning, the stimulus that elicits the unconditioned response is called the ____________________.

34. The day-to-day operation of the family system is called ____________________.

35. A voluntary and controllable behavior that "operates" on an individual's environment is called a(n) ____________________.

36. The process of learning by observing models and imitating them is called ____________________.

FACTUAL MULTIPLE-CHOICE QUESTIONS

1. A psychologist who believes that genetics, brain chemistry, and damage to the nervous system are the major causes of mental disorder subscribes to the ____________________ model.
   a. psychoanalytic
   b. existential
   c. biological
   d. multicultural

2. According to Freud, ____________________ is present at birth and impulsively seeks immediate gratification of pleasure needs.
   a. the id
   b. the ego
   c. the superego
   d. fixation

3. According to Freud, fixation in a psychosexual stage
   a. cannot be overcome.
   b. reduces the person's need for ego defense mechanisms.
   c. explains the development of conscience.
   d. arrests future emotional development.

4. According to Freud, when id impulses threaten to break through ego controls, we experience
   a. neurotic anxiety.
   b. moral anxiety.
   c. heightened consciousness.
   d. defensiveness.

5. Conditions of worth, conditional positive regard, and incongruence are all associated with the ____________________ approach to abnormal behavior.
   a. humanistic
   b. diathesis-stress
   c. psychodynamic
   d. object relations

6. Because they are voluntary behaviors, social skills are learned through
   a. classical conditioning.
   b. operant conditioning.
   c. extinction.
   d. the pairing of conditioned and unconditioned stimuli.

7. Research indicates that when children watch television violence, they often imitate the aggressive actions in their own lives. This illustrates
   a. classical conditioning.
   b. modeling.
   c. operant conditioning.
   d. the cognitive model of psychopathology.

8. According to Albert Ellis, negative emotions are the result of
   a. irrational beliefs about events that occur in our lives.
   b. modeling inappropriate behaviors.
   c. pairing certain conditioned stimuli with negative unconditioned responses.
   d. faulty communications in which verbal messages contradict nonverbal messages.

9. In ____________________ therapy, problems are seen in terms of power struggles, control, and the need to reestablish boundaries.
   a. strategic family
   b. conjoint family
   c. rational-emotive
   d. cognitive restructuring

10. Early theories that attempted to account for cultural differences in psychopathology
    a. relied on what Thorndike called "the law of effect."
    b. balanced European-American concepts of mental health with non-Western ones.
    c. looked at ethnic minorities as inferior to or deprived of white middle-class values.
    d. explained the differences in terms of bias in diagnosis.

CONCEPTUAL MULTIPLE–CHOICE QUESTIONS

1. The biological model of schizophrenia would be supported if researchers found that
   a. schizophrenia occurred most frequently among those from the lower socioeconomic groups.
   b. a specific neurotransmitter imbalance occurred only in people with the disorder.
   c. people with the disorder had a forebrain that controlled higher mental functions.
   d. people who suffered from the disorder came from families with great marital conflict.

2. Genotype is to ____________________ as phenotype is to ____________________.
   a. genetic makeup; observable behavioral or physical characteristics
   b. abnormal; normal
   c. environmental forces; biological inheritance
   d. observable behavioral or physical characteristics; genetic makeup

3. Which of the following is emphasized in neo-Freudian theories but not in psychodynamic theory?
   a. Anxiety as related to psychopathology
   b. Freedom of choice and future goals
   c. Psychosexual stages of development
   d. Unconscious childhood memories having an effect on adult behavior

4. Psychodynamic theory has been criticized because
   a. it has failed to have much impact on the field of psychology.
   b. it relies too heavily on evidence from scientific, laboratory investigations.
   c. it fails to examine the impact of the unconscious on psychopathology.
   d. its form of therapy cannot be applied to a range of disturbed people.

5. Which statement about the humanistic and existential theories is *accurate*?
   a. They believe that biological and instinctual forces determine each individual's behaviors.
   b. They argue that the individual's subjective view of events is more important than the events themselves.
   c. They emphasize the need to break down personality into its component parts.
   d. They reject the idea of an actualizing tendency.

6. In classical conditioning, the ____________________ is initially neutral, but can evoke a response if it is paired with the ____________________.
   a. unconditioned stimulus; conditioned response
   b. operant stimulus; classical stimulus
   c. unconditioned response; conditioned stimulus
   d. conditioned stimulus; unconditioned stimulus

7. Which of the following is probably best explained by classical conditioning?
   a. Learning how to use chopsticks in a Chinese restaurant
   b. Becoming silent when your friend continually interrupts anything you say
   c. Two people getting the same grade on a test, but only one of them feeling proud of it
   d. Developing a fear of cars after being in a traffic accident

8. In ____________________, behavior is controlled by preceding stimuli; in ____________________, learning is based on the consequences of behavior.
   a. modeling; cognitive-behavioral theory
   b. classical conditioning; operant conditioning
   c. operant conditioning; modeling
   d. classical conditioning; cognitive-behavioral theory

9. Which statement is *accurate* concerning the family systems model?
   a. It suggests that all phenomena can be understood in terms of learning based on associations between stimuli.
   b. It suggests that abnormal behavior in an individual reflects unhealthy dynamics in the family.
   c. It suggests that family dynamics can not be changed once they have been established.
   d. It assumes that genetics explains why some families have certain behavior problems generation after generation.

10. The terms *African-American, American Indian, Asian-American,* and *Hispanic-American*
    a. are universally recognized as appropriate labels to define ethnic minorities in the U.S.
    b. are convenient labels recognized by the U.S. government, but they are not without controversy.
    c. are most preferred by ethnic minority groups regardless of age.
    d. are the most comprehensive and accurate description of all ethnic groups.

APPLICATION MULTIPLE–CHOICE QUESTIONS

1. Dr. Chapman thinks of the brain as a kind of computer that takes in data, processes it, stores it, and retrieves it at a later date. Dr. Chapman is
   a. an eclectic thinker.
   b. taking a humanistic view of the brain.
   c. a supporter of the biological approach.
   d. using a model to think about the brain.

2. Dr. Mandler says, "We know that this patient has a high genetic vulnerability to the disorder. Given the current difficulties in his life, it is logical that he would develop a severe case of the disorder." Which perspective does Dr. Mandler's statement illustrate?
   a. Psychoanalytic
   b. Diathesis-stress
   c. Behavioral
   d. Humanistic

3. Dr. Layton says, "I cannot agree with you. I think that social forces are much more important than primitive sexual impulses in determining behavior." With whom is Dr. Layton disagreeing?
   a. A humanistic psychologist
   b. A Freudian psychologist
   c. A neo-Freudian such as Erich Fromm
   d. An existential psychologist

4. Kate is an outspoken feminist. With which perspective is she likely to have the most disagreements?
   a. Eclectic
   b. Biopsychosocial
   c. Humanistic
   d. Psychodynamic

5. Paula R. says, "I cannot decide on anything! I am drifting, and I have no direction." Dr. Pratt responds by reflecting Paula's feelings, but not by providing her with advice. What type of therapy does this illustrate best?
   a. psychoanalysis
   b. Rogers's person-centered therapy
   c. modeling therapy
   d. cognitive therapy

6. In the Case of Steven V., Steven becomes sexually aroused when watching violent movies. From a classical conditioning viewpoint, a violent movie is a(n) ____________________ for Steven.
   a. conditioned response
   b. conditioned stimulus
   c. operant behavior
   d. schema

7. Dr. Lawrence says to a client, "Your phobia of spiders came about because your mother set an example by jumping on a chair and shrieking any time a spider was within twenty yards of her." Dr. Lawrence's explanation follows the ____________________ model.
   a. family systems
   b. cognitive
   c. operant conditioning
   d. observational learning

8. Dr. McNally says to a depressed client, "You are not depressed because of bad events; you are depressed because you have the irrational belief that any bad event is a catastrophe that is totally unfair and inhumane." Dr. McNally's statement illustrates
   a. Ellis's A-B-C theory of personality.
   b. what Beck refers to as the law of effect.
   c. the strategic approach to depression.
   d. the humanistic approach to psychopathology.

9. Mr. and Mrs. Juarez are very concerned about their daughter's performance in school. They see her as "sick," but their therapist thinks they are diverting attention from their own troubled marriage. What kind of therapist are the Juarez'es probably seeing?
   a. A cognitive therapist
   b. A behavior therapist
   c. A family systems therapist
   d. A psychoanalytic therapist

10. A psychologist who agrees with the contemporary multicultural model would be most likely to make which of the following statements?
   a. "Minority groups experience more psychopathology than whites do because minority group children are deprived of a cultural background rich in good values."
   b. "The strongest reason for cultural differences in psychopathology is genetics."
   c. "The best way to understand human personality is to examine the individual at a micro level: his or her personal experiences, impulses, and thoughts."
   d. "Culture is central to all theories of pathology and must balance European concepts with non-European ones."

ANSWER KEY: KEY TERMS REVIEW

1. humanistic perspective (54)
2. defense mechanisms (43)
3. psychoanalysis (40)
4. diathesis-stress theory (40)
5. psychopathology (33)
6. existential approach (55)
7. model (33)
8. neo-Freudians (44)
9. psychodynamic model (40)
10. genotype (38)
11. phenotype (38)
12. pleasure principle (40)
13. reality principle (40)
14. self-actualization (54)
15. concept of the self (54)
16. psychosexual stages (41)
17. synapse (36)
18. dendrites (36)
19. axon (36)
20. neurons (35)
21. neurotransmitters (37)
22. cognitive model (50)
23. observational learning theory (48)
24. classical conditioning (46)
25. family systems model (56)
26. operant conditioning (46)
27. behavioral models (44)
28. conditioned response (46)
29. conditioned stimulus (46)
30. law of effect (47)
31. schema (50)
32. unconditioned response (46)
33. unconditioned stimulus (46)
34. family dynamics (57)
35. operant behavior (46)
36. modeling (49)

ANSWER KEY: FACTUAL MULTIPLE–CHOICE QUESTIONS

1. a. Psychoanalysts emphasize unconscious conflicts and childhood sources of anxiety.
   b. Existentialists take a psychogenic view that emphasizes personal freedom and responsibility.
   *c. The biological model assumes that biological factors such as genetics, brain chemistry, hormones, and nervous system damage account for abnormal behavior. (p. 35)
   d. The multicultural model emphasizes social factors and is, therefore, a variant of the psychogenic view.

2. *a. The id is the portion of personality that psychoanalysts describe as pleasure-seeking, impulsive, and unable to delay gratification. We can see this sort of behavior in newborns. (p. 41)
   b. The ego develops out of the id and is reality oriented.
   c. The superego develops at age five or six and is oriented toward morality.
   d. Fixation occurs when traumas arrest emotional development at any of the psychosexual stages.

3. a. Healthy individuals can overcome or transcend fixation that occurs earlier. In part, this is why therapy provides hope.
   b. Fixation arrests emotional development and, if anything, increases the need for defenses against anxiety.
   c. Conscience is one aspect of the superego.
   *d. Psychoanalytic theorists stress how fixation arrests emotional development and contributes to symptoms in adults. (p. 41)

4. *a. Neurotic anxiety occurs when unacceptable id impulses threaten to overwhelm ego control. (p. 41)
   b. Moral anxiety stems from failing to live up to one's moral code.
   c. Heightened consciousness is achieved by uncovering material about one's past buried in the unconscious.
   d. Defensiveness is the ego's unconscious attempt to protect the person from anxiety. It may occur when id impulses threaten, but it may not and it can occur in response to other sources of anxiety.

5. *a. All three are important concepts in Rogers's theory. When there are conditions of worth, incongruence is likely—resulting in behavior disorders. (p. 54)
   b. Diathesis-stress theory combines genetic vulnerability and environmental factors to explain abnormal behavior.
   c. Freud's psychodynamic approach emphasizes unconscious impulses and sources of anxiety.
   d. Object relations theorists stress early mother-child relationships.

6. a. Classical conditioning involves the learning of involuntary behaviors.
   *b. Operant conditioning involves the learning of voluntary behaviors. (p. 47)
   c. Extinction decreases the frequency of a behavior.
   d. The pairing of stimuli is a part of classical conditioning.

7. a. Classical conditioning involves the pairing of stimuli and the learning of associations to make involuntary responses.
   *b. These children are imitating others, the essence of modeling. (p. 49)
   c. Operant conditioning occurs when behavior is changed by experiencing direct consequences.
   d. Cognitive models emphasize irrational or maladaptive thought processes.

8. *a. Ellis's rational-emotive therapy says that negative emotions are the result of irrational beliefs. (p. 51)
   b. Modeling involves imitation of others.
   c. The pairing of stimuli is the essence of classical conditioning.
   d. Virginia Satir stresses faulty communications in families.

9. *a. Strategic family therapy attempts to change the power relationships and boundaries in distressed families. (p. 58)
   b. Conjoint family therapy tries to change the communication patterns in distressed families.
   c. Rational-emotive therapy focuses on the irrational thoughts of individuals.
   d. Cognitive restructuring helps clients identify and change their thought processes.

10. a. Thorndike's "law of effect" was an early behavioral explanation of how we learn through operant conditioning.
   b. Contemporary multicultural approaches balance European and non-European concepts; older approaches did not.
   *c. Two of the earlier ways of looking at cultural differences (inferiority and deprivation) placed white, middle-class values as the standard and looked at nonwhite cultures as inadequate. (p. 59)
   d. Contemporary multicultural approaches consider diagnostic bias as an explanation for apparent cultural differences in psychopathology.

ANSWER KEY: CONCEPTUAL MULTIPLE–CHOICE QUESTIONS

1. a. The biological model downplays the role of socioeconomic factors and emphasizes brain structure and chemistry.
   *b. The linking of specific neurotransmitter imbalances and mental disorders is a major theme of the biogenic model. (p. 36)
   c. The forebrain controls higher mental functions in all people so it would not be additional evidence for a biogenic model of schizophrenia.
   d. Marital conflict is an environmental and psychological factor that is not included in a purely biogenic perspective.

2. *a. The definition of genotype is one's genetic makeup; the phenotype is how genetic makeup and environmental factors interact to produce an observable set of physical and behavioral characteristics. (p. 38)
   b. Genotype can be abnormal or normal; phenotype can be abnormal or normal.
   c. Genotype is what we inherit; phenotype is what can be seen (the product of genes and environment).
   d. Genotype is defined as one's genetic makeup; phenotype is the observable pattern of physical and behavioral characteristics in a person.

3. a. Freud stressed the role of anxiety in the development of psychopathology; neo-Freudians did not challenge this idea.
   *b. Freedom of choice and being goal-directed were central themes of Alfred Adler and Carl Jung, two neo-Freudians. (p. 45)
   c. Freud originated the idea of psychosexual stages of development.
   d. The influence of unconscious childhood memories is central to Freud and all neo-Freudians.

4. a. Psychoanalytic thinking has had a tremendous impact on the field of psychology.
   b. Psychoanalytic theory has been criticized for relying on case studies and for putting no importance on laboratory investigations.
   c. Psychoanalytic theory puts heavy emphasis on the unconscious.
   *d. Psychoanalysis, which relies on talking and abstraction, is not appropriate for people with poor verbal skills. (p. 44)

5. a. Humanistic and existential thinkers suggest that people are free to make life choices; they reject the ideas of biological destiny and instinctual forces.
   *b. Central to both humanistic and existential theories is the importance placed on how the individual subjectively views the world. (p. 53)
   c. Humanistic and existential thinkers value the integrity of the human personality and argue against breaking it down into components or formulas.
   d. The actualizing tendency is a core idea in humanistic theory.

6. a. The unconditioned stimulus is not neutral; it automatically elicits the unconditioned response.
   b. *Operant* is a word used to describe behavior in the operant conditioning model.
   c. Stimuli are paired in classical conditioning, not responses and stimuli.
   *d. The conditioned stimulus is neutral with respect to a response until it has been paired with the unconditioned stimulus that can elicit the response in question. (p. 46)

7. a. Using chopsticks is voluntary behavior, and it is therefore more related to operant or modeling approaches.
   b. Talking is a voluntary behavior being affected by consequences.
   c. This illustrates how individuals interpret events—a component of the cognitive-behavioral approach.
   *d. Classical conditioning involves an involuntary response (fear) that is paired with previously neutral stimuli (cars). (p. 46)

8. a. Modeling is part of observational learning; cognitive-behavioral theory stresses thinking processes.
   *b. Behaviors learned through classical conditioning are controlled by stimuli preceding the response. In operant conditioning, behaviors are controlled by events that follow them. (p. 47)
   c. Operant conditioning is based on consequences; modeling is a part of observational learning.
   d. Stimuli that precede responses do control classical conditioning, but cognitive-behavioral theory stresses thinking processes.

9. a. Classical conditioning emphasizes the pairing of stimuli.
   *b. Family systems theory suggests that symptoms in an individual reflect unhealthy family dynamics. (p. 56)
   c. Although family systems theory recognizes that change that threatens homeostasis is unwelcome, the whole thrust of therapy is to produce change toward healthy dynamics.
   d. The biological model stresses genetics; the family systems approach would emphasize parents' rules and behavior patterns.

10. a. While commonly used, these categories are practical choices, and do not reflect the more complex cases where individuals have mixed ancestry.
    *b. Although overgeneralization and some inaccuracy may result from using the labels, the U.S. Census Bureau and Office of Management and Budget use these terms. (pp. 60–61; Focus On)
    c. Particular terms may be accepted by some generations but not others; for example, the term *African-American* may be less accepted to Blacks holding strong political views developed during the 1960s.
    d. These descriptions are generalizations and do not account for the nuances and differences that exist between ethnic groups; for example, there are about thirty distinct Asian-American subgroups.

ANSWER KEY: APPLICATION MULTIPLE–CHOICE QUESTIONS

1. a. An eclectic approach uses ideas from different theories to find whatever works best to explain and treat a condition.
   b. Humanistic thinkers do not consider the human mind to be like a machine.
   c. Nothing indicates whether Dr. Chapman believes that biological factors cause disorders, so it is unclear whether the doctor supports the biogenic view.
   *d. A model is an analogy; the analogy between computer and brain may help Dr. Chapman understand the brain better. (p. 33)

2. a. Psychoanalytic theorists put little emphasis on genetics.
   *b. Diathesis-stress theory emphasizes just these ideas: that inherited vulnerability combines with environmental stress to cause disorders. (p. 40)
   c. Behavioral theorists emphasize learning.
   d. Humanistic theorists highlight freedom, individuality, and self-actualization.

3. a. Humanistic psychologists do not suggest that sexual impulses determine behavior. In fact, they do not believe that any unconscious or outside forces determine behavior.
   *b. The chief criticism of Freud by neo-Freudians is his emphasis on sexual motivation for all behavior. (p. 43)
   c. Erich Fromm and other neo-Freudians diminished the importance of sexual motivation.The quotation might have *come* from a neo-Freudian, rather than being targeted at one.
   d. Existential psychologists are much like humanistic psychologists. They, too, deemphasize the idea of unconscious forces determining our behavior.

4. a. Eclectic professionals borrow from a variety of theories, so it is unlikely that an outspoken feminist would be in disagreement with behavioral, cognitive, biological, and systems models.
   b. The biopsychosocial perspective accepts the importance of sociocultural factors as well as biological and psychological ones.
   c. The humanistic approach has not proposed any concepts inconsistent with a feminist approach.
   *d. Psychoanalytic theory has been criticized by feminists for taking a biased view of women, particularly seeing males as the standard against which normality is based. (p. 44)

5. a. Psychoanalysis makes unconscious impulses conscious through projective techniques and other methods.
   *b. Rogers's person-centered therapy gives the client unconditional positive regard by reflecting feelings and allowing the person to find his or her own direction. (p. 55)
   c. Modeling therapy presents the client with behaviors to imitate and directs the person to do so.
   d. Cognitive therapy challenges the irrational beliefs of the client.

6. a. Sexual arousal would be an example of a conditioned response.
   *b. The movies were probably initially neutral (with respect to sex), but were paired with situations for sexual arousal and came to be a conditioned stimulus for arousal. (p. 46)
   c. Operant behaviors are voluntary actions that "operate" on the environment.
   d. A schema is a set of personal assumptions that influences how we see, value, and experience the world.

7. a. Family systems would examine the relationships and communications in the family.
   b. A cognitive approach would look at the irrational beliefs the client has about spiders.
   c. Operant conditioning involves direct learning, not observation.
   *d. Observational learning involves learning through modeling; in this case, from the mother. (p. 49)

8. *a. Ellis's A-B-C theory of personality holds that negative emotions stem not from events but from the irrational beliefs we have about them. (p. 51)
   b. Beck is a cognitive theorist, but the "law of effect" is an early operant conditioning idea.
   c. The strategic approach to family therapy emphasizes power relationships.
   d. The humanistic approach emphasizes incongruence, conditions of worth, and blocked self-actualization.

9. a. A cognitive therapist would help them to examine their thinking about their daughter's performance and to develop more realistic expectations.
   b. A behavior therapist would stress the environmental factors that reduce their daughter's school performance.
   *c. Family systems therapists see individual pathology stemming from faulty family dynamics. (pp. 57–58)
   d. Psychoanalytic therapists focus on the individual's unconscious conflicts.

10. a. This statement reflects the deprivation approach of Reissman; it suggests that non-European cultures are lacking appropriate values; the multicultural approach values all cultures.
    b. Genetic inferiority is not a viable explanation in the multicultural model.
    c. The multicultural model proposes that development be seen at multiple levels including the family and culture.
    *d. The multicultural model notes that all behavior has a cultural influence and that non-European perspectives are as valid as European ones. (pp. 59–60)

CHAPTER 3
Assessment and Classification of Abnormal Behavior

LEARNING OBJECTIVES

1. Define the term *psychodiagnosis* and describe its functions. (p. 72)
2. Identify the characteristics of good tests, including reliability and validity. Define *reliability*, and differentiate among test-retest, internal, and interrater reliability. Define *validity*, and differentiate among predictive, criterion-related, construct, and content validity. (pp. 72–73)
3. Define *assessment* and discuss its role in clinical psychology. Describe and discuss various psychological assessment techniques and their strengths and limitations, including observation of behavior, clinical interviews, and tests and inventories. (pp. 73–87; Table 3.1)
4. Describe the nature and purposes of projective personality tests, including the Rorschach, Thematic Apperception Test (TAT), sentence-completion test, and draw-a-person test. Discuss the strengths and weaknesses of projective tests. (pp. 76–78)
5. Describe the nature and purposes of self-report inventories, including the Minnesota Multiphasic Personality Inventory (MMPI-2). Discuss the strengths and weaknesses of personality inventories. (pp. 78–80; Figure 3.1)
6. Describe the purposes and characteristics of the Wechsler and Stanford-Binet intelligence tests and the Kaufman Assessment Battery for Children (K-ABC). Discuss the strengths and limitations of these tests. (pp. 80–83; Table 3.2)
7. Describe methods for assessing cognitive impairments due to brain damage (*organicity*), including the WAIS-R, Bender-Gestalt Visual-Motor Test, Halstead-Reitan Neuropsychological Test Battery, and Luria-Nebraska Neuropsychological Battery. (p. 83)
8. Describe neurological procedures for detecting brain damage, including CAT and PET scans, EEGs, and MRIs. (pp. 84–85)
9. Discuss ethical issues involved in assessment, particularly how cultural differences may influence clinical judgments. (pp. 85–87; Critical Thinking)
10. Explain the goals of classifying abnormal behaviors and review the history of classification systems. Discuss how validity problems have been raised and dealt with. (pp. 88–89)
11. Describe the characteristics of the DSM-IV, including its five axes, the broad categories of mental disorders, and how the DSM-IV places diagnosis in a cultural context. (pp. 89–93; Focus On)
12. Discuss the objections to the DSM classification system and the arguments supporting its use. (pp. 93–97)
13. Describe four problems associated with classification and labeling and the research related to these problems. Discuss how the findings of Rosenhan (1973) relate to the impact of labeling. (pp. 95–97; Focus On)

CHAPTER OUTLINE

1. **Reliability and validity** (pp. 72–73) Evaluation of information about an individual leads to a *psychodiagnosis,* which involves describing and drawing inferences about the person's psychological state. The psychodiagnosis clarifies the picture of that state, may lead to a treatment program, provides a way of communicating about disorders, and serves to standardize assessment procedures. To be useful, assessment tools must show *reliability,* the ability to get the same results across time or across different observers. Measures that are reliable can also demonstrate *validity*. Predictive validity indicates how well a measure predicts future behavior. Three other aspects of validity are criterion-related, construct, and content validity. Standardization in administration and the presence of standardization samples affect reliability and validity.

2. **The assessment of abnormal behavior: Observations and interviews** (pp. 73–76) *Assessment* requires obtaining information from many sources: observations, interviews, psychological tests, and neurological tests. Clinical observations in either controlled or naturalistic settings are usually made in conjunction with an interview and can have diagnostic significance. A person who is aware of being observed may show *reactivity,* altering normal responses. Interviews stress different information depending on the interviewer's theoretical orientation. Standardized interviews such as the Composite International Diagnostic Interview and the mental status examination produce fewer errors but may not yield usable information.

3. **The assessment of abnormal behavior: Psychological tests and inventories** (pp. 76–80) Psychological tests have a wide range of application. They provide a standard situation for responses and allow comparison of results with normative samples. *Projective personality tests* present ambiguous stimuli and ask for responses that "project" the person's motives. The *Rorschach technique* is a series of cards displaying inkblots. What people see in the blots and why they see what they do are interpreted in terms of psychoanalytic symbolism. The *Thematic Apperception Test (TAT)* uses pictures of people and asks the person to tell a story about each picture. The style and themes of the stories are used to gain insight into conflicts and personality. The sentence-completion test and the Draw-a-Person test are other examples of projective tests. Projectives tend to have low reliability and validity.

   Self-report inventories supply the test taker with a list of alternative answers. The *Minnesota Multiphasic Personality Inventory (MMPI)* consists of 567 statements that are answered "true," "false," or "cannot say," and was revised to become the MMPI-2. MMPI-2 responses are scored on ten clinical and three validity scales. Profiles of scale results indicate personality styles. The Beck Depression Inventory is an example of a test focused on a particular trait or problem. Inventories have been criticized for being restrictive, pathology oriented, and easily faked. Still, inventories are widely used, and some show both reliability and validity since the techniques used in making mental measurement—*psychometrics*—are becoming increasingly sophisticated.

4. **The assessment of abnormal behavior: Intelligence tests** (pp. 80–83) Intelligence tests are designed to measure cognitive functioning, called the intelligence quotient (IQ), and to detect organic brain disorders. The *Wechsler Adult Intelligence Scale* (revised to become the WAIS-R), and two other forms for children (WISC-III) and preschoolers (WPPSI-R) are widely used. Also used is the *Stanford-Binet Scale*. Ethnic groups have attacked IQ tests for being culturally biased, and it is clear that reliance on IQ has led to discrimination. Social competency cannot be adquately assessed with IQ tests. The *System of Multicultural Pluralistic Assessment (SOMPA)* and the *Kaufman Assessment Battery for Children (K-ABC)* are tests that address this and other criticisms.

5. **The assessment of abnormal behavior: Tests for cognitive impairment and neurological tests** (pp. 83–85) Tests to detect and assess brain damage to the central nervous system (*organicity*) include the WAIS-R, the *Bender-Gestalt Visual-Motor Test*, the *Halstead-Reitan Neuropsychological Test Battery*, and the *Luria-Nebraska Neuropsychological Battery*. Neurological medical procedures such as *computerized axial tomography* (CAT scan), *positron emission tomography*

(PET scan), the *electroencephalograph* (EEG), and *magnetic resonance imaging* (MRI) are also used to assess brain conditions.

6. **The ethics of assessment** (pp. 85–87) There is a strong antitesting movement in the United States. Criticisms include the undesirable social consequences of using test results and problems of using tests on people from non-Western cultures. Computer assessment has been viewed as a potential substitute for some testing. Studies of computer assessment have yielded encouraging results, but its validity must be established.

7. **The classification of abnormal behavior** (pp. 88–89) The goal of a *classification system* is to provide distinct categories for different behavior problems. Classification systems should provide distinct categories that are used consistently but that still accommodate imperfect cases. Kraepelin's system and the original DSM were based on medical model principles and the hope that similar disorders would have a common *etiology* (cause). The *Diagnostic and Statistical Manual of Mental Disorders (DSM)* was first published in 1952 and is now revised (DSM-IV). Interrater reliability of recent editions of the DSM has been good for broad categories, but less reliable for specific diagnoses. Older editions of the DSM were criticized for having poor reliability and validity, including an inability to adequately predict the future course of a disorder (*prognosis*).

8. **The current system: DSM-IV** (p. 89; Focus On) This newest version (1994) evaluates an individual on five dimensions or axes: Axis I, clinical syndromes; Axis II, personality or specific developmental disorders; Axis III, general medical conditions; Axis IV, psychosocial problems; and Axis V, global assessment of the highest level of adaptive functioning. The reliability of DSM-IV continues to be studied.

9. **DSM-IV mental disorders** (pp. 89–93) The broad categories of mental disorders discussed in the text are disorders usually first diagnosed in infancy, childhood, or adolescence; delirium, demential, amnestic, and other cognitive disorders; mental disorders due to a general medical condition; substance-related disorders; schizophrenia and other psychotic disorders; mood disorders; anxiety disorders; somatoform disorders; factitious disorders; dissociative disorders; sexual and gender identity disorders; eating disorders, sleep disorders, impulse control disorders not elsewhere classified; adjustment disorders; and personality disorders. The DSM-IV addresses cross-cultural assessment more than previous DSM versions.

10. **Evaluation of the DSM classification system** (pp. 93–95) It is too soon to provide an evaluation of DSM-IV; however, critics of past DSMs argue it is biased toward the medical model, will not adequately classify psychopathology in non-Western cultures, and classifies people into categories rather than seeing them as having more or less of certain characteristics. There is also controversy over a proposed condition, premenstrual dysphoric disorder. Supporters suggest that weaknesses in the DSM merely reflect current gaps in knowledge.

11. **Objections to classification and labeling** (pp. 95–97; Focus On) Classification can exaggerate the differences between normal and abnormal. It can also lead people to misinterpret normal behavior as pathological, affect the way people treat those who are labeled, change the behavior of people who are labeled (self-fulfilling prophecies), and fail to provide the information emphasized by managed-care organizations. Rosenhan's study with pseudopatients illustrates some of these problems.

KEY TERMS REVIEW

1. The degree to which a procedure or test yields the same result repeatedly under the same circumstances is called ________________________.

2. An assessment tool in which the test taker answers specific questions or responds to specific self-descriptive statements is called a(n) ________________________.

3. A variety of standardized test instruments used to assess personality, maladaptive behavior, social skills, intellectual abilities, vocational interests, and cognitive impairment are called ________________________.

4. The process of gathering information about an individual's traits, skills, abilities, emotional functioning, and psychological problems is called ________________________.

5. The cause or origin of a disorder is called the disorder's ________________________.

6. A personality assessment technique in which the test taker is presented with ambiguous stimuli to which he or she is asked to respond is called a(n) ________________________.

7. The degree to which a procedure or test actually performs the function that it was designed to perform is called ________________________.

8. With regard to psychopathology, a system of distinct categories, indicators, and nomenclature for different patterns of behavior, thought processes, and emotional disturbances is called a(n) ________________________.

9. Damage or deterioration in the central nervous system is called ________________________.

10. The study and techniques of mental measurement are called ________________________.

11. The change in the way people usually respond, caused by their awareness that they are being observed is called ________________________.

12. A prediction of the future course of a particular disorder is called ________________________.

13. An individual diagnosed with two or more mental disorders is said to show ________________________.

FACTUAL MULTIPLE–CHOICE QUESTIONS

1. When different observers of the same individual agree on a diagnosis, this illustrates
   a. high predictive validity.
   b. low construct validity.
   c. high test-retest reliability.
   d. high interrater reliability.

2. Projective personality tests are most likely to be used by psychologists who agree with the
   a. psychodynamic perspective.
   b. medical model.
   c. behavioral perspective.
   d. family systems model.

3. Exner's system has become the standard way of scoring
   a. the Rorschach inkblot test.
   b. intelligence tests so that they are culturally unbiased.
   c. such projective tests as the Draw-a-Person and the sentence-completion test.
   d. the MMPI–2.

4. Which personality test has more than 550 items and reports results on ten clinical scales and three validity scales?
   a. The TAT
   b. The Wechsler scales
   c. The MMPI–2
   d. The Bender-Gestalt

5. The Beck Depression Inventory is an example of a
   a. projective personality test.
   b. self-report inventory covering many traits.
   c. test for assessing organicity.
   d. self-report inventory aimed at detecting one specific problem.

6. Unlike the Stanford-Binet, the WAIS-R
   a. gives separate verbal IQ and performance IQ scores.
   b. is a structured interview as well.
   c. is used to assess children's intelligence.
   d. does not examine verbal IQ.

7. Which method of assessing brain function records brain wave patterns?
   a. Electroencephalograph (EEG)
   b. Bender-Gestalt Visual-Motor Test
   c. Computerized axial tomography (CAT) scan
   d. Magnetic resonance imaging (MRI)

8. Which statement about computer assessment is *accurate*?
   a. Computers tend to make more errors in scoring than humans.
   b. There is an abundance of research evidence assuring the scientific precision of computer assessment.
   c. Computer assessment tends to increase the cost of mental health care.
   d. Many clients enjoy being assessed by computer.

9. If a classification system provided useful information about the etiology and prognosis of disorders, it would be
   a. based on the behavioral model of abnormality.
   b. low in reliability but high in validity.
   c. considered a standardized instrument.
   d. telling about the cause and future course of disorders.

10. What information is revealed on Axis II of DSM-IV?
    a. Level of functioning now and in the past year
    b. Any personality or specific developmental disorder
    c. Level of stress experienced in the past year
    d. The clinical syndrome which is the focus of treatment

CONCEPTUAL MULTIPLE–CHOICE QUESTIONS

1. Which of the following statements about assessment is *accurate*?
   a. Assessment uses a wide range of information sources to get a clear picture of a client's problem.
   b. Assessment occurs when information is synthesized into a particular category.
   c. Assessment must use psychological tests in order to be valid.
   d. Assessment methods are not necessary for research.

2. Reactivity is a major problem for which of the following assessment methods?
   a. Observation
   b. Neurological procedures to detect brain damage
   c. Projective intelligence tests
   d. Structured interviews

3. The mental status examination and the Composite International Diagnostic Interview are likely to
   a. have low reliability because they employ naturalistic observation.
   b. produce very little reactivity because they employ naturalistic observation.
   c. have higher reliability because they are structured.
   d. be used for the same purposes as the CAT-scan and the electroencephalograph.

4. Which of the following statements about clinical interviews is *accurate*?
   a. Despite differences in theoretical orientations, psychologists tend to interview clients in the same way.
   b. Clinical interviews do not make use of observations.
   c. The quality of the relationship between interviewer and interviewee has a strong effect on the value of the interview.
   d. Interviews are most likely to be highly structured if performed by psychodynamically oriented psychologists.

5. Which of the following is characteristic of psychological tests?
   a. They predominantly measure intellectual functioning.
   b. They are given in standard situations, and norms exist for making assessments of individuals.
   c. They typically allow the examiner to use his or her own judgment about how to administer and score the test.
   d. They are typically used for research purposes only.

6. What did Kraepelin's system and the original DSM classification system have in common?
   a. High reliability
   b. An eclectic approach that described disorders rather than proposing specific causes for them
   c. Overreliance on the behavioral perspective
   d. Overreliance on the medical model

7. The poor reliability of the original DSM was mostly due to
   a. the poor training of the people who used it.
   b. its excessive use of specific behavior to define categories.
   c. inadequacies in the system itself.
   d. faking in the clients who were examined.

8. Anxiety disorders, mood disorders, and substance-related disorders are all categories of behavior that appear on which axis of the DSM-IV?
   a. Axis I
   b. Axis III
   c. Axis V
   d. None; these categories have been omitted from the DSM- IV

9. Diagnostic labels create all of the following problems *except* one. Which?
   a. They influence the behavior of the people who are labeled.
   b. They provide more information than is required by managed-care organizations.
   c. They influence others to treat the labeled person differently.
   d. They imply that the labeled person is qualitatively different from normal people.

10. What did the Rosenhan study with pseudopatients illustrate?
    a. The high reliability of the new DSM-IV
    b. The ability of professionals to detect faking
    c. How self-fulfilling prophecies can make even normal people act "insane"
    d. How labels influence us to see abnormality even when people act normally

APPLICATION MULTIPLE–CHOICE QUESTIONS

1. A psychologist records the posture, facial expressions, and language patterns of adolescents in a local bowling alley. This represents assessment based on
   a. controlled observation.
   b. structured interviews.
   c. projective personality testing.
   d. naturalistic observation.

2. Gary thinks that projective tests are excellent because they reveal underlying conflicts and motives. Gary is probably in agreement with the ________________________ perspective on abnormal behavior.
   a. behavioral
   b. neuropsychological
   c. humanistic
   d. psychodynamic

3. A psychologist gives Larry two tests. In one test, Larry draws a picture of a person. In the other, he tells what he sees in ten symmetrical inkblots. The psychologist is assessing Larry by using
   a. objective personality tests.
   b. intelligence tests.
   c. projective personality techniques.
   d. one intelligence and one projective test.

4. Dr. Shaw says, "The more sophisticated we get at mental measurement, the higher the reliability and validity of our assessment instruments." Dr. Shaw is discussing
   a. the problem of classification and labeling.
   b. changes in the DSM that include cultural sensitivity.
   c. improving the cultural sensitivity of intelligence tests.
   d. psychometrics.

5. Alan is given the Luria-Nebraska Neuropsychological Battery and an MRI. We can assume that
   a. Alan is being assessed for brain damage.
   b. Alan is a young child.
   c. Alan's clinical psychologist is a behaviorist.
   d. Alan's clinical psychologist is a psychoanalyst.

6. Dr. Ireland asks, "Who will use the test results you ask for; for what purpose is this assessment requested?" These questions highlight ________________________ concerns about testing.
   a. standardization
   b. psychometric
   c. ethical
   d. biomedical

7. ______________________ will probably be less costly than traditional assessment methods because it does not require person-to-person contact. However, we are a long way from knowing whether it increases assessment validity.
   a. The Rorschach inkblot technique
   b. Computerized assessment
   c. Electroencephalograph (EEG)
   d. Brain imaging techniques

8. Ross has a phobia about going out in public. He was recently and unexpectedly divorced by his wife, and he has a heart condition. How would this information about Ross's life show up on the DSM-IV?
   a. His phobia would be given on Axis II.
   b. His heart condition would be considered a form of organicity.
   c. His divorce would add to his stress rating on Axis IV.
   d. The phobia would not show up since it is not a disorder.

9. Oscar says, "The current diagnostic system is biased against minorities. No guidelines are given to help clinicians understand the cultural context of the client." Is Oscar correct?
   a. No, because the DSM-IV has emphasized cross-cultural assessment.
   b. No, because previous editions of the DSM had specific guidelines for cultural contexts.
   c. Yes, Axis III and Axis IV of the DSM are biased against minorities.
   d. Yes, the diagnostic system relies solely on culturally biased IQ tests.

10. After Ellen is diagnosed as "schizophrenic," she begins to act so bizarrely that she seems more schizophrenic than before. This illustrates the problem of
    a. self-fulfilling prophecies.
    b. poor reliability in the DSM-IV.
    c. diagnosis without the use of norms.
    d. reactivity in controlled observations.

ANSWER KEY: KEY TERMS REVIEW

1. reliability (72)
2. self-report inventory (78)
3. psychological tests and inventories (76)
4. assessment (73)
5. etiology (88)
6. projective personality test (76)
7. validity (72)
8. classification system (88)
9. organicity (83)
10. psychometrics (80)
11. reactivity (74)
12. prognosis (88)
13. comorbidity (92)

ANSWER KEY: FACTUAL MULTIPLE–CHOICE QUESTIONS

1. a. Predictive validity is shown when a test accurately foretells future performance or behavior.
   b. Low construct validity means that the measure fails to reliably detect a theoretically coherent pattern of behavior.
   c. Test-retest reliability is consistency across time.
   *d. Interrater reliability is the degree of agreement in measurements or judgments made by two or more observers. (p. 72)

2. *a. Because they reveal unconscious conflicts and symbolic behaviors, projective tests are favored by psychoanalysts. (pp. 76–78)
   b. The medical model would emphasize neurophysiological functioning.
   c. The behavioral perspective would favor observations of behavior and its consequences.
   d. The family systems model would examine actual communications in family settings.

3. *a. Exner's scoring system, a more reliable method than previous systems, is now the standard way to score the Rorschach. (p. 76)
   b. Intelligence tests themselves have been revised to be less culturally biased; Exner's system is used strictly with the Rorschach.
   c. Exner's system is used strictly with the Rorschach.
   d. The MMPI-2 is scored by computer.

4. a. The TAT is a projective test that uses pictures of people and asks the test taker to tell a story about them.
   b. The Wechsler scales are intelligence tests.
   *c. The MMPI–2 consists of 567 statements and yields scores on ten scales to indicate abnormal behavior and three scales to see whether the test taker gave accurate answers. (p. 78)
   d. The Bender-Gestalt asks test takers to copy designs.

5. a. Because it asks the test taker specific questions, the Beck Depression Inventory cannot be a projective personality test.
   b. Unlike the MMPI-2, the Beck Depression Inventory is focused on only one problem: depression.
   c. The Beck Depression Inventory was not designed to assess brain damage (organicity).
   *d. The Beck Depression Inventory asks for specific responses to items involving depression. (p. 80)

6. *a. The Wechsler Adult Intelligence Scale, Revised (WAIS-R), like all Wechsler scales, yields both verbal and performance IQ scores. (p. 80)
   b. The WAIS-R is an IQ test, not a diagnostic interview.
   c. The Stanford-Binet can be given to children, but the WAIS-R is usually given to people over age fifteen.
   d. The WAIS-R, like all Wechsler scales, has a verbal and a performance component.

7. *a. An electroencephalograph involves attaching electrodes to the scalp so that brain wave activity patterns can be recorded. (p. 84)
   b. The Bender-Gestalt involves copying a number of designs.
   c. CAT scans involve the use of multiple x-rays of the brain; they produce images of the brain, not recordings of brain wave activity.
   d. MRI produces a clear picture of the brain (or other structure) by surrounding the area with powerful magnetic fields.

8. a. Computers are likely to make fewer scoring errors than humans.
   b. A chief criticism of computer assessment is the absence of definitive evidence that such assessments are precise.
   c. Because machines can do the scoring tirelessly, costs are likely to be reduced.
   *d. Research shows that many clients enjoy, even prefer, being assessed by computer. (p. 85)

9. a. The behavioral model is not uniquely interested in the causes and course of disorders.
   b. One cannot have high validity without also having high reliability.
   c. Standardization requires giving a test in the same manner each time and using data from a large comparison group (a set of norms).
   *d. *Etiology* is the cause of a disorder; *prognosis* refers to the future course of the disorder. (p. 88)

10. a. Functioning level is indicated on Axis V.
 *b. Axis II indicates personality disorders or, in the case of children, developmental disorders. (p. 89)
 c. Stress level is indicated on Axis IV.
 d. The clinical syndrome—the main mental disorder—is listed on Axis I.

ANSWER KEY: CONCEPTUAL MULTIPLE–CHOICE QUESTIONS

1. *a. Assessment involves collecting as much information as possible so that the clinician gains a better understanding of the client. (p. 73)
 b. When assessment information is synthesized, classification or psychodiagnosis is being done.
 c. Tests are a possible source of information, but they are not required.
 d. Assessment is critical for research.

2. *a. Observation can lead to reactivity—the problem of people changing the way they act because they know someone is watching. (pp. 73–74)
 b. Neurological procedures do not change the way people act, or at least they don't change the way people's *brains* act.
 c. Projective techniques are used in personality testing, not in intelligence testing.
 d. Structured interviews ask very specific questions, so although people may fake their answers, they do not change their actual behavior in response to the interviewer.

3. a. Neither interview employs naturalistic observation.
 b. Interviews involve face-to-face contact, not naturalistic observation, so reactivity is always a possibility.
 *c. These interviews are fairly structured—predetermined questions are asked in a specific order—so reliability is likely to be higher than in unstructured interviews. (pp. 74–75)
 d. CAT scans and electroencephalographs are used to detect brain damage; these interviews are to assess general mental status.

4. a. Different perspectives lead to different interview strategies: psychoanalysts use less structured formats than behaviorists.
 b. Interviews rely on the combination of observation and verbal information.
 *c. According to Kleinmuntz, the relationship between interviewer and interviewee is one of three main reasons for interviewing errors. (p. 76)
 d. Psychoanalysts are least likely to use structured interviews.

5. a. Psychological tests usually look for underlying traits, not intellectual functioning.
 *b. Tests commonly have these two characteristics: a standard situation in which they are given, and the use of norms for making comparisons. (p. 76)
 c. Tests are usually standardized, so that they are given in a uniform manner.
 d. Tests are used for both research and clinical purposes.

6. a. The failing of both the original DSM and Kraepelin's system was poor reliability.
 b. Both systems relied on the medical model, not a broad range of ideas as occurs with an eclectic approach.
 c. Neither system relied on a behavioral approach; behaviorists are the prime movers of the alternative system.
 *d. Both the original DSM and Kraepelin's system were based on the biogenic idea that common symptoms have the same cause. (pp. 88–89)

7. a. In the Ward et al. (1962) study of the DSM, poor training was not a major reason for poor reliability.
   b. The DSM's poor reliability was traced to a *lack* of specific behavioral guidelines for diagnosis.
   *c. In the Ward et al. (1962) study, 62.5 percent of the errors came from inadequacies in the system itself. (p. 88)
   d. Faking has not been found to be a major source of errors.

8. *a. The principal mental disorders are listed on Axis I. (p. 89)
   b. Axis III lists physical illnesses or disorders that relate to the clinical syndrome (for example, a thyroid condition).
   c. Axis V rates the person's level of functioning currently and in the past year.
   d. The categories listed are included in DSM-IV.

9. a. Labels often influence the people who are given the labels to act differently, something called a self-fulfilling prophecy.
   *b. A criticism of labeling is that a single phrase fails to provide the detailed information on clients desired by managed-care organizations. (p. 97)
   c. One problem with labels is that labeled individuals are treated differently by others.
   d. Labeling has the problem of seeming to segregate people into qualitatively different groups.

10. a. Rosenhan's study undercut the field's faith in the DSM's reliability because professionals could not detect faked symptoms.
   b. The results were the reverse of this: Patients on the ward could tell that the pseudopatients were faking, whereas professionals could not.
   c. The pseudopatients never acted insane; they continued to act normally while in the hospital.
   *d. Hospital staff started to see abnormal behavior ("excessive note-taking") in those labeled as schizophrenic. (Focus On; p. 97)

ANSWER KEY: APPLICATION MULTIPLE–CHOICE QUESTIONS

1. a. Although this illustrates observation, it is not being done in a controlled setting such as a laboratory or clinic.
   b. A structured interview would involve a predetermined list of questions and a limited set of responses.
   c. Projective tests such as the Rorschach or TAT present test takers with ambiguous stimuli.
   *d. A bowling alley is a "real world" place where natural behavior can be observed without interference. (p. 73)

2. a. Behaviorists do not stress underlying conflicts, and they are unlikely to use projective tests.
   b. Neuropsychologists focus on brain function, so they would be more likely to use the Luria-Nebraska or a medical test.
   c. Humanists are interested in the current, conscious, subjective world of clients more than in their underlying conflicts.
   *d. Psychoanalysts have developed and used projective tests to get a general picture of functioning, underlying motives, and conflicts. (p. 76)

3. a. Objective tests offer set responses (e.g., "true" or "false") to predetermined, written items.
   b. Intelligence tests also offer structured problems with a limited range of alternative responses.
   *c. Larry is completing the Draw-a-Person test and the Rorschach test; both are projective because the stimuli presented to him are ambiguous. (pp. 76–78)
   d. Because both tests Larry is completing are projective, this cannot be the best answer.

4. a. Classification and labeling are activities that are separate from assessment and the instruments used in assessment.
   b. The cultural sensitivity of the DSM is not directly related to issues of reliability and validity in assessment.
   c. Improved cultural sensitivity of IQ testing is not directly related to issues of reliability and validity.
   *d. Mental measurement, including the reliability and validity of assessment devices, is the subject called psychometrics. (p. 80)

5. *a. The Luria-Nebraska is a test battery used to assess brain damage; an MRI is also able to detect brain lesions, tumors, and other problems associated with brain damage. (pp. 83–84)
   b. Neither the Luria-Nebraska nor MRI is limited to being used with children.
   c. A behaviorist would be interested in observable behaviors; Alan's clinical psychologist is probably a specialist in brain disorders with a biogenic orientation.
   d. A psychoanalyst would be interested in unconscious conflicts; Alan's clinical psychologist is probably a specialist in brain disorders with a biogenic orientation.

6. a. When tests are standardized, the questions are asked and responses are scored in a consistent manner.
   b. Psychometric concerns involve reliability and validity.
   *c. These questions reflect the ethical concerns that many have about psychological tests. (pp. 85–87)
   d. Biomedical concerns would highlight the impact of tests on the human body.

7. a. The Rorschach involves person-to-person contact.
   *b. Computerized assessment can be done without personal contact, and Farrell et al.'s (1987) study says clients accept it. (pp. 85–86)
   c. EEG requires one-on-one interaction.
   d. Brain imaging techniques involve person-to-person contact.

8. a. Axis II lists personality and developmental disorders, not the clinical syndrome (in this case, phobia).
   b. Organicity is restricted to brain damage, not damage to other organs.
   *c. The divorce is a strong stressor and would contribute to a high stress level rating on Axis IV. (p. 88)
   d. Phobias are considered disorders and are shown on Axis I.

9. *a. The DSM-IV emphasizes cross-cultural assessment far more than previous versions of DSM. (p. 93)
   b. Earlier editions of the DSM failed to include information on relevant cultural features of disorders.
   c. These axes record information on health and stress, issues that are unrelated to culture.
   d. IQ tests are not crucial to the diagnostic system except in matters of diagnosing mental retardation.

10. *a. Labels can change people's behavior in a process called self-fulfilling prophecy. (p. 97)
   b. We would see poor reliability if one doctor diagnosed Ellen as schizophrenic and another considered her depressed.
   c. Diagnosis without norms would occur if Ellen were considered schizophrenic without being compared with other schizophrenics.
   d. Reactivity would occur if, knowing she was being observed, Ellen began to act differently.

CHAPTER 4
The Scientific Method in Abnormal Psychology

LEARNING OBJECTIVES

1. Explain the roles of skepticism and replication in science. Discuss the current status of scientific "facts" in abnormal psychology that have received subsequent investigation, including facilitated communication and the identification of an alcoholism gene. (pp. 100–101)
2. Discuss the characteristics of the scientific method in clinical research, including the proper stating of hypotheses, operational definitions, and the need for reliable and valid measures and observations. (pp. 101–104)
3. Describe the concepts of base rates, statistical significance, and clinical significance. (p. 104)
4. Identify the components of a basic experiment, and describe the need for placebos, blind and double-blind research designs. (pp. 104–107)
5. Discuss the characteristics of correlational studies and their strengths and limitations, specifically their ambiguous conclusions with respect to causality. Use the Sanders and Giolas (1991) study to discuss how correlational research can be improved. (pp. 107–110)
6. Describe analogue and field studies, and discuss their strengths and limitations. (pp. 110–112)
7. Define the nomothetic and idiographic orientations toward research. Discuss the characteristics and limitations of case studies and single-subject experiment designs. (pp. 112–113)
8. Discuss the biological research strategies, including genetic linkage studies, biological markers, iatrogenic effects, genetic penetrance, pathognomonic symptoms, and biological challenge tests. (pp. 113–116)
9. Describe various research strategies used in the study of abnormal behavior, including epidemiological research. Differentiate between prevalence and incidence. (pp. 116–117)
10. Discuss the ethical issues in conducting research and the American Psychological Association's guiding principles on ethics, including the use of animals, and research with culturally diverse populations. (pp. 117–119)

CHAPTER OUTLINE

1. **Reasons for skepticism** (pp. 100–101) News articles, such as the recent "discovery" of facilitated communication, frequently describe research findings as "conclusive," but after use of the *scientific method,* these claims are often proven unfounded. Firm scientific information requires the replication of results, good research methods, and a skeptical attitude. Initial reports that a specific gene for alcoholism existed were questioned when subsequent studies found no difference in the prevalence of the gene in controls and samples of alcoholics and when equal or greater numbers of nonalcoholic clinical populations showed the "alcoholism" gene.

2. **The scientific method in clinical research** (pp. 101–104) The most general characteristic of science is its potential for self-correction. *Hypotheses* must be clearly stated and variables given definitions. Recent studies of child sexual abuse illustrate the range of definitions used. Measures must show reliability and validity. Appropriate comparison frequencies for a phenomenon (*base rates*) should be considered. For instance, if eating problems and child abuse are both commonly occurring events but one is unaware of this, one could mistakenly conclude that abuse causes eating problems. Finally, results should be evaluated in terms of both statistical significance (whether the results were due to a factor other than chance) and clinical significance (whether the results have clinical value). In large-sample studies, statistically significant differences are sometimes clinically meaningless.

3. **Experiments** (pp. 104–107) Experiments include experimental and control groups. Only the experimental group participants are exposed to the *independent variable* (the possible cause of behavior the experimenter manipulates). Measures of the *dependent variable* (the behavior believed to be controlled by the independent variable) are taken for participants in both groups. *Placebo groups* can be included to rule out the possibility that participants' expectations alter their behavior in the experimental group. Experimenter expectations can also be controlled by making the clinicians in a study blind (uninformed) as to the experimenter's hypothesis. To reduce the impact of both experimenter and participant expectations, there are double-blind designs where neither the individual working directly with the participant nor the participant is aware of who is in the experimental group. When changes in the dependent variable can unambiguously be attributed to the changes in the independent variable, a study is said to have *internal validity*. When results of a study can be generalized to other populations or situations, the study is said to have *external validity*.

4. **Correlations** (pp. 107–110) Correlations measure the degree to which changes in one variable are associated with changes in another variable. Statistically, these associations are symbolized by *r*, which ranges from –1.00 to +1.00. Even if a correlational study shows a strong association, it is often difficult to determine whether Variable A caused changes in Variable B, Variable B caused changes in Variable A, or some third variable affected the other two.

5. **Analogue studies and field studies** (pp. 110–112) When the study of real-life situations is impractical or unethical, *analogue studies* are conducted in simulated, but controlled, circumstances. When analogue studies are too contrived, observations can be made in the real-life situation in what is called a *field study*.

   These are limited research strategies because they cannot determine the direction of causality and they introduce the potential for observers influencing behavior.

6. **Single-subject studies** (pp. 112–113) Although most research methods are aimed at making general statements about behavior and, therefore, use groups of people (the *nomothetic* orientation), in-depth studies are sometimes done on individuals (the *idiographic* orientation). The *case study* is used extensively by clinicians, and although it lacks control and objectivity, it examines and analyzes conditions over a period of time. The *single-subject experiment* measures an individual's behavior over time. It observes changes that occur after some behavior modification has been applied.

7. **Biological research strategies** (pp. 113–116) *Genetic linkage studies* determine if a disorder follows a genetic pattern by identifying the family members of a person with a disorder (proband) who also suffer from it. *Biological marker studies* identify a biological characteristic (for example, blood flow patterns or brain size) that are associated with a disorder in family members of a proband.

   Researchers must be on guard for *iatrogenic* effects—those negative effects brought on by treatment. For example, traumatic events recalled during hypnosis may be a function of hypnotic suggestion more than accurate recollection. When a person carries a gene for a characteristic but fails to show the characteristic, there is incomplete *penetrance*. Symptoms that are distinctive for a disorder are considered *pathognomonic*. Finally, when clinical researchers use *biological challenge tests,* they observe for changes in behavior when chemicals (foods, allergens, or drugs) are introduced and for those behaviors to disappear when the chemical is absent.

8. **Epidemiological and other forms of research** (pp. 116–117; Focus On) A variety of research types including survey research, longitudinal research, historical research, twin studies, treatment outcome and treatment process studies, and program evaluation can use experimental, correlational, or single-subject methods. An important type of research is *epidemiological research,* which examines the rate and distribution of mental disorders. It can reveal the rate of new cases (*incidence*) or the total rate of cases (*prevalence*) as well as risk factors associated with the disorder.

9. **Ethical issues in research** (pp. 117–119) The scientific method can be abused and misused. The American Psychological Association has adopted the principle that the likely benefits of research must outweigh the risk or discomfort to its participants. Deception should be used only when alternatives are not possible. Only when alternatives are unavailable should animals be used as subjects, and then they should be treated in humane ways. Guidelines for research sensitive to minority ethnic and religious groups are also in place.

KEY TERMS REVIEW

1. The degree to which variations in one variable are associated with increases or decreases in a second variable is called the ____________________.

2. The research technique in which behaviors are observed or recorded in non-laboratory conditions, in the natural environment is called a(n) ____________________.

3. The method of inquiry that involves systematic collection of data through controlled observation and provides for the testing of hypotheses based on those data is called the ____________________.

4. An investigation that attempts to simulate, as closely as possible, under controlled conditions a situation that occurs in real life is called a(n) ____________________.

5. The biological research method that attempts to determine whether a disorder follows a genetic pattern is called a(n) ____________________.

6. A technique of scientific inquiry in which an independent variable is differentially manipulated for an experimental group and a control group, and the changes in a dependent variable are measured, is called a(n) ____________________.

7. Frequencies of phenomena that occur without treatment and that are used for comparing populations are called ____________________.

8. Research that studies the rate and distribution of mental disorders in a population is called ____________________.

9. In a psychological experiment, the variables (e.g., attitudes or behaviors) that are expected to change as a result of the manipulation of an independent variable are called ____________________.

10. The variable or condition that is manipulated by the experimenter and tested for its effects on the dependent variable is called the ____________________.

11. A description of variables under study in terms of the specific procedures used to measure them is called a(n) ____________________.

12. The intensive study of one individual that relies on observation, psychological tests, and historical data is called a(n) ____________________.

13. The unintended effects of treatment are considered ____________________ effects.

14. An experiment performed on a single individual in which the individual's own behavior is used as the control is called a(n) ____________________.

15. Biological indicators of a disorder that may or may not be causal are called ____________________.

16. A prediction concerning how an independent variable affects a dependent variable in an experiment is called a(n) ____________________.

17. A conjectural statement describing a relationship between two variables is called a(n) ____________________.

18. A group of principles that together explain some aspect of a specific area of study is called a(n) ____________________.

19. When a study is shown to be caused by changes in the independent variable, the study is said to have ____________________.

20. The degree to which findings of a particular study are generalizable to other populations or situations is known as ____________________.

FACTUAL MULTIPLE–CHOICE QUESTIONS

1. Epidemiological studies are concerned with
   a. independent and dependent variables.
   b. internal validity.
   c. incidence and prevalence.
   d. control groups and placebo groups.

2. Freud built his theories and developed his therapy with the use of a relatively small number of clients. His research was based on
   a. case studies.
   b. field studies.
   c. longitudinal studies.
   d. historical studies.

3. In very large samples, you can have statistically significant results without having
   a. measured any variables.
   b. employed the nomothetic approach.
   c. clinically significant results.
   d. used numerical measurements.

4. The ____________________ is the best research method for making cause-and-effect inferences.
   a. correlation
   b. historical research method
   c. case study
   d. experiment

5. In an experiment, which group is exposed to the independent variable?
   a. The control group
   b. The experimental group
   c. Both the control group and the experimental group
   d. The placebo group

6. Double-blind experimental designs are necessary
   a. when the control group's characteristics are unlike the experimental group's.
   b. to control for the effect of subjects' expectations.
   c. when no pretest has been done on the experimental group.
   d. to reduce the impact of both experimenter and participant expectations.

7. ______________________ are the research methods most often used in the study of rare conditions or when ethical standards only allow research in simulated, controlled situations.
   a. Longitudinal studies
   b. Correlations
   c. Case studies
   d. Analogue studies

8. When researchers go into a real-life situation and observe people's behavior, they are using the research method called the
   a. analogue study.
   b. correlation.
   c. field study.
   d. historical study.

9. A single-subject study that measures changes in behaviors before and after a particular modification is applied is called the
   a. analogue experiment.
   b. case study.
   c. single-subject experiment.
   d. double-blind correlational study.

10. Prevalence and incidence rates are two concepts related to
   a. epidemiology.
   b. analogue studies.
   c. single-subject experiments.
   d. idiographic research.

CONCEPTUAL MULTIPLE–CHOICE QUESTIONS

1. Why is it premature to say that alcoholism is caused by the A1 allele on a specific chromosome?
   a. The relationship between the gene and alcoholism is iatrogenic.
   b. The A1 allele proved to be pathognomonic for alcoholism.
   c. The A1 allele finding was replicated in other populations of alcoholics.
   d. Later studies showed no difference in the likelihood of the A1 allele in control and alcoholic samples.

2. What are the main characteristics of the scientific method?
   a. Personal values and belief in rationality
   b. Personal belief and emotion
   c. Skepticism and self-correction
   d. Subjectivity and personal values

3. A researcher interested in thumb sucking and later adult personality would need to know how common thumb sucking is among children. The researcher would need to know
   a. if thumb sucking is genetic.
   b. the base rate for thumb sucking.
   c. whether there is a biological marker for thumb sucking.
   d. what is a placebo for thumb sucking.

4. Unlike an experiment, in a correlational study,
   a. only the control group is exposed to the independent variable.
   b. there is no dependent variable.
   c. statistics are not used to determine the strength of association between variables.
   d. variables are not manipulated by the researcher.

5. If the results of a correlation study showed that $r = -0.73$, what could be said?
   a. There is a strong inverse relationship between the factors that were studied.
   b. The association between the two factors is so weak that the study was a failure.
   c. In 73 percent of the cases, one variable causes the other.
   d. As the scores on one of the factors go up, scores on the other factor go up, too.

6. The Sanders and Giolas (1991) study of child abuse and dissociation illustrates
   a. that good science permits little debate about how variables should be operationally defined.
   b. the value of a double-blind experimental design.
   c. that third-variable explanations still exist after correlational studies are done.
   d. that control groups are unnecessary once an association between variables is established in a clinical population.

7. Which statement about field studies is *accurate*?
   a. The primary technique for data collection in field studies is observation.
   b. The participants in field studies are most often individual cases.
   c. Field studies occur in laboratories where variables and conditions can be controlled.
   d. Researchers doing field studies need little special training.

8. Correlations and experiments are to the ____________________ orientation as case studies and single-subject experiments are to the ____________________ orientation.
   a. common-sense; scientific
   b. scientific; nomothetic
   c. idiographic; nomothetic
   d. nomothetic; idiographic

9. A study examining the level of certain neurotransmitters in people with a disorder and in a control group without the disorder is attempting to identify
   a. biological markers.
   b. iatrogenic effects.
   c. double-blind effects.
   d. penetrance.

10. Which statement below accurately summarizes the American Psychological Association's guidelines for ethical research?
   a. "Any research effort that might hurt a person or animal cannot be allowed."
   b. "Most of human behavior is best left as a mystery."
   c. "The value of any research effort must outweigh its potential risks."
   d. "Animals may be treated in any manner as long as scientific truths are the result."

APPLICATION MULTIPLE–CHOICE QUESTIONS

1. Jenny reads in the paper that scientists have found unusually high levels of a certain hormone in women who develop cancer. What information does Jenny need before she can believe the hormone increases her risk of cancer?
   a. Evidence of statistical significance on huge samples.
   b. Replication of the results by other scientists.
   c. Evidence that the hormone has a very high base rate in the general population.
   d. A correlation of about 0.00 between hormone concentrations and cancer.

2. In a research study, "alcoholism" is defined as a score of five or more on the Michigan Alcoholism Screening Test. This illustrates
   a. the use of an operational definition.
   b. a low-reliability measure.
   c. an iatrogenic effect.
   d. a base rate.

3. In an experiment to see whether diet influences depression, participants are randomly selected to eat either a high-protein–low-carbohydrate diet or their usual diet. At the end of six weeks on the diets, the experimental group is significantly less depressed. What is missing in this experiment?
   a. A control group
   b. A dependent variable
   c. An independent variable
   d. A placebo condition

4. In a study of the effects of a drug on anxiety, neither the participants nor the people dispensing the drug know who is getting a placebo and who is getting the drug being tested. This kind of study is considered
   a. correlational.
   b. a double-blind design.
   c. an analogue study.
   d. idiographic.

5. The longer Stephanie stays awake at night, the less efficient her study becomes. Which of the following best expresses the relationship between hours staying awake and study efficiency?
   a. $r = +1.00$
   b. A negative correlation
   c. A positive correlation
   d. $r = -1.00$

6. If a research study shows that life stress correlates positively with alcohol consumption, what can we conclude about the relationship between these two variables?
   a. That stress causes drinking
   b. That drinking causes stress
   c. That genetics cause both stress and drinking
   d. Nothing

7. Dr. Keys reports that one of her patients has sixteen distinct personalities. There are both male and female personalities. She reports that, through hypnosis, she has helped the personalities fuse into one competent individual. This report illustrates
   a. a correlation between sex-role typing and hypnosis.
   b. an analogue study, because the person did not receive hypnosis in the "real world."
   c. a case study.
   d. a single-subject experiment.

8. In order to study hyperactivity, a researcher asks Jimmy's teacher to keep track of how often he is out of his chair for five straight school days. Then, over the next twenty days, Jimmy is rewarded when he stays in his chair. His behavior improves. When the teacher stops the rewards, Jimmy gets worse, so rewards are returned, and his behavior improves again. This illustrates
   a. a positive correlation between reward and hyperactivity.
   b. an analogue study.
   c. a single-subject experiment.
   d. historical research.

9. Researchers interested in phobias identify 100 people who have a fear of animals. They assess the presence of a similar phobia in the parents and grandparents of all 100 people. This is an example of a(n) ____________________ study.
   a. longitudinal
   b. analogue
   c. biological challenge
   d. genetic linkage

10. Dr. Szezch is interested in the rate of new cases of childhood autism in Poland. Dr. Szezch is
   a. doing an analogue experiment.
   b. interested in the incidence of childhood autism.
   c. interested in the prevalence of childhood autism.
   d. doing unethical research.

ANSWER KEY: KEY TERMS REVIEW

1. correlation (107)
2. field study (111)
3. scientific method (101)
4. analogue study (110)
5. genetic linkage study (113)
6. experiment (104)
7. base rates (104)
8. epidemiological research (117)
9. dependent variables (105)
10. independent variable (105)
11. operational definition (102)
12. case study (112)
13. iatrogenic (115)
14. single-subject experiment (113)
15. biological markers (114)
16. experimental hypothesis (105)
17. hypothesis (101)
18. theory (101)
19. internal validity (105)
20. external validity (105)

ANSWER KEY: FACTUAL MULTIPLE–CHOICE QUESTIONS

1. a. These studies are not concerned with treatment of a disorder.
   b. These studies are concerned more so with external validity and representativeness.
   *c. Epidemiological studies yield information on the incidence (the number of new cases) and prevalence (the percentage of cases in a population during a specified time period). (p. 117)
   d. Control groups and placebo groups apply to experimental research.

2. *a. Freud relied on case studies; while this method provides in-depth information about a single case, it lacks control and objectivity. (p. 112)
   b. Freud did his work in his office and used his clinical experiences as his laboratory.
   c. Freud's case studies involved relatively short periods of time.
   d. Freud was concerned with insight, not history.

3. a. There can be no statistical analyses unless there are variables that have been measured.
   b. The nomothetic approach uses groups of people as participants.
   *c. In very large samples, statistically significant differences can have no clinical or real-world significance. (p. 104)
   d. Statistics can only be computed using numbers.

4. a. Correlational studies can only show an association between two variables, not what caused what.
   b. Historical research cannot create the experimental and control groups necessary to infer cause.
   c. Case studies examine individuals, provide no control groups, and make causal inferences impossible.
   *d. The greatest strength of the experiment is the manipulation of one factor by the experimenter and the consequent ability to make causal inferences. (p. 105)

5. a. The control group experiences the same factors as the experimental group *except* for the independent variable.
   *b. The definition of an experimental group is that it is exposed to the independent variable. (p. 105)
   c. If both groups were exposed to the independent variable, there would be no basis for comparing the two groups.
   d. The placebo group is led to believe it gets the independent variable, but it does not.

6. a. Control group characteristics should be the same as the experimental group's except for the independent variable; double-blind strategies can only reduce expectation effects, not influence sample characteristics.
   b. Double-blind studies control for both experimenters' and participants' expectations.
   c. A lack of a pretest will make it impossible to tell whether a treatment made a difference; placebos cannot help with this problem.
   *d. Double-blind studies make it impossible for either participants or those who interact with them to know whether the independent variable is being dispensed; this reduces the impact of expectations on both groups. (p. 106)

7. a. Longitudinal studies follow individuals across time; they do not involve simulated situations.
   b. Correlations involve an examination of how two factors are associated.
   c. Case studies involve an examination of one person or situation.
   *d. Analogue studies are used when it is impractical to study behavior in real-life situations, either because the behavior is rare or because control over the situation is impossible. (p. 110)

8. a. Analogue studies are done when researchers *cannot* go into a real-life situation.
   b. Correlations involve an examination of how two factors are associated.
   *c. Field studies involve "going into the field" to examine behavior in "the real world." (p. 111)
   d. Historical research involves the collection of documents to shed light on behavior in a prior period.

9. a. Analogue studies are simulations of naturally occurring situations and involve multiple subjects.
   b. Case studies look at individuals in depth but do not systematically alter conditions.
   *c. The single-subject experiment looks at one person's behavior at baseline (before the introduction of some intervention) and again afterward. The modification is often a form of treatment. (p. 113)
   d. Double-blind correlations do not exist since "blind" experiments involve the hiding of independent variables.

10. *a. Epidemiology is research that examines the distribution of cases, including new ones (incidence) and the total number (prevalence) within a given time period. (pp. 116–117)
    b. Analogue studies involve the simulation of real-life situations under more controlled circumstances.
    c. Single-subject experiments look at one person's behavior, not that of many people.
    d. The idiographic approach involves the in-depth study of individuals.

ANSWER KEY: CONCEPTUAL MULTIPLE–CHOICE QUESTIONS

1. a. An iatrogenic effect is one caused by treatment; there was no treatment and genes cannot be changed that way.
   b. If the gene were pathognomonic (specific to the disorder) it would support the idea that it causes alcoholism.
   c. If the finding were replicated in other alcoholic populations, the genetic cause of alcoholism would have been supported.
   *d. Lack of replication has led to reduced confidence that the A1 allele is a marker for alcoholism. (p. 100)

2. a. Scientists emphasize objective data rather than personal values.
   b. Scientists seek ways to reduce the influence of personal belief and emotion on their search for answers.
   *c. The hallmarks of the scientific method are skepticism (cautiousness) and self-correction (replication and efforts directed at ruling out alternative explanations). (p. 101)
   d. Scientists try to be as free from subjectivity and personal values as possible.

3. a. Genetics would have no relevance to this study.
   *b. Base rates are the frequencies of phenomena and are used to compare groups; if thumb sucking is very common, it may mean that there is little relationship between it and adult personality. (p. 104)
   c. Since the researcher is using thumb sucking as a predictor, it is unnecessary to find a biological marker for it.
   d. Placebos are only necessary in experiments; this is not an experiment.

4. a. There are no control groups in correlational studies.
   b. Dependent variables are measures of behavior; they are found in both experiments and correlational studies.
   c. The statistic called the correlation coefficient (*r*) is used to assess the strength of associations in correlational studies.
   *d. In correlations, the researcher does not manipulate a variable, but examines the association between scores on two or more variables that happen "naturally." (p. 108)

5. *a. When $r = -0.73$, there is a strong negative correlation, which indicates that as scores on one variable increase, scores on the other decrease—an inverse relationship. (p. 108)
   b. A weak association would be indicated by an r around 0.00.
   c. The correlation coefficient r is not a percentage, it is a measure of association.
   d. This kind of positive correlation would yield a positive r, such as $r = +0.66$.

6. a. The Sanders and Giolas study used a highly debatable operational definition of abuse; good science encourages debate about operational definitions.
   b. The Sanders and Giolas study was a correlational study so it could not illustrate double-blind design.
   *c. Since it is a correlational study, the findings leave open the possibility that some third variable accounts for whatever association there may be between dissociation and abuse. (p. 108)
   d. Unless we know whether abuse occurs rarely in non-dissociating populations (control groups), it is impossible to say whether abuse is a significant contributor to dissociation. Therefore such comparison groups are quite necessary.

7. *a. Field studies emphasize the observation of behavior in natural settings, so observation is a primary technique, although interviews and surveys are other possible means of recording data. (p. 111)
   b. Field studies usually focus on groups of people in organizations or communities.
   c. Field studies are done in naturalistic settings and never in laboratories.
   d. Since observation is crucial to field studies, these researchers must be trained in making careful observations and in how not to influence the behaviors of others.

8. a. Correlations and experiments are part of the scientific method; they do not necessarily rely on common sense.
   b. Case studies and single-subject experiments use one person and are therefore the opposite of the nomothetic orientation, which looks for universal behavior from many subjects.
   c. These are reversed.
   *d. Correlations and experiments use groups of people (a nomothetic approach); case studies and single-subject experiments focus on the individual (idiographic orientation). (p. 112)

9. *a. A biological characteristic such as neurotransmitter level is a biological marker that might identify those who are at risk for developing a disorder. (p. 114)
   b. Iatrogenic effects are the side effects of treatment; there is no treatment in this study.
   c. *Double-blind* refers to a study design where neither the subjects nor the individuals who work directly with them know who is in the experimental or control groups.
   d. Penetrance refers to the degree to which people having a specific gene also have a specific characteristic.

10. a. APA guidelines accept that some studies may induce embarrassment or pain in some subjects.
   b. APA guidelines encourage the pursuit of complete knowledge.
   *c. APA guidelines try to strike a balance between the need to learn and the need to protect subjects; they suggest that any risk to the subject must be overshadowed by potential benefits. (p. 119)
   d. APA guidelines have policies for the humane care of animal subjects.

ANSWER KEY: APPLICATION MULTIPLE–CHOICE QUESTIONS

1. a. Ironically, statistically significant results based on huge samples may mean that there is little clinical significance. Without clinical significance she has little reason to believe the factor increases her personal risk of cancer.
   *b. Only with replication of findings can we believe that there is stability in a scientific outcome; Jenny would be wise to be as skeptical as scientists are. (p. 101)
   c. If the base rate is high in the population, we will have a hard time seeing the hormone as causing a specific disorder since it will be present in many without the disorder.
   d. Correlations near 0.00 indicate no association between variables.

2. *a. Operational definitions define concepts in terms of how they are measured; in this case, alcoholism is defined in terms of a score on a questionnaire. (p. 102)
   b. Reliability refers to the consistency of a measure; the Michigan Alcoholism Screening Test has very strong reliability.
   c. An iatrogenic effect is caused by treatment; no treatment exists in this study.
   d. Base rates involve the frequency of a phenomenon; if the study looked at how often people score 5 on the Michigan Alcoholism Screening Test, that would entail base rates.

3. a. All experiments include control groups; in this case, it is the group that eats its normal diet.
   b. All experiments include a measure of behavior (the dependent variable); in this case, it is depressive symptoms.
   c. All experiments include an independent variable; in this case, it is the high-protein–low-carbohydrate diet.
   *d. Without controlling for expectations about how diet will alter mood, we cannot tell whether it is the diet or expectations that cause changes in feelings. We need to disguise from participants the type of food they are eating—we need a placebo condition. (p. 105)

4. a. Experimental groups receive the independent variable (the drug).
   *b. *Double-blind* means that neither the participants nor those who come in contact with them know who is getting the independent variable. (p. 106)
   c. Analogue studies look at behavior in simulated situations.
   d. Idiographic studies examine individuals in great detail; groups are being studied here.

5. a. An r of +1.00 would be a perfect positive correlation; it would mean that every minute she was awake, her studying would get consistently *better* by a uniform amount.
   *b. As her time awake increases, study efficiency decreases; that is a negative correlation. (p. 108)
   c. A positive correlation would mean that as she stays awake longer, her efficiency increases.
   d. A perfect negative correlation ($r = -1.00$) would mean that for every minute of staying awake, her efficiency would decrease by a set amount.

6. a. With correlational studies, no direction of causality can be determined.
   b. With correlational studies, no direction of causality can be determined.
   c. Correlational studies cannot determine whether a third variable causes the relationship in the other two.
   *d. Correlations tell nothing about causality. (p. 108)

7. a. Since only one person is being examined, a correlation is impossible.
   b. An analogue study would look at therapy in some simulated environment, not an actual therapy.
   *c. Since only one person is being examined, it is a case study. (p. 112)
   d. An experiment requires a control group or the use of a person's own behavior as a control (in the case of single-subject experiments).

8. a. Correlations use data from groups of people, not an individual person.
   b. This work is taking place in an actual classroom, so it is not an analogue study, which would use a simulated setting.
   *c. Single-subject experiments examine behavior before and after a treatment is introduced. (p. 113)
   d. Historical research would collect data from the past on a group of individuals.

9. a. A longitudinal study would repeatedly observe the same 100 people over time.
   b. An analogue study would put individuals in a simulated situation so that an independent variable could be introduced.
   c. A biological challenge test would introduce some chemical into the bodies of individuals to see if behavior changed.
   *d. Genetic linkage studies examine the frequency of a disorder in the family members of those who have the disorder. (p. 113)

10. a. An analogue study puts subjects in simulated situations.
   *b. Incidence is the number of new cases of a disorder in a population over a period of time. (p. 117)
   c. Prevalence is the total number of cases of a disorder (old and new) in a population over a period of time.
   d. There is nothing unethical about doing epidemiological research.

CHAPTER 5
Anxiety Disorders

LEARNING OBJECTIVES

1. Describe the nature and cognitive, behavioral, and somatic manifestations of anxiety in anxiety disorders and list the five major groups of anxiety disorders. (pp. 122–123)
2. Describe the symptoms and discuss the prevalence of panic disorder. (pp. 123–126)
3. Describe the symptoms and frequency of generalized anxiety disorder. (p. 126)
4. Discuss the psychodynamic, cognitive-behavioral, and biological theories of cause for panic disorder and generalized anxiety disorder. (pp. 126–130)
5. Compare the biochemical and behavioral treatment approaches for panic disorder and generalized anxiety disorder and discuss their relative efficacy in treating these disorders. (pp. 130–131)
6. Discuss the symptoms and prevalence of phobias, including agoraphobia, specific phobia, and social phobia. (pp. 131–140)
7. Discuss the psychodynamic, behavioral, cognitive, and biological theories for the cause of phobias. (pp. 136–140)
8. Discuss the biochemical and behavioral treatment of phobias, including systematic desensitization, exposure, and modeling therapy. (pp. 140–143)
9. Distinguish between obsessions and compulsions and describe the symptoms and prevalence of obsessive-compulsive disorder. (pp. 143–146)
10. Discuss the psychodynamic, behavioral, and biological theories of the cause of obsessive-compulsive disorder. (pp. 146–148)
11. Describe and discuss the biological, behavioral, and cognitive treatment of obsessive-compulsive disorder. (pp. 148–149)
12. Differentiate between acute stress disorders (ASD) and posttraumatic stress disorders (PTSD) and the DSM-IV's criteria for their diagnoses. (pp. 149–155)
13. Discuss the causes and treatment of PTSD, including prolonged exposure and eye movement desensitization and reprocessing. (pp. 155–157)

CHAPTER OUTLINE

1. **Manifestations of anxiety** (pp. 122–123) Anxiety is a fundamental human emotion that has an adaptive function. *Anxiety disorders* meet one of the following criteria: the anxiety is a major disturbance, the anxiety is manifested only in a particular situation, or anxiety results from attempts to master other symptoms. *Anxiety* is manifested cognitively, behaviorally, and somatically. Cognitive symptoms range from mild worry to panic; behaviors include avoidance

of feared situations; somatic signs include shallow breathing, perspiring, and muscular tension. In the current diagnostic system, anxiety disorders consist of *panic disorder, generalized anxiety disorder (GAD), phobias, obsessive-compulsive disorder,* and *acute* and *posttraumatic stress disorders.* In each of these disorders, a person can experience panic attacks—intense fear with symptoms such as a pounding heart and fear of losing control. There are three types of attacks: (1) situationally bound (occurring in response to a stimulus); (2) situationally predisposed (usually occurring in response to a stimulus); and (3) unexpected attacks. Most attacks are of the first two types.

2. **Panic disorder and generalized anxiety disorder** (pp. 123–130) Free-floating anxiety characterizes both panic disorder and generalized anxiety disorder. Panic disorder is diagnosed when a person has recurrent panic attacks that alternate with periods of low anxiety. Such attacks are terrifying and may lead to agoraphobia. While attacks are fairly common, the disorder is not; the lifetime prevalence is 3.8 percent. Generalized anxiety disorder is characterized by persistent anxiety, heart palpitations, tension, and restlessness, together lasting over six months. People with GAD worry over major and minor events and have more persistent but less severe physical symptoms than people with panic disorder. Estimated lifetime prevalence of GAD in the United States is 6.6 percent for females and 3.6 percent for males.

   Psychoanalysts suggest that internal (sexual) conflicts are expressed in outward anxiety. The effectiveness of defenses used determines whether the person develops panic disorder or generalized anxiety disorder. The cognitive behavioral thinkers argue that catastrophic thoughts and overattention to internal signals maintain and inflate anxiety symptoms. Research in which subjects had marked increases in cardiovascular activity after focusing on negative thoughts supports this argument. The biogenic perspective focuses on panic disorder and notes that such factors as oxygen-monitoring receptors and response to sodium lactate influence panic attacks. Dysfunction in the locus ceruleus, a part of the central anxiety system in the brain, may account for panic disorders. Genetics also seem to play a role, particularly in panic disorder.

3. **Treatment of panic disorder and generalized anxiety disorder** (pp. 130–131) Medications, particularly the antidepressants, have proven useful in treating panic disorder, although relapse rates after ceasing the drugs is high. Benzodiazepines (Valium and Librium) have been used successfully to treat generalized anxiety disorder, but psychological treatment is also necessary. Behavior therapies, including relaxation training and cognitive restructuring, show promise. Treatment for panic disorder can include educating the client about the disorder, training in relaxation techniques, altering unrealistic thoughts, facing the symptoms, and developing coping strategies. Cognitive therapy seems particularly effective for generalized anxiety disorder.

4. **Phobias: Agoraphobia, social phobias, and specific phobias** (pp. 131–136) A *phobia* is an intense, persistent, and unwarranted fear of an object or situation. Attempts to avoid the fear-inducing situation interfere with the person's life. Phobias are the most common mental disorder in the United States. *Agoraphobia* is a fear of being in public places without the availability of help. Lifetime prevalence is 7 percent for females and 3.5 percent for males. The disorder, more common in females than males, often has a precipitating event, and thoughts play a key role. People with agoraphobia tend to react more intensely to anxiety symptoms than people with other anxiety problems. *Social phobia* is an intense fear of being watched and humiliated. There are three types of social phobias: performance (involving such activities as public speaking), limited interactional (involving such interactions as going out on a date), and generalized (where extreme anxiety occurs in most social situations). The last category has been criticized for being too similar to avoidant personality disorder. Except for public speaking, social phobias are somewhat rare. Despite knowing that their fears are irrational, people with social phobias curtail many activities. The distinction between social phobias and normal social fears is a difficult one to make. *Specific phobias* are fears of specific objects and include a long list of disorders. In DSM-IV there are five types: animal, natural environmental (for example, thunder); blood/injections or injury; situational (for example, heights); and other (a range of

situations that may lead to choking or illness). The most common phobias involve small animals, heights, the dark, and lightning. They are twice as prevalent in women as in men and are rarely incapacitating.

5. **Etiology and treatment of phobias** (pp. 136–143) Psychoanalysts see phobias as symbolic of unconscious sexual or aggressive conflicts. The case of little Hans is used to explain a youth's fear of horses. Classical conditioning explains the development of some phobias. Observational learning and operant conditioning principles may explain some phobias. Retrospective reports indicate that conditioning experiences play a major causative role. However, in one study, 36 percent of phobics could not remember how their fear was acquired. Catastrophic thoughts may cause strong fears to develop and phobic individuals are more likely than other people to overestimate the odds of unpleasant events occurring, supporting a cognitive-behavioral perspective. Genetic evidence indicates that phobias may stem from a predisposition to excessive autonomic reaction to stress, but genetic vulnerability has only a modest relationship to specific phobias. The notion of prepared learning is also related to the existence of certain phobias and the nonexistence of others.

   Biochemical treatment of the phobias usually involves antidepressants, although a beta blocker has been used to treat social phobias. Behavioral treatment seems necessary in addition to medication when treating agoraphobia. *Exposure therapy* (the gradual presentation of the feared situation) has been helpful in reducing fears and panic attacks in agoraphobic individuals and those with specific phobias. Multimodal treatment that includes cognitive, behavioral, and physiological components is increasingly used. *Systematic desensitization* is often used to treat social and simple phobias. *Modeling therapy* and cognitive-behavioral approaches are also highly effective with certain phobias.

6. **Obsessive-compulsive disorder** (pp. 143–146) Obsessive-compulsive disorder is an anxiety disorder characterized by intrusive thoughts (*obsessions*) and the need to perform ritualistic actions *(compulsions)*. The symptoms are "ego-dystonic"—they are involuntary and are perceived as alien. Once thought to be rare, obsessive-compulsive disorder has an estimated lifetime prevalence of between 2 and 3 percent. Common *obsessions* among adults involve bodily wastes, dirt or germs, and environmental contamination. Many "normal" individuals have obsessions, but those with obsessive-compulsive disorder report thoughts that last longer, produce more discomfort, and cannot be easily controlled. *Compulsions* are behaviors that are designed to reduce anxiety but that cause distress if not performed correctly. To the compulsive, these actions have the magical ability to ward off danger.

7. **Etiology and treatment of obsessive-compulsive disorder** (pp. 146–149) The causes of obsessive compulsive disorder are unclear. One theory, favored by psychoanalysts, suggests that obsessions substitute for unconscious conflicts and that compulsions are based on defense mechanisms such as undoing and reaction formation. The behavioral perspective emphasizes the anxiety-reducing functions of compulsions. Biogenic models emphasize differences in brain function, genetic vulnerability, and effects of medication on individuals with obsessive-compulsive disorder. Recent research shows that people with obsessive-compulsive disorder have higher levels of glucose metabolism in the frontal lobes.

   Antidepressant medication is the chief biological treatment for obsessive-compulsive disorder, but only 60 to 80 percent of obsessive-compulsives respond to these drugs, relief is only partial, and relapse is a problem. Behavioral treatments, including systematic desensitization, *flooding*, and response prevention, have been effective. Cognitive approaches identify and challenge the irrational thoughts of obsessive-compulsives.

8. **Acute (ASD) and posttraumatic stress disorders (PTSD): Diagnosis, etiology, and treatment** (pp. 149–157) Acute stress disorder produces dissociation, a reliving of a traumatic experience, and avoidance of reminders of the experience. It lasts for less than thirty days and occurs within four weeks of the stressful event. PTSD is an anxiety disorder involving delayed reactions, lasting thirty or more days, to extraordinarily distressing events. Symptoms include reexperiencing the event, intrusive memories and dreams, emotional numbing, and heightened autonomic arousal.

Diagnosis is subjective and difficult because it depends on the definition of the stressor. Recent research suggests that some extreme stressors may produce PTSD in almost everyone. Although men are more likely to be exposed to stressors, women seem to be more likely than men to suffer from PTSD. Roughly 80 percent of women in one sample developed PTSD after being raped. Classical conditioning combined with poor coping styles seems a good explanation for the development of this disorder. Preexisting anxiety disorder or a family history of anxiety occurs in many with PTSD. A range of treatments for PTSD exists. Extinction through prolonged exposure has helped individuals with PTSD. A new treatment is called *eye movement desensitization and reprocessing* (EMDR), in which the individual visualizes the disturbing situation and then visually tracks back and forth the clinician's finger while keeping the head immobile. It is not clear how this treatment has its therapeutic effects and some studies are questioning its effectiveness.

KEY TERMS REVIEW

1. A strong subjective need to perform an act in order to reduce anxiety is called a(n) ____________________.

2. A strong, persistent, and unwarranted fear of a specific object or situation is called a(n) ____________________.

3. The therapeutic technique that involves continued actual or imagined exposure to a feared situation is called ____________________.

4. An excessive fear of being scrutinized in social situations is called a(n) ____________________.

5. Feelings of fear and apprehension are also called ____________________.

6. The disorder characterized by persistent high levels of anxiety and excessive worry over many life circumstances is called ____________________.

7. The anxiety disorder that is characterized by intrusive memories of a traumatic event, emotional withdrawal, and increased arousal levels, and that lasts more than thirty days, is called ____________________.

8. The therapy technique of gradually exposing the client to a feared situation is called ____________________.

9. An extreme fear of a specific object that is not classified as agoraphobia or a social phobia is called a(n) ____________________.

10. Disorders such as phobias and panic disorder that are characterized by irrational feelings of fear and apprehension are called ____________________.

11. The anxiety disorder that involves intrusive and uncontrollable thoughts, the need to perform specific acts repeatedly, or both is called ____________________.

12. The anxiety disorder characterized by severe episodes of apprehension and feelings of impending doom is called ____________________.

13. An intrusive, uncontrollable, and persistent thought or image is called a(n) ____________________.

14. The disorder involving an intense fear of open spaces or of being alone where help may not be available is called ________________________.

15. The therapeutic approach to phobias in which the phobic client observes a fearless individual coping with the fear-producing situation is called ________________________.

16. The behavior therapy technique in which relaxation is used to eliminate the anxiety associated with phobias and other fear-evoking situations is called ____________________.

17. The disorder, lasting less than thirty days, in which a traumatic stressor results in dissociation, reliving the experience, and attempts to avoid reminders of the event is called ________________________.

FACTUAL MULTIPLE–CHOICE QUESTIONS

1. When anxiety produces changes in breathing, perspiration, and muscle tension, these changes reflect ____________________ manifestations of anxiety.
   a. behavioral
   b. somatic
   c. cognitive
   d. neurological

2. Which statement below concerning panic attacks is *accurate*?
   a. They always occur in specific situations and are preceded by warning signs of their occurrence.
   b. They are fairly common.
   c. They are extremely rare and occur only in people who suffer from panic disorder.
   d. They involve behavioral aspects of anxiety but not cognitive or somatic ones.

3. The chemical ____________________ seems to induce panic attacks in clients with panic disorder.
   a. imipramine.
   b. serotonin.
   c. alcohol.
   d. sodium lactate.

4. Which statement about the biological treatment of generalized anxiety disorder is *accurate*?
   a. The first effective treatment was a form of brain surgery called leucotomy.
   b. Medication helps reduce anxiety, but psychological treatment is also necessary for successful treatment.
   c. Antidepressants are more helpful than benzodiazepines.
   d. The most effective medication is sodium lactate.

5. Agoraphobia is
   a. much more common in men than in women.
   b. characterized by persistent unwanted thoughts and rituals.
   c. an intense fear of being in public places without available help.
   d. so similar to panic attack that the two have been merged in the DSM-IV.

6. What makes it difficult to diagnose the generalized type of social phobia?
   a. The phobic individual is only frightened in the presence of a specific situation.
   b. The phobic individual does not believe that his or her fears are irrational.
   c. The symptoms overlap with many other disorders.
   d. The lifetime prevalence rate is so high (about 20 percent) that it seems as if everyone has the disorder.

7. The behavior therapy that teaches clients to relax while imagining a feared stimulus is called
   a. systematic desensitization.
   b. cognitive restructuring.
   c. flooding.
   d. modeling therapy.

8. An effective multimodal approach for treating agoraphobia might include
   a. sodium lactate and exposure therapy.
   b. antidepressants and exposure to public places.
   c. social isolation and eye movement desensitization and reprocessing.
   d. flooding and preparedness learning.

9. The preferred behavioral treatment for obsessive-compulsive disorder is
   a. relaxation training and biofeedback.
   b. biofeedback and response prevention.
   c. cognitive restructuring and positive reinforcement.
   d. flooding and response prevention.

10. A new treatment for posttraumatic stress disorder involves
    a. the use of the tranquilizer imipramine.
    b. visually tracking the clinician's finger back and forth.
    c. repeated exposure and response prevention.
    d. avoidance of the distressing situation.

CONCEPTUAL MULTIPLE–CHOICE QUESTIONS

1. Recurrent unexpected panic attacks and at least one month of worry over having another are the criterion for diagnosing
   a. agoraphobia.
   b. panic disorder.
   c. generalized anxiety disorder.
   d. posttraumatic stress disorder.

2. Constant worry over major and minor life events, poor concentration, and physiological symptoms that are less extreme than a panic attack but last more than six months are the chief characteristics of
   a. acute stress disorder.
   b. social phobia.
   c. obsessive-compulsive disorder.
   d. generalized anxiety disorder.

3. Cognitive behavioral theorists suggest that generalized anxiety disorder develops when
   a. people discover they can avoid the negative consequences of panic attacks by avoiding situations in which they occur.
   b. the consequence of a fear response is punished or extinguished.
   c. a feedback loop between catastrophic thoughts and somatic symptoms increases anxiety.
   d. people mistakenly believe they have control over situations and their internal arousal level.

4. A psychodynamic explanation for specific phobias stresses
   a. prepared learning.
   b. irrational beliefs that mistakenly predict negative events.
   c. how symptoms are a compromise between the ego and the id's need to gratify sexual impulses.
   d. how parents provide modeling for the fears that develop in early childhood.

5. Research on the genetic cause of agoraphobia
   a. suggests that both heredity and modeling may account for it being prevalent in first-degree relatives of agoraphobics.
   b. has shown no higher vulnerability in parents or siblings of agoraphobic patients than in control groups.
   c. indicates that what is inherited is an underactive autonomic nervous system.
   d. suggests that the neurotransmitter imipramine is deficient in these clients.

6. If preparedness were not an issue in the development of phobias,
   a. it would be unlikely that we would find any phobias for cars or airplanes.
   b. we would find that any object was as likely as any other to be a source of terror.
   c. genetics would be the sole reason for phobias.
   d. classical conditioning could no longer be considered a reason for phobias.

7. A persistent and unwanted fear of being contaminated by dirt and germs illustrates ________________ and is often associated with the ________________ of handwashing.
   a. a phobia; obsession
   b. an obsession; compulsion
   c. a compulsion; phobia
   d. preparedness; compulsion

8. Which of the following statements about the psychoanalytic theory of obsessive-compulsive disorder is *accurate*?
   a. It is based on observational learning.
   b. It adequately explains the majority of cases of obsessive-compulsive disorder.
   c. It is essentially the same thing as preparedness theory.
   d. It assumes that symptoms originate out of defenses against unconscious conflicts.

9. Which theory and concept pairing concerning the cause of obsessive-compulsive disorder is *accurate*?
   a. Biological: orbital frontal cortex activity
   b. Biological: sodium lactate sensitivity
   c. Behavioral: reaction formation and undoing
   d. Behavioral: catastrophic thinking

10. Anxiety disorders that stem from extraordinarily distressing events such as living through tornadoes and incest or rape, and that last more than thirty days, are considered
    a. forms of social phobia.
    b. generalized anxiety disorder.
    c. forms of obsessive-compulsive disorder.
    d. posttraumatic stress disorder.

APPLICATION MULTIPLE–CHOICE QUESTIONS

1. Dr. Thomas says, "They can occur in response to a specific feared stimulus or come on unexpectedly. When you have one, you think you might be dying of a heart attack. They are fairly common: Between one-quarter and one-third of college students report having had one in the past year." What is Dr. Thomas referring to?
   a. Obsessions
   b. Compulsions
   c. Posttraumatic stress reactions
   d. Panic attacks

2. Gene is diagnosed as suffering from generalized anxiety disorder, whereas Paul is diagnosed with panic disorder. What is the main difference between the two diagnoses?
   a. In panic disorder, the person shows relatively low anxiety levels between panic episodes.
   b. In panic disorder, the person is constantly worried about a wide range of life situations.
   c. In generalized anxiety disorder, the person primarily experiences the somatic aspects of anxiety.
   d. In generalized anxiety disorder, the person performs rituals as a way of reducing anxiety.

3. Ben is being treated for panic disorder. His therapist tells him, "You need to change from thinking 'I'll pass out if I walk into that store' to 'I can control my anxiety.'" What perspective on anxiety disorders does this illustrate?
   a. Classical conditioning
   b. Psychoanalytic
   c. Cognitive-behavioral
   d. Biological

4. Dr. Harlan is a researcher investigating the relationship between the locus ceruleus and a specific anxiety symptom. Which symptom is she most likely interested in?
   a. Obsessions
   b. Fear of being in public
   c. Compulsions
   d. Panic attack

5. Charlene is receiving biological treatment for her panic disorder. It is most likely that she is getting
   a. electroshock treatments.
   b. antidepressants.
   c. biofeedback.
   d. sodium lactate.

6. Laurie is terribly afraid of being seen in restaurants or movie theaters because she fears she will make a complete fool of herself in some way. She recognizes that her fear is irrational, but the fear completely controls her. Laurie's problem best illustrates
   a. a social phobia.
   b. agoraphobia.
   c. phobophobia.
   d. generalized anxiety disorder.

7. A psychologist says, "The case of little Hans (and his 'widdler') illustrates that classical conditioning might cause phobias. Unfortunately, other attempts to replicate that study have failed." What part of the psychologist's statement is *inaccurate*?
   a. It is inaccurate to say that the case of little Hans illustrates classical conditioning.
   b. It is inaccurate to say that the case of little Hans involved phobias.
   c. It is inaccurate to say that the case of little Hans examined the cause of a disorder.
   d. It is inaccurate to say that the results of the case were not replicated.

8. Suppose we found that, of 100 people with phobias, 80 percent had a fear of animals, 10 percent had a fear of germs and dirt, and the remainder feared enclosed places. None of the people had phobias about machinery. This finding would support the ____________________ approach to phobias.
   a. cognitive-behavioral
   b. psychoanalytic
   c. exposure
   d. preparedness

9. A psychiatrist says, "Even in normal populations, there are people who are fearful of contamination and of being out of control. They check everything to lessen their worries." What kind of problem is the psychiatrist describing?
   a. Posttraumatic stress disorder
   b. Obsessions
   c. Panic disorder
   d. Reaction formation

10. After being unsuccessfully treated with antidepressants for obsessive-compulsive disorder, Wayne is looking for a treatment technique that is both effective and takes little time. A psychologist might suggest ____________________ to Wayne.
    a. biofeedback
    b. psychoanalytic psychotherapy
    c. flooding and response prevention
    d. systematic desensitization

ANSWER KEY: KEY TERMS REVIEW

1. compulsion (143)
2. phobia (131)
3. flooding (149)
4. social phobia (133)
5. anxiety (122)
6. generalized anxiety disorder (126)
7. posttraumatic stress disorder (150)
8. exposure therapy (141)
9. specific phobia (134)
10. anxiety disorders (122)
11. obsessive-compulsive disorder (143)
12. panic disorder (123)
13. obsession (143)
14. agoraphobia (132)
15. modeling therapy (143)
16. systematic desensitization (142)
17. acute stress disorder (150)

ANSWER KEY: FACTUAL MULTIPLE–CHOICE QUESTIONS

1. a. Behavioral aspects of anxiety involve avoidance of places where anxiety has occurred in the past.
   *b. Sweating, muscular tension, heart palpitations, cold hands and feet, perspiration, and diarrhea are all somatic manifestations of anxiety. (p. 122)
   c. Cognitive manifestations of anxiety include worrying, indecisiveness, and confusion.
   d. There are no neurological manifestations of anxiety, but if there were, they would involve changes in nervous system structures.

2. a. Panic attacks can occur in specific situations, but can also come on without warning.
   *b. Although panic disorder is uncommon, many people report having had at least one panic attack; nearly 45 percent of college women report an attack in the past year. (p. 125)
   c. Panic disorder is defined by recurrent panic attacks, but many "normal" people have one or two such attacks over a lifetime.
   d. Panic attacks are so distressing because they affect behavior, thought, and physical functioning.

3. a. Imipramine is an antidepressant drug that reduces symptoms of anxiety.
   b. Serotonin is a neurotransmitter that appears to regulate emotional experience.
   c. Alcohol does not increase anxiety; it tends to reduce it.
   *d. Sensitivity to sodium lactate appears to be a biological difference between those who are vulnerable to panic disorder and those who are not. (p. 130)

4. a. Leucotomy was originally used as a surgical treatment for obsessive-compulsive disorder.
   *b. Medication, such as benzodiazepines, helps reduce symptoms, but anxiety management training seems necessary to alter avoidance responses. (p. 131)
   c. Benzodiazepines have proven to be more effective than antidepressants when treating generalized anxiety disorder.
   d. Sodium lactate increases the likelihood of panic attack, rather than reducing it.

5. a. Agoraphobia is two or three times more likely in women.
   b. Persistent thoughts and rituals are symptoms of obsessive-compulsive disorder.
   *c. Agoraphobia is an intense fear of being in public without support or assistance, and leads to avoidance of such situations. (p. 132)
   d. Agoraphobia may develop after panic attacks, but the two are separate disorders.

6. a. The generalized type does not respond with anxiety to a specific situation.
   b. All phobic individuals know that their fears are irrational, but they are controlled by them anyway.
   *c. Several researchers report complete overlap in the symptoms of generalized anxiety disorder and avoidant personality disorder. (p. 133)
   d. Overall, the lifetime prevalence for social phobias is 11 to 15 percent, but generalized social phobia is just one of three subtypes of the disorder.

7. *a. Systematic desensitization involves teaching relaxation skills and then pairing relaxation with imagined or real anxiety-producing situations on a gradual basis. (p. 142)
   b. Cognitive restructuring focuses on how we think about situations and our behavior in them.
   c. Flooding represents "cold turkey" extinction and high levels of anxiety; it is the opposite of systematic desensitization.
   d. Modeling therapy involves imitation of effective individuals and does not rely on relaxation training or classical conditioning.

8. a. Sodium lactate induces panic attacks; it is unrelated to treating agoraphobia.
   *b. Successful treatment of agoraphobia has included antidepressants, which appear to reduce anxiety, and behavior therapy, which gets individuals to face fearful situations. (p. 141)
   c. Social isolation would intensify agoraphobia; eye movement desensitization and reprocessing treatment is used for PTSD.
   d. Flooding is used for obsessive-compulsive disorder, and preparedness is an explanation for the cause of phobias, not a treatment method.

9. a. Relaxation training may be helpful, but biofeedback will have little effect on reducing ritualistic actions.
   b. Biofeedback will have little effect on reducing ritualistic actions.
   c. Positive reinforcement will not reduce the likelihood of ritualistic actions.
   *d. It is necessary to extinguish both anxiety (through flooding) and ritualistic actions (through response prevention). (p. 149)

10. a. Imipramine is an antidepressant that is most effective in treating panic disorder and agoraphobia.
   *b. Eye movement desensitization and reprocessing, which involves visualizing the disturbing situation and tracking the clinician's finger or pencil as it moves from side to side, is a new but controversial treatment for PTSD. (p. 157)
   c. Repeated exposure may reduce the anxiety of the remembered situation, but there is no ritualistic action that must be prevented.
   d. Continued avoidance of disturbing situations maintains an anxiety disorder rather than effectively treating it.

ANSWER KEY: CONCEPTUAL MULTIPLE–CHOICE QUESTIONS

1. a. Agoraphobia involves intense fear of going out in public without assistance.
   *b. Panic disorder is diagnosed when there are recurrent panic attacks and at least one month of worry about another occurring or about the consequences of a previous one. (p. 124)
   c. Generalized anxiety disorder is characterized by constant worry and anxiety symptoms that are less intense than those in panic disorder.
   d. Posttraumatic stress disorder is diagnosed when symptoms occur after an event outside the normal range of life stressors (for example, experiencing a tornado)

2. a. Psychogenic amnesia is a dissociative disorder characterized by memory loss.
   b. Panic disorder is characterized by intermittent yet terrifying episodes, but relatively low anxiety levels otherwise.
   c. Obsessive-compulsive disorder is diagnosed when a person has worrisome thoughts that lead to ritualistic actions such as handwashing or repetitive checking.
   *d. Generalized anxiety disorder is characterized by constant worry over both minor and major events, indecisiveness and poor concentration, and physiological manifestations of anxiety such as sweating and muscle tension. (p. 126)

3. a. Generalized anxiety disorder is not associated with panic attacks; the anxiety in the disorder is constant and at a low level.
   b. Consequences are the focus of operant conditioning principles, and if a response is extinguished it should disappear rather than strengthen.
   *c. Cognitive behaviorists say that when individuals think catastrophic thoughts or pay extra attention to bodily changes, they trigger somatic symptoms, which foster more negative thoughts and greater anxiety. (p. 128)
   d. Thoughts before and during panic attacks involve being out of control.

4. a. Preparedness is a biological concept.
   b. Irrational beliefs are cognitive concepts.
   *c. Psychodynamic explanations stress unconscious conflicts between id and ego. (p. 136)
   d. Modeling is a social learning concept.

5. *a. Just because a disorder runs in families does not mean that inheritance is the cause; imitation of parents is just as likely an explanation. (p. 139)
   b. First-degree relatives do show higher percentages of cases.
   c. If anything is inherited, it is an overactive autonomic nervous system.
   d. Imipramine is an antidepressant medication, not a neurotransmitter.

6. a. Preparedness suggests that posttechnical-age objects (such as cars) do not easily become conditioned stimuli.
   *b. If preparedness did not enter into the equation, every object would have an equal chance of being a source of phobia if it were paired with anxiety. (p. 139)
   c. Preparedness only suggests that certain categories of objects are easily associated with anxiety; no prediction is made as to the importance of genetics as the cause.
   d. Classical conditioning could still be the explanation; all that changes is the object that induces terror.

7. a. A phobia is an intense, irrational fear of an object, not an unwanted thought.
   *b. An obsession is an unwanted and unstoppable thought; a compulsion is a ritualistic behavior to ward off the worry. (p. 143)
   c. A phobia is an intense, irrational fear, not a ritualistic action.
   d. Preparedness deals with the likelihood of certain stimuli becoming the target of a phobia, not with persistent thoughts.

8. a. Substitution, not observation, is a psychoanalytic explanation.
   b. Although psychoanalytic explanations have clinical appeal, they do not explain the majority of cases.
   c. Preparedness is a concept used to explain the cause of specific phobias.
   *d. As a psychodynamic explanation, substitution says that symptoms at the surface substitute for conflicts below the surface. (p. 146)

9. *a. Research shows that higher glucose metabolism is found in the orbital frontal cortex of people with obsessive-compulsive disorder than in controls. (p. 148)
   b. Sodium lactate is a biogenic explanation for panic disorder.
   c. Psychoanalysts, not behaviorists, would emphasize these defense mechanisms.
   d. Cognitive theorists, not behaviorists, would emphasize catastrophic thinking.

10. a. Social phobias involve intense fears of activity in public (such as using public toilets) and are not related to severe traumatic events.
   b. Generalized anxiety disorder rarely develops out of a particular traumatic event.
   c. Obsessive-compulsive disorder is characterized by unwanted thoughts and ritualistic actions.
   *d. Posttraumatic stress disorder is a delayed reaction to a stressful event outside the normal range of human experience. (p. 150)

ANSWER KEY: APPLICATION MULTIPLE–CHOICE QUESTIONS

1. a. Obsessions are unwanted, persistent anxiety-arousing thoughts. They do not come on without warning.
   b. Compulsions are stereotyped, ritualistic actions that reduce anxiety.
   c. Posttraumatic stress disorder occurs in response to a specific, highly stressful event.
   *d. Panic attacks involve heart palpitations and can occur in response to a specific situation or be unexpected; college students report they are fairly common. (p. 126)

2. *a. In between panic attacks, those with panic disorder are relatively low in anxiety; those with generalized anxiety disorder are never low in anxiety. (p. 126)
   b. It is in generalized anxiety disorder that worry is constant.
   c. In both disorders, anxiety produces somatic complaints; in panic disorder, the anxiety is so great the patient may think he or she will die.
   d. Rituals are associated with obsessive-compulsive disorder.

3. a. Classical conditioning focuses on the external stimuli that are associated with fear responses.
   b. Psychoanalytic explanations look for the unconscious conflicts that surface in symbolic symptoms.
   *c. Cognitive-behavioral theorists stress how thinking influences the experience of anxiety. (p. 127)
   d. Biological explanations stress the genetics of patients and their sensitivity to such chemicals as sodium lactate.

4. a. Obsessions are associated with heightened frontal cortex activity.
   b. Social phobias have no clear relationship to brain abnormalities.
   c. Compulsions are associated with heightened frontal cortex activity.
   *d. People with panic disorder have been found to have unusually high sensitivity in the locus ceruleus, a portion of the central anxiety system of the brain. (p. 129)

5. a. Electroshock treatments may be helpful in depression, but not in panic disorder.
   *b. Antidepressants such as imipramine have been helpful in reducing the frequency and intensity of panic attacks. (p. 131)
   c. Biofeedback is not actually a biological treatment; it is based on operant conditioning.
   d. Sodium lactate seems to increase panic attacks in patients, but not in controls.

6. *a. Social phobias are characterized by irrational fears of performing actions in public that will be evaluated. (p. 133)
   b. Agoraphobia is an intense fear of being in public (in general) without available help.
   c. Phobophobia is a fear of having a phobia.
   d. Generalized anxiety disorder involves worry about almost everything, not a specific target as in phobias.

7. *a. The case of little Hans underscored psychodynamic explanations, and was unrelated to classical conditioning. (p. 137)
   b. The case of little Hans was used by Freud to explain how the surface symptoms of a phobia stemmed from unconscious (oedipal) conflicts.
   c. The case of little Hans was about the causes of phobia.
   d. As a case, the results have not been replicated; evidence does not sustain Freud's analysis of phobia.

8. a. Cognitive-behavioral explanations focus on thoughts.
   b. Psychoanalytic explanations focus on unconscious conflicts.
   c. Exposure is the treatment technique of extinguishing anxiety through habituation.
   *d. Preparedness is the concept that pretechnical objects related to evolution are more likely to be objects of phobic fear than technical ones such as cars and machinery. (p. 139)

9. a. Posttraumatic stress disorder involves events, not thoughts.
   *b. Contamination worries and checking behaviors are seen in the obsessional activities of many people. (p. 144)
   c. Panic disorder involves fears of attacks, not worries over contamination.
   d. Reaction formation is a defense mechanism, not a disorder.

10. a. Biofeedback has not been helpful in treating obsessive-compulsive disorder.
   b. Psychoanalytic therapy takes a long time.
   *c. Flooding (arousal of intense fear) and response prevention (stopping avoidance of the object) is a quick and effective treatment. (p. 149)
   d. Systematic desensitization may be helpful, but it is more time-consuming than flooding.

CHAPTER 6
Dissociative Disorders and Somatoform Disorders

LEARNING OBJECTIVES

1. Discuss the fundamental characteristics involved in dissociative disorders, and list the four types of dissociative disorders. (p. 160)
2. Discuss the characteristics of the four types of dissociative amnesia and the process by which they occur. (pp. 160–161)
3. Describe the characteristics of dissociative fugue and depersonalization disorder. (pp. 161–165)
4. Discuss the controversy over the validity of "repressed memories" and research that indicates the possibility of false memories. (pp. 164–167; Critical Thinking; First Person)
5. Describe the characteristics of dissociative identity (multiple personality) disorder and its prevalence. (pp. 165–167)
6. Discuss the diagnostic controversies concerning dissociative identity disorder. (pp. 167–169)
7. Discuss and distinguish the psychodynamic, behavioral, and iatrogenic (therapist-produced) explanations for dissociative disorders. (pp. 169–172)
8. Discuss the treatment of dissociative amnesia and fugue, depersonalization disorder, and dissociative identity disorder. (pp. 172–174)
9. Describe the basic characteristics of somatoform disorders and distinguish them from malingering and factitious disorders. (pp. 174–175, 178; Focus On)
10. List and describe the five subtypes of somatoform disorder, including somatization disorder, conversion disorder, pain disorder, hypochondriasis, and body dysmorphic disorder. (pp. 175–182; Focus On)
11. Describe and discuss the causes of somatoform disorders from the psychodynamic, behavioral, sociocultural, and biological perspectives, and the diathesis-stress model. (pp. 182–186)
12. Describe and discuss the treatment of somatoform disorders with psychoanalytic, behavioral, and family systems therapies. (pp. 186–187)

CHAPTER OUTLINE

1. **Dissociative and somatoform disorders** (p. 160) The *dissociative disorders* show altered or disrupted identity, memory, or consciousness; the *somatoform disorders* involve physical symptoms that have no physiological basis. Both disorders occur because of some psychological need and both rely on self-reports, and so are subject to faking. There are four dissociative disorders: dissociative amnesia, dissociative fugue, dissociative identity disorder (formerly

called multiple-personality disorder), and depersonalization disorder. Except for depersonalization, dissociative disorders are rare, although there has been a dramatic increase in reports of dissociative identity disorder.

2. **Dissociative amnesia** (pp. 160–161) *Dissociative amnesia* is the partial or total loss of important personal information, often occurring in response to a stressful event. There are four types. *Localized amnesia* is characterized by total memory loss for a particular, short time period, and is the most common form. In *selective amnesia,* the memory loss is for details about an incident. Total loss of memory for one's past life is the criterion for *generalized amnesia*, and total loss of memory from one point in time to another occurs in *continuous amnesia*. Repression seems to be the main reason for psychogenic amnesia; a similar process occurs in *posthypnotic amnesia.* There is great controversy about the validity of uncovered, repressed memories for child abuse.

3. **Dissociative fugue and depersonalization disorder** (pp. 161–165) In *dissociative fugue*, memory loss is accompanied by flight to another area and establishment of a new identity. Recovery from this and from psychogenic amnesia is usually abrupt and spontaneous.

   Depersonalization disorder is characterized by feelings of unreality or distorted perceptions of the body or environment. It is more common than the other dissociative disorders and can be precipitated by stress.

4. **Dissociative identity disorder (multiple-personality disorder)** (pp. 165–169) In *dissociative identity disorder,* two or more (often many more) distinct personalities exist in one individual. Not all personalities are aware of one another. However, even objective testing with physiological measurements produces conflicting findings about the existence of distinct personalities. Although this condition was once thought to be rare, there has been a dramatic increase in reported cases, perhaps because of the influence of therapists while clients are under hypnosis. People with dissociative identity disorder often report a history of childhood abuse. Diagnosis in childhood is possible, but misdiagnosis is common, both by seeing the disorder in people who have other problems and by failing to see multiple personality in people diagnosed with other disorders. Diagnosis is much more common in the United States and Canada than in other parts of the world.

5. **Etiology and treatment of dissociative disorders** (pp. 169–174) The causes of dissociative disorders are subject to a good deal of conjecture because faking is always a possibility. The psychodynamic perspective sees repression of unpleasant emotions as the cause of dissociative disorders. Splits in consciousness protect the individual from anxiety and pain. Behavioral theorists suggest that avoidance of stress is the main causative factor. Role playing and selective attention also help explain dissociative identity disorder. The disorder may also be the unintended effect of treatment, an *iatrogenic* condition. The expectations of therapists and their use of hypnosis, which increases suggestibility, may create memories of abuse and personalities.

   Recovery from dissociative amnesia, dissociative fugue, and depersonalization disorder often occurs spontaneously; therefore, treatment often aims at reducing the depression or anxiety these conditions produce. Dissociative identity disorder is usually treated with psychotherapy and hypnosis, but not with notable success. Behavior therapists use contingent reinforcement for the "healthy personality" and extinction for the others.

6. **Somatoform disorders** (pp. 174–175; Focus On) The principal symptoms of *somatoform disorders* are complaints of physical symptoms that have no apparent physiological cause. Faking is possible, but when symptoms such as fever are consciously induced, they are considered *factitious disorders* rather than *malingering,* which involves voluntary faking for monetary or other rewards. Somatic complaints are far more common in non-Western cultures where a somatopsychic view (physical problems produce emotional symptoms) is more prevalent than the Western psychosomatic view (internal conflicts are expressed as physical symptoms).

7. **Somatization disorder and conversion disorder** (pp. 175–179) In *somatization disorder,* individuals have physical complaints in four or more different sites in the body, symptoms for which there are no physiological explanations. Complaints include gastrointestinal, sexual, and pseudoneurological symptoms. Patients shop around for doctors and often have unneeded surgery. Somatization disorder, formerly called hysteria, is rarely diagnosed in men although over one-third of males referred for unexplained somatic complaints meet the criteria for the disorder.

   In *conversion disorder,* there is a significant physical impairment, such as paralysis in a limb or sensory problems, without physical basis. When neurological or other processes prove the symptoms impossible (such as in glove anesthesia), diagnosis is readily made; otherwise, it is quite hard to differentiate conversion disorder from actual illnesses or faking.

8. **Pain disorder, hypochondriasis, and body dysmorphic disorder** (pp. 179–182) Pain that is excessive, lingers too long, or is unrelated to a physiological cause is characteristic of *pain disorder*. As with ordinary pain, there is a complex interaction among perception, thinking, and behavior.

   In *hypochondriasis,* there is a consistent preoccupation with illness in the face of doctors' repeated assurances of health. Those with hypochondriasis often have a history of illness and parents who focused on illness. Fear, anxiety, and depression are common complaints.

   Body dysmorphic disorder involves an excessive concern with an imagined or slight physical defect such as facial features, excessive hair, or the shape of genitals. Individuals with this disorder frequently check their appearance in the mirror and fear that others are looking at the defect. They make frequent requests for plastic surgery regardless of the treatment's outcome. Because the disorder involves obsessive thinking and delusions, its placement in the diagnostic category of somatoform disorders has been questioned. It is also not clear where normal concerns about appearance end and the disorder begins.

9. **Etiology and treatment of somatoform disorders** (pp. 182–187) A *diathesis-stress* view of somatoform disorders suggests that individuals are hypersensitive to bodily sensations and are predisposed to react strongly to somatic sensations. In the event of a stressor, they develop intense bodily complaints and symptoms. Psychoanalysts believe that repression accounts for the process of converting unconscious conflicts into physical symptoms. There is *primary gain* in the reduction of anxiety and *secondary gain* in the sympathy the individual receives. Behavioral theorists contend that a "sick role" is reinforced by others and helps the person escape from responsibilities. The sociocultural perspective stresses that, historically, social norms did not provide women with appropriate channels for the expression of aggressive or sexual needs. As a result, women developed hysterical symptoms. The biological perspective notes that individuals with somatoform disorders are unusually sensitive to bodily sensations and have higher arousal levels than others.

   Psychoanalytic treatment emphasizes the need to relive unpleasant experiences so that they can be mastered rather than converted into symptoms. Behavioral therapists advise extinction for complaints and reinforcement for healthy behavior. Cognitive-behavioral treatments focus on changing the conscious thoughts and expectations of clients. Family therapists teach family members to support one another without resorting to physical symptoms and to anticipate such problems.

KEY TERMS REVIEW

1. The somatoform disorder characterized by a persistent preoccupation with one's health is called __________________________.

2. The dissociative disorder in which psychogenic amnesia is accompanied by flight from familiar surroundings and adoption of a new identity is called __________________________.

3. The dissociative disorder in which an individual reports feelings of unreality or distortions of self and the environment is called ________________________.

4. The disorder that involves chronic complaints about a number of physical symptoms for which there is no physical basis is called ________________________.

5. The somatoform disorder in which there appears to be a significant impairment of physical function without an underlying organic cause is called ________________________.

6. Mental disorders characterized by disruption or alteration of one's identity, memory, or consciousness are called ________________________.

7. Mental disorders involving complaints of physical symptoms that mimic authentic medical conditions but have no physical basis are called ________________________.

8. The somatoform disorder characterized by severe physical discomfort that has a psychological rather than a physical basis is called ________________________.

9. The dissociative disorder characterized by an inability to recall information of personal significance, usually after a traumatic event, is called ________________________.

10. The dissociative disorder in which two or more relatively distinct personalities exist in one individual is called ________________________.

11. The somatoform disorder that involves preoccupation with an imagined physical defect is called ________________________.

12. The inability to recall events from a period in the past to present is called ________________________.

13. The inability to recall the entire past, due to some psychosocial crisis, is called ________________________.

14. The inability to recall all events during a specific period is the most common type of amnesia and is called ________________________.

15. The inability to recall information as a result of a suggestion made during a hypnotic state is called ________________________.

16. When some psychosocial stress results in the inability to recall only some aspects of a situation, the condition is called ________________________.

17. A problem that is the result of the therapist's treatment is considered ________________________.

18. Deliberately self-induced or simulated physical or mental conditions without apparent incentive are called ________________________.

19. Faking an illness to obtain a goal is called ________________________.

FACTUAL MULTIPLE–CHOICE QUESTIONS

1. Amnesia, fugue, and depersonalization disorder are all examples of
   a. somatoform disorders.
   b. anxiety disorders.
   c. dissociative disorders.
   d. iatrogenic disorders.

2. In localized amnesia, the memory loss is
   a. total; nothing can be remembered about one's past life.
   b. almost always due to a biological cause.
   c. only for specific details of a specific event.
   d. complete for a specific period in one's life.

3. When people develop amnesia and then travel to a new area where they establish a new identity, the problem is called
   a. dissociative fugue.
   b. generalized amnesia.
   c. dissociative identity disorder.
   d. dissociative phobia.

4. The most common dissociative disorder involves feelings of unreality about one's body or the environment. These intense experiences may lead sufferers to wonder whether they are losing their minds. The disorder being described is called
   a. dissociative identity disorder.
   b. dissociative fugue.
   c. somatoform disorder.
   d. depersonalization disorder.

5. The majority of people with dissociative identity disorder report a history of
   a. vague physical complaints.
   b. excessively permissive upbringing.
   c. physical and sexual abuse.
   d. having one traumatic incident in adulthood.

6. In recent years, the number of ________________________ cases reported by mental health professionals has increased.
   a. conversion disorder
   b. depersonalization disorder
   c. hypochondriasis
   d. dissociative identity disorder

7. Somatization disorder was previously called
   a. hysteria.
   b. iatrogenic.
   c. dementia praecox.
   d. manic-depression.

8. Because it involves symptoms that mimic physical disorders, it is difficult to differentiate ________________________ from faking and from organic problems.
   a. depersonalization disorder
   b. body dysmorphic disorder
   c. conversion disorder
   d. dissociative amnesia

9. A history of physical illness, a low pain threshold, and parents who focused on the symptoms of illness are all believed to be factors related to
   a. body dysmorphic disorder.
   b. hypochondriasis.
   c. dissociative identity disorder.
   d. factitious disorder.

10. Family therapists would see somatoform complaints as a way of
   a. avoiding family responsibilities.
   b. crying for help.
   c. responding to childhood abuse and neglect.
   d. repressing unpleasant emotions related to an earlier trauma.

CONCEPTUAL MULTIPLE–CHOICE QUESTIONS

1. Why is it difficult to tell whether the personalities in dissociative identity disorder truly exist?
   a. The personalities usually exhibit dissociative amnesia.
   b. Not even physiological measures produce consistent results.
   c. The personalities almost always appear at the same time.
   d. One personality typically does not have memory of what another personality has experienced.

2. In dissociative identity disorder, it is rare to find
   a. more than three distinct personalities.
   b. that the personalities are distinct from one another.
   c. that every personality is aware of every other one.
   d. evidence that there is dissociation.

3. Among the dissociative disorders, the development of ________________ is thought to be partially iatrogenic (induced by certain treatment methods).
   a. dissociative identity disorder
   b. depersonalization disorder
   c. dissociative amnesia
   d. body dysmorphic disorder

4. Avoidance of stress is the main factor in the ________________ theorist's explanation of dissociative disorders.
   a. iatrogenic
   b. biological
   c. behavioral
   d. psychodynamic

5. Long-term psychotherapy is usually not necessary for ________________ because it usually stops spontaneously.
   a. dissociative amnesia
   b. dissociative identity disorder
   c. hypochondriasis
   d. factitious disorders

6. In somatoform disorders, the fundamental symptom is
   a. the involuntary separation of consciousness in response to traumatic events.
   b. irrational fears of specific objects.
   c. physical symptoms, such as ulcers and diabetes, that develop in response to stress.
   d. involuntarily produced physical symptoms that occur in the absence of organic causes.

7. Unlike somatoform disorders, factitious disorders
   a. are complicated by depression and anxiety.
   b. are under voluntary control.
   c. involve a separation of consciousness.
   d. stem from repression of psychological conflicts.

8. Which statement about somatization disorder is *accurate*?
   a. The disorder is defined in terms of numerous physical complaints.
   b. The disorder's main symptom is exaggerated or lingering pain.
   c. The disorder is related to physical and sexual abuse during childhood.
   d. The disorder is more common in men than in women.

9. Primary gain and secondary gain are concepts that ____________________ theorists use to explain the adaptive qualities of somatoform disorders.
   a. psychodynamic
   b. biological
   c. learning
   d. sociocultural

10. Hypnotherapy is used to treat somatoform disorders because
   a. it prevents others from reinforcing the patient's symptom complaints.
   b. it helps the patient understand the physical causes of his or her complaints.
   c. it raises the patient's pain threshold.
   d. it helps the patient relive feelings associated with a traumatic event.

APPLICATION MULTIPLE–CHOICE QUESTIONS

1. Nora has no recollection of the events just before her house burned down, although she recalls running to a neighbor's house to call for the fire department. Nora's amnesia illustrates
   a. dissociative fugue.
   b. continuous amnesia.
   c. selective amnesia.
   d. depersonalization disorder.

2. Paula is diagnosed as having dissociative identity disorder. One personality, Mark, protects her from trouble, while another personality, Kim, is sexually promiscuous. All three personalities are aware of one another. What is unusual about Paula's case of multiple personality?
   a. There are rarely three separate personalities.
   b. Rarely are all personalities aware of one another.
   c. A male personality is rarely found in a female patient.
   d. Sexually promiscuous personalities are rare.

3. "Dissociative identity disorder is an adaptive response to unbearable psychological torture: the repression is so complete that distinct personalities are protected from any memory of the trauma." What kind of psychologist would say this?
   a. A behavior therapist
   b. A biologically oriented psychologist
   c. A therapist who believes the disorder is iatrogenic
   d. A psychoanalyst

4. Dr. Greise says to a patient's husband, "Whenever she says she is feeling as though she or the world is getting distorted and unreal, you should ignore her. Make sure you show attention, though, when she is in control." The disorder being treated is ________________, and Dr. Greise is a ________________ theorist.
   a. depersonalization disorder; behavioral
   b. dissociative identity disorder; psychoanalytic
   c. pain disorder; behavioral
   d. depersonalization disorder; biological

5. Dr. O'Neil says, "These disorders involving physical symptoms are diagnosed by what they *aren't:* they aren't under voluntary control, they aren't faked, and they aren't due to physiological causes." What is Dr. O'Neil talking about?
   a. Dissociative disorders
   b. Anxiety disorders
   c. Factitious disorders
   d. Somatoform disorders

6. Sharon has complained about more than fifteen physical problems over the past year and has had surgery four times even though there is no evidence of physiological causes. She constantly "shops around" for doctors. Sharon suffers from
   a. conversion disorder.
   b. dissociative amnesia.
   c. somatization disorder.
   d. hypochondriasis.

7. Milton began complaining of leg paralysis after he lost his job. There is no evidence of a physical cause. He does not stand to benefit from having these symptoms. Milton suffers from
   a. conversion disorder.
   b. malingering.
   c. somatization disorder.
   d. hypochondriasis.

8. Dr. Wimsey says, "There is no doubt that this patient is preoccupied with health concerns and possible death, and that there are no physiological reasons behind the complaints. However, the insistence on one complaint (chest pains) means that the diagnosis should be ________________ rather than ________________."
   a. hysteria; malingering
   b. conversion disorder; somatization disorder
   c. hypochondriasis; somatization disorder
   d. malingering; hypochondriasis

9. Dr. Blue notes that women have more somatoform disorders than men, perhaps because they experience few situations in which they are in control of their lives. It is likely that Dr. Blue is a ________________ theorist.
   a. sociocultural
   b. behavioral
   c. biological
   d. psychodynamic

10. "Physicians, nurses, and eventually, spouses are trained to respond to complaints of pain. Unless attention to (and reinforcement for) such complaints is ended, you cannot expect the somatoform pain patient to improve." Who might say this?
   a. A psychoanalyst
   b. A psychiatrist who treats disorders with medication
   c. A behavior therapist
   d. A humanistic psychotherapist

ANSWER KEY: KEY TERMS REVIEW

1. hypochondriasis (180)
2. dissociative fugue (or fugue state) (161)
3. depersonalization disorder (162)
4. somatization disorder (175)
5. conversion disorder (176)
6. dissociative disorders (160)
7. somatoform disorders (160)
8. pain disorder (179)
9. dissociative amnesia (160)
10. dissociative identity disorder (165)
11. body dysmorphic disorder (180)
12. continuous amnesia (161)
13. generalized amnesia (161)
14. localized amnesia (161)
15. posthypnotic amnesia (161)
16. selective amnesia (161)
17. iatrogenic (168)
18. factitious disorders (175)
19. malingering (174)

ANSWER KEY: FACTUAL MULTIPLE–CHOICE QUESTIONS

1. a. Somatoform disorders involve physical complaints; they include such problems as hypochondriasis and conversion disorder.
   b. Anxiety disorders do not produce memory problems; they include phobias and panic disorder.
   *c. Dissociative disorders involve a division of consciousness, usually producing memory problems, as is seen in amnesia and dissociative identity. (p. 160)
   d. Although some believe dissociative identity disorder can be iatrogenic (therapist-caused), the other disorders are seen as originating in the individual's inadequate response to stress.

2. a. Complete loss of previous experience occurs in generalized dissociative amnesia.
   b. Localized amnesia can be caused by psychosocial stressors. Dissociative disorders, by definition, are psychogenic.
   c. Selective amnesia involves loss of memory of specific aspects of a traumatic incident, such as amnesia for some events related to a devastating tornado.
   *d. Localized amnesia is complete memory loss for a specific time; for example, one may not remember being robbed and threatened. (p. 161)

3. *a. The central characteristic of fugue is dissociative amnesia together with travel to a new region to establish a new identity. (p. 161)
   b. Generalized amnesia involves complete loss of memory of previous experience.
   c. Dissociative identity disorder is characterized by distinct personalities, not by travel to another area.
   d. *Dissociative phobia* is a made-up term; *dissociative* is usually associated with amnesia or fugue, and *phobia* is a disorder on its own.

4. a. Dissociative identity disorder is characterized by distinct personalities, not a sense of unreality; it is also considered rather rare.
   b. Dissociative fugue is characterized by travel to a new region and establishment of a new identity.
   c. Somatoform disorders involve physical complaints such as anesthesia, paralysis, or dizziness.
   *d. Depersonalization disorder is characterized by feeling unreal, seeing distortions in the environment or one's body parts, and fear of going crazy; such reactions in times of stress are common. (p. 162)

5. a. Vague physical complaints are more likely to be related to hypochondriasis or somatization disorder than to dissociative identity disorder.
   b. Dissociative identity disorder is not associated with permissive upbringing.
   *c. Most cases of dissociative identity disorder seem to develop out of childhood abuse, as in the case of Sybil. (pp. 167–169)
   d. Single traumatic events are more likely to be associated with dissociative amnesia; dissociative identity disorder usually involves a childhood full of trauma.

6. a. There is no evidence that conversion disorder has increased recently.
   b. There is no evidence that depersonalization disorder has increased recently.
   c. There is no evidence that hypochondriasis has increased recently.
   *d. There has been an enormous upsurge in reported cases of dissociative identity disorder recently; one clinician alone reported 130 cases. (p. 167)

7. *a. An older name for somatization disorder was *hysteria;* until the DSM-III it was lumped together with conversion disorder. (p. 175)
   b. *Iatrogenic* is a term for disorders that are the unintended effect of treatment.
   c. *Dementia praecox* is the older term for schizophrenia.
   d. *Manic-depression* is the older term for the mood disorder called bipolar disorder.

8. a. Depersonalization is a dissociative disorder, not a somatoform disorder, which would involve physical complaints.
   b. Body dysmorphic disorder involves exaggerated concern about a body part, such as too much hair or too long a nose.
   *c. Conversion disorder involves somatic complaints that might be due to organic causes or sheer fakery. (pp. 176–179)
   d. Dissociative amnesia is a memory problem, not one connected with somatic complaints.

9. a. Too little is known about body dysmorphic disorder to speculate on preexisting factors.
   *b. Hypochondriasis is a preoccupation with illness and death that stems from actual illness and parental modeling. (p. 180)
   c. The major preexisting factors in dissociative identity disorder seem to be child abuse, an ability to dissociate, and a lack of environmental support.
   d. Too little is known about factitious disorders to speculate on preexisting factors.

10. *a. The impact of these complaints is to disrupt family functioning by taking the patient "off the hook" for his or her responsibilities. (p. 187)
    b. Family therapists do not see these physical complaints as cries for help.
    c. Family therapists tend to focus on current relationships, not childhood issues; also, abuse is more related to dissociative disorder.
    d. Psychoanalysts, not family therapists, would stress the repression of emotions.

ANSWER KEY: CONCEPTUAL MULTIPLE–CHOICE QUESTIONS

1. a. Dissociative amnesia is another DSM–IV disorder; this fact is unrelated to the case in detecting the existence of separate personalities.
   *b. Current attempts to identify the disorder through EEGs, cerebral blood flow, and other physiological measures have been inconclusive and contradictory (Miller & Triggiano, 1992). (p. 167)
   c. Personalities typically appear one at a time.
   d. The asymmetry in awareness is not complete; this fact is unrelated to the ease in detecting the existence of separate personalities.

2. a. Many more than three personalities have been reported: Chris Sizemore (the real "Eve") had more than twenty, and one clinician says the average is thirteen to fourteen!
   b. The diagnosis of dissociative identity disorder rests on the notion that the personalities are distinct.
   *c. Usually one personality has limited or no awareness of the others; this is the basic dissociation of consciousness. (p. 165)
   d. Dissociative identity disorder is a form of dissociative disorder because one part of the person (along with memories for that part) dissociates itself from the rest.

3. *a. Research indicates that the suggestion of a therapist can influence the reporting of multiple-personality-like symptoms. (pp. 166–169; 171; Focus On)
   b. Depersonalization disorder does not seem to be induced by therapy.
   c. Dissociative amnesia is triggered by traumatic events, not by therapy.
   d. Body dysmorphic disorder does not seem to be induced by therapy.

4. a. Iatrogenic refers to a problem that is the result of the therapist's treatment.
   b. Biological theory does not emphasize avoidance; it emphasizes genetics and body processes.
   *c. Behavioral theory looks at dissociative symptoms in terms of rewards and punishments, the rewards being attention and avoidance of stressful situations. (p. 171)
   d. Psychodynamic theory emphasizes repression of traumatic events.

5. *a. Dissociative amnesia often ends as abruptly as it begins. (p. 173)
   b. Dissociative identity disorder is often a lifelong problem; it is difficult to treat even with extensive psychotherapy.
   c. Hypochondriasis is usually a lifelong problem; it is as much a lifestyle as a psychological disorder.
   d. Factitious disorders are poorly understood but are believed to be linked to deep-seated and enduring problems.

6. a. The separation of consciousness is a fundamental symptom of the dissociative disorders.
   b. Irrational fears of objects are associated with phobias.
   c. Actual physical damage associated with stress is called stress-related illness or psychophysiological illness.
   *d. When physical symptoms are not caused by organic factors and do not seem to be voluntarily induced (as they are in factitious disorders), the diagnosis is somatoform disorder. (p. 174)

7. a. It is not believed that factitious disorders are complicated by depression and anxiety.
   *b. In factitious disorders the person may either inject himself/herself with agents that produce fever or consciously mimic physical disorders. (p. 175; Focus On)
   c. Dissociative disorders involve the division of consciousness.
   d. Factitious disorders are poorly understood, but repression is more involved in somatoform disorders.

8. *a. In the DSM-IV, the criteria for somatization disorder are pain complaints in four different sites, two gastrointestinal symptoms, one sexual symptom, and one pseudoneurological symptom. The range of complaints is a prime way of differentiating this disorder from hypochondriasis. (p. 175)
   b. Lingering and exaggerated pain are symptoms of pain disorder.
   c. Childhood abuse is more related to dissociative identity disorder than to somatization disorder.
   d. Somatization disorder is more common in women than in men.

9. *a. Psychoanalysts consider the primary gain in somatoform disorders to be relief from unconscious conflicts and the secondary gain to be attention from others, which meets dependency needs. (p. 183)
   b. Biological theory stresses the pain and sensory thresholds of people with somatoform disorders.
   c. Learning theory highlights the positive consequences of making physical complaints.
   d. Sociocultural theorists argue that women develop somatoform disorders because they have typically had social restrictions placed upon them.

10. a. The behavioral concept of extinction is more likely to prevent reinforcement from being given to the patient; hypnotherapy highlights the individual's inner world.
   b. Since there are few, if any, physical causes for the complaints, hypnotherapy is not used to explain these.
   c. Although biological theorists suggest that hypochondriacs have low pain thresholds, hypnotherapy is not used to raise the threshold.
   *d. Hypnotherapy is usually used as a way of bringing unconscious feelings to consciousness. (p. 186)

ANSWER KEY: APPLICATION MULTIPLE–CHOICE QUESTIONS

1. a. Dissociative fugue is characterized by amnesia, travel to a new place, and the establishment of a new identity.
   b. Continuous amnesia is a rare form of dissociative disorder in which there is complete memory loss for the past until a specific point in time.
   *c. Selective amnesia involves partial memory loss for a specific traumatic event. (p. 161)
   d. Depersonalization disorder is characterized by feelings of body distortion and unreality.

2. a. Three or more separate personalities are commonly found in multiple personality.
   *b. Typically, one or more of the separate personalities are unaware of the existence of the others. (p. 165)
   c. In many cases, male personalities are found in females (as in the case of Sybil) and female personalities are found in males (as in the case of Billy Milligan).
   d. Often, one of the personalities is sexually promiscuous or aggressive (taking on id qualities).

3. a. Behavior therapists stress how dissociation is a coping strategy for daily stress.
   b. Biological theorists have rarely commented on multiple personality, but would emphasize brain function or genetics if they did.
   c. Those who believe dissociative identity disorder is iatrogenic would discount the importance of trauma and repression.
   *d. Psychoanalysts emphasize the function of repression in all dissociative disorders. (p. 169)

4. *a. Depersonalization disorder involves complaints of feeling unreal; behaviorists would treat the problem through extinction of the complaints and rewards for "healthy talk." (pp. 162, 173)
   b. Dissociative identity disorder does not involve feelings of unreality; psychoanalysts would try to unlock unconscious factors.
   c. Pain disorder is about pain, not body distortions or feelings of unreality.
   d. The biological viewpoint would use medication for treatment.

5. a. Dissociative disorders involve a split in consciousness, usually involving memory loss, not physical symptoms.
   b. Anxiety disorders are not thought to be faked and involve only physical complaints that are secondary to the anxiety.
   c. Factitious disorders *are* under voluntary control.
   *d. Part of the problem of diagnosing somatoform disorders (particularly conversion) is that the factors Dr. O'Neil mentions are other possible explanations for the complaints. (p. 174)

6. a. Conversion disorder usually involves paralysis or sensory problems (blurred vision, for instance), and there is rarely much "doctor shopping."
   b. Dissociative amnesia is characterized by memory loss, not physical complaints.
   *c. Somatization disorder involves multiple physical complaints that often lead to unnecessary surgery. (p. 175)
   d. Hypochondriasis involves a preoccupation with health problems and often centers on one vague complaint.

7. *a. Conversion disorder often involves paralysis in an extremity and begins shortly after a major stressor. (pp. 176–179)
   b. *Malingering* is when a person consciously fakes his or her symptoms.
   c. Somatization disorder involves multiple complaints.
   d. Hypochondriasis is characterized by a preoccupation with illness; rarely is the complaint about a specific dysfunction like leg paralysis.

8. a. *Hysteria* is an older name for both conversion and somatization disorder.
   b. Conversion disorder usually involves one complaint (extremity paralysis or sensory loss), not the multiple complaints seen in somatization disorder.
   *c. Chest pains and fear of death are the kinds of complaints associated with hypochondriasis; in somatization disorder, many more diverse and vague complaints would be made. (p. 180)
   d. Malingering is unlikely to involve a fear of death.

9. *a. Sociocultural theorists note that hysteria was more common when women had fewer social roles in which they could express aggression or sexuality. (p. 185)
   b. Behavioral theorists highlight the reinforcements for sick behavior.
   c. Biological theorists stress the lower pain tolerance and heightened internal awareness of somatoform patients.
   d. Psychoanalysts relate the physical complaints to repressed unpleasant memories and conflicts.

10. a. Psychoanalysts would stress the repression behind such complaints and the need for unconscious feelings to become conscious.
    b. Psychiatrists (medical doctors) are likely to be attentive to pain complaints rather than to suggest that they be ignored.
    *c. Behavior therapists want to extinguish pain complaints by reducing the attention patients receive for them. (p. 186)
    d. Humanistic therapists would accept as valid the subjective experience of the patient and would not encourage this kind of selective attention.

CHAPTER 7

Psychological Factors Affecting Medical Conditions

LEARNING OBJECTIVES

1. Describe the sudden death syndrome and the factors related to it. Discuss how culture shock can lead to sudden death among Hmong immigrants. (pp. 190–191)
2. List the DSM-IV criteria for diagnosis of psychological factors affecting medical conditions. Explain the rationale for changes in terminology from "psychosomatic" to "psychophysiological." (pp. 190–192)
3. Discuss the three models for understanding stress, including Selye's general adaptation syndrome, the life change model, and Lazarus's transaction model. (pp. 192–196)
4. List some of the biological and psychological consequences of stress. (pp. 192–193)
5. Discuss the research linking emotional states to vulnerability to infection. Discuss the evidence for and against the claim that stress influences the development of Acquired Immune Deficiency Syndrome (AIDS). (pp. 196–199)
6. Describe the components of the immune system and evidence that stress decreases its functioning. (pp. 199–200)
7. Describe the mediating effects of control and hardiness on stress. (pp. 200–201)
8. Discuss the evidence linking personality, mood, and cancer. (pp. 201–204; Focus On)
9. Describe the relationship between stress and coronary heart disease and the influence of the Type A personality on CHD. (pp. 204–207)
10. Describe the relationship between stress and essential hypertension, and the ethnic and social factors associated with it. (pp. 207–210)
11. Describe the nature of migraine, tension, and cluster headaches. (pp. 210–212)
12. Describe asthma and the psychological factors related to it. (pp. 212–213)
13. Discuss the psychodynamic and biological perspectives on psychophysiological disorders, including the somatic weakness, autonomic response specificity, and the general adaptation hypotheses. (pp. 213–215)
14. Discuss the behavioral perspective on psychophysiological disorders, including the influence of classical conditioning and operant conditioning. Describe how sociocultural factors influence coronary heart disease. (pp. 215–216)
15. Define behavioral medicine and describe various interventions for psychophysiological disorders, including medical, relaxation training, biofeedback, and cognitive-behavior therapy. (pp. 216–218)

CHAPTER OUTLINE

1. **Psychological factors affecting medical conditions** (pp. 190–193; Focus On) Anxiety and stress have some role in *sudden death syndrome*, unexpected death that often seems to have no physical basis. Sudden death is related to the likelihood of blood clotting, blood pressure rising and tearing off fat deposits, and heart rhythm changes. Sudden death among Hmong immigrants in the United States may be due to severe culture shock.

   In earlier versions of the DSM, certain disorders (psychosomatic disorders) were seen as stemming from psychological problems. Now, psychological problems are believed to be potential factors in almost any physical problem. Disorders that include both psychological and physical problems are called *psychophysiological disorders*. Unlike in conversion disorders, the tissue damage is real. The DSM-IV diagnosis of psychological factors affecting medical condition requires a medical condition and one of the following: a relationship in time between the psychological factor and the condition; the psychological factor interferes with treatment; and the psychological factor adds to the individual's health risk.

2. **Models for understanding stress** (pp. 192–196) *Stress* is an internal response to an external, threatening event, or *stressor*. Stressors can be biological, psychological, or social. In the *general adaptation syndrome,* formulated by Selye, the body automatically reacts to prolonged stress in three stages: alarm, resistance, and exhaustion. Sustained stress may not only reduce resistance to disease, but also alter its course. De La Fuente presents a parallel three-stage psychological response to crisis, including impact, attempted resolution, and *decompensation*.

   The *life change model* emphasizes the frequency and characteristics of the stressors. Cumulative changes, both positive and negative, are measured on the Social Readjustment Rating Scale (Holmes and Rahe) in life change units. The more units, the greater the likelihood and severity of illness, although it is too soon to say if stressors are the cause of illness. Evidence shows that negative events have greater impact.

   Lazarus's *transaction model* suggests that both the situation and the person's reaction to it explain stress-related illnesses. Perceptions of events are critical; those who deny any negative effect of a disease do more poorly than those who cope.

3. **Stress and the immune system** (pp. 196–200) Viral conditions such as herpes infections and even Acquired Immune Deficiency Syndrome (AIDS) may be influenced by emotional factors. Stress may reduce resistance to infections, trigger the expression of existing pathogens, or contribute to the disease process or change health habits of the individual. Over short periods of time, depression seems to have no influence on the development of AIDS in infected individuals, but over longer time periods, depression is associated with weaker immune function. This relation may be moderated by various psychosocial variables such as self-efficacy and social support. Stress reactions release chemicals that suppress such immune system components as lymphocytes (B-, T-, and natural killer cells) and phagocytes. Divorce, bereavement, and other stressors can impair immune functioning directly or indirectly through such poor health practices as sleeping less or drinking more. In Western culture, emotional states are seen as contributing to illness. In non-Western cultures, emotional states are not seen as having as much impact as the stressors themselves.

4. **Mediating the effects of stressors** (pp. 200–201) Perception of control over the environment seems to reduce stress effects, as evidenced by rats' ability to reject cancer cells and by reduced mortality rates in nursing home patients given additional responsibilities. *Hardiness*, a personality trait characterized by openness to change, commitment, and a sense of personal control, appears to protect individuals against stress-related illness. However, the reduction in immune functioning caused by psychological factors is often quite small.

5. **Personality, mood states, and cancer** (pp. 201–204; Focus On) Positive emotions and the expression of such negative ones as anger may be involved in the development, course, and recurrence of cancer. However, research and methodological problems make these propositions controversial. Even well-designed studies linking anger expression and breast cancer have

alternative explanations. However, in one prospective study, MMPI depression scores predicted cancer even when lifestyle and family history factors were taken into account.

6. **Psychological involvement in specific physical disorders** (pp. 204–213) *Coronary heart disease (CHD),* a narrowing of arteries in or to the heart, kills nearly 400,000 people in the United States annually. Stress plays a role: job stress is associated with increases in a blood-clotting compound; a prospective study found that anxiety symptoms predicted death due to cardiac arrest. The Type A personality pattern is also involved in CHD. Type A's are time-pressured, hostile, and competitive. Hostility, either expressed or hidden, seems to be the most significant risk factor.

   Essential hypertension (high blood pressure) can lead to heart attacks and other fatal disorders. Higher stress levels correlate with higher blood pressure. Anger, expressed and unexpressed, may be related to chronic hypertension, particularly for men. Hypertension is a greater problem for blacks than for whites, perhaps because of differences in psychosocial resources. High-status jobs together with the perception that hard work is needed for success are associated with high blood pressure in women and African-American men, but not in white men.

   Stress contributes to all three types of headaches: *migraine headaches, tension headaches,* and *cluster headaches.* The classic migraine headache has neurological warning signs, such as distorted vision or numbness in the body, followed by intense, throbbing pain. In the common migraine, there may be no neurological symptoms. Although the name implies it, tension headaches are not necessarily caused by muscular tension; psychological factors are often the precipitants. Cluster headaches are excruciating and center on the area around the eye. Relaxation, biofeedback, and cognitive therapy show promise in treating headaches.

   Asthma is a chronic inflammatory disease that makes breathing difficult. There has been a recent and unexplained rise in deaths resulting from asthma. Most sufferers are adolescents or young children who have allergies. However, psychological factors involving family dynamics can also be involved.

7. **Perspectives on etiology** (pp. 213–216) According to Alexander (1950), a psychoanalyst, each type of psychophysiological disorder is caused by a specific unconscious conflict. Research support for this is not strong.

   There is some evidence that genetics influences the rate of psychophysiological disorder. Somatic weakness theory proposes that certain organs are weakened by earlier experience and are vulnerable to disease under stress. The autonomic response specificity hypothesis argues that each person has a unique way of responding to stressors. The *general adaptation syndrome* may be combined with the previous two theories to understand illness as a disease of adaptation.

   Classical conditioning may explain how certain stress reactions can generalize to a wide range of stressful stimuli. However, this perspective cannot account for the original reaction. Operant approaches note that internal processes originally thought to be involuntary can be influenced by external reinforcement and biofeedback.

   Japanese who retain close social and emotional ties and maintain traditional values seem to have lower coronary heart disease levels than acculturated Japanese Americans.

8. **Treatment of psychophysiological disorders: Relaxation training, biofeedback, and cognitive-behavioral interventions** (pp. 216–218) *Behavioral medicine* comprises a range of disciplines that study the social and psychological issues in health and apply that knowledge to stress management approaches. In *relaxation training,* individuals are taught to alternately tense and relax muscle groups in the body. In *biofeedback* training, clients are informed about small internal changes (such as in blood pressure and heart rate). They learn to control these internal processes and eventually do not need the monitoring devices. Essentially an operant technique, biofeedback has been used to treat a range of psychophysiological disorders, from headache to asthma. Stress management programs often include such cognitive-behavioral interventions as self-instructional techniques and cognitive restructuring.

KEY TERMS REVIEW

1. A number of disciplines that study social, psychological, and lifestyle influences on health are collectively called behavioral medicine

2. The concept developed by Kobasa and Maddi that refers to an individual's ability to deal well with stress is called hardiniss. Page 201

3. Severe headaches that result from the dilation of cerebral blood vessels after an initial contraction of cranial arteries are called migraine headaches

4. The chronic inflammatory disease characterized by attacks in which breathing becomes extremely difficult as a result of constriction of lung airways is called asthma.

5. The therapeutic technique in which the individual acquires the ability to relax the muscles of the body is called Relaxtion training

6. The cardiovascular disease in which the flow of blood and oxygen to the heart is restricted because of narrowed arteries in or near the heart is called coronary heart disease

7. Unexpected death that may be brought on by stress and in most cases is also due to an underlying coronary condition is called ____________________.

8. A physical or psychological demand placed on an individual by some external situation is called a(n) ____________________.

9. The therapeutic technique in which the individual receives information about internal physiological functions and learns to control them is called ____________________.

10. A headache that may be produced by prolonged contraction of scalp and neck muscles is called a(n) ____________________.

11. High blood pressure with no known organic cause is called ____________________.

12. A model that assumes that the body's physical and psychological reaction to biological stressors involves three stages of response (alarm, resistance, exhaustion) is called the ____________________.

13. A physical disorder that has a strong psychological basis or component is called a(n) ____________________.

14. An individual's internal reaction to the physical or psychological demands placed on him or her by the environment is called ____________________.

15. The loss of the ability to successfully deal with stress, resulting in more primitive coping methods, is called ____________________.

16. The hypothesis that all life changes can act as stressors is called the ____________________.

17. The hypothesis that stress is best viewed as an interaction between the situation and the person's responses is called the ____________________.

18. An excruciating headache that tends to occur near the eye or cheek and produces tears or a blocked nose is called a(n) ____________________.

FACTUAL MULTIPLE–CHOICE QUESTIONS

1. Because any physical disorder can have a psychological component, the term now being used by psychologists to describe stress-related illnesses is
   a. psychosomatic.
   b. adaptive.
   c. somatopsychic.
   d. psychophysiological.

2. *Alarm, resistance,* and *exhaustion* are terms associated with the ____________________ model of stress-related illness.
   a. general adaptation
   b. life change
   c. decompensation
   d. transaction

3. In the stages of crisis decompensation, the first stage is characterized by ____________________, whereas the second features ____________________.
   a. increases in catecholamine levels; an increase in NK cells
   b. dependency on others for support; panic and confusion
   c. panic and confusion; attempted resolution of the problem
   d. panic and confusion; tissue damage and illness

4. The greater the number of life change units experienced in a year's time,
   a. the lower the likelihood of illness.
   b. the more serious the illness that might be experienced.
   c. the hardier the personality will become.
   d. the stronger the immune system will become.

5. As a result of marital separation or bereavement, people often experience
   a. an increase in NK cells.
   b. impairments in the immune system.
   c. an increase in phagocytes and lymphocytes.
   d. a lowering of their life change units.

6. Openness to change, commitment, and a sense of personal control are all components of the personality pattern called
   a. hardiness.
   b. Type A.
   c. general adaptation.
   d. Type B.

7. The key element in the relationship between Type A and coronary heart disease seems to be
   a. the Type A's tendency to do everything quickly.
   b. the Type A's tendency to be perfectionistic.
   c. the fact that Type A behavior reduces catecholamine levels.
   d. the Type A's tendency to be hostile.

8. When a person has high blood pressure without physiological reason, the disorder is called
   a. coronary heart disease.
   b. essential hypertension.
   c. angina pectoris.
   d. psychosomatic blood pressure.

9. An African American who is excessively angry and deficient in psychosocial resources is believed to be at particularly high risk for developing
   a. tension headaches.
   b. asthma.
   c. high blood pressure.
   d. defective NK cells.

10. Headaches that are preceded by neurological symptoms such as blurred vision and that are caused by uncontrolled blood flow to the brain are called
    a. tension headaches.
    b. classic migraine headaches.
    c. cluster headaches.
    d. common migraine headaches.

CONCEPTUAL MULTIPLE–CHOICE QUESTIONS

1. According to the life change model of psychophysiological disorders,
   a. only positive life changes produce stress.
   b. the accumulation of even small changes increases the likelihood of illness.
   c. the way a person interprets the stressfulness of an event determines the likelihood of illness.
   d. after a stage of resistance, the body "gives out," and tissue damage results.

2. The transaction model of stress argues that
   a. a person's upbringing determines how he or she will respond to stressors.
   b. the greater the number of negative life events, the greater the risk of serious illness.
   c. biology plays almost no role in the development of psychophysiological disorders.
   d. stressors negatively affect people because of the way people perceive and cope with them.

3. Research on nursing home residents indicates that those who live the longest
   a. have the highest catecholamine levels.
   b. relinquish most of their decision-making power to the nursing home staff.
   c. tend to suppress their anger.
   d. are allowed to make certain decisions that increase their sense of control.

4. The majority of psychologists and physicians believe that psychological moods
   a. have no effect on the progression of cancer.
   b. determine whether or not a person develops cancer.
   c. are an important factor in the development of cancer only for women.
   d. may have an impact on cancer, but research is too inconclusive to be sure.

5. Recent research examining depression before a diagnosis of cancer found that
   a. the cancer death rate was two times greater for people with high depression scores than for those with low depression scores.
   b. cancer was unrelated to depression scores.
   c. the cancer death rate was two times lower for people with high depression scores than for those with low depression scores.
   d. high depression scores predicted cancer death, but only when people were also anger suppressors.

6. The relationship between stress and the development of various psychophysiological disorders is best understood by understanding the effect of stress on
   a. HPA dysregulation.
   b. passive coping.
   c. the immune system.
   d. somatization disorders.

7. The autonomic response specificity hypothesis suggests that
   a. if a stressor goes on long enough, any person's body will become exhausted.
   b. each individual has a unique way of reacting to stressors.
   c. each type of psychophysiological disorder has a specific conflict associated with it.
   d. certain body parts respond to certain levels of life change.

8. The concept of ____________________ explains how bronchial irritation can become associated with stressors and other stimuli so that conflicts produce asthma attacks.
   a. operant conditioning
   b. the hardy personality
   c. general adaptation
   d. classical conditioning

9. The voluntary control of a physiological response such as heart rate can be demonstrated by using
   a. biofeedback.
   b. progressive relaxation.
   c. classical conditioning.
   d. modeling.

10. Psychophysiological disorders differ from somatoform disorders in that
    a. somatoform disorders involve actual bodily disease, whereas psychophysiological disorders are psychogenic.
    b. psychophysiological disorders involve actual bodily disease, whereas somatoform disorders are psychogenic.
    c. somatoform disorders are caused by immune system dysregulation, whereas psychophysiological disorders are psychogenic.
    d. somatoform disorders are treated successfully with behavioral therapy, whereas psychophysiological disorders are not successfully treated.

APPLICATION MULTIPLE–CHOICE QUESTIONS

1. Dr. Morgan is trying to decide if a medical condition is affected by a psychological factor. She thinks that as long as there is a temporal relationship between psychological factors and the onset of or the delay in recovery from a medical condition, the diagnosis that it is an affected condition can be made. Is she correct?
   a. No, the psychological factor must interfere with treatment.
   b. No, the psychological factor must add to the health risk of the individual.
   c. No, the psychological factor must interfere with treatment and add to health risk.
   d. Yes, she is correct.

2. Gina's reactions to a snarling dog are a rapid heartbeat and the secretion of hormones by her adrenal glands that temporarily reduce the efficiency of her immune system. These reactions are
   a. an illustration of the somatic weakness hypothesis.
   b. the exhaustion stage of the general adaptation syndrome.
   c. an illustration of the hardy personality.
   d. the alarm stage of the general adaptation syndrome.

3. In the past three months, Vera has changed jobs twice, has learned that her parents plan to divorce, and has gone on a vacation. The life change model of stress suggests that
   a. only the job changes are stressors.
   b. the way she interprets these events will determine whether or not she becomes ill.
   c. all these changes increase her chances of becoming ill.
   d. she is now in the alarm stage of adapting to stressors.

4. Mr. Panzano, upon learning that he has lung cancer, considers his life to be a failure. He gives up all hope of being successfully treated and becomes depressed. Mr. Panzano's reaction illustrates what the ________________________ perspective on stress emphasizes.
   a. life change
   b. transaction
   c. classical conditioning
   d. somatic weakness

5. Jill is being transferred to Tokyo. She sees this as a challenge and an opportunity. She believes that she is in control of her life and that she must remain open to change. Jill illustrates
   a. the Type A personality.
   b. learned helplessness.
   c. the hardy personality.
   d. classically conditioned adaptation.

6. Barbara has never outwardly expressed anger in her life. On the MMPI, she shows a very high depression score. What physical illness is she at higher risk for developing?
   a. General paresis
   b. Coronary heart disease
   c. Cancer
   d. Asthma

7. John, age 36, is a poor black man with a Type A personality. He is almost always angry and upset. John is at highest risk for developing which disorders?
   a. Asthma and migraine headaches
   b. Essential hypertension and coronary heart disease
   c. Cancer and migraine headaches
   d. Sudden death syndrome and asthma

8. A health psychologist plans to give a lecture on stress and coping to employees at a large electronics manufacturing company. Whom should she highlight as particularly prone to developing CHD?
   a. Type A men who are married to Type B women
   b. Middle managers who are responsible for production outcomes of a department.
   c. Type A men who have essential hypertension.
   d. Type B men who pursue pleasurable hobbies with friends outside the work situation.

9. Don says, "When I was small, I was exposed to severe air pollution that damaged my lungs. Now, whenever I am under stress, I develop a bad cough and wheezing." Don's explanation reflects the ________________________ hypothesis on psychophysiological illnesses.
   a. operant conditioning
   b. psychodynamic
   c. neurotransmitter
   d. autonomic weakness

10. To treat his hypertension, Carl is hooked up to a machine that shows small changes in his blood pressure. The information that he is lowering his blood pressure acts as reinforcement. Carl's treatment is
    a. progressive relaxation.
    b. cognitive restructuring.
    c. biofeedback.
    d. implosive therapy.

ANSWER KEY: KEY TERMS REVIEW

1. behavioral medicine (216)
2. hardiness (201)
3. migraine headaches (210)
4. asthma (212)
5. relaxation training (217)
6. coronary heart disease (204)
7. sudden death syndrome (190)
8. stressor (192)
9. biofeedback training (217)
10. tension headache (212)
11. essential hypertension (208)
12. general adaptation syndrome (192)
13. psychophysiological disorder (190)
14. stress (192)
15. decompensation (193)
16. life change model of stress (194)
17. transaction model of stress (196)
18. cluster headache (212)

ANSWER KEY: FACTUAL MULTIPLE–CHOICE QUESTIONS

1. a. *Psychosomatic* is the old term that implied that only some disorders were related to psychological states.
   b. *Adaptive* may be related to the general adaptation syndrome view of psychophysiological illnesses, but this represents only one viewpoint.
   c. *Somatopsychic* is a term that describes a non-Western view that illness produces emotional disorder.
   *d. To convey the idea that any physical condition can be related to psychological states, the new term used is *psychophysiological*. (p. 190)

2. *a. There are three stages in the general adaptation syndrome: alarm, resistance, and exhaustion. (p. 192)
   b. The life change model stresses the role of small and large life events; it predicts that higher life change scores lead to greater illness.
   c. Decompensation is a model of psychological response to stress, developed by De La Fuente, that has three stages, too: impact, attempted resolution, and decompensated adjustment.
   d. The transaction model emphasizes actual situations and the appraisal of events.

3. a. Catecholamines and NK (natural killer) cells are related to biological processes in stress; NK cells decrease during stress.
   b. Panic and confusion are early responses to stress in decompensation theory.
   *c. Decompensation theory suggests that panic and confusion are first responses, followed by attempts at resolution and, if these are unsuccessful, a stage of apathy and withdrawal. (p. 193)
   d. Decompensation deals with psychological consequences, not physical ones such as tissue damage.

4. a. The correlation is positive between life change units and likelihood of illness.
   *b. There is a positive correlation between life change units and severity of illness. (p. 195)
   c. Life change theory does not examine such personality variables as hardiness.
   d. As the number of life changes increases, the immune system is weakened.

5. a. When people are under stress, their NK cells are less responsive.
   *b. A variety of impairments in the immune system, including decreased NK cell responsiveness, are found during stress. (p. 199)
   c. Phagocytes and lymphocytes are immune system components weakened by stress.
   d. Separation and bereavement are life events associated with high numbers of life change units.

6. *a. The hardy personality features an openness to change, a commitment to a life course, and a sense of being able to control future events. (p. 201)
   b. The Type A personality is characterized by hostility, time pressure, and competitiveness.
   c. *General adaptation* is a term used to describe a generic response to stress that involves the stages of alarm, resistance, and exhaustion.
   d. The Type B personality is characterized by the ability to sequence tasks and relax between work efforts.

7. a. Although Type A's work fast, this is not the key element in the personality's relationship to heart disease.
   b. While Type A's may seek perfection, it is their hostility (expressed and unexpressed) that is related to increased coronary heart disease risk.
   c. Type A behavior seems to increase catecholamine levels, a biological sign of the stress response.
   *d. Hostility is the component of the Type A personality that is most closely associated with heart disease. (p. 207)

8. a. *Coronary heart disease* is a more general term for conditions that reduce the efficiency and longevity of the heart.
   *b. Essential hypertension exists when blood pressure is high but cannot be traced to a direct cause. (p. 208)
   c. *Angina pectoris* is a term for pains in the chest caused by heart disease.
   d. *Psychosomatic blood pressure* is a made-up term.

9. a. Episodic tension headaches are not overrepresented by African-Americans.
   b. Asthma is primarily a problem in youths and is not related to any particular personality pattern or ethnicity.
   *c. Poor blacks (who have fewer psychosocial resources) and those who express or suppress either anger excessively are most likely to have essential hypertension. (pp. 206–207)
   d. There is no evidence that defective NK cells are related to ethnicity or personality.

10. a. Tension headaches are characterized by a feeling of pressure and by lower intensity than migraine headaches, and they do not have neurological symptoms.
   *b. Classic migraines have such neurological signs as blurred vision and tingling sensations prior to appearance of the headache itself. (p. 210)
   c. Cluster headaches are not believed to be related to blood flow; they involve excruciating pain around the eye.
   d. Common migraine headaches do not have the neurological symptoms of classic migraines.

ANSWER KEY: CONCEPTUAL MULTIPLE–CHOICE QUESTIONS

1. a. The life change model originally looked at both positive and negative changes as stressors; more recent work considers negative events as the sole influence.
   *b. Life changes, regardless of type, are seen as piling together to reduce the person's coping ability. (p. 194)
   c. The transaction model stresses the cognitive aspects of coping, such as interpretation.
   d. The general adaptation model consists of alarm, resistance, and exhaustion stages.

2. a. Psychodynamic theory would stress early childhood experiences, although it is conceivable that individual differences in coping could be related to such experiences.
   b. Life change theory emphasizes the role of negative life events.
   c. The transaction model accepts the importance of biology, but adds the influence of cognitions and coping strategies.
   *d. Perceptions and methods of coping are central to the transaction model of stress. (p. 196)

3. a. High catecholamine levels are a sign of stress and may lead to early death rather than long life.
   b. Reduced personal control is associated with shortened life span in nursing homes.
   c. Suppression of anger is, if anything, related to an increased likelihood of essential hypertension.
   *d. Research by Rodin and Langer indicates that personal control in nursing-home residents is associated with longer life. (p. 200)

4. a. There is too much evidence linking personality and cancer to dismiss the entire topic.
   b. Cancer is related to diet, pollution, genetics, and many other nonpersonality dimensions.
   c. There is no evidence that women alone develop cancer because of emotions.
   *d. There are too many methodological problems in the current research to permit definite conclusions about the role of moods in cancer. (pp. 201–203; Focus On)

5. *a. Research shows that high depression scores on the MMPI predict future mortality due to cancer. (p. 202)
   b. Cancer is related to high scores on the depression scale of the MMPI.
   c. The reverse of this is true: As depression scores increase, so does the risk of later cancer (at least in one study).
   d. The research reports no interaction between depression and anger suppression.

6. a. Stress may activate the hypothalamic-pituitary-adrenocortical (HPA) axis, which mobilizes energy, but this effect may be positive or negative.
   b. Passive coping occurs when the individual cannot attempt to minimize exposure to the stressor and must tolerate it.
   *c. Research indicates that prolonged stress negatively affects the immune system. (pp. 197–198)
   d. Somatization disorder occurs when a person has a long-standing history of physical complaints for which medical tests indicate the person is normal.

7. a. The general adaptation model predicts that exhaustion occurs after a stressor has gone on too long.
   *b. Autonomic response specificity argues that each person has a unique way of reacting to stressors. (p. 215)
   c. Psychoanalytic theory (Alexander) suggests that each disorder is associated with a particular unconscious conflict.
   d. There is no theory that suggests that body parts react differently to different levels of stress.

8. a. Operant conditioning stresses the consequences of responses; it would examine the rewards for having an attack.
   b. Hardiness is associated with reduced risk of illness in the face of stressors.
   c. General adaptation is a model that proposes a generic response to stressors.
   *d. Classical conditioning focuses on the pairing of stimuli and would explain the generalization of attacks to a variety of stimuli. (p. 215).

9. *a. Biofeedback is an operant procedure that gives one control over autonomic responses such as heart rate and skin temperature. (p. 217)
   b. Progressive relaxation (Jacobson) involves tensing and relaxing muscle groups throughout the body.
   c. Classical conditioning is a passive process, unlike the operant conditioning that occurs in biofeedback.
   d. Modeling entails the imitation of others; none of this occurs in biofeedback.

10. a. The reverse is true; psychophysiological disorders involve tissue damage, whereas somatoform disorders are psychogenic in nature.
   *b. Psychophysiological disorders involve tissue damage, whereas somatoform disorders are psychogenic in nature. (pp. 190–191)
   c. Psychophysiological disorders are not psychogenic; they involve tissue damage.
   d. Psychophysiological disorders may be treated with cognitive-behavioral techniques, relaxation, biofeedback, and medications.

ANSWER KEY: APPLICATION MULTIPLE–CHOICE QUESTIONS

1. a. The DSM-IV says that any *one* of three relationships between psychological factors and the medical condition must exist: a temporal relationship or interference with treatment or additional health risk.
   b. The DSM-IV says that any *one* of three relationships between psychological factors and the medical condition must exist: a temporal relationship or interference with treatment or additional health risk.
   c. The DSM-IV says that any *one* of three relationships between psychological factors and the medical condition must exist: a temporal relationship or interference with treatment or additional health risk.
   *d. Because she sees a temporal relationship, the diagnostic criterion has been met. (pp. 190–191)

2. a. The somatic weakness hypothesis would be illustrated by Gina having heart trouble after this episode.
   b. The exhaustion stage is illustrated by the breakdown of tissues that have experienced prolonged resistance.
   c. The hardy personality is one that shows openness to change, commitment, and a sense of personal control.
   *d. The first stage of the general adaptation syndrome (alarm) involves a general mobilization of body functions that reduces immune system strength. (p. 192)

3. a. The life change model would consider all the events as examples of stressors.
   b. The interpretation of events is a key component of the transaction model.
   *c. The life change model suggests that all events—negative and positive, large and small—increase the likelihood of illness. (p. 194)
   d. The general adaptation syndrome suggests that alarm occurs soon after a stressor.

4. a. The life change perspective emphasizes the external environment.
   *b. The transaction perspective suggests that the way we interpret life events affects how stressed we become and how we cope with those reactions. (p. 196)
   c. Classical conditioning explains how a range of stimuli can produce the same stress reactions.
   d. Somatic weakness theory proposes that, after an earlier illness, certain body parts are vulnerable to impairment during stress.

5. a. The Type A personality is hostile and time-pressured.
   b. Learned helplessness involves a sense that personal control is lost.
   *c. According to Maddi and Kobasa, people like Jill are hardy in that they seem less vulnerable to stress-related illness than others. (p. 201)
   d. Classical conditioning may explain stress responses to various stimuli, but it has nothing to do with the cognitive factors described here.

6. a. There is no evidence that general paresis (deterioration of the brain due to syphilis) is related to a particular personality pattern.
   b. Coronary heart disease is related to hostility, but not to suppressed anger.
   *c. Cancer has been found to be more common both in people who are extreme anger suppressors and in those with high depression scores on the MMPI. (p. 202)
   d. Asthma is primarily a biological disorder, although fear of separation from others is related to some attacks.

7. a. Ethnicity and personality are unrelated to asthma and migraines.
   *b. Essential hypertension is related to race and anger expression; coronary heart disease is related to Type A personality. (pp. 206–209)
   c. Cancer may be related to depression and anger suppression, but migraines are not related to any of the factors listed in John's case.
   d. Sudden death syndrome is found among Hmong males; ethnicity and personality are not strongly related to asthma.

8. a. A husband's Type A status alone is not sufficient to produce the heightened hostile dominance pattern between spouses. It also requires a Type A spouse.
   b. Recurrent, uncontrollable stressors are related to CHD. This may be a risk factor if the manager is not given appropriate tools or resources to do a high-demand job.
   *c. Type A personality characteristics and essential hypertension both contribute to CHD. (pp. 204–207)
   d. Relaxation, meditation, and social support are effective buffers to stress.

9. a. Operant conditioning would focus on the consequences of a wheezing attack, such as increased attention.
   b. Psychodynamic thinking would examine the unconscious conflicts underlying a wheezing attack.
   c. Neurotransmitters play no role in the development of a cough.
   *d. Autonomic weakness theory suggests that each person has a unique physiological reaction to all types of stressful situations. (p. 214)

10. a. Progressive relaxation involves the tensing and relaxing of muscle groups.
   b. Cognitive restructuring features changing the way people think about stressors and about their ability to cope.
   *c. Biofeedback is an operant procedure that uses machinery to give information that leads to the voluntary altering of internal processes. (p. 217)
   d. Implosive therapy is used to extinguish fears by having people experience high levels of anxiety.

CHAPTER 8
Personality Disorders and Impulse Control Disorders

LEARNING OBJECTIVES

1. Discuss the general characteristics of personality disorders, the factors involved in considering a personality pattern a disorder, how they are diagnosed in the DSM-IV, and why they are difficult to diagnose. (pp. 221–223)
2. Discuss the prevalence and gender distribution of personality disorders and possible reasons for gender differences. (pp. 221–222; Critical Thinking, Focus On)
3. Discuss the causal considerations for personality disorders, including the five-factor model and its relevance. Explain why we know little about treating personality disorders. (pp. 223–224)
4. Describe the three clusters of personality disorders. (p. 224)
5. Describe and differentiate among the characteristics of paranoid, schizoid, and schizotypal personality disorders. Discuss how schizoid and schizotypal personality disorders are differentiated from schizophrenia. (pp. 225–228)
6. Describe and differentiate among the characteristics of histrionic, narcissistic, antisocial, and borderline personality disorders. (pp. 229–233)
7. Describe and differentiate among the characteristics of avoidant, dependent, and obsessive-compulsive personality disorders. (pp. 233–235)
8. Describe the characteristics and incidence of antisocial personality disorder and how it is differentiated from criminal behavior. Explain why it is a difficult population to study. (pp. 235–238)
9. Describe and discuss the etiological theories of antisocial personality disorders, including psychodynamic, family and socialization, and genetic theories. (pp. 238–240)
10. Discuss the relationship between central nervous system and autonomic nervous system abnormalities and antisocial personality disorder. Discuss the role of fearlessness, lack of anxiety, underarousal, learning deficits, and thrill-seeking in the disorder. (pp. 240–245; Focus On)
11. Describe treatments for antisocial personality and their success. (pp. 245–246)
12. Define impulse control disorders. Describe and differentiate among the following impulse control disorders: intermittent explosive disorder, kleptomania, pathological gambling, pyromania, and trichotillomania. (pp. 246–250)
13. Discuss how impulse control disorders overlap with other conditions. Describe the two explanatory "camps" for these disorders. Review the treatments for impulse control disorders and their success. (pp. 250–251)

CHAPTER OUTLINE

1. **The personality disorders** (pp. 221–223; Critical Thinking, Focus On) *Personality disorders* involve longstanding, inflexible, and maladaptive behavior patterns that produce personal and social difficulties, personal distress, or problems in functioning in society. They account for about 5 to 15 percent of admissions to hospitals and outpatient clinics; lifetime prevalence for all of them is 10 to 13 percent. Men are more likely than women to be diagnosed with some of the personality disorders, whereas women are more likely to be diagnosed with others. There are reasons to suggest that the gender distribution may be due to bias in diagnosing. Diagnosis is made on Axis II of the DSM, but diagnosis is difficult because symptoms represent extremes of normal personality traits, are rarely stable across situations, and may overlap with other disorders. Further, clinicians often render diagnoses inconsistent with DSM criteria. To be considered disorders personality patterns must cause significant impairment in functioning or subjective distress. Further, there may be questions about the universality of these disorders and the cultural validity of DSM-IV personality disorders.

2. **Etiological and treatment considerations for personality disorders** (pp. 223–224) There is insufficient empirical research pertaining to the personality disorders. Researchers have found the five-factor model (FFM) may be a good way to describe personality and personality disorders. The five factors are neuroticism, extraversion, openness to experience, agreeableness, and conscientiousness. Personality disorders may be exaggerations of these traits. Heredity partially explains the development of personality styles, but family environment is also crucial. As varied as the theories of cause may be, so are the treatment approaches. Many people with personality disorders resist treatment, and there is little research on success rates for the full range of disorders. DSM-IV lists ten personality disorders in three clusters: odd or eccentric behaviors; dramatic, emotional, or erratic behaviors; and anxious or fearful behaviors.

3. **Disorders characterized by odd or eccentric behaviors** (pp. 225–228) *Paranoid personality disorder* is characterized by suspiciousness, hypersensitivity, and reluctance to trust others. DSM-IV estimates the prevalence of paranoid personality disorder as between 0.5 and 2.5 percent. Psychodynamic explanations emphasize the role of projection in the disorder. *Schizoid personality disorder* is marked by aloofness and voluntary social isolation. To avoid conflicts and emotional involvements, these people withdraw from others or comply superficially with requests from others. The relationship between this disorder and schizophrenia is not clear. *Schizotypal personality disorder* involves odd thoughts and actions, such as speech oddities or beliefs in personal magical powers. It occurs in approximately 3 percent of the population. Odd though their behaviors are, individuals with this disorder are not as impaired as people with schizophrenia. There is some evidence of genetic links between the two disorders.

4. **Disorders characterized by dramatic, emotional, or erratic behaviors** (pp. 228–233) *Histrionic personality disorder* is marked by self-dramatization, exaggerated emotional expression, and attention-seeking behaviors. It affects 2 to 3 percent of the population. *Narcissistic personality disorder* involves an exaggerated sense of self-importance. People with this disorder may use denial to ward off feelings of inferiority. Prevalence is about 1 percent. *Antisocial personality disorder* involves exploitation of others, irresponsibility, and guiltlessness, and is far more common in men than women. *Borderline personality disorder* is characterized by extreme fluctuations in mood: friendly one day, hostile the next. People with this disorder also lack identity, feel lost and empty; they engage in self-destructive behaviors. The core aspects seem to be difficulty in regulating emotions, and intense, unstable relationships. This disorder is the most commonly diagnosed personality disorder and is estimated to occur in 2 percent of the population, with females three times more likely to receive the diagnosis than men. The disorder has been conceptualized from a psychodynamic perspective (object splitting—either people are completely good or completely bad), a social learning viewpoint (conflict between attachment to others and avoidance of such engagement), and a cognitive approach (distorted attributions and assumptions). There is much more theory than research evidence.

5. **Disorders characterized by anxious or fearful behaviors** (pp. 233–235) Individuals with *avoidant personality disorder* desire interpersonal contact but fear social rejection; they avoid situations that might lead to criticism. Their primary defense mechanism is fantasy, and their social skills are weak. People with *dependent personality disorder* are characterized by an extreme lack of self-confidence, reliance on others for decisions, and an ingrained assumption that they are inadequate and must be cared for by others. Prevalence of the disorder is about 2.5 percent. *Obsessive-compulsive personality disorder* is marked by excessive perfectionism, devotion to details, rigidity, and indecisiveness. Unlike in obsessive-compulsive disorder, there are no recurrent unwanted thoughts or ritualistic actions.

6. **Antisocial personality disorder** (pp. 235–238) Other terms for this disorder are *sociopathic* and *psychopathic personality*. Cleckley's (1976) classic description of *antisocial personality disorder* includes superficial charm, shallow emotions and lack of guilt, unplanned actions, failure to learn from experiences, absence of anxiety, and irresponsibility. DSM-IV criteria do not include lack of anxiety, shallow emotions, failure to learn, and superficial charm. They do include being at least eighteen years old, having a history of breaking laws since age fifteen, aggressiveness, impulsivity, and lack of remorse. Cleckley's traits seem to be retained as psychopathic criminals age, the DSM-IV characteristics seem to decline with age. The prevalence in the United States is about 2 percent, with three times more men than women being diagnosed. Although there are socioeconomic differences, there are no racial differences in prevalence. Criminals are not necessarily antisocial personalities; they often have a sense of loyalty to others and feelings of guilt, which are missing in antisocial personalities. Primary psychopaths feel no guilt over antisocial behaviors, secondary psychopaths do.

7. **Explanations of antisocial personality disorder** (pp. 238–245; Focus On) Psychoanalytic theory stresses a lack of parental identification and consequent superego deficiency. Family and socialization theory stresses parental rejection and modeling of antisocial behavior by fathers. Poor parental supervision predicts delinquency better than poverty or divorce. Genetic theory is supported by evidence of MZ twin concordance and greater likelihood of the disorder in the adoptees of antisocial biological parents. Central nervous system theory maintains that antisocial personalities have abnormal EEGs. Autonomic nervous system theory stresses antisocial personalities' low anxiety level and thrill seeking to counteract general underarousal. Eysenck and Lykken have done research to support these ideas. Lykken and Farley suggest that psychopaths and heroes have traits of fearlessness or thrill seeking in common (they are called "Big T's"). "Little t's" prefer certainty and low conflict. Antisocial personalities are also influenced by the kind and timing of punishment. Psychopaths may also have an emotional imagery deficit: they have trouble forming associations between perceptual memory and responding.

8. **Treatment of antisocial personality disorder** (pp. 245–246) Owing to their lack of anxiety, antisocial personalities are poorly motivated to change. Behavior modification and cognitive therapies have been somewhat helpful, but effective treatments for antisocial personality are rare. The focus might be placed on youths, who are more amenable to treatment.

9. **Disorders of impulse control** (pp. 246–250) *Impulse control disorders* are unrelated to personality disorders and are included in this chapter for the sake of convenience. These disorders involve an inability to resist the temptation to perform some act, a feeling of tension before the act, and a sense of excitement, release, and sometimes guilt afterward. *Intermittent explosive disorder* is marked by brief episodes of losing control, leading to destruction of property or assaults on other people. *Kleptomania* involves stealing, even when the article is not needed. It appears to be more common in women than men. *Pathological gambling* involves an inability to resist impulses to gamble and afflicts 1 to 3 percent of American adults. *Pyromaniacs* repeatedly and deliberately set fires without the motive of revenge. Children who are fire-setters are more often boys than girls and have problems with impulsivity and hostility. *Trichotillomania* is the

inability to refrain from pulling out one's hair. It is probably more common in women than men; about 1 to 2 percent of college students have a past or current history of the disorder.

10. **Etiology and treatment of impulse control disorders** (pp. 250–251) Little research has been done on the causes of these disorders. In some ways, impulse control disorders are similar to obsessive-compulsive, substance abuse, and sexual disorders. Psychodynamic theory stresses sexual symbolism; behavioral theory focuses on classical conditioning, reinforcement, and modeling; and biological theory points out greater thrill seeking in pathological gamblers. Lesieur (1989) notes two schools of thought: impulse control problems range on a continuum, or they are disease-like (one either has the disorder or not). Behavioral and cognitive treatments have had some success, as have insight therapies and self-help groups such as Gamblers Anonymous.

KEY TERMS REVIEW

1. The personality disorder characterized by intense fluctuations in mood, self-image, and interpersonal relationships is called ____________________.

2. The personality disorder characterized by failure to conform to social rules, lack of guilt feelings for wrongdoing, and superficial relationships is called ____________________.

3. The impulse control disorder in which there is a recurrent failure to resist impulses to steal objects is called ____________________.

4. The personality disorder characterized by self-dramatization, exaggerated emotions, and attention-seeking behavior is called ____________________.

5. The group of maladaptive behavior patterns that are longstanding and interfere with productive living and that stem from distorted personality structure are called ____________________.

6. The personality disorder characterized by unwarranted suspiciousness, hypersensitivity, and a reluctance to trust others is called ____________________.

7. The disorders characterized by a failure to resist the temptation to perform an act that is harmful to oneself or others are called ____________________.

8. The personality disorder characterized by such oddities of thinking and behavior as frequent digressions in speech or a belief in personal magical powers is called ____________________.

9. The impulse control disorder that is marked mainly by deliberate fire setting is called ____________________.

10. The impulse control disorder characterized by an inability to resist pulling out one's hair is called ____________________.

11. The personality disorder characterized by a fear of rejection and humiliation and, as a result, reluctance to enter into social relationships, is called ____________________.

12. The personality disorder characterized by extreme reliance on others and an unwillingness to assume responsibility is called ____________________.

13. The impulse control disorder characterized by an inability to refrain from gambling is called ____________________.

14. The personality disorder characterized by social isolation and emotional coldness is called ____________________.

15. The personality disorder characterized by perfectionism, indecision, devotion to details, and rigidity in behavior is called ____________________.

16. The personality disorder characterized by egocentrism and an exaggerated sense of self-importance is called ____________________.

17. The impulse control disorder marked by loss of control over aggressive impulses is called ____________________.

FACTUAL MULTIPLE-CHOICE QUESTIONS

1. Which statement below is *accurate* concerning the personality disorders?
   a. They are recorded on Axis I of the DSM-IV.
   b. They have symptoms that can overlap with those of other disorders.
   c. Symptoms first appear in young adulthood.
   d. They are characterized by an inability to resist temptation.

2. Neuroticism, extraversion, and agreeableness are
   a. characteristics of the antisocial personality disorder.
   b. components of the five-factor model of personality.
   c. personality characteristics that are not influenced by cultural norms.
   d. characteristics found in all personality disorders.

3. Which of the following statements about histrionic personality disorder is *accurate*?
   a. It involves attention-seeking behavior and exaggerated emotional expression.
   b. It is characterized by withdrawal from other people.
   c. It is related to abnormally low levels of arousal.
   d. It is considered a disorder involving odd or eccentric behaviors.

4. How do narcissistic personalities relate to other people?
   a. Narcissistic personalities do not trust others.
   b. Narcissistic personalities rely on others' opinions.
   c. Narcissistic personalities feel superior to others.
   d. Narcissistic personalities avoid other people.

5. Extreme fluctuations in mood, an unstable identity, a sense of being empty, and intense but erratic interpersonal relationships are characteristics of ____________________ personality disorder.
   a. borderline
   b. antisocial
   c. histrionic
   d. dependent

6. Which description of antisocial personality is *accurate*?
   a. It is three times more common in women than in men.
   b. It is characterized by marked irresponsibility and lack of empathy.
   c. Attention to details and lack of expressed warmth are common symptoms.
   d. Development of symptoms usually occurs after the age of eighteen.

7. What is the incidence of antisocial personality in males in the United States?
   a. .5 percent
   b. 2 percent
   c. 20 percent
   d. 45 percent

8. ____________________ psychologists would explain the cause of antisocial personality in terms of inadequate superego development.
   a. Behavioral
   b. Physiological
   c. Humanistic
   d. Psychoanalytic

9. Both Lykken and Farley assume that antisocial personalities
   a. are fearless.
   b. are able to learn from punishment.
   c. have an excessively active autonomic nervous system.
   d. have an underlying fear of being humiliated by others.

10. According to psychodynamic theory, the irresistible actions and the feelings of excitement and guilt related to them in the impulse control disorders are evidence of
    a. traumatic experiences in early childhood.
    b. the sexual symbolism in these disorders.
    c. excessive superego development.
    d. anal fixation.

CONCEPTUAL MULTIPLE–CHOICE QUESTIONS

1. The principal feature of paranoid personality disorder is
   a. excessive attention to details and general perfectionism.
   b. wide fluctuations in mood and self-image.
   c. unwarranted suspiciousness.
   d. a desire to be alone.

2. Schizoid personality disorder differs from schizotypal personality disorder in that in schizoid personality disorder there
   a. is a withdrawal from other people.
   b. is a possible genetic relationship to schizophrenia.
   c. is unwarranted suspiciousness of other people.
   d. are odd thoughts that border on delusions.

3. In this personality disorder, people believe they are innately inadequate and must rely on others for protection and information. They rarely express their own opinions. What is being described?
   a. Borderline personality disorder
   b. Dependent personality disorder
   c. Narcissistic personality disorder
   d. Obsessive-compulsive personality disorder

4. Perfectionism is to ____________________ personality disorder as fear of humiliation is to ____________________ personality disorder.
   a. borderline; obsessive-compulsive
   b. obsessive-compulsive; avoidant
   c. narcissistic; histrionic
   d. obsessive-compulsive; histrionic

5. Cleckley's indicators include lack of anxiety and superficial charm; the DSM-IV criteria include breaking social norms and acting impulsively. What is being described?
   a. Narcissistic personality disorder
   b. Histrionic personality disorder
   c. Antisocial personality disorder
   d. Impulse control disorders

6. Which of the following is a problem when criminal psychopaths are used in research on antisocial personality disorder?
   a. Very few antisocial personalities engage in criminal behavior.
   b. Criminals, unlike antisocial personalities, tend to request treatment for psychological problems.
   c. Criminals may not be representative of nonprison psychopaths.
   d. Criminals tend to be male, whereas noncriminal psychopaths tend to be female.

7. Twin and adoption studies of antisocial personalities tend to
   a. support the idea that the disorder is inherited.
   b. reject the idea that the disorder is inherited.
   c. explain why females are especially likely to develop the disorder.
   d. highlight the role of the superego in the disorder.

8. Research on antisocial personalities shows that they make fewer errors in avoiding punishment when
   a. they are given tranquilizers.
   b. punishment means losing money.
   c. punishment is highly uncertain.
   d. their arousal level is low.

9. In general, there are few effective treatments for antisocial personality disorder because
   a. there are so few people with the disorder.
   b. antisocial personalities suffer from extreme anxiety.
   c. the neurotransmitter imbalance of antisocial personalities cannot be offset by medication.
   d. antisocial personalities are unmotivated for treatment.

10. What do pyromania, kleptomania, and trichotillomania have in common?
   a. They all affect women more than men.
   b. They are all personality disorders.
   c. They all involve lower than normal levels of arousal.
   d. They are all impulse control disorders.

APPLICATION MULTIPLE–CHOICE QUESTIONS

1. Irma, age twenty-nine, spends her days alone in her room playing records and looking at magazines. She has no desire to talk with others, and has had no intimate relationships in her life. Irma illustrates which personality disorder?
   a. Avoidant
   b. Obsessive-compulsive
   c. Schizoid
   d. Antisocial

2. Dr. Clopper says, "Georgette is an unusual case of histrionic personality. She constantly seeks attention, dramatically 'performs' emotions, and demands perfection of herself and others." What is unusual about the case?
   a. Most histrionics are shy and withdrawn.
   b. Most histrionics are not perfectionistic.
   c. Most histrionics are unable to express emotions.
   d. Most histrionics are men.

3. "The incompetence of my subordinates upsets me. If I didn't have ignorant people holding me down, I'd get the promotions I deserve." People with which personality disorder are most likely to make such statements?
   a. Narcissistic
   b. Dependent
   c. Obsessive-compulsive
   d. Avoidant

4. A psychologist says, "Because of early childhood experiences, these people see others as either all good or all bad. That accounts for their tremendous swings in mood and self-image." The psychologist is giving a ____________ explanation for ____________ personality disorder.
   a. behavioral; antisocial
   b. psychodynamic; borderline
   c. psychodynamic; avoidant
   d. behavioral; borderline

5. Shandra is an accountant with a passion for details. She is so perfectionistic, she drives everyone else crazy. These behaviors best illustrate the ____________ personality disorder.
   a. schizotypal
   b. avoidant
   c. narcissistic
   d. obsessive-compulsive

6. Juan is diagnosed as a primary psychopath. He exploits other people and feels guilt about it. He has been imprisoned repeatedly for small crimes because he acts impulsively and fails to learn from his mistakes. What is unusual about this case?
   a. Most antisocial personalities are women.
   b. Most antisocial personalities learn from mistakes.
   c. Most antisocial personalities experience no guilt.
   d. Most antisocial personalities plan their crimes carefully.

7. While interviewing a client whom he suspects should be diagnosed with ____________, Dr. Hill asks many questions about whether the client's father was an impulsive criminal, a hostile and rejecting parent, or physically abusive.
   a. borderline personality disorder
   b. kleptomania
   c. antisocial personality disorder
   d. pathological gambling

8. Tom is diagnosed as an antisocial personality. He takes several psychological tests and is measured for physiological arousal when under stress. What ought to be the results of the tests and physiological measures?
   a. He is highly fearful, but has a low arousal level.
   b. He is a "Big T" and has a low arousal level.
   c. He is a "little t" and has a high arousal level.
   d. He is fearless and has a high arousal level.

9. A psychologist says, "Unlike pyromania and kleptomania, this impulse control disorder does not involve an action that is harmful to others. Indeed, the irresistible response in this disorder is physically painful to the person with the disorder." What disorder is being discussed?
   a. Trichotillomania
   b. Intermittent explosive disorder
   c. Antisocial personality disorder
   d. Pathological gambling

10. A student goes to the library to study about impulse control disorders. The student is likely to find that
   a. there is little research on their cause.
   b. they are very similar to anxiety disorders.
   c. behavioral and cognitive behavioral therapies are totally ineffective.
   d. the cause of these disorders is neurological.

ANSWER KEY: KEY TERMS REVIEW

1. borderline personality disorder (230)
2. antisocial personality disorder (230)
3. kleptomania (248)
4. histrionic personality disorder (229)
5. personality disorders (221)
6. paranoid personality disorder (225)
7. impulse control disorders (246)
8. schizotypal personality disorder (226)
9. pyromania (249)
10. trichotillomania (250)
11. avoidant personality disorder (233)
12. dependent personality disorder (234)
13. pathological gambling (248)
14. schizoid personality disorder (225)
15. obsessive-compulsive personality disorder (235)
16. narcissistic personality disorder (229)
17. intermittent explosive disorder (247)

ANSWER KEY: FACTUAL MULTIPLE–CHOICE QUESTIONS

1. a. The major clinical syndrome is recorded on Axis I; personality disorders are listed on Axis II.
   *b. One problem with diagnosing personality disorders is that symptoms, such as suspiciousness, overlap with those of other disorders, such as paranoia or paranoid schizophrenia. (p. 222)
   c. Personality disorders usually become evident during adolescence or earlier.
   d. An inability to resist temptation is associated with the impulse control disorders.

2. a. The antisocial personality disorder is characterized by impulsivity, thrill seeking, and law breaking; it is not associated with neuroticism or agreeableness.
   *b. The five-factor model (FFM) of personality includes neuroticism, extraversion, openness to experience, agreeableness, and conscientiousness. (p. 224)
   c. People from different cultures exhibit different personality characteristics; it is unlikely that these three are immune from cultural forces.
   d. Some of the components of the five-factor model may be present in some of the personality disorders; what all personality disorders have in common are inflexible, maladaptive patterns of behavior that cause distress or functional impairment.

3. *a. Histrionic personality disorder is characterized by attention-seeking behavior, exaggerated emotional displays, and egocentric self-dramatization. (p. 229)
   b. Histrionics need the attention of others; they seek out people rather than withdrawing from them.
   c. There is no evidence that low arousal is related to histrionic personality disorder.
   d. Histrionic personality disorder is categorized with those disorders involving "emotional or erratic behaviors."

4. a. Paranoid personalities do not trust other people.
   b. Dependent personalities rely on others' opinions.
   *c. Narcissistic personalities feature inflated self-importance, which is propped up by devaluing others. (p. 230)
   d. Schizoid personalities tend to avoid other people.

5. *a. Extreme fluctuations in mood and self-image, impulsivity, and underlying feelings of purposelessness are key symptoms of borderline personality disorder. (p. 230)
   b. Antisocial personalities use other people and do little self-evaluation, so there is rarely a time of low self-image.
   c. Histrionic personalities can have mood swings, but this is coupled with attention-seeking behavior, seductiveness, and shallowness.
   d. Dependent personalities rely on others for advice and information.

6. a. The reverse is true: antisocial personality is three times more likely in men than in women.
   *b. Irresponsibility, impulsivity, lack of empathy, and lack of remorse are key features of antisocial personality. (pp. 236–237)
   c. Attention to details is a sign of obsessive-compulsive personality disorder.
   d. All personality disorders show symptoms in adolescence or earlier.

7. a. One percent or less is the incidence for females in the United States.
   *b. Although this may be an underestimate, 2 percent is the approximate rate of new cases in males. (p. 238)
   c. Twenty percent is roughly seven times the U.S. male incidence rate.
   d. Forty-five percent is roughly fifteen times the U.S. male incidence rate.

8. a. Behaviorists would stress modeling and inconsistent reinforcement.
   b. Physiological psychologists would stress nervous system abnormalities.
   c. Humanistic psychologists are not typically concerned with antisocial personalities but might stress social conditions.
   *d. Psychoanalysts see morality and self-control as stemming from the superego; lack of parental identification produces a faulty superego. (p. 238)

9. *a. Lykken and Farley report that psychopaths enjoy taking risks and showing their fearlessness. (pp. 241–242; Focus On)
   b. Eysenck's research shows that they learn slowly.
   c. Fearlessness and lack of anxiety stem from underarousal in the autonomic nervous system.
   d. Fear of humiliation is a problem for people with avoidant personality disorder.

10. a. Early traumatic experiences are not necessarily associated with these disorders.
    *b. Psychoanalysts see each forbidden behavior as linked to sex; for instance, gambling and masturbation or stealing and sexual gratification. (p. 251)
    c. Excessive superego concern is expressed in perfectionism and a need to obey all rules.
    d. Anal fixation is associated with stinginess and stubbornness.

ANSWER KEY: CONCEPTUAL MULTIPLE–CHOICE QUESTIONS

1. a. Excessive attention to details is a feature of obsessive-compulsive personality disorder.
   b. Wide fluctuations in mood and self-image are related to borderline personality disorder.
   *c. Paranoid personality disorder is characterized by suspiciousness without cause and by emotional distance from others. (p. 225)
   d. A desire to be alone can be associated with the schizoid personality disorder and with complete normality.

2. *a. Although both personality disorders have some symptoms in common with schizophrenia, schizoid personality disorder is marked by the social withdrawal that is seen in schizophrenia. (p. 225)
   b. The genetic links to schizophrenia are not as clear for schizoid personality disorder as they are for schizotypal.
   c. Unwarranted suspiciousness is most important in paranoid personality disorder.
   d. Odd thoughts are the key symptom of schizotypal personality disorder; social withdrawal is seen as secondary to cognitive difficulties.

3. a. Borderline personalities have mood swings; they have no trouble expressing opinions.
   *b. Dependent personalities rely on others for their ideas because they have low self-confidence. (p. 234)
   c. Narcissistic personalities devalue others to inflate their own self-concept and feel superior to others.
   d. Obsessive-compulsives take on many responsibilities and attempt to execute them perfectly.

4. a. Perfectionism is a characteristic of obsessive-compulsive personalities, not borderlines.
   *b. Perfectionism is a core feature of people with obsessive-compulsive personality disorder, and avoidant personalities fear criticism from and embarrassment in front of others. (p. 235)
   c. Narcissistic personalities do not strive for perfectionism; if they are sloppy, they blame others.
   d. Histrionic personalities seek attention from others; they do not fear being humiliated.

5. a. Narcissistic personality involves an inflated self-concept; there is no alternative diagnostic criteria.
   b. Histrionics are attention seekers who have exaggerated emotional displays.
   *c. Antisocial personality disorder has these two sets of symptoms, which overlap somewhat. (p. 237)
   d. Impulse control disorders only involve recurrent failure to resist an urge.

6. a. Research with nonprison populations shows that antisocials engage in a great deal of criminal behavior.
   b. Antisocials both inside and outside of prison do not feel there is anything wrong with them.
   *c. Imprisoned psychopaths have been studied because they are clearly a captive audience, but it is unclear whether they are representative; they might be more impulsive than others, since they got caught. (p. 238)
   d. There is no evidence that nonprison psychopaths are any more likely to be female, but even if there were this bias, c is a more general answer.

7. *a. Both kinds of studies find that the greater the genetic similarity of one person to an antisocial personality, the greater the likelihood that that person is antisocial, too. (p. 240)
   b. Twin and adoption studies support genetic theory.
   c. Females are less likely to develop the disorder.
   d. The superego is related to psychoanalysis.

8. a. Tranquilizers would further reduce the already low arousal level of antisocial personalities.
   *b. When punishment was defined as losing money (rather than electric shock), antisocial personalities learned the avoidance task better. (p. 244)
   c. Antisocial personalities learn less well when there is high uncertainty about when punishment will occur.
   d. A reason that they learn poorly is that their arousal level is too low.

9. a. With an incidence of 2 percent among males in the United States, antisocial personality disorder is fairly common.
   b. Antisocial personalities experience abnormally low levels of anxiety.
   c. There is no clear neurotransmitter imbalance.
   *d. Because of underarousal, antisocial personalities are not motivated for treatment; they usually consider therapy a joke. (p. 245)

10. a. There is no evidence for a sex difference in these disorders.
   b. None of them is a personality disorder.
   c. Antisocial personality involves abnormally low levels of arousal; there is no evidence for such a deficit in these disorders.
   *d. Since all these disorders involve both an inability to resist some behavior and excitement or guilt when engaged in that behavior, they are impulse control disorders. (p. 246)

ANSWER KEY: APPLICATION MULTIPLE–CHOICE QUESTIONS

1. a. Although avoidant personalities may spend time alone, they crave attention and uncritical acceptance.
   b. Obsessive-compulsive personality disorder is marked by attention to detail and perfectionism.
   *c. Social isolation is the key symptom of schizoid personality disorder. (pp. 225–226)
   d. Antisocial personalities seek others out so that they can exploit them.

2. a. Histrionics seek attention, so they are rarely withdrawn.
   *b. Histrionics are impressionistic and vague; they are not perfectionists. (p. 229)
   c. Histrionics are constantly expressing emotions that appear, after a while, to be superficial.
   d. More women are diagnosed with histrionic personality disorder than men, perhaps because it is a caricature of traditional femininity.

3. *a. The central feature of narcissistic personality disorder is inflated self-importance, which is demonstrated by devaluing others. (p. 229)
   b. Dependent personalities would not make a statement like this; they have very low self-confidence.
   c. Obsessive-compulsive personality disorder is marked by perfectionism and a lack of warmth.
   d. Avoidant personality disorder involves hypersensitivity to criticism by others.

4. a. Behaviorists would stress the reinforcements for exploiting others (antisocial personality).
   *b. Psychoanalysts believe that the borderline person has split the world into "good objects" and "bad objects," which accounts for the extreme mood swings seen in the disorder. (p. 231)
   c. Avoidant personality disorder does not involve such wide fluctuations of mood.
   d. Behaviorists would stress the reinforcements for being changeable.

5. a. Schizotypal personalities have odd thoughts and ways of speaking.
   b. Avoidant personality disorder involves hypersensitivity to criticism and fantasies of being loved.
   c. Inflated self-importance is the hallmark of narcissistic personality disorder.
   *d. Individuals diagnosed with obsessive-compulsive personality disorder are devoted to details and insist that everything be done perfectly. (p. 235)

6. a. Most antisocial personalities are men.
   b. Most antisocial personalities fail to learn from mistakes.
   *c. Primary psychopaths feel no guilt over their antisocial actions. (p. 238)
   d. Impulsivity is a central feature of antisocial personality disorder; antisocial personalities rarely plan their crimes carefully.

7. a. Borderline personality disorder may be related to splitting the world into "all good" and "all bad."
   b. There is no evidence that kleptomania stems from parental rejection or the modeling of impulsivity.
   *c. Family and socialization theory suggests that antisocial personality develops in families where fathers model antisocial behavior and parents are hostile and rejecting. (p. 239)
   d. Pathological gambling is too little understood to suggest this pattern of development.

8. a. Research shows that antisocial personality is associated with fearlessness.
   *b. Farley has coined the term "Big T" for thrill seekers such as psychopaths; Lykken's and other research show psychopaths to be low in autonomic arousal. (pp. 241–243)
   c. "Little t's" avoid reckless activity, making them the opposite of antisocial personalities.
   d. High arousal during stress is true of nonpsychopaths; psychopaths keep their cool when everyone else would be emotional.

9. *a. Trichotillomania—uncontrolled hair pulling—harms only oneself, not others. (p. 250)
   b. The physical and verbal aggression of intermittent explosive disorder certainly hurts others.
   c. Antisocial personality disorder involves the exploitation of others and invariably produces harmful consequences for others.
   d. Pathological gambling may be harmful to oneself, but cannot be seen as *physically* damaging.

10. *a. There is very little research on the cause of impulse control disorders. (p. 250)
    b. Impulse control disorders have more similarities with substance abuse disorders and sexual deviations.
    c. Booth's (1988) review shows that behavioral and cognitive behavioral methods can be helpful.
    d. There is no evidence that impulse control disorders are caused by neurological factors.

CHAPTER 9
Substance-Related Disorders

LEARNING OBJECTIVES

1. Distinguish substance-related disorders from substance-use cognitive disorders, substance abuse from substance dependence, and define the terms *tolerance*, *withdrawal*, and *intoxication*. Discuss the overlap in criteria for dependence and abuse. (pp. 254–255)
2. Describe the nature and scope of substance use and describe the types and prevalence of substance-use disorders in the United States. (pp. 255–257)
3. Categorize the psychoactive drugs according to their properties (sedative, stimulant, or hallucinogenic). (pp. 255–260)
4. Discuss the nature and magnitude of drinking problems in the United States and the short- and long-term physiological and psychological effects of alcohol. (pp. 256–262; Focus On)
5. Describe the effects of narcotics, barbiturates, and benzodiazepines. Define polysubstance use and explain why it causes special problems. (pp. 262–264)
6. Describe and discuss the problems of stimulant-use disorders, including amphetamines, caffeine, nicotine, cocaine, and crack. Evaluate the controversy concerning nicotine addiction and its treatment. (pp. 264–266)
7. Describe and discuss the problems of hallucinogen-use disorders, including marijuana, LSD, phencyclidine (PCP), and "other substance-use disorders." Evaluate evidence concerning marijuana's harmful effects. (pp. 266–268)
8. Describe the two general types of etiological theories of substance-related disorders. Describe and evaluate the evidence for specific genes and risk factors related to alcoholism and other forms of substance dependence. (pp. 268–270)
9. Describe and discuss the various explanations for alcoholism and other substance-related disorders, including psychodynamic, personality, and sociocultural explanations. Evaluate research evidence on the relation between drug use and maladjustment. (pp. 270–272; Critical Thinking)
10. Describe and discuss behavioral explanations for alcohol abuse and dependence, including the anxiety-reduction hypothesis, learned expectations, and cognitive influences. (pp. 273–275)
11. Discuss explanations for relapse among alcoholics and people who are dependent on other substances. Describe and distinguish opponent process, two-factor, and automatic processing theories of the addiction process. (pp. 275–278)
12. Describe the nature and effectiveness of alcohol and drug treatment programs, including self-help groups, pharmacological approaches to substance-use treatment, and controlled-drinking. (pp. 278–281)
13. Describe and compare the cognitive and behavioral approaches to treating substance-related disorders, including aversion therapy, covert sensitization, rapid smoking, nicotine fading,

relaxation and social learning methods, and cognitive-change treatments. (pp. 280–284; Focus On)

14. Discuss what is meant by multimodal treatment. Describe and evaluate the evidence concerning treatment effectiveness for alcohol, smoking cessation, and other substance-related disorders. (pp. 281–285)

CHAPTER OUTLINE

1. **Substance-use disorders** (pp. 254–255) In the United States, there is widespread use of drugs that alter mood and consciousness. *Substance-related disorders* involve drug use that alters one's psychological state and causes significant physical, social, or occupational problems and sometimes results in abuse or dependence. Substance-use disorders involve abuse or dependence; substance-induced disorders (discussed in Chapter 15) involve withdrawal or delirium.

   DSM-IV defines *substance abuse* as recurrent use over twelve months that leads to impairment or distress, and continues despite problems. *Substance dependence* adds the concepts of tolerance (needing increased dosages) and *withdrawal* (physical or emotional symptoms after reduced intake). Further, *intoxication* refers to central nervous system effects, following ingestion of a drug, that involve maladaptive behaviors or thinking. Dependence is the more serious condition.

   Prescription drugs and legal and illegal substances can lead to abuse or dependence. Such disorders are most prevalent among youths and young adults. Overall lifetime prevalence of drug abuse/dependence (excluding nicotine and alcohol) is 6.2 percent. Women are much less likely to take drugs than men; whites have higher lifetime prevalence for drug abuse than African Americans or Hispanic Americans.

2. **Depressants or sedatives: alcohol** (pp. 255–262) Depressants cause generalized depression of the central nervous system and slowing of responses. They induce feelings of calm but also make people more sociable and open because of lowered inhibitions. People with alcohol abuse or alcohol dependence are popularly referred to as alcoholics, their disorder as alcoholism. Problem drinking often begins as a way to reduce anxiety and expands to heavier drinking. Some drink daily, others "binge." About 35 percent of Americans abstain from alcohol, but 10 percent of the drinkers consume 50 percent of all alcohol consumed in this country. Men drink two to five times as much as women; and heavy drinking is most common between eighteen and twenty-five years of age. Lifetime prevalence for alcohol dependence is 14 percent. Consumption patterns are associated with cultural and racial background. Alcohol abuse is associated with medical costs, lowered productivity, and problems in children of alcoholic parents. Alcohol has short-term physiological effects, such as impaired speech and motor coordination, because it is a central nervous system depressant. Its short-term psychological effects include poor judgment, feelings of happiness, and reduced concentration, but the precise effects are influenced by the situational context. The long-term effects are serious: Some drinkers become preoccupied with thoughts of alcohol, experience blackouts, lose control over their consumption, and deteriorate. However, most research has been based on male alcoholics, and effects may be different for females. Physiological effects can include liver damage, heart disease, and cancers of the mouth and throat. Moderate use is associated with lowered risk of heart disease.

3. **Depressants or sedatives: narcotics, barbiturates, and benzodiazepines** (pp. 262–264) Narcotics, which include opium and its derivatives morphine, heroin, and codeine act as sedatives and are addictive. Tolerance builds rapidly and withdrawal is severe. Prevalence of addiction decreases with age. *Barbiturates* are legal medications and are used mostly by middle-aged and older people to induce sleep and relaxation. Combined with alcohol, barbiturates can lead to fatal overdoses. DSM-IV lists a diagnosis of polysubstance dependence in which three or more substances (not including nicotine and caffeine) are abused for at least twelve months. Benzodiazepines, including Valium, a widely prescribed drug, are overused to deal with stress.

4. **Stimulants** (pp. 264–266) A *stimulant* energizes the central nervous system. One example is an *amphetamine,* which increases alertness and inhibits both appetite and sleep. Tolerance builds quickly, and chronic high doses can lead to aggressive behavior. Lifetime prevalence of amphetamine abuse or dependence is about 2 percent. Caffeine and nicotine are both legal and widely used stimulants. Caffeine has mild effects; nicotine is the single most preventable cause of death in the United States. About 30 percent of the U.S. population currently smokes. Nicotine dependence symptoms are unsuccessful attempts to stop, withdrawal symptoms after stopping, and continued use despite such illnesses as emphysema. *Cocaine* induces feelings of self-confidence in users. It is a fashionable drug, and there are from one to three million cocaine abusers in need of treatment in the United States. Cocaine is typically snorted. Crack, a rock-like, purified form of cocaine, is smoked, resulting in rapid euphoria followed by depression. Cocaine and amphetamines alter moods by increasing brain dopamine levels. Crack is a major social concern because it is inexpensive, easy to acquire, produces an intense high, leads to rapid addiction, and is associated with crime.

5. **Hallucinogens** (pp. 266–268) *Hallucinogens* are not believed to be physically addicting, although psychological dependence may occur. They produce hallucinations, vivid sensory awareness, and perceptions of increased insight. Over 33 percent of the U.S. population has used *marijuana,* although it is illegal. Technically, the DSM-IV does not consider marijuana a hallucinogen. Marijuana is a mild hallucinogen that produces euphoria, passivity, and memory impairment. There is considerable controversy concerning its short- and long-term physical and psychological effects. *Lysergic acid diethylamide (LSD)* is a psychotomimetic drug that alters visual and auditory perceptions and can produce flashbacks. It does not produce physical dependence. *Phencyclidine (PCP)* is an extremely dangerous hallucinogen because it often leads to assaultive and suicidal behavior. Other DSM-IV categories for substance-related disorders include anabolic steroids and nitrous oxide ("laughing gas").

6. **Etiology of substance-use disorders** (pp. 268–273; Critical Thinking) There are two major perspectives on substance-related disorders, biogenic and cultural, although integration of the two is growing. The genetic transmission of alcoholism is supported by evidence with children of alcoholics adopted by nonalcoholics and by twin research. No specific genes have been found to explain the causes of alcoholism. The search for specific genes has used quantitative trait loci (QTL) and the selective breeding of animals that prefer alcohol. Biological markers for alcoholism have been suggested in the form of neurotransmitter differences and insensitivity to alcohol but firm causal links are yet to be found. There is less research on the hereditary basis for other substances.

   Psychodynamic explanations stress childhood traumas, dependency needs, and the need to release inhibitions concerning repressed conflicts. While reviews of the research show no single alcoholic personality, antisocial behavior and depression have been associated with drinking problems. Emotionality and sociability may also be associated. Longitudinal research indicates that maladjustment in teens may be associated with both abstinence from drug use and frequent drug use.

   Sociocultural explanations note differences in consumption based on sex, age, social class, ethnicity, and religion. France and Italy both have high alcohol consumption, but the U.S. and Russia have high rates of alcoholism. In the United States, European Americans are more likely to use hallucinogens and PCP but less likely to use heroin than African Americans or Latinos, a probable reflection of sociocultural influences. Peer group influences predict adolescent drug use.

   Behavioral explanations originally focused on the tension-reducing properties of alcohol. However, the Marlatt et al. (1973) study, in which alcoholics and social drinkers were led to believe they were drinking alcohol when they actually got tonic, showed that expectation has a strong influence on use. Alcohol seems either to increase or decrease anxiety, depending on whether there is a distraction to divert the drinker's attention from his or her anxiety. A longitudinal study showed that adolescents who expected social benefits from drinking drank more and endorsed even more positive expectancies about alcohol. Coping responses and expectancy exert a combined effect to predict alcohol and drug use.

Relapse is a crucial topic for substance-related disorders. Certain feelings and situations increase the risk for relapse, although recent research found that relapse was least likely when users set goals of absolute abstinence and had positive moods, rather than when they were in stress-free environments. Relapse is not merely caused by physiological withdrawal effects; cognitive, behavioral, and biological factors interact.

7. **Overall theories of the addiction process** (pp. 276–278) Solomon (1977) argues that addiction is an acquired motivation. His opponent process theory says that chronic use decreases the initial effects of a drug but increases the intensity of withdrawal reactions. Motivation for drug use changes from positive to aversive control. Wise (1988) believes that positive and negative reinforcement combine to explain addiction. Finally, Tiffany (1990) suggests that drug use is largely an automatic process, where urges and plans play little role.

8. **Intervention and treatment of substance-use disorders** (pp. 278–285) A first step in most treatment programs is *detoxification*, the elimination of the chemical from the body. The second step tries to prevent the person from returning to the substance. Self-help groups, such as Alcoholics Anonymous, which stress support, spiritual awareness, and public self-revelations, are often helpful, but less so than members assert. Chemicals such as Antabuse for alcohol and methadone for heroin treatment can be useful but have the problem of individuals ceasing to take the medication. However, in smoking cessation, nicotine patches hold promise. Reasons for resuming smoking include physiological and psychological factors. Cognitive and behavioral therapies include aversion therapy, *covert sensitization*, rapid smoking, nicotine fading, spacing of cigarettes, relaxation training, and coping-skills training. There is considerable controversy about treatment for *controlled drinking* for alcoholics. In addition to the problem of retraining patients to drink socially, the researchers themselves have been attacked. Most treatment uses a multimodal effort, including inpatient individual and group therapy followed by outpatient treatment and support groups.

   Prevention programs often seek to educate the public about the negative consequences of substance use. One junior high school smoking-prevention program that used resistance training, information about physical consequences, and information on the social image of smokers was able to reduce the likelihood of students becoming smokers, compared with a control group not participating in the program.

   Treatment is effective but only modestly so. One-third of alcoholic clients are abstinent at one year; most smokers have relapsed within a year of treatment. However, some individuals recover on their own.

KEY TERMS REVIEW

1. The treatment aimed at removing all alcohol (or other substance) from a user's body is called ____________________.

2. Excessive use of a substance leading to lack of control over use and impaired functioning is called ____________________.

3. Substance abuse or dependence in which the substance being used is alcohol is called ____________________.

4. The physical or emotional symptoms, such as shaking and irritability, that appear when intake of a regularly used substance is halted are called ____________________.

5. A substance that causes general depression of the central nervous system and a slowing of responses is called a sedative or a(n) ____________________.

6. The pathological pattern of excessive use of a substance that results in impaired social and occupational functioning but not tolerance or withdrawal is called ____________________.

7. When a substance is ingested and causes central nervous system effects involving maladaptive behaviors or thinking, this state is called ____________________.

8. A behavioral strategy designed to promote the abstinence of drugs is called ____________________.

9. People who abuse and depend on alcohol are called ____________________.

10. Substances known as "uppers" that speed up central nervous system activity and produce increased alertness and euphoria and, in chronic users, paranoia are called ____________________.

11. Substances known as "downers" that powerfully depress the central nervous system and can induce physical dependency and lethal overdose are called ____________________.

12. A drug that induces feelings of euphoria and self-confidence in users and is usually inhaled is called ____________________.

13. An aversive conditioning technique in which the individual imagines a noxious stimulus in the presence of a behavior is called ____________________.

14. The conditioning procedure in which the response to a stimulus is decreased by pairing it with an aversive stimulus is called ____________________.

15. A substance that produces hallucinations, vivid sensory awareness, or feelings of increased insight is called a(n) ____________________.

16. The mildest and most commonly used hallucinogen is called ____________________.

17. An addictive substance that depresses the central nervous system, provides relief from pain and anxiety, and is derived from opium is called a(n) ____________________.

18. A psychoactive substance that energizes the central nervous system and causes elation, hyperactivity, and appetite suppression is called a(n) ____________________.

19. A maladaptive pattern of use extending over a twelve-month period and characterized by inability to control use and by tolerance or withdrawal symptoms is called ____________________.

20. The condition in which increasing doses of a substance are necessary to achieve a desired effect is called ____________________.

21. Substance dependence based not on any single substance but on the repeated use of at least three groups of substances for a period of twelve months is called ____________________.

22. Behavioral techniques used in drug treatment programs that are designed to improve one's communication, problem solving, and peer pressure refusal abilities are called ____________________.

FACTUAL MULTIPLE–CHOICE QUESTIONS

1. When increasing doses of a substance are necessary to achieve a desired effect, this
   a. is considered a substance-induced disorder.
   b. indicates tolerance for the drug.
   c. shows that the user will experience withdrawal.
   d. indicates the key symptom of substance abuse.

2. In the United States, substance-related disorders would *most* likely be expected in which population?
   a. Females under age thirty
   b. African Americans and Hispanic Americans
   c. Males under age thirty
   d. White males over age forty-five

3. Which statement about alcohol consumption is *accurate*?
   a. Roughly 50 percent of the alcohol consumed in the United States is consumed by 10 percent of the drinkers.
   b. Women drink more frequently than men.
   c. About 50 million Americans have been problem drinkers at some time in their lives.
   d. Less than 10 percent of American adults abstain from drinking.

4. Which of the following is a physiological effect of chronic alcohol use?
   a. Intoxication
   b. Flashbacks
   c. Liver cirrhosis
   d. Lung disease

5. ____________________ are a category of drug that is widely prescribed for reduction of anxiety and muscle tension.
   a. Hallucinogens
   b. Opiates
   c. Amphetamines
   d. Benzodiazepines

6. Which statement about marijuana is *accurate*?
   a. It is the least commonly used hallucinogen.
   b. When intoxicated, users are excited and time seems to pass quickly.
   c. Prior experience and the setting in which it is used influence its effects.
   d. It produces serious physiological withdrawal effects.

7. The hallucinogen that is most related to uncontrolled aggression and delusional states is called
   a. PCP.
   b. marijuana.
   c. LSD.
   d. crack cocaine.

8. Results from the study in which alcoholics and social drinkers drank either tonic or alcohol indicate that
   a. alcoholism is a disease in which one loses control over drinking.
   b. a subject's expectations have little effect on how much he or she drinks.
   c. expectations are important only for social drinkers.
   d. the disease concept of loss of control is inaccurate.

9. According to Schachter, most smokers have difficulty quitting because of
   a. expectation, since nicotine cannot be physically addicting.
   b. the drug's ability to produce hallucinations.
   c. physical addiction to nicotine.
   d. the social pressures that smokers feel to fit in with their peers.

10. Multimodal treatment for substance-related disorders entails
    a. working with people who are addicted to several different chemicals.
    b. extinguishing behaviors to many different cues and situations.
    c. detoxifying people before they become involved with Alcoholics or Narcotics Anonymous.
    d. inpatient treatment group therapy, individual psychotherapy, self-help groups, and behavior therapy.

CONCEPTUAL MULTIPLE–CHOICE QUESTIONS

1. The major difference between substance abuse and substance dependence is that in substance dependence,
   a. the problem has lasted one month or more.
   b. social functioning has been affected.
   c. there are signs of tolerance or withdrawal symptoms.
   d. the person shows other signs of mental disorder.

2. Heroin, barbiturates, and benzodiazepines have what in common?
   a. They are all depressants or sedatives.
   b. They are all illegal.
   c. None of them produces tolerance.
   d. None of them can be lethal.

3. Which drugs have their stimulant effect by increasing dopamine levels?
   a. Amphetamine and cocaine
   b. Alcohol and narcotics
   c. Marijuana and LSD
   d. Barbiturates and cocaine

4. There are two general explanations for substance-related disorders: ____________________ and ____________________.
   a. personality; environment
   b. biology; psychological/cultural factors
   c. social class; education
   d. learning; psychoanalytic factors

5. Results of twin and adoption studies tend to
   a. support the idea that alcoholism is due to preexisting personality characteristics.
   b. reject the idea that alcoholism is hereditary.
   c. support the idea that alcoholism is a sociocultural phenomenon.
   d. support the idea that alcoholism is hereditary.

6. Which of the following is a biological marker related to alcoholism?
   a. Central nervous system functioning differences between alcoholics and nonalcoholics
   b. High concordance among identical twins
   c. The fact that children of alcoholics have a higher rate of alcoholism themselves
   d. Physiological response to Antabuse

7. Research by Shedler and Block compared the psychological adjustment of adolescents who abstained from drugs, experimented with drugs, or used drugs heavily. The results showed that
   a. heavy drug use caused maladjustment.
   b. abstainers were the least likely to have adjustment problems.
   c. those who experimented with drugs were best adjusted.
   d. all the "experimenters" became maladjusted, heavy users.

8. Which of the following statements strengthens the belief that cultural values play an important role in drinking patterns?
   a. Alcohol is a central nervous system depressant in all races.
   b. Although France and Italy have high rates of alchol consumption, the rate of alcoholism is high in the U.S. and Russia.
   c. Recent research demonstrates that pregnant women who drink heavily have higher risk of giving birth to children with FAS.
   d. Antisocial behavior and depression are frequently associated with alcoholism.

9. Early behavioral explanations for alcoholism emphasized findings that
   a. cats placed in approach-avoidance conflicts learn to prefer milk mixed with alcohol over regular milk.
   b. rats will refuse to drink alcohol-spiked water when they are under stress.
   c. in conditioning experiments, rats' responses indicate that alcohol is a more aversive stimulus than electric shocks.
   d. responses to alcohol in stress-producing situations are more a function of our expectations than of the chemical's effect.

10. The problem with methadone treatment is that
   a. it is part of an aversive behavior therapy that clients drop out of before completing treatment.
   b. it substitutes one addiction for another.
   c. it relies heavily on the Alcoholics Anonymous requirement of spiritual awareness.
   d. it intensifies the experience of narcotic withdrawal.

APPLICATION MULTIPLE–CHOICE QUESTIONS

1. Karen has been using marijuana for several months. Using the drug has led to several minor traffic accidents and a marked drop in her school grades. Her friends find her uninvolved and unhappy. She can go for several days without using pot and feels no craving. What diagnosis is appropriate for Karen?
   a. Substance use without abuse
   b. Substance abuse
   c. Substance dependence
   d. Addiction to stimulants

2. You hear that an acquaintance smokes a drug that comes in the form of small pieces he calls "rocks." When he has smoked the drug he becomes euphoric, but when it is out of his system he feels depressed. What drug is he using?
   a. Cocaine
   b. LSD
   c. Crack
   d. Marijuana

3. Fran looks back on her days of drug use and says, "The good trips were filled with startling hallucinations and feelings of ecstasy. But weeks later, I'd have 'flashbacks' at truly inopportune times, like when I was driving on the freeway." What drug did Fran use?
   a. Heroin
   b. Marijuana
   c. LSD
   d. Crack cocaine

4. Dr. Enberg says, "Alcoholism is caused by frustration of oral dependency needs in infancy. Alcohol allows the expression of repressed feelings and gratification of oral needs." These remarks reflect the ____________________ perspective.
   a. behavioral
   b. family systems
   c. biological-physical
   d. psychodynamic

5. Dr. Gomez says, "There are two personality factors that are associated with drinking problems: low intelligence and a tendency to become depressed." Is anything wrong with the doctor's statement?
   a. Yes, the personality factors associated with alcoholism are repression and antisocial behavior.
   b. No, the doctor's statement is accurate.
   c. Yes, *no* personality factors are associated with drinking problems.
   d. Yes, the personality factors associated with alcoholism are antisocial behavior and depression.

6. Jane quit smoking cigarettes in July and promised not to smoke another one. Now, in August, having had one cigarette, she feels guilty. Losing all sense of personal control, she smokes two packs of cigarettes the same day. According to behavioral explanations, what happened?
   a. Nicotine sets up a physiological chain reaction that no one can stop.
   b. She fell victim to the abstinence violation effect.
   c. She experienced what is called covert sensitization.
   d. She had stopped taking her Antabuse tablets.

7. Sima says that when she first used narcotics, they produced a euphoric high, and that after the drug was out of her system there were only mild problems "coming down." Now, however, she only uses narcotics because they control the intense withdrawal effects of not using them. Her story best matches ____________________ model of drug use.
   a. the cognitive-behavioral learned expectancy
   b. Tiffany's automatic processes
   c. the biogenic detoxification
   d. Solomon's opponent-process

8. Alvin says, "My treatment was successful because I became a part of a fellowship that provides support and increases spiritual awareness. That group saved my life!" What kind of treatment is Alvin describing?
   a. Methadone maintenance
   b. Systematic desensitization
   c. Alcoholics Anonymous
   d. Group behavior therapy

9. Stanley is being treated for a substance-related disorder with a patch of medication he wears on his arm. The patch slowly helps him overcome the withdrawal effects of the substance he is trying to stop using. What is Stanley's problem?
   a. LSD
   b. Marijuana
   c. Nicotine
   d. Caffeine

10. The mayor of a town says, "Drug prevention programs have never been shown to work. We must put our efforts into treatment of drug problems. Even so, treatment is only modestly effective, since only one-third of treated alcoholics remain abstinent, and most treated narcotics addicts are readdicted within a year of treatment." What portion of the mayor's statement is *inaccurate*?
    a. It is inaccurate to say that prevention has never been shown to work.
    b. It is inaccurate to say that drug treatment has been modestly effective.
    c. It is inaccurate to say that one-third of treated alcoholics are using again within a year of treatment.
    d. It is inaccurate to say that most treated narcotic addicts are using again within a year of treatment.

ANSWER KEY: KEY TERMS REVIEW

1. detoxification (278)
2. substance-related disorder (254)
3. alcoholism (256)
4. withdrawal symptoms (255)
5. depressant (256)
6. substance abuse (254)
7. intoxication (255)
8. reinforcing abstinence (280)
9. alcoholics (256)
10. amphetamines (264)
11. barbiturates (262)
12. cocaine (265)
13. covert sensitization (280)
14. aversion therapy (280)
15. hallucinogen (266)
16. marijuana (266)
17. narcotic (262)
18. stimulant (264)
19. substance dependence (255)
20. tolerance (255)
21. polysubstance dependence (264)
22. skills training (280)

ANSWER KEY: FACTUAL MULTIPLE–CHOICE QUESTIONS

1. a. Substance-induced disorders are those that cause delirium and other cognitive disorders.
   *b. Tolerance is defined as the need for increased doses of a drug to achieve a particular effect. (p. 255)
   c. Withdrawal occurs when there is distress when drug use stops.
   d. Substance abuse involves impairment due to drug use but does not require signs of tolerance; substance dependence involves tolerance.

2. a. Females are much less likely to have substance-related disorders than men.
   b. White Americans have higher lifetime prevalence for drug abuse and dependence than African Americans or Hispanic Americans.
   *c. Substance-related disorders are most prevalent in youths and young adults and far more so in men than women. (p. 255)
   d. Although white males are more prone to substance-related disorders than nonwhites and women, the chief age groups for disorders are youths and young adults.

3. *a. Statistics show that a small number of drinkers (10 percent) account for half of all alcohol consumed. (p. 258)
   b. Men drink two to five times as much as women.
   c. The estimate is closer to 10 to 15 million; about 14 percent of the adults in the United States have drinking problems.
   d. Roughly one-third of Americans do not drink at all.

4. a. Intoxication is the physical and psychological effect of acute doses of a substance.
   b. Flashbacks are symptoms of LSD use only.
   *c. Liver cirrhosis is one of the many serious physiological effects of chronic alcohol use; heart failure and cancers of the mouth and throat are others. (p. 261)
   d. Lung disease is an outcome of smoking, not drinking.

5. a. Hallucinogens are all illegal drugs, so they are not prescribed.
   b. Opiates are narcotics; they are not prescribed for anxiety reduction.
   c. Amphetamines are stimulants; they increase muscle tension.
   *d. Benzodiazepines, such as Valium, are prescribed frequently for anxiety and tension reduction. (p. 264)

6. a. Marijuana is the most commonly used hallucinogen.
   b. The main effects of marijuana are calm, euphoria, passivity, and a feeling that time has slowed down.
   *c. The exact effects that marijuana has on the user are influenced by the person's past experience with the drug and by the setting in which it is taken. (pp. 266–267)
   d. There is no evidence of physiological withdrawal effects when people stop using marijuana.

7. *a. Phencyclidine (PCP or "angel dust") is a hallucinogen that can produce homicidal aggression and delusions of such invincibility that people jump out of windows expecting to fly. (p. 268)
   b. Marijuana is a mild hallucinogen that causes passivity, not aggressiveness.
   c. Heroin is not a hallucinogen; it usually promotes relaxation rather than aggression.
   d. Crack is a stimulant, not a hallucinogen.

8. a. If alcoholism were a disease involving loss of control, the only thing that would have influenced drinking would have been drinking alcohol, not expectation.
   b. The subjects' expectations had a great impact on the amount they drank.
   c. Expectations were important for both groups.
   *d. That alcoholics primed with alcohol did *not* drink more alcohol when they thought it was tonic undercuts the disease notion of loss of control. (p. 274)

9. a. Schachter's work suggests that nicotine is strongly addicting.
   b. Nicotine is not a hallucinogen.
   *c. Schachter's work suggests that the body craves nicotine, and that continued smoking is an attempt to avoid withdrawal. (p. 282; Focus On)
   d. Schachter's work stresses the physiological needs of smokers, not their psychological needs.

10. a. The term for people who are addicted to several substances is *polysubstance abusers.*
   b. Extinction connotes only behavior therapy; multimodal treatment may use behavior therapy and several others.
   c. Detoxification is not a form of treatment per se; Alcoholics Anonymous is only one method of treatment.
   *d. Multimodal treatment uses a wide range of individual, group, and self-help measures to stop substance abuse and find alternative behaviors. (p. 281)

ANSWER KEY: CONCEPTUAL MULTIPLE-CHOICE QUESTIONS

1. a. Both substance abuse and substance dependence are associated with use over a period of at least twelve months.
   b. Substance abuse and substance dependence both impair social functioning.
   *c. The key feature of substance dependence is tolerance or withdrawal symptoms. (p. 255)
   d. Mental disorders may or may not be associated with abuse or dependence.

2. *a. All three are depressants or sedatives—they slow down the working of the brain. (pp. 262–264)
   b. Barbiturates are prescribed drugs but are often obtained illegally; benzodiazepines (such as Valium) are widely available from doctors.
   c. All three produce tolerance.
   d. All three can be lethal, particularly barbiturates.

3. *a. Amphetamines and cocaine are central nervous stimulants that prevent the reuptake of dopamine and therefore increase its concentration in certain brain synapses. (p. 264)
   b. Alcohol and narcotics are depressants.
   c. Marijuana and LSD are hallucinogens, not stimulants.
   d. Barbiturates are depressants.

4. a. Both personality and environment are part of the psychological/cultural viewpoint.
   *b. Causes are usually seen as internal and biogenic (especially genetics) or psychological/cultural (personality and social factors); however, an integration of the two schools of thought is quite common. (p. 268)
   c. Social class and education are both cultural factors.
   d. Learning and psychodynamic perspectives are both psychological; biogenic factors are important in understanding substance-related disorders.

5. a. Support for personality factors comes from longitudinal studies, which find that impulsive and antisocial youths are more likely than others to develop drinking problems.
   b. Evidence from this work tends to support the genetic position.
   c. Support for the sociocultural position comes from evidence that different cultures have different rates of consumption and alcoholism.
   *d. Concordance ratios of MZ twins are higher than those of DZ twins, and children of alcoholics who are adopted by nonalcoholics have higher rates of drinking problems—both support the role of heredity. (p. 269)

6. *a. Research shows that the central nervous system functioning of sons of alcoholics differs from that of sons of nonalcoholics, which suggests a biological marker for alcoholism. (p. 270)
   b. Concordance shows that the disorder may be inherited or may be the product of similar expectations; it does not indicate a biological marker.
   c. Children of alcoholics may learn to be alcoholics; this does not indicate a biological marker.
   d. As far as we know, all individuals have a negative physiological reaction to Antabuse when they drink.

7. a. Shedler and Block found that maladjustment preceded heavy drug use in adolescents.
   b. Abstainers had more adjustment problems than experimenters; they tended to be inflexible and had poorer social skills.
   *c. Much to the surprise of many, those who experimented with drugs but did not use heavily had the best social adjustment. (p. 272; Critical Thinking)
   d. Experimenters did not become heavy users.

8. a. If alcohol has the same physiological effect on all people, culture is irrelevant.
   *b. If cultures differ in their rates of alcoholism, it *may* be because the cultures teach different values concerning what is deviant drinking. (p. 271)
   c. Fetal alcohol syndrome is a physiological effect that appears to be unrelated to cultural values.
   d. That antisocial behavior and depression are related to drinking is support for a personality explanation.

9. *a. Early behaviorists stressed the role of alcohol as an anxiety-reducing chemical, which was supported by the research with cats. (p. 273)
   b. If rats did this (and they don't), it would undercut the early behaviorist position, which stressed anxiety reduction.
   c. Such a finding would undercut the behaviorist position.
   d. The importance of expectation is a *recent* behavioral explanation for why alcohol sometimes has anxiety-reducing properties and sometimes doesn't.

10. a. Methadone treatment is unrelated to behavior therapy and is far from aversive since it produces a euphoria.
   *b. Because methadone produces a euphoria and is addictive, it substitutes one substance-related problem for another. (p. 279)
   c. Methadone treatment is unrelated to Alcoholics Anonymous.
   d. The goal of methadone is to do the opposite—to reduce the impact of heroin withdrawal.

ANSWER KEY: APPLICATION MULTIPLE–CHOICE QUESTIONS

1. a. Karen's drug use has led to social and occupational (school) impairments; this cannot be considered nonabusive use.
   *b. Karen's use is clearly pathological and the symptoms have occurred during the same twelve-month period, so she shows signs of substance abuse; since there are signs of neither tolerance or withdrawal, we need to rule out substance dependence. (p. 255)
   c. Without signs of tolerance or withdrawal, one cannot diagnose this as substance dependence.
   d. Marijuana is not a stimulant; it is a mild hallucinogen.

2. a. Cocaine is usually snorted (inhaled into the nose) rather than smoked; it occurs in a powder form, not small, solid pieces.
   b. LSD is not smoked and it produces hallucinations rather than euphoria and depression.
   *c. Crack is a purified form of cocaine that is sold as small "rocks" that are smoked; its effects are sudden euphoria followed by depression once the drug is out of the system. (p. 265)
   d. Although marijuana is smoked, it is not in solid pieces, nor does it produce depression when it is out of the person's system.

3. a. Heroin does not produce hallucinations, and there is no evidence of it producing flashbacks.
   b. Marijuana produces only the mildest of hallucinations and no flashbacks.
   *c. One of LSD's unique properties is that hallucinations can occur weeks after use has stopped; these are called flashbacks. (p. 267)
   d. Crack cocaine produces a strong and rapid high, but there is no evidence of hallucinations or flashbacks.

4. a. The behavioral perspective stresses modeling, anxiety reduction, and expectations.
   b. The family systems perspective stresses the adaptive role of drunkenness in the family.
   c. The biological-physical perspective emphasizes the role of genetic vulnerability.
   *d. The psychodynamic perspective emphasizes early childhood influences and the symbolic nature of adult drinking. (p. 270)

5. a. This is inaccurate because, although psychoanalysts focus on repression, no empirical relationship between it and alcoholism has been documented.
   b. This is inaccurate because intelligence has no relationship to alcoholism.
   c. This is inaccurate; two personality factors *have* been related to alcoholism.
   *d. Peter Nathan (1988) has shown that antisocial behavior and depression are the two factors most related to drinking problems. (p. 271)

6. a. Behaviorists do not believe that physiological loss of control occurs when people relapse.
   *b. The abstinence violation effect is the feeling of having "blown it" when one gives in to temptation once; according to Marlatt, it is a principal reason for relapses. (p. 275)
   c. Covert sensitization is a treatment method using imagery.
   d. Antabuse is used in the treatment of alcoholism.

7. a. A cognitive-behavioral learned expectancy approach would emphasize the beliefs she had about narcotics—their social benefits.
   b. Tiffany's automatic processes model highlights that lack of thinking marks chronic drug use.
   c. Detoxification is a first stage in treatment and is not an explanation for chronic drug use.
   *d. Opponent process theory says that initial drug use has positive effects, but that chronic use involves a lessened high and a dramatically intensified withdrawal effect; chronic use is therefore motivated by avoidance of the withdrawal effects. (pp. 276–277)

8. a. Methadone maintenance is not done in groups; it is administered individually on a daily basis to offset the craving for heroin.
   b. Systematic desensitization is an individual treatment that uses classical conditioning principles.
   *c. Alcoholics Anonymous is a group treatment that uses self-revelation, support, and spiritual involvement. (p. 278)
   d. Behavior therapy, if done in groups, would not focus on the spiritual, but would teach coping skills.

9. a. LSD does not produce withdrawal effects.
   b. Marijuana does not produce withdrawal effects.
   *c. Transdermal nicotine patches have proven to be useful in weaning cigarette smokers from their addiction to nicotine. (pp. 279–280)
   d. Caffeine does not produce serious withdrawal effects and is not treated with transdermal patches.

10. *a. Prevention programs can be successful; the text describes one that reduced smoking in junior high students (p. 284).
   b. Treatment of drug problems has been modestly effective since a minority of those treated remain drug-free for a period of time after treatment.
   c. One-third of alcoholics getting treatment remain abstinent one year after treatment.
   d. Most treated narcotics addicts are readdicted within a year of treatment.

CHAPTER 10
Sexual and Gender Identity Disorders

LEARNING OBJECTIVES

1. Distinguish between sexual dysfunctions, paraphilias, and gender identity disorders. (p. 288)
2. Discuss the problems of defining "normal" sexual behavior. (pp. 288–290)
3. Indicate the contributions of Kinsey, Masters and Johnson, Kaplan, and the Janus Report in the history of studying human sexuality. (pp. 290–291)
4. Describe and discuss the four stages of the human sexual response cycle. (pp. 291–293)
5. Explain why homosexuality is not considered a mental disorder. (pp. 291–294)
6. Discuss the results of research on sexuality among those over age sixty. (pp. 294–296)
7. Describe and differentiate sexual desire disorders in men and women, sexual arousal disorder in men and women, and male and female orgasmic disorder. Describe and discuss the causes of sexual pain disorders. (pp. 297–301)
8. Discuss the biological causes and treatments for psychosexual dysfunctions. (pp. 301–304)
9. Discuss the psychological factors that cause, and the behavioral therapy techniques used to treat, sexual dysfunctions. (pp. 304–307)
10. Define gender identity disorders and describe their symptoms. Discuss the biological, psychodynamic, and behavioral explanations for these disorders and how gender identity disorders are treated. (pp. 307–310)
11. Define paraphilias and list the three categories of these disorders. Describe and differentiate fetishism, transvestic fetishism, exhibitionism, voyeurism, frotteurism, pedophilia, sadism, and masochism. (pp. 310–318)
12. Discuss the problems of people who were childhood victims of sexual abuse. (pp. 314–315)
13. Discuss the biological, psychodynamic, and behavioral etiological theories of paraphilia and how those theories lead to different forms of treatment. (pp. 318–319)
14. Differentiate the terms *sexual coercion, sexual aggression, rape,* and *incest.* Describe the effects of rape on victims, including the acute and long-term phases of rape trauma syndrome. Discuss what is known about the cause of rape, including the three motivational types of rapists. (pp. 319–324)
15. Discuss the effects of media portrayals of sexual violence and sociocultural variables. (pp. 324–326; Critical Thinking)
16. Describe and evaluate the conventional and controversial treatments provided for incest offenders and rapists. (p. 326)

CHAPTER OUTLINE

1. **What is "normal" sexual behavior?** (pp. 288–290) This chapter discusses sexual dysfunctions, gender identity disorders, and paraphilias, as well as sexual coercion. The sexual and gender identity disorders are the hardest to distinguish from "normal" sexual behavior because of cultural differences as well as moral and legal judgments. Normal sexual behavior is poorly understood and differs depending upon the historical period and one's culture. The first reliable information concerning human sexuality came from the survey research work of Alfred Kinsey. Masters and Johnson used laboratory research to study physiological sexual responses. More recently, the Janus Report described sexual practices in the United States. Because it is a lethal infectious disease and is transmitted, at least in part, sexually, AIDS has affected current sexual behavior. (pp. 285–288, Focus On)

2. **The sexual response cycle** (pp. 290–291) The sexual response cycle has an *appetitive (desire) phase,* when fantasies about sex increase. The *excitement phase* occurs when direct sexual stimulation (not necessarily physical) increases blood flow to the genitals. The *orgasm phase* produces involuntary contractions and the release of sexual tension. Men ejaculate then have a refractory period where additional stimulation does not produce orgasm; women are capable of multiple orgasms. The body then returns to relaxation during the *resolution phase.* Decreased functioning in any of these phases can be criteria for a sexual dysfunction.

3. **Homosexuality, aging, and sexual activity** (pp. 291–296) Homosexuality is not a mental disorder. There are no physiological differences in sexual arousal, no differences in psychological disturbance, no gender identity distortions that differentiate homosexuals and heterosexuals.

   Sexuality continues into old age, although sexual dysfunction increases. Patterns of sexuality during middle age are maintained. The recent (1993) Janus survey suggests that sexual activity and enjoyment remain high among those sixty-five and older.

4. **Sexual dysfunctions** (pp. 297–301) Psychosexual dysfunction disorders involve any persistent disruption in the normal sexual response cycle. DSM-IV requires that factors such as frequency, chronicity, distress, and impact on functioning be considered in the diagnosis. *Sexual desire disorders* involve a lack of interest in or aversion to sex. These are more common in women than in men, and there are many questions about what "normal" sexual interest is (about 20 percent of the adult population is believed to suffer from this disorder).

   Sexual arousal disorders are problems occurring during the excitement phase of the sexual response cycle. *Erectile disorder* is the man's inability to maintain an erection sufficient for intercourse. Physical conditions may account for a large minority of cases. Distinguishing biogenic erectile dysfunction from psychogenic cases is difficult. Primary dysfunction is when a man has never been successful in intercourse; secondary dysfunction means the problem is situational.

   Female sexual arousal disorder involves lack of vaginal lubrication or erection of the nipples. This disorder, too, can be primary or secondary.

   Orgasmic disorders involve the inability to achieve orgasm after receiving adequate stimulation in the excitement phase. *Female orgasmic disorder* means a woman is unable to achieve orgasm. Many questions arise about whether the lack of an orgasm is a normal variant of sexual behavior or a disorder. This sexual dysfunction can be primary (no orgasm ever experienced) or secondary (situational problems). Some argue the disorder should not be diagnosed until all experiences conducive to orgasm have proven ineffective. *Male orgasmic disorder,* the inability to ejaculate intravaginally, is relatively rare and little is known about it. *Premature ejaculation* is a common disorder involving an inability to delay ejaculation during intercourse, but definitions of "premature" vary. *Sexual pain disorders* include *dyspareunia* (persistent pain in the genitals before, during, or after intercourse) and *vaginismus* (involuntary muscular contraction of the outer vagina). DSM-IV also notes sexual dysfunction owing to a general medical condition and substance-induced sexual dysfunction.

5. **Etiology and treatment of sexual dysfunctions** (pp. 301–307) Many dysfunctions are due to a combination of biological and psychological factors. Organic factors include sex hormone levels (although this is not well understood), blood flow in the genitals, hypersensitivity to physical stimulation, vascular diseases, and the side effects of medications. Medical treatments include exercise, oral medication (Viagra), surgery, and injections into the penis of substances that induce erection. Psychological factors include predisposing causes, such as early experiences and upbringing, and current concerns, such as poor marital relations and performance anxiety. Research shows that anxiety and self-focus impair performance.

   Treatment often includes education, anxiety reduction, structured behavioral exercises, and improved communication. Specific treatments for dysfunctions include masturbation as treatment for female orgasmic disorder, the "squeeze technique" for premature ejaculation, and relaxation and insertion of dilators for vaginismus. The glowing reports of success for these methods have been called into question recently. Long-term success requires relapse prevention.

6. **Gender identity disorders** (pp. 307–310) *Gender identity disorders*, often called transsexualism, involve a conflict between anatomical sex and gender self-identification. A second disorder is called gender identity disorder not otherwise specified. Transsexuals have a lifelong conviction that they are in the body of the wrong sex. Sex role conflicts start at an early age; they are more common in boys than in girls. Prevalence estimates range from 1 in 100,000 to 1 in 37,000 among males and about one-quarter that rate among females. The not-otherwise-specified disorder may involve preoccupation with castration without desire to acquire the characteristics of the other sex, stress-related cross-dressing, or persistent cross-dressing without the other criteria of gender identity disorder.

   Because it is rare, we do not know much about the disorder's cause. Some animal research supports the biological view that neurohormones explain gender identity disorders. However, children have adopted the gender identity that their parents imposed rather than that of their genetic makeup. Psychoanalysts suggest that sexual deviations symbolize unconscious conflicts involving separation from the mother. Behaviorists note that parental encouragement to act like the opposite sex and cross-dress may lead to gender identity disorder.

   Most treatment programs with children having gender identity disorder assign boys to male therapists, to facilitate identification with a male, and teach behavior modification skills to the parents. Sex conversion treatment involving hormones and surgery can alter the apparent sex of transsexuals; woman-to-man changes seem to have more positive outcomes. Behavior therapy, including aversive conditioning, reinforcing heterosexual fantasies has been used. Controversy exists whether sex-conversion surgery or psychotherapy should be advanced in treating individuals with gender identity disorders.

7. **Paraphilias involving nonhuman objects** (pp. 310–311) *Paraphilias* are sexual disorders lasting at least six months in which repeated intense sexual urges exist for nonhuman objects, real or simulated suffering, or nonconsenting others. Either the urge is acted upon or causes severe distress. Sex offenders often have multiple paraphilias. They are overwhelmingly male problems.

   Fetishism is a strong sexual attraction to inanimate objects, such as shoes or underwear. As a group, fetishists are not dangerous. In *transvestic fetishism*, the person obtains sexual arousal by dressing in the clothes of the opposite sex. Most transvestites are heterosexual males who use cross-dressing to facilitate sexual intercourse, but many transvestites feel they have both male and female personalities.

8. **Paraphilias involving nonconsenting persons** (pp. 311–315) *Exhibitionism* involves urges, acts, or fantasies about exposing one's genitals to strangers. Women commonly report being victims. Most exhibitionists are young married men who want no further contact with the women to whom they expose themselves. Most have fantasies of being admired by female observers. *Voyeurism* is sexual gratification obtained primarily from observing others' genitals or others engaged in sex. Acts are repetitive and premeditated. *Frotteurism* involves intense sexual urges to touch and rub against nonconsenting individuals. *Pedophilia* is characterized by adults obtaining erotic

gratification from sexual fantasies about or involving sexual contact with children. DSM-IV criteria include being at least sixteen years old and five or more years older than the victim. The disorder is not rare; 20 to 30 percent of women report having had a childhood sexual encounter with an adult man. Victims often have long-term psychological difficulties. Molesters tend to be impulsive, passive, and alcoholic. Social skill deficits and below-average intelligence are also reported. More than half of one sample used "hard core" pornography to excite themselves into committing an offense.

9. **Paraphilias involving pain or humiliation** (pp. 315–318) *Sadism* and *masochism* involve associations between pain or humiliation and sex. Sadists inflict pain; masochists receive it. Often people engage in both roles. Some cases develop from early experiences with pain, but causal explanations are currently weak.

10. **Etiology and treatment of paraphilias** (pp. 318–319) Some research findings suggest biological causes for paraphilias but replication is needed. Psychodynamic theory links paraphilias to unresolved oedipal conflicts, particularly castration anxiety. Treatment involves making these unconscious conflicts conscious. Behavioral theory stresses early conditioning experiences, masturbation fantasies, and a lack of social skills. Conditioning must overcome preparedness—the fact that some stimuli become associated more readily than others because of evolutionary pressures. Treatment seeks to extinguish inappropriate behaviors and reinforce appropriate ones. One example is aversive behavior rehearsal, in which the exhibitionist exposes himself to a prepared female audience and must explain his fantasies. Results of behavioral treatments are positive but largely based on single-subject reports.

11. **Sexual aggression: Rape and incest** (pp. 319–326; Critical Thinking) *Sexual coercion* refers to all forms of sexual pressure. *Sexual aggression* is restricted to sexual actions that are performed against a person's will by way of force, argument, pressure, authority, or drugs. *Rape* is forced intercourse. It can be seen as either a sexual act, a violent act, or both. Rape is common: An estimated one-fifth of all U.S. women will be raped in their lifetime. Many rapists are friends or acquaintances of the victims. Many young men who do not rape try to coerce women into intercourse. Both rapists and their victims tend to be young. Victims may experience prolonged distress and sexual dysfunction. Consistent with posttraumatic stress disorder, survivors may experience rape trauma syndrome. It consists of an acute phase involving fear, self-blame, and depression, and a long-term phase that slowly leads to reorganization. Flashbacks during sex are common. Rapists are most often motivated by power and anger, not by sex. Nonrapists report being aroused by aggressive sex; a significant proportion of university men report some likelihood they would rape if they could get away with it. Where there is general acceptance of violence, there is a spillover effect on rape. The cause of rape can be seen as sociocultural (male sex roles and general social violence) or sociobiological (innate sex differences in sexual motivation).

    Incest is sexual relations between close relatives. Most common is father-daughter incest. Estimates of incidence rates range from 48,000 to 250,000 cases per year. Incestuous fathers are more likely than nonincestuous fathers to have been victims of childhood sexual abuse, although this is not common. Survivors have a range of difficulties, continuing into adulthood.

    Treatment for incest offenders and rapists traditionally involves imprisonment, although punishment is more common than therapy. Behavioral therapy, surgical castration, and drug therapies have all been used. Results are mixed, with more success treating child molesters and exhibitionists than rapists. Biological treatments, in particular, have been very controversial.

KEY TERMS REVIEW

1. The disorder characterized by an extremely strong sexual attraction to a particular nongenital part of the anatomy or an inanimate object is called ____________________.

2. The disorder in which an adult obtains erotic gratification through fantasies about or sexual contact with children is called ___________________.

3. The paraphilia characterized by the sexual desire to rub against or the act of rubbing against the body of a nonconsenting individual is called ___________________.

4. The disorder characterized by conflict between an individual's anatomical sex and his or her sexual identity is called ___________________.

5. The condition in which there is recurrent or persistent pain in the genitals before, during, or after sexual intercourse is called ___________________.

6. The sexual disorder in which erotic or sexual gratification is obtained by receiving pain or punishment is called ___________________.

7. An act of intercourse accomplished through force or the threat of force is called ___________________.

8. Sexual relations between close relatives is called ___________________.

9. The sexual dysfunctions characterized by a lack of interest in or aversion to sexual arousal are called ___________________.

10. The disorder in which sexual gratification is obtained by inflicting pain or punishment on others is called ___________________.

11. The sexual dysfunction in which a woman has a persistent delay or inability to achieve orgasm despite adequate stimulation is called ___________________.

12. Sexual disorders in which unusual or bizarre acts or objects are required for sexual arousal or in which such urges are distressing are called ___________________.

13. The sexual dysfunction in which men experience persistent delay or inability to achieve orgasm despite adequate stimulation is called ___________________.

14. The inability of a male to attain or maintain an erection that is sufficient for sexual intercourse is called ___________________.

15. The dysfunction characterized by ejaculation before penile entry into the vagina or so soon after entry that sexual relations are unsatisfactory is called ___________________.

16. The disorder in which sexual gratification is obtained by secretly observing strangers disrobe or engage in sex is called ___________________.

17. The paraphilia in which a person derives sexual gratification from cross-dressing is called ___________________.

18. The disorder characterized by urges, acts, or fantasies about exposing one's genitals to strangers is called ___________________.

19. Sexual dysfunctions that occur during the excitement phase and relate to difficulties in feeling sexual pleasure are called ___________________.

20. The condition in which strong cross-gender identification exists and in which there is persistent discomfort with one's own anatomical sex, causing impairments in social and other areas of functioning, is called ___________________.

21. The sexual pain disorder in which there are involuntary spasms of the outer third of the vagina wall is called ____________________.

22. Emotional symptoms such as distress, phobic reactions, and sexual dysfunction following unwanted coerced sexual contact defines the ____________________.

23. A disruption of any part of the normal sexual response cycle is known as a ____________________.

24. A woman who experiences persistent delays or inability to achieve an orgasm even though there is adequate stimulation is said to have ____________________.

FACTUAL MULTIPLE–CHOICE QUESTIONS

1. Who of the following is *not* an important contributor to the study of sex research and therapy?
   a. Kinsey
   b. Masters & Johnson
   c. Kaplan
   d. Beck

2. Research with nonclinical samples of homosexuals suggests that
   a. they are more inclined to develop psychoses than are heterosexuals.
   b. lesbians are far more disturbed than male homosexuals.
   c. distress over being homosexual rarely, if ever, occurs.
   d. there is no more psychopathology in homosexuals than in heterosexuals.

3. Which of the following is *not* a DSM-IV disorder?
   a. Premature ejaculation
   b. Sexual addiction
   c. Hypoactive sexual desire disorder
   d. Dyspareunia

4. A woman who has experienced orgasm in the past but currently cannot be brought to orgasm should be diagnosed as having
   a. a sexual desire disorder.
   b. primary vaginismus.
   c. secondary female orgasmic disorder.
   d. a secondary paraphilia.

5. Which of the following are related to sexual pain disorders?
   a. Lack of sexual desire and lack of orgasm
   b. Vaginismus and dyspareunia
   c. Premature ejaculation and erectile dysfunction
   d. Hypoactive sexual desire and erectile dysfunction

6. The inability to obtain sexual arousal unless one is wearing the clothes of the opposite sex indicates
   a. transvestic fetishism.
   b. gender identity disorder.
   c. exhibitionism.
   d. fetishism.

7. Contrary to popular belief, most ____________________ tend to be people who are relatives or friends of their victims.
   a. exhibitionists
   b. pedophiles
   c. masochists
   d. transvestites

8. Which of the following is a paraphilia that involves intentional pain or humiliation?
   a. Transvestic fetishism
   b. Premature ejaculation
   c. Voyeurism
   d. Sadomasochism

9. The behavioral treatment called aversive behavior rehearsal involves shame and is most appropriate for treating
   a. gender identity disorder.
   b. exhibitionism.
   c. premature ejaculation.
   d. homosexuality.

10. Anger and power are two of the more common motivations for
   a. sadomasochists.
   b. rapists.
   c. transvestic fetishists.
   d. exhibitionists.

CONCEPTUAL MULTIPLE-CHOICE QUESTIONS

1. Sexual deviation disorders
   a. are unaffected by legal or moral judgments.
   b. can be reliably diagnosed because they all entail personal distress.
   c. are difficult to define because they involve legal and moral judgments.
   d. involve an inability to perform at some stage in the normal sexual response cycle.

2. Which sexual dysfunction, believed to affect 20 percent of the adult population, is difficult to diagnose because we know little about the "normal" frequency of sexual fantasies and activities?
   a. Paraphilia
   b. Premature ejaculation
   c. Sexual desire disorder
   d. Primary erectile dysfunction

3. Which of the following is a current psychological factor that increases the likelihood of erectile dysfunction?
   a. Excessive levels of testosterone
   b. A strict moral upbringing
   c. Unresolved castration anxiety
   d. Pressure to perform sexually

4. Transsexuals tend to
   a. show sex role conflicts at an early age.
   b. be women.
   c. outgrow their gender identity disorder.
   d. engage in gender-inappropriate behavior, but have no desire to change their physical characteristics.

5. Absence of a male role model, lack of male playmates, and parental encouragement of cross-dressing are psychological factors in the development of
   a. pedophilia.
   b. premature ejaculation.
   c. sexual desire disorders.
   d. gender identity disorders.

6. Rubbing against a nonconsenting person is to ____________________ as observing others in sexual activity is to ________________.
   a. transvestic fetishism; exhibitionism
   b. frotteurism; voyeurism
   c. transvestic fetishism; voyeurism
   d. frotteurism; exhibitionism

7. According to psychoanalytic theory, sadomasochism and other sexual deviations are caused by
   a. the pairing of certain stimuli with sexual arousal in early childhood.
   b. cultural requirements of males and females.
   c. unconscious conflicts related to castration anxiety.
   d. a lack of superego controls.

8. Behavioral approaches to treating pedophilia would focus on
   a. strengthening the association between sexual arousal and children.
   b. bringing to consciousness unconscious fears and conflicts.
   c. the need to imprison convicted offenders.
   d. extinguishing sexual responses to fantasies about children.

9. "Cultural spillover" theory suggests that a culture where violence is encouraged or condoned will have
   a. very few incidents of sexually deviant behavior.
   b. a high rate of sexually dysfunctional men.
   c. a high rate of exhibitionism, voyeurism, and other paraphilias.
   d. more rapes than in other cultures.

10. Which statement about the treatment of sex offenders is *true*?
    a. Imprisonment is the main form of "treatment."
    b. Controlled research shows that psychotherapy is more effective than biological treatments.
    c. Treatment for rapists is far more successful than for any other type of offender.
    d. Surgical castration has been found to have no effect on sexual fantasies or recidivism rates.

APPLICATION MULTIPLE–CHOICE QUESTIONS

1. Kara has inhibited sexual desire, whereas Fred occasionally has problems maintaining an erection. Kara's problem is an example of a disorder in the ____________________ stage of the sexual response cycle; Fred's problem is in the ____________________ stage.
   a. excitement; orgasm
   b. appetitive; excitement
   c. appetitive; resolution
   d. excitement; appetitive

2. Dr. Knowlton says, "By masturbating, women can completely eliminate this common problem. However, there is good reason to believe that, without manual stimulation, the problem will continue during normal intercourse." What problem is Dr. Knowlton discussing?
   a. Functional vaginismus
   b. Transvestic fetishism
   c. Primary inhibited sexual orgasm
   d. Gender identity disorder in women

3. John received a penile implant as treatment for a sexual problem. It is likely that the problem was
   a. premature ejaculation.
   b. low sexual desire.
   c. pedophilia.
   d. erectile dysfunction.

4. Mrs. Johnson is instructed by a therapist to stimulate her husband's penis while it is outside the vagina until he senses an ejaculation about to occur. She is then to stop stimulation and continue only after a short time has gone by. What sexual dysfunction is probably being treated?
   a. Mrs. Johnson's sexual pain disorder
   b. Mr. Johnson's premature ejaculation
   c. Mr. Johnson's erectile dysfunction
   d. Mrs. Johnson's sexual desire disorder

5. At an early age, Albert avoided all traditionally male activities and felt that he was a girl trapped in the body of a boy. As an adult, he had a sex change operation and is now called Alberta. This case illustrates
   a. gender identity disorder.
   b. sexual desire disorder.
   c. pedophilia.
   d. transvestic fetishism.

6. Doris derives sexual gratification from fondling men's underwear. She is a shy, married woman who also must dress in men's clothes to have satisfactory intercourse with her husband. What is unusual about Doris's case?
   a. Men are more likely to have paraphilias than women.
   b. People rarely have more than one paraphilia.
   c. Transvestites are almost always homosexuals.
   d. People with paraphilias are rarely shy or married.

7. Todd, age twenty-six, responds to attractive women in public by fantasizing about exposing his genitals, then returning to the same place and actually exposing himself. Todd would probably be diagnosed with
   a. gender identity disorder.
   b. sexual dysfunction of the arousal stage.
   c. voyeurism.
   d. exhibitionism.

8. Donald, who likes to look at attractive women, wonders whether he is really a voyeur. Which incident below would indicate that he is?
   a. He drove fifty miles to see bottomless dancers.
   b. He bought ten copies of nudist magazines.
   c. He prefers "peeping" to having sex with his wife.
   d. He spends the summer at a swimming pool so that he can watch women in swimsuits.

9. Harold is in behavior therapy for exhibitionism. His therapist is helping him learn appropriate ways of deriving sexual gratification and is modeling improved social skills. What component of Harold's therapy, common in a learning approach, is missing?
   a. Harold is not examining unconscious castration anxieties.
   b. Harold is not receiving medical treatment to reduce his sex drive.
   c. Harold is not receiving the "squeeze technique."
   d. Harold's inappropriate behaviors are not receiving aversive conditioning.

10. Gina has become intensely fearful of the dark. Since a particular incident occurred, she has little desire for sex, and when she has sex, there are flashbacks of that incident. It's a good bet that Gina
    a. has survived a rape.
    b. has a husband with erectile dysfunction.
    c. was a victim of an exhibitionist.
    d. has a paraphilia.

ANSWER KEY: KEY TERMS REVIEW

1. fetishism (311)
2. pedophilia (314)
3. frotteurism (314)
4. gender identity disorder (307)
5. dyspareunia (301)
6. masochism (315)
7. rape (320)
8. incest (324)
9. sexual desire disorders (297)
10. sadism (315)
11. female orgasmic disorder (300)
12. paraphilias (310)
13. male orgasmic disorder (inhibited orgasm) (300)
14. male erectile disorder (298)
15. premature ejaculation (300)
16. voyeurism (314)
17. transvestic fetishism (311)
18. exhibitionism (312)
19. sexual arousal disorders (298)
20. transsexualism (307)
21. vaginismus (301)
22. rape trauma syndrome (321)
23. sexual dysfunction (297)
24. female sexual arousal disorder (inhibited female orgasm) (299)

ANSWER KEY: FACTUAL MULTIPLE–CHOICE QUESTIONS

1. a. Kinsey published a study of male sexuality (1948) and female sexuality (1953).
   b. Masters & Johnson published several studies in the 1960s and 1970s.
   c. Kaplan's research deals with the treatment of sexual dysfunctions.
   *d. Beck is associated with the cognitive therapy for depression. (pp. 290–291)

2. a. Comparisons of nonclinical samples of homosexuals and heterosexuals show no significant difference in psychological adjustment.
   b. If anything, lesbians show better psychological adjustment than male homosexuals.
   c. Most psychologists agree that ego dystonicity (distress) over one's homosexual orientation affects every homosexual at some point.
   *d. Nonclinical homosexual samples are no more disturbed than nonclinical heterosexual samples. (pp. 292–293)

3. a. Premature ejaculation is considered a male orgasm disorder.
   *b. DSM–IV does not recognize sexual addiction as a disorder. (p. 289)
   c. About 20% of the population are thought to suffer from hypoactive sexual desire disorder.
   d. Dyspareunia is painful intercourse.

4. a. Sexual desire disorders involve a lack of interest in sexual behavior.
   b. Vaginismus involves uncontrolled spasms.
   *c. A secondary disorder is one that is currently a problem but was not at some previous time. (p. 297)
   d. A paraphilia is arousal associated with a bizarre object or situation; inhibited orgasm is not a paraphilia but a dysfunction.

5. a. Lack of sexual desire is a problem in the appetitive stage, not during excitement and orgasm, as is true with vaginismus.
   *b. Vaginismus (spasms in the vagina) and dyspareunia (pain during intercourse) are forms of sexual pain disorders. (p. 298)
   c. Premature ejaculation and erectile dysfunction are male dysfunctions unrelated to pain.
   d. Erectile dysfunction is unrelated to pain.

6. *a. Transvestic fetishism involves sexual arousal when cross-dressing, but not as a function of gender identity disorder. (p. 307)
   b. Cross-dressing related to gender identity disorder is not done for sexual arousal; the person feels he or she is trapped in the body of the wrong sex.
   c. Exhibitionism is revealing one's genitals in order to shock someone else.
   d. Fetishism involves extremely strong attraction to an inanimate object (bras, shoes, and so on).

7. a. Exhibitionists almost always expose themselves to strangers.
   *b. Pedophiles tend to be fathers, stepfathers, or friends of the children they abuse. (p. 310)
   c. Masochists receive pain and humiliation; they do not victimize others.
   d. Transvestites do not victimize others; they merely cross-dress to obtain sexual gratification.

8. a. Transvestites do not victimize others.
   b. Premature ejaculation, a sexual dysfunction, causes anguish to the premature ejaculator.
   c. Voyeurs tend to be harmless; they want only to "peep," not to have sex.
   *d. Sadomasochism may be scripted and mutual, but pain, humiliation, and helplessness are its goals. (p. 312)

9. a. ABR involves getting the patient to see his effect on a victim; those with gender identity disorder have no victims.
   *b. ABR helps exhibitionists see the impact they have on victims, and it controls compulsive exposing. (p. 314)
   c. Premature ejaculation is shaming enough without additional "treatment."
   d. Homosexuality is a life lived in an atmosphere of unacceptance; there are no intended victims in this lifestyle.

10. a. The motivation behind most sadomasochism is helplessness.
   *b. Three common motives for rapists are power, anger, and sadism. (pp. 317–318)
   c. Transvestic fetishism is motivated by sexual arousal, not power.
   d. Exhibitionists may want to impress and shock women, but anger is not a common motive.

ANSWER KEY: CONCEPTUAL MULTIPLE–CHOICE QUESTIONS

1. a. Religious and legal authorities have made many pronouncements about which sexual acts are moral or illegal, and these color definitions of sexual deviation.
   b. Not all sexual deviations involve personal distress; for example, fetishists can be quite content with their behavior.
   *c. Because there are many conflicting legal and moral perspectives on acceptable sex, definitions of deviance are difficult. (p. 285)
   d. Only the sexual dysfunctions involve an inability to perform; gender identity disorders and paraphilias involve no such problem.

2. a. Paraphilias are relatively rare, occur in men more than in women, and are not sexual dysfunctions.
   b. Premature ejaculation is a dysfunction that occurs exclusively in men.
   *c. Perhaps the most common of the sexual dysfunctions, sexual desire disorders are more common in women, but without knowing what is "normal," the diagnosis is difficult. (pp. 295–296)
   d. Females do not achieve erections.

3. a. Excessive levels of testosterone would increase masculine behavior.
   b. Childhood upbringing is an example of a predisposing factor.
   c. Unresolved castration anxiety is an example of a predisposing factor.
   *d. Pressure and anxiety over performance are current factors that are particularly important causes of erectile dysfunction. (p. 300)

4. *a. Transsexuals show gender identity abnormalities at a young age. (p. 303)
   b. Most transsexuals are men.
   c. Transsexuals maintain their gender identity disorder throughout adulthood.
   d. Transsexuals feel trapped in the wrong body and desire a change in physical characteristics.

5. a. Pedophilia, sexual involvement with children, is unrelated to cross-dressing.
   b. Premature ejaculation is a sexual dysfunction unrelated to male role models or cross-dressing.
   c. Sexual desire disorders are unrelated to cross-dressing.
   *d. Lack of male role models and cross-dressing are early experiences in many cases of gender identity disorder. (p. 304)

6. a. Rubbing against a nonconsenting person is the core symptom of frotteurism.
   *b. Rubbing against a nonconsenting person is the core symptom of frotteurism; voyeurism involves watching others engage in sexual activity or observing unsuspecting undressed people. (p. 309)
   c. Transvestic fetishism is deriving sexual arousal from cross-dressing.
   d. Exhibitionism involves exposing one's genitals to unsuspecting individuals for shock value.

7. a. Classical conditioning proposes that certain stimuli are paired.
   b. Sociocultural theory would stress the roles of men and women.
   *c. Psychoanalytic theory asserts that all sexual deviations stem from unconscious fears of castration that go back to the oedipal stage of development. (p. 313)
   d. Masochism would not involve too *few* superego controls, but excessively harsh controls.

8. a. Learning approaches would want to weaken and eliminate any association between children and sexual arousal.
   b. Only in psychoanalytic therapy would raising unconscious issues be important.
   c. Imprisonment is not a form of behavioral treatment since it teaches nothing.
   *d. Behavioral treatment would extinguish sexual responses to fantasies about children and later introduce social skills and sexual responses to more appropriate adult stimuli. (p. 314)

9. a. Cultural spillover theory is associated with increased rates of one sexually deviant behavior: rape.
   b. Cultural spillover theory is unrelated to sexual dysfunction.
   c. Cultural spillover theory is unrelated to the paraphilias.
   *d. Research indicates that where violence is condoned, there is a "spillover effect" and rape is more common. (p. 318)

10. *a. Imprisonment is the "treatment" most sex offenders get; it does not usually change their behavior. (p. 321)
   b. There has been no controlled research comparing psychotherapy and biological treatment.
   c. Rapists have *not* been found to be effectively treated; child molesters and exhibitionists seem to be treated more effectively.
   d. In one study, surgical castration led to reduced sexual activity and fantasy; results from Europe indicate low recidivism rates after castration.

ANSWER KEY: APPLICATION MULTIPLE–CHOICE QUESTIONS

1. a. Erectile dysfunctions are associated with the excitement stage.
   *b. Sexual desire is part of the appetitive stage, and erections are part of the excitement stage in the normal sexual response cycle. (p. 290)
   c. Erectile dysfunctions are associated with the excitement stage.
   d. Sexual desire is part of the appetitive stage, not the excitement stage.

2. a. Functional vaginismus usually stems from partners suffering from impotence, strict upbringing, sexual trauma, or dyspareunia.
   b. Transvestic fetishism is a male problem.
   *c. Female orgasmic disorder is often seen as a problem of insufficient stimulation; Wakefield (1988) claims it exists in less than 1 percent of women. (p. 297)
   d. Gender identity disorders in women would stem from very early childhood upbringing or biological differences, not from masturbatory practices.

3. a. Premature ejaculation is treated with the squeeze technique.
   b. Low sexual desire is a problem caused by relationship stress or medication, not physical equipment.
   c. Pedophilia is not a sexual dysfunction.
   *d. Penile implants are frequently a successful treatment for erectile dysfunction when hormone replacement therapies and psychological treatments have failed. (p. 299)

4. a. A sexual pain disorder (vaginismus) would be treated by relaxation and insertion of successively larger dilators.
   *b. Premature ejaculation is treated by increasing the time during which stimulation occurs prior to ejaculation. (p. 301)
   c. Treatment of erectile dysfunction would increase stimulation, not stop it.
   d. Sexual desire disorder is treated with education, relaxation, and couples therapy.

5. *a. Gender identity disorder involves the feeling of being trapped in the body of the wrong sex. (pp. 301–303)
   b. The term *sexual desire disorder* is reserved for adults who have no interest in sexual activity or who avoid it.
   c. Pedophiles do not feel trapped; they sexually abuse children.
   d. Transvestites cross-dress, but they do so for sexual arousal, not because they identify with the opposite sex.

6. *a. Paraphilias are quite rare in females. (p. 306)
   b. In most cases, people have more than one paraphilia; for example, child molesters often commit rape or expose themselves.
   c. Most transvestites are married heterosexual males.
   d. Most people with paraphilias are socially unskilled.

7. a. Gender identity disorders involve a conflict between genetic sex and preferred sex-appropriate dress and behavior.
   b. Exposing one's genitals constitutes a paraphilia, not a sexual dysfunction.
   c. Voyeurism involves observing sexual behavior in unsuspecting individuals or looking at disrobed people who do not consent to being observed.
   *d. The key symptom of exhibitionism is fantasizing about and actually exposing one's genitals in the manner Todd illustrates. (p. 308)

8. a. This does not illustrate the risk taking and exclusive preference shown in the disorder.
   b. This does not illustrate the risk taking and exclusive preference shown in the disorder.
   *c. When observing is preferred over sex, the disorder can be diagnosed. (p. 309)
   d. This does not illustrate the risk taking and exclusive preference shown in the disorder.

9. a. Psychoanalytic, not behavior, therapy would emphasize unconscious castration anxieties.
   b. Behavior therapists do not rely on medicine to alter this behavior.
   c. The squeeze technique is used to treat premature ejaculation.
   *d. Behavior therapists would first ensure that the problem behavior had been extinguished before moving on to more appropriate alternatives. (p. 314)

10. *a. Rape trauma syndrome is a cluster of negative consequences following rape, such as sexual dysfunction, fear reactions, and psychological distress, including flashbacks, during sex, of the rape. (p. 317)
    b. Erectile dysfunction may be upsetting, but fears and flashbacks in women are unheard-of.
    c. Victims of exhibitionism may be distressed, but there are no reports of either effects on the desire for sex or the production of flashbacks.
    d. Few women have paraphilias.

CHAPTER 11
Mood Disorders

LEARNING OBJECTIVES

1. Describe the mood disorders and distinguish them from normal mood changes. Recall prevalence rates for these disorders. (p. 329)
2. Describe the symptoms of depression, including the affective, cognitive, behavioral, and physiological domains. (pp. 329–332)
3. Describe the symptoms of mania. Differentiate the two levels of manic intensity. (pp. 332–333)
4. Describe and differentiate among the following mood disorders and the symptom features that may accompany these disorders: major depressive disorder, dysthymic disorder, the bipolar disorders, cyclothymic disorder, and mood disorders associated with a medical condition or substance use. (pp. 333–337)
5. Describe and differentiate course specifiers including cycling type, seasonal, postpartum, and longitudinal patterns of mood disorders. Compare unipolar and bipolar disorders. (pp. 336–337)
6. Contrast the various theories of depression, including psychodynamic, behavioral, and Lewinsohn's comprehensive view of depression. (pp. 337–341)
7. Discuss the cognitive and cognitive-learning approaches to depression. Give examples of the logical errors depressives make and the pessimistic attributions they might use. (pp. 341–345)
8. Describe various sociocultural explanations for mood disorders, including cross-cultural differences, the role of stress, and social support in depression. (pp. 345–347; Focus On)
9. Describe what is known about sex differences and depression and the explanations for any differences. (pp. 347–350).
10. Describe the biological theories of mood disorders, including genetic and neurotransmitter theories, the role of cortisol and REM sleep in depression. (pp. 350–354)
11. Evaluate the strengths and weaknesses of the various causal theories of depression. (p. 354)
12. Indicate the kinds of biological therapies that have been used to treat depression, including medication and electroconvulsive therapy (ECT). Discuss the effectiveness of these treatments and their side effects. (pp. 354–355; Critical Thinking)
13. Describe psychological treatments for mood disorders, including interpersonal psychotherapy and cognitive-behavioral therapy. Evaluate the effectiveness of these treatments. (pp. 355–359)
14. Describe the use of lithium and its problems in treating bipolar disorders. (pp. 359–361)

CHAPTER OUTLINE

1. **Mood disorders** (p. 329) *Mood disorders* are disturbances in emotions that cause discomfort or hinder functioning. *Depression* is by far the most common mood disorder and is characterized by

sadness, feelings of worthlessness, and social withdrawal. *Mania* is characterized by elevated mood, expansiveness, and irritability. Depression and mania are different from normal mood changes because they are more intense, last longer, and may occur for no apparent reason. Lifetime prevalence for depression ranges from 10 to 25 percent for women and 5 to 12 percent for men. A recent study puts the overall lifetime prevalence for all mood disorders at nearly 20 percent. Prevalence for depression is more than ten times that for mania. Severe depression occurs in all socioeconomic and educational groups.

2. **The symptoms of depression and mania** (pp. 329–333) The affective (emotional) symptoms of depression are sadness, dejection, crying spells, and feelings of worthlessness. Cognitive symptoms include profound pessimism, loss of interest, and suicidal thoughts. The cognitive triad (negativism about self, others, and the future) is found in depressives. Behavioral symptoms include poor personal hygiene, slowed speech and movement (psychomotor retardation), and social withdrawal. Physiological symptoms of depression include disturbances of eating, sleeping, sexual activity, and menstruation.

   The affective symptoms of mania are elation or irritability and grandiosity. Cognitive symptoms include accelerated and disjointed speech. Behaviorally, at the level of hypomania, people are overactive but not delusional. Mania involves increased levels of activity, incoherence, and sleeplessness. In severe forms, hallucinations and delusions appear and the person is uncontrollable.

3. **Classification of mood disorders** (pp. 333–337) Depressive disorders are considered *unipolar*, whereas disorders with manic and depressive episodes are *bipolar disorders*. Depressive disorders include major depressive disorder, dysthymic disorder, and depressive disorders not otherwise specified. Symptoms must be present for at least two weeks and must represent a change from typical functioning to be considered signs of a mood disorder. About half of those who have a depressive episode have another. Some depressions have psychotic features such as hallucinations and delusions. *Dysthymic disorder* is a chronic condition (at least two years) involving depressed mood, low self-esteem, fatigue, and apathy. *Bipolar disorders* are identified when manic episodes last one week or, in the case of hypomania, four days. Depression almost always follows a manic period. *Bipolar I* disorders include those in which a manic episode occurs; *Bipolar II* is reserved for hypomania that alternates with major depression. If hypomanic and depressed mood swings do not meet the criteria for bipolar disorder, the diagnosis is *cyclothymic disorder*, a disorder more common than bipolar and less common than dysthymic disorder.

   Mood disorders owing to general medical conditions and substance-induced mood disorders are also categories in the DSM-IV. DSM-IV also lists *symptom features*—characteristics that accompany mood disorders but are not criteria for diagnosis. These include *melancholia* (loss of pleasure, depression worse in the morning) and *catatonia* (immobility and negativism). *Course specifiers* in DSM-IV indicate whether the mood disorder is *cyclic* (how quickly moods shift from manic to depressive), *seasonal, postpartum* (after giving birth), or *longitudinal* (length between relapses).

   Unipolar and bipolar disorders are distinguished from one another because in bipolar, inheritance plays a bigger role, the age of onset is earlier, depressive episodes involve greater motor retardation, and lithium provides effective relief. Lifetime prevalence of bipolar disorder is roughly 1 percent. Finally, there is no sex difference for bipolar disorder, but major depression is far more common in women.

4. **The etiology of mood disorders: Psychological and sociocultural approaches to depression** (pp. 337–350) There are few theories explaining the cause of bipolar disorders. For depression, psychoanalysts suggest that separation and anger are potent causal factors. Separation can be real or symbolic, but is different from normal mourning. Guilt can account for some depressive symptoms, and anger (at the lost person) turned against the self accounts for others.

   Behaviorists suggest that reduced reinforcements lead to reduced reinforceable activity, thus producing a downward spiral. A lack of self-reinforcement, social skills, and a tendency to create more stressors are also associated with depression. Lewinsohn and his colleagues have developed a comprehensive view of depression: Stress disrupts established behavior patterns, positive reinforcement declines, self-critical and low-confidence thoughts produce depressed affect, which makes functioning more difficult.

Cognitive theorists suggest that depressives' *schemas* for interpreting events produce low self-esteem. According to Beck, depressives operate from a primary triad involving negative expectations about self, others, and the future. Four errors in logic typify this schema: arbitrary inference, selected abstraction, overgeneralization, and magnification and minimization. Cognitive-learning approaches include *learned helplessness* and attributional theories. Learned helplessness argues that depression occurs when, after experiencing uncontrollable stressors, a person comes to believe that he or she has no effect on the environment. Coupled with a certain attributional style, learned helplessness leads to the passivity that characterizes depression. The pessimistic attributional style sees the causes of bad events as internal, global (true for many situations), and stable (a permanent condition). Attributional style may be related to achievements, health, and depression although the causal relationships are not established.

Sociocultural explanations stress differences in prevalence rates and symptom pictures across cultures. Stress theory argues that individuals have a vulnerability to depression (diathesis), exposure to stressors, and limited resources such as social supports. Gender differences in depression may not be real because women are more likely to be seen in treatment and may report their symptoms more readily than men. Diagnostic bias and misdiagnosis of male depression are other explanations. Real differences may be due to biology, gender roles, or social restrictions on women. Nolen-Hoeksema concluded that women are more likely than men to ruminate in response to depressed mood.

5. **The etiology of mood disorders: Biological perspectives** (pp. 350–354) Biological explanations of the causes of mood disorders emphasize evidence that genetic factors play a role, particularly in bipolar disorder. Concordance rates for bipolar disorder average 72 percent for identical twins and 14 percent for fraternals; the percentages are 40 and 11 for unipolar mood disorders. Genetic factors may predispose people to a deficit of activity in certain neurotransmitters called catecholamines. The *catecholamine hypothesis* proposes that low levels of norepinephrine, dopamine, or serotonin make individuals vulnerable to depression. The problem may involve dysfunction in the reception of the neurotransmitter rather than insufficient concentrations of it. Other biological factors related to depression are abnormally high cortisol levels (as measured by the dexamethasone suppression test) and rapid onset of and increased REM sleep among depressives.

6. **Evaluating the causation theories** (p. 354) Our knowledge has been increased by using longitudinal research designs, advanced technologies, and an awareness that there are subtypes of mood disorders. All current causation theories have weaknesses. Some seem oversimplistic, whereas others are unable to explain all forms of depression. It is likely that at the mild end of the continuum, psychological factors explain many disorders, but, as severity increases, the influence of biological factors increases, too.

7. **The treatment of mood disorders** (pp. 354–361) The principal medications used to treat depression are *tricyclic antidepressants, monoamine oxidase (MAO) inhibitors*, and *SSRIs* such as fluoxetine *(Prozac)*. Tricyclics are effective but cause side effects—drowsiness, insomnia, and agitation. MAO inhibitors have a serious interaction with tyramine, found in many cheeses and other fermented products. Prozac, a widely used medication, blocks the reuptake of serotonin. *Electroconvulsive therapy (ECT)*, usually reserved for severe depressives who do not respond to medications, works rapidly but can cause memory loss and so is controversial. Interpersonal psychotherapy is a short-term, psychodynamic-eclectic treatment that focuses on current conflicts in relationships and links these to earlier life experiences and traumas. Cognitive-behavioral therapy teaches the patient to identify, examine, and replace distorted negative thoughts with more realistic ones. Patients increase their activity level and improve their social skills. Both forms of treatment are effective and equal to medication. Cognitive-behavioral training reduces the risk of relapses and can be helpful in preventing depression.

Drugs such as lithium are often used in the treatment of bipolar disorder, although there are side effects. Patient compliance with lithium treatment is another impediment.

KEY TERMS REVIEW

1. A pattern of thinking or a cognitive set that determines an individual's reactions and responses is called a(n) ____________________.

2. The DSM-IV category including major depressive disorder, dysthymic disorder, and depressive disorders not otherwise specified and generally known as the unipolar disorders is also called ____________________.

3. The emotional state characterized by great elation, seemingly boundless energy, and irritability is called ____________________.

4. Severe disturbances of emotions or affect involving depression, mania, or both are called ____________________.

5. The disorders in which both depression and mania are exhibited and those in which only mania has been exhibited are called ____________________.

6. A disorder whose symptoms include depressed mood, loss of interest, sleep disturbances, and an inability to concentrate, lasting at least two weeks, is called ____________________.

7. The emotional state characterized by intense dysphoria, sadness, feelings of futility and worthlessness, and withdrawal from others is called ____________________.

8. A mild, chronic mood disorder characterized by nonpsychotic mood swings is called ____________________.

9. A mild, chronic mood disorder characterized by nonpsychotic depression is called ____________________.

10. Acquiring the belief that one is impotent and cannot control the outcomes in one's life is called ____________________.

11. Substances that help transmit nerve impulses from one neuron to another are called ____________________.

FACTUAL MULTIPLE–CHOICE QUESTIONS

1. The prevalence of mania is ____________________ that of major depression.
   a. about one-half
   b. about the same as
   c. more than two times
   d. about one-tenth

2. When a mild depression continues for most days over a two-year period and includes symptoms of social withdrawal, pessimism, and loss of interest, the appropriate diagnosis is
   a. dysthymic disorder.
   b. exogenous depression.
   c. cyclothymic disorder.
   d. major depression.

3. Mood disorders that occur during certain seasons of the year or after a woman gives birth are considered disorders
   a. that are endogenous.
   b. with certain symptom features.
   c. that are bipolar.
   d. with course specifiers.

4. Symbolic loss, grief work, and anger turned inward are central concepts in the ______________ theory of depression.
   a. psychodynamic
   b. cognitive
   c. learned helplessness
   d. operant conditioning

5. When things are going poorly, depressives make attributions that are
   a. external, unstable, and global.
   b. internal, global, and stable.
   c. internal, unstable, and specific.
   d. external, stable, and global.

6. Low levels of ______________ are most commonly found in people suffering from major depression.
   a. REM sleep
   b. norepinephrine
   c. dexamethasone
   d. Prozac and lithium carbonate

7. What does the dexamethasone suppression test measure?
   a. Degree of norepinephrine reuptake
   b. The degree of "high" and depth of "low" in bipolar patients
   c. The cortisol levels of depressives
   d. The contribution of genetic factors to chronic depression

8. One type of drug used to treat unipolar depression has a number of serious side effects related to diet. These drugs are known as
   a. MAO inhibitors.
   b. catecholamines.
   c. tricyclics.
   d. Prozac.

9. Electroconvulsive therapy (ECT) is usually used for treating ______________, but it causes side effects, such as ______________.
   a. bipolar disorder; gastrointestinal difficulties
   b. severely depressed patients; confusion and memory loss
   c. dysthymic individuals; increased REM sleep and decreased norepinephrine
   d. mildly depressed individuals; dependency on the therapist and increasing apathy

10. Lithium carbonate is usually used in the treatment of
    a. dysthymic disorder.
    b. bipolar disorder.
    c. unipolar depression.
    d. melancholia.

CONCEPTUAL MULTIPLE–CHOICE QUESTIONS

1. When a person's mood disturbance involves hyperactivity, irritability, and expansiveness, the problem is considered
   a. depression.
   b. dysthymia.
   c. mania.
   d. schizophrenia.

2. Difficulty in concentration, suicidal thoughts, and loss of motivation are
   a. physiological signs of depression.
   b. cognitive signs of depression.
   c. elements of the cognitive triad.
   d. affective signs of hypomania.

3. Which of the following symptoms is characteristic of hypomania?
   a. Slowed movements and speech
   b. Extreme irritability, sleeplessness, and hallucinations
   c. "High" mood, poor judgment, and grandiosity
   d. Weight loss, feelings of worthlessness, and apathy

4. When family and friends are sympathetic toward a depressed person, according to behavioral psychologists,
   a. the person develops a negative cognitive schema.
   b. the family shows a negative attributional style.
   c. the depression will deepen.
   d. this will challenge the depressive's irrational beliefs.

5. According to ________________, the cure for depression requires increased activity levels and improved social skills; according to ________________, the cure for depression is changed schemas and improved self-esteem.
   a. Beck; Seligman
   b. Seligman; Lewinsohn
   c. Freud; Beck
   d. Lewinsohn; Beck

6. If we see depression as a mistaken belief that outcomes are independent of our actions and that the disorder is a motivational problem, we are seeing it as a problem involving
   a. unconscious conflicts.
   b. sociocultural norms.
   c. learned helplessness.
   d. illogical attributional thoughts.

7. The gender difference in ________________ may be either "real" and due to hormonal differences or caused by ________________.
   a. bipolar disorder; diagnosticians' expectations about women
   b. major depression; women's greater likelihood to ask for help
   c. major depression; men's tendency to ruminate about their symptoms
   d. bipolar disorder; women's greater likelihood to ask for help

8. Studies to determine the biological factors that cause mood disorders have shown that
   a. concordance rates for MZ and DZ twins are about the same for bipolar disorder.
   b. the incidence of major depression is higher in individuals' adoptive families than in their biological families.
   c. concordance rates for bipolar disorder are higher for MZ twins than for DZ twins.
   d. biological factors are more potent predictors of major depression than of bipolar disorder.

9. The client monitors his or her thoughts and emotions, then increases pleasurable activities and social skills. These processes are components of
   a. psychoanalytic therapy for depression.
   b. psychoanalytic therapy for bipolar disorder.
   c. cognitive-behavioral therapy for bipolar disorder.
   d. cognitive-behavioral therapy for depression.

10. Which statement about cognitive therapy for depression is *accurate*?
    a. Cognitive therapy is less effective than medication but more effective than interpersonal psychotherapy.
    b. With cognitive therapy the risk of relapse is less than with medication.
    c. Cognitive therapy relates the person's current conflicts with traumas from the past.
    d. Cognitive therapy accepts the client's attributional style but changes their activity level.

APPLICATION MULTIPLE–CHOICE QUESTIONS

1. Jon is so depressed that if he thinks about himself or the future, all he can imagine is failure. He does not believe that anyone else can help him, either. Jon's symptoms illustrate
   a. the physiological symptoms of depression.
   b. the affective symptoms of depression.
   c. what Beck calls the cognitive triad of depression.
   d. what Freud calls learned helplessness.

2. Frank is diagnosed with bipolar disorder. His symptoms are elevated mood, disjointed talk, excessive sleep, and irritability at others. Which aspect of Frank's case is unusual?
   a. Most people with bipolar disorder are female.
   b. Most people with bipolar disorder remain awake for long periods.
   c. Most people with bipolar disorder are calm rather than irritable.
   d. Disjointed talk never occurs in bipolar disorder.

3. Sarah has had many mild swings of mood over the past two years. She has never been hypomanic so the correct diagnosis is
   a. dysthymic disorder.
   b. cyclothymic disorder.
   c. Bipolar I.
   d. Bipolar II.

4. Richard is depressed, and his therapist says, "The best way to feel better is to do more. Doing more increases your chances of being rewarded and finding pleasure in your activities." Richard's therapist illustrates
   a. the psychodynamic approach to treatment.
   b. Lewinsohn's learning approach to treatment.
   c. Beck's cognitive approach to treatment.
   d. the humanistic-existential approach to treatment.

5. Cathy throws a party one evening, but it rains so hard that the party must be canceled. Cathy concludes that she is worthless. According to Beck's cognitive theory, this error in logic is called
   a. magnification and minimization.
   b. undergeneralization.
   c. the cognitive triad.
   d. arbitrary inference.

6. Seligman suggests that depressives make a certain type of attribution for failure. Which statement below best illustrates that attributional style?
   a. "I didn't work hard enough, but tomorrow I will work harder."
   b. "The job was too hard for anyone to do; I can't blame myself."
   c. "I am stupid and I always will be stupid; it shows in everything I do."
   d. "Just because I fail in one area of life doesn't mean I'll fail in others."

7. Dr. Nemmah says, "Depressed women respond to some stressors by creating more crises for themselves. Their lack of effective coping makes the depression continue and get worse." This statement suggests that
   a. the gender difference for depression is more imagined than real.
   b. depressed women consciously try to further their depression.
   c. women who are depressed seek treatment at an earlier time than men.
   d. stress triggers depression and depression triggers stress.

8. Verne suffers from major depression. What can we predict about his sleep habits?
   a. He may have trouble getting to sleep or awaken earlier than he wants.
   b. He may have slower onset and less frequent REM sleep than others.
   c. He can fall asleep only when he uses cortisol.
   d. He will feel fatigued at night but rested during the day.

9. Kim is being treated for depression by a therapist who focuses on her current relationships and makes links to earlier life experiences and traumas. The treatment is briefer than traditional psychoanalytic therapy but uses some of the same concepts. What kind of therapy is Kim receiving?
   a. Beck's cognitive therapy
   b. Electroconvulsive therapy
   c. Seligman's attributional therapy
   d. Interpersonal psychotherapy

10. Martha has major depressive disorder. She was treated with tricyclics and MAO inhibitors without success. Her therapist tells her, "The only effective treatment left is ECT." What is incorrect about this advice?
    a. ECT is only effective with people suffering from bipolar disorder.
    b. ECT is ineffective if tricyclic medication has been ineffective.
    c. Cognitive therapy is as successful as drug therapy.
    d. Lithium is the most successful treatment for major depressive disorder.

ANSWER KEY: KEY TERMS REVIEW

1. schema (341)
2. depressive disorders (333)
3. mania (329)
4. mood disorders (329)
5. bipolar disorders (333)
6. major depression (333)
7. depression (329)
8. cyclothymic disorder (335)
9. dysthymic disorder (333)
10. learned helplessness (343)
11. neurotransmitters (351)

ANSWER KEY: FACTUAL MULTIPLE–CHOICE QUESTIONS

1. a. The prevalence of depression is more than 10 times that of mania.
   b. Mania is much less common than depression.
   c. Mania is much less common than depression.
   *d. The prevalence of depression is more than 10 times that of mania. (p. 329)

2. *a. Dysthymic disorder is a mild depression that goes on for at least two years, so long that it seems congruent with the person's personality. (p. 333)
   b. An exogenous depression is triggered by outside events and usually ends when the stressor does.
   c. Cyclothymic disorder involves mild, but chronic, mood swings.
   d. Major depression has more severe symptoms than those described here and must elicit behaviors foreign to the person's personality.

3. a. Endogenous mood disorders are ones that are unrelated to environmental changes.
   b. Symptom features include catatonia (lack of movement) and melancholia (lack of motivation) and focus on the behaviors of the individual, not the circumstances under which the disorders occur.
   c. Bipolar disorders involve mood swings.
   *d. Course specifiers describe the circumstances under which the disorders occur—seasonal, postpartum, cycling, and longitudinal patterns are examples. (p. 336)

4. *a. Psychoanalysts believe that early childhood losses, incomplete grieving, and angry feelings turned toward oneself are important in depression. (p. 338)
   b. The cognitive perspective emphasizes illogical thinking, negative schemas, and inappropriate attributions.
   c. Learned helplessness argues that depression occurs when individuals mistakenly generalize, from a circumstance in which inescapable negative consequences occurred, the belief they have no control over the events in their lives.
   d. The operant conditioning approach to depression highlights poor social skills, lack of reinforcement for actions, and reinforcement for inaction.

5. a. Depressives tend to blame themselves (make internal attributions) when things go poorly.
   *b. Depressives are depressed because they blame themselves (internal) for everything (global) and assume that their inability is unchanging (stable). (p. 344)
   c. If people say that they are at fault (internal) but that the fault is specific to one situation and may change, they are less apt to become depressed.
   d. Depressives tend to blame themselves, not outside factors.

6. a. In major depression, REM sleep appears to be excessive.
   *b. Supporting the catecholamine hypothesis, low levels of norepinephrine activity are found in major depression and are changed by antidepressant drugs. (p. 351)
   c. Dexamethasone usually suppresses cortisol levels, but only in certain kinds of depression.
   d. Prozac is an antidepressant medication; lithium carbonate is a treatment for bipolar disorder.

7. a. There is no test for norepinephrine reuptake; tricyclic antidepressants work by decreasing such reuptake.
   b. Mood swings are evaluated by observation of behavior.
   *c. The dexamethasone suppression test detects abnormally high levels of cortisol in some kinds of depression. (p. 353)
   d. The dexamethasone suppression test cannot assess genetic influence.

8. *a. MAO inhibitors are antidepressants that interact with tyramine (an amino acid found in many foods) and cause side effects that can be lethal. (p. 355)
   b. Catecholamines are neurotransmitters that are associated with mood disorders; they are not drugs.
   c. Tricyclics are antidepressants, but they have no known side effects resulting from food interactions.
   d. Prozac is an antidepressant that does not, as far as we know, have any interaction with chemicals in the diet.

9. a. Electroconvulsive therapy is reserved almost exclusively for treating severe unipolar depression.
   *b. ECT is used when drugs have not helped seriously depressed people. Common side effects include memory loss, and in about 1 in every 1000 cases there are serious medical complications. (p. 355)
   c. Dysthymic disorder is too mild a depression for ECT to be used.
   d. ECT's major side effect is memory loss, not dependency.

10. a. Dysthymic disorder is a mild, chronic depression; medical treatment would probably involve antidepressants.
   *b. Lithium carbonate is used almost exclusively to treat bipolar disorder; it brings down the highs and lifts the lows. (p. 359)
   c. Unipolar depression is most often treated with antidepressants.
   d. Melancholia is a symptom feature of depressive disorders.

ANSWER KEY: CONCEPTUAL MULTIPLE–CHOICE QUESTIONS

1. a. Depression is characterized by sadness, feelings of worthlessness, and reduced activity.
   b. Dysthymia is a mild depression that goes on for long periods.
   *c. Mania involves uncontrollably "high" moods that include excessive activity, sleeplessness, and irritability because others cannot keep up. (p. 329)
   d. Schizophrenia is a thought disorder rather than a mood disorder.

2. a. Physiological (bodily) symptoms of depression include gastrointestinal problems, weight loss, and sleep problems.
   *b. Cognitive (thought) symptoms of depression include poor concentration, thoughts of suicide and worthlessness, and negative self-statements. (p. 330)
   c. The cognitive triad involves illogical ways of viewing oneself.
   d. The affective signs of hypomania are hyperactivity and grandiosity.

3. a. Hypomania is a form of bipolar disorder involving excessive and rapid activity.
   b. Mania is the more severe form of bipolar disorder during which people are delusional, stay up for long hours, and speak wildly.
   *c. Hypomania, a milder form of mania, is marked by hyperactivity and poor judgment, but no hallucinations or delusions. (p. 332)
   d. Feelings of worthlessness and apathy are key symptoms of depression.

4. a. Negative cognitive schemas are persistent thoughts that cause depression; kindness will not help one develop.
   b. The depressive has a negative attributional style (gives internal and stable, global trait, reasons for any failure), not the family or friends.
   *c. According to operant theorists, when depressive behavior is rewarded through sympathetic attention, the depressed person will probably withdraw further and get worse. (p. 339)
   d. Sympathy does not challenge irrational beliefs; in fact, it may strengthen them.

5. a. Increases in social skills are more the concern of an operant therapist than of a cognitive therapist like Beck.
   b. Lewinsohn is a believer in operant conditioning and puts less emphasis on cognitive issues like schemas and self-esteem.
   c. Freud stressed the symbolic, not the social skills or activity levels of patients.
   *d. Lewinsohn is an operant theorist and emphasizes what people do; Beck is a cognitive theorist concerned with what they think. (pp. 339–340)

6. a. Unconscious conflicts suggest a psychodynamic approach: seeing depression as a function of separation and anger turned inward.
   b. Sociocultural norms would highlight the ways depression is to be expressed and the situations in which members of the society are "permitted" to be depressed.
   *c. The concept of learned helplessness involves believing (mistakenly) that our actions have no impact on outcomes and that there is nothing to motivate us. (p. 343)
   d. No attributional thoughts are illogical; depressives tend to see their failures as due to their own actions—the opposite of thinking that their actions have no consequences.

7. a. There is no sex difference in rates of bipolar disorder.
   *b. There is a considerable sex difference in reported rates of major depression, but this may only be an illusory difference because women are more likely to request help. (pp. 347–350)
   c. The sex difference in major depression is that women have a higher reported rate than men; women tend to ruminate about their symptoms more than men.
   d. There is no sex difference in rates of bipolar disorder.

8. a. Higher concordance rates for MZ (70+ percent) than for DZ twins (10+ percent) indicate a strong genetic contribution.
   b. Rates are higher in biological families than in adoptive ones.
   *c. Higher concordance rates for MZ (70+ percent) than for DZ twins (10+ percent) indicate a strong genetic contribution. (p. 351)
   d. Biological factors appear to be better predictors of bipolar disorder than of major depression.

9. a. Psychoanalysts would be interested in dreams and the symbolic meaning of depression, not in activities and social skills.
   b. Psychoanalysts would be interested in dreams and the symbolic meaning of bipolar disorder, not in activities and social skills.
   c. Bipolar disorder is usually treated with drugs, particularly lithium carbonate, since bipolar disorder appears to be an endogenous mood disorder.
   *d. Cognitive-behavioral therapy stresses irrational thoughts and the need to change both those thoughts and the behaviors that typically reduce opportunities for pleasure. (pp. 358–359)

10. a. In general, interpersonal therapy, cognitive-behavioral therapy, and imipramine treatment were equally effective in treating depressive disorder.
    *b. Cognitive-behavioral therapy tends to yield lower relapse rates than medication treatment alone. (p. 359)
    c. Psychodynamic treatment addresses past events and their effect on current mood.
    d. Cognitive-behavior therapy focuses on changing one's maladaptive thinking processes.

ANSWER KEY: APPLICATION MULTIPLE–CHOICE QUESTIONS

1. a. Physiological symptoms include weight loss, sleeplessness, and gastrointestinal problems.
   b. Affective symptoms include sadness and crying, slumped posture, and a sense of defeat.
   *c. Beck stresses the cognitive aspects of depression; the cognitive triad consists of negative views of others, of oneself, and of the future. (p. 331)
   d. Seligman, not Freud, is associated with learned helplessness.

2. a. There is no sex difference in rates of bipolar disorder.
   *b. When in the midst of a manic episode, bipolar patients can stay awake for days on end. (p. 333)
   c. When people experience mania, they speed up activity and become irritable with others who cannot keep up.
   d. As mania becomes more severe, the speed of speech increases and its coherence decreases.

3. a. Dysthymic disorder is a mild form of depression that can last for years but does not involve mood swings.
   *b. Cyclothymic disorder is a mild form of bipolar disorder, with repeated mood swings, but without ever reaching the criteria for hypomania or depression. (p. 335)
   c. Bipolar I disorders involve a manic episode.
   d. Bipolar II disorder is characterized by a hypomanic episode and periods of major depression.

4. a. The therapist's comments stress activity rather than separation, anger, or other symbolic issues that psychoanalysts would emphasize.
   *b. The therapist's remarks mirror Lewinsohn's behavioral approach, which sees depression as a lack of reinforced activity. (p. 340)
   c. Beck's cognitive approach would examine and seek to change Richard's illogical thinking.
   d. A humanistic-existential approach would not highlight the reinforcing aspects of activity.

5. a. Magnification is an exaggeration of limitations, and minimization is a diminution of achievements.
   b. The logical error is *over*generalization.
   c. The cognitive triad is a negative schema for self, others, and the future.
   *d. Arbitrary inference occurs when a depressive draws a conclusion without evidence (for example, a rainy day does not indicate that one is worthless). (p. 342)

6. a. How hard one works is an internal attribution, and suggesting the possibility for change makes the attribution unstable.
   b. Blaming an external factor (task difficulty) for failure contradicts the depressive's attributional tendency.
   *c. The depressive attributional style involves making internal and stable attributions for failure. (p. 344)
   d. Specific attributions are unlike the global attributions of the depressive attributional style.

7. a. Differences in diagnostic criteria and help-seeking are reasons the gender difference may be more imagined than real; this describes a real difference in behavior.
   b. The statement does not suggest that there is a conscious attempt to bring more pain into their lives.
   c. If anything, this statement suggests that depressives would get help later, after they have used inadequate coping methods.
   *d. Hammen's longitudinal research shows that depressive women respond to stress in ways that foster depression, but also that their depressive actions bring on more stress. (p. 348)

8. *a. Insomnia and early waking are classic symptoms of depression. (p. 331)
   b. Depressives demonstrate more rapid onset and greater frequency of REM sleep.
   c. Cortisol is a naturally occurring hormone and levels are higher in depressives.
   d. Fatigue during the day is a classic symptom of depression; depressives rarely feel well rested.

9. a. Beck's cognitive therapy focuses on examining and changing illogical schemas.
   b. Electroconvulsive therapy is a biological treatment rather than a talk therapy.
   c. Seligman's attributional therapy focuses on the mistaken causal explanations a depressive uses.
   *d. Interpersonal psychotherapy is a short-term, psychodynamic-eclectic treatment that looks at current relationships and their links to earlier life experiences. (p. 357)

10. a. ECT is used with severely depressed people and is much less effective with bipolar disorder.
   b. ECT is often successfully used when antidepressant medication is ineffective.
   *c. Research shows that cognitive therapy is as effective as medication; the two together are no more effective than either separately. (p. 359)
   d. Lithium is only effective in treating bipolar disorder.

CHAPTER 12
Suicide

LEARNING OBJECTIVES

1. Discuss such facts about suicide as its frequency, prevalence, and its correlation with gender, marital status, occupation, socioeconomic level, religious affiliation, ethnicity, historical periods, and communication of intent. (pp. 364–369)
2. Identify some of the possible reasons for suicide and discuss the relationships among hopelessness, depression, and suicide. (pp. 369–371)
3. Discuss the relationship between suicide and other psychological factors, including alcohol abuse and other DSM-IV disorders. (p. 371)
4. Describe the sociocultural factors in suicide, including egoistic, altruistic, and anomic suicide. (pp. 371–373)
5. Describe the psychodynamic and biological factors related to suicide and the different types of suicide notes. (pp. 373–375; Focus On)
6. Describe and discuss research on child and adolescent suicide, including characteristics of suicidal children, family issues, and copycat suicides. (pp. 375–378)
7. Discuss research on college student suicide, including the characteristics of the victims and reasons for student suicide. (pp. 378–380)
8. Discuss suicide among special populations, including the elderly and among Asian Americans. (pp. 380–381)
9. Describe clues to suicide intent and crisis intervention efforts to prevent it. (pp. 381–383)
10. Describe the methods used by workers in suicide prevention centers and the effectiveness of these efforts. (pp. 383–386)
11. Describe how community prevention programs may help to reduce the stress of suicide on survivors, with a focus on school-based interventions. (p. 386)
12. Discuss the moral, ethical, and legal implications of the right to suicide. Clarify your own position on the legality of doctor-assisted suicide. (pp. 386–390; Critical Thinking)

CHAPTER OUTLINE

1. **Problems in the study of suicide** (pp. 364–369) People may commit suicide if they feel depressed, like a failure, as though the quality of their life is poor, unwanted, as though their death is for a greater good, and for many other reasons. Suicide is not a disorder in DSM-IV, but is important in abnormal psychology. Suicide and suicidal ideation (thinking about it) may be separate from depression. As a topic, suicide has been hidden, but it is now emerging as a focus of research and social discussion.

2. **Correlates of suicide** (pp. 366–369) Those who complete suicide attempts cannot be asked their reasons. Patterned after medical autopsies, a psychological autopsy attempts to make psychological sense of suicide by examining the person's case history, interviewing family and friends, and analyzing suicide notes. However, these sources of information are often unavailable or unreliable.

   More than 30,000 people in the United States kill themselves each year, but the real number may be 25 to 30 percent higher. In addition, for each suicide completed, eight to ten people make an attempt. Suicides among the young have increased dramatically in the past decade. Suicide is twice as common among college students as among those of the same age who are not in college. One in five students think about suicide sometime during their college career. Men complete suicide three times as often as women, but women attempt suicide three times as often. High-risk people are unmarried, divorced, and widowed individuals, professionals, and those living in countries where religious authority is weak. The rate is 12.2 per 100,000 in the United States; Hungary's rate is highest at 40.7 per 100,000. Firearms in suicide are most often used by men although their use by women is increasing. Most people communicate their intent to kill themselves within three months of the suicide.

3. **Correlates of suicide: Hopelessness, alcohol, and other factors** (pp. 369–371) Depression and suicide are strongly correlated. From half to two-thirds of all suicides are related to mood disorders. However, most depressives do not commit suicide, and the risk of suicide increases after a depression has lifted. Negative expectations about the future—hopelessness—may be the major catalyst for suicide. Hopelessness predicts suicidal behavior better than depression and better than thoughts about suicide *(suicidal ideation)*. There is a strong correlation between alcohol consumption and suicide: intoxication may lower inhibitions or constrict thought and make negative moods or thoughts more intense. Those who commit suicide are more likely than others to suffer from mood disorders, schizophrenia, or substance abuse. A variety of stressors are associated with suicide.

4. **Theoretical perspectives** (pp. 371–375; Focus On) Emile Durkheim, a sociologist, proposed that suicide was related to sociocultural influences. He concluded that three categories of suicide exist: *egoistic* (when the person is unable to integrate with society), *altruistic* (when self-destruction is for the culture's greater good), and *anomic* (when a major life event leaves a person unable to cope). Psychodynamic explanations stress the idea of anger turned inward on the self. However, psychological autopsies show this to be a cause of suicide in only a minority of cases. Suicide notes have been classified into three types: egoistic, dyadic, and ageneratic. The chemical 5HIAA, a metabolite of the neurotransmitter serotonin, is found to be at abnormally low levels in people who commit suicide. This raises the possibility that suicides have a biological basis. Low 5HIAA levels occur in suicidal individuals who are not depressed.

5. **Victims of suicide** (pp. 375–381) Children and adolescents take their lives at an alarming rate. Approximately 3000 teens end their lives each year. There was a 200-percent increase in adolescent suicide from 1960 to 1988. Recent polls indicate that 8 or 9 percent of teens have engaged in self-harm behavior. Those who attempt suicide tend to show clinical symptoms of psychological disturbance, to use drug overdose as the method, to make their attempt at home, and to come from families with high levels of stress as a result of economic instability, substance abuse, or other life events. Copycat suicides, in which adolescents imitate media portrayals of other adolescents' suicides, are less common than the media suggest and tend to occur among those already contemplating suicide. However, highly publicized suicides can increase the chances of attempts. Fortunately, 41 percent of schools report having programs aimed at suicide prevention.

   Seiden's research at the University of California at Berkeley has helped to clarify which college students are at greatest risk for suicide. They appear to be older students, foreign-born students, undergraduates with extremely good grades but many self-doubts, and postgraduates with poor grades. Reasons for college student suicides include shifting sex roles, unrealistic standards for excellence, shame and disgrace, and emotional disturbance.

   The many stresses of life among the elderly place them at high risk for suicide. Suicide rates are particularly high for white males and first-generation Asian Americans. Native Americans and African Americans show low rates of suicide among older adults, although both groups are at high risk during young adulthood.

6. **Preventing suicide** (pp. 381–386; Focus On) People who attempt suicide have a wish to live along with a wish to die. They usually leave verbal or behavioral clues of their intentions, although these may be subtle. A clinical approach to suicide intervention stresses that most individuals are ambivalent about ending their lives and that counselors must be comfortable discussing the subject. Crisis intervention strategies are used to assess lethality, and to abort suicide attempts by offering intensive counseling to the individual and stabilizing him or her in a hospital environment while clarifying ways to deal with the crisis. Suicide prevention centers usually use paraprofessionals to take telephone calls from potentially suicidal individuals. These paraprofessionals are trained to establish rapport with the caller, evaluate suicidal potential, clarify the nature of the problem and the caller's ability to cope, and recommend a plan of action. There is no conclusive evidence for the effectiveness of suicide prevention centers. Little research has been conducted, and alternative explanations for results are possible. Community prevention efforts can involve going into a school where a suicide has occurred and educating and providing counseling to survivors. Such an institutional response serves to minimize the mental health problems of survivors and can prevent future suicides.

7. **The right to suicide: Moral, ethical, and legal implications** (pp. 386–390) The Catholic Church sees suicide as a sin. On the other hand, Thomas Szasz criticizes suicide prevention programs because they limit individual options and personal responsibility. Some people contend that the elderly have the right to end their lives when they suffer terminal illness or an incapacitating illness that causes others misery. The quality of life is a significant moral and ethical issue that has led to right-to-die legislation and "living wills" that are recognized in several states. Dr. Jack Kevorkian, a physician in Michigan, has assisted patients to commit suicide, an act that a new law states is illegal. In 1992, Californians voted on a bill to allow physicians to help terminally ill patients die. Mental health professionals, like their medical colleagues, must face the issue of treating people who want to die. Practicing therapists must consider their responsibility to keep someone alive who wants to die and the legal consequences of allowing someone to die. The Constitution appears to provide a basis for the right to refuse treatment, but therapists who fail to prevent suicides can anticipate that they will be sued.

KEY TERMS REVIEW

1. Suicide that results from a maladaptive relation to society is called ____________________.

2. A systematic examination of information in order to explain the behavior of a person prior to his or her death is called a(n) ____________________.

3. Suicide that is motivated by a desire to further group goals or to achieve some greater good is called ____________________.

4. Suicide that results from an inability to integrate oneself with society is called ____________________.

5. Thoughts about suicide are called ____________________.

6. The taking of one's own life is called ____________________.

7. The probability that a person will end his or her life is called ____________________.

FACTUAL MULTIPLE–CHOICE QUESTIONS

1. A psychological autopsy
   a. is difficult to perform because suicide notes provide little information.
   b. seeks to make psychological sense of a homicide or suicide.
   c. is the first step in treatment programs for people who are suicidal.
   d. is relatively easy to perform because more than 90 percent of suicides leave notes and other written explanations behind.

2. Which of the following statistics about suicide is *accurate*?
   a. Roughly two million people commit suicide in the United States each year.
   b. Men are six times as likely to attempt suicide as women.
   c. Suicides among people aged fifteen to twenty-four have stayed about the same over the past ten years.
   d. The suicide rate for men is three times that for women.

3. Which of the following increases the risk of suicide?
   a. Being an American Indian adolescent or young adult
   b. Living in a country where the Catholic Church has strong influence
   c. Being married
   d. Living in a time of warfare or natural disaster

4. According to Durkheim's sociological perspective on suicide, when a person is unable to integrate himself or herself with society, the result may be an ____________________ suicide.
   a. anomic
   b. altruistic
   c. existential
   d. egoistic

5. Abnormally low amounts of ____________________ have been found in the spinal fluid of patients who are at high risk for killing themselves.
   a. 5HIAA
   b. phenylalanine
   c. Thorazine
   d. dopamine

6. Research on adolescent suicide attempters indicates that
   a. they are unlikely to show any symptoms of psychological disturbance.
   b. most attempts occur at home.
   c. they represent fewer than 1 percent of all adolescents.
   d. almost all attempts occur during spring and summer.

7. Which statement about adolescent suicide attempters is *accurate*?
   a. They experience traumatic events in chaotic families.
   b. The majority are determined to end their lives.
   c. Most come from economically well-off families.
   d. Most use firearms or hanging.

8. Among the elderly in the United States, which group has the *highest* rate of suicide?
   a. Black females
   b. Black males
   c. First-generation Asian Americans
   d. Males of northern European backgrounds

9. Making or rewriting a will and giving away one's personal possessions are examples of
   a. verbal clues to suicide.
   b. lethality of suicide intent.
   c. learned helplessness.
   d. behavioral clues to suicide.

10. Studies of the effectiveness of suicide prevention centers have shown that
    a. callers feel that the service is far more helpful than discussions with friends.
    b. few suicidal people use the centers and those who do call only once.
    c. cities with centers have one-half the suicide rate of those without centers.
    d. approximately one-half of the callers do commit suicide.

CONCEPTUAL MULTIPLE–CHOICE QUESTIONS

1. What mental state seems to increase one's risk of suicide?
   a. Being in the depths of a severe depression
   b. Negative expectations about the future
   c. An inflated sense of self-importance
   d. Cognitive slippage

2. When explaining suicidal behavior, Freud stresses ____________________, whereas Durkheim stresses ____________________.
   a. lack of social support; economic influences
   b. genetic factors; environmental factors
   c. anger turned inward; economic influences
   d. sexual symbolism; discrimination and prejudice

3. According to Seiden's research on college student suicide, which category of student is most likely to take his or her own life?
   a. Math and science majors
   b. Black students
   c. Students who commute to school
   d. Very-high-achieving students at large universities

4. Which of the following reasons for college student suicide is *most* plausible?
   a. As final examinations approach, stress levels become unbearable.
   b. Highly successful students are filled with doubt about their ability to succeed.
   c. Men are confused about the new roles society has pressured them to adopt.
   d. Foreign students are discriminated against by teachers and administrators.

5. Which of the following is *not* characteristic of suicide?
   a. A common emotion in suicide is hopelessness.
   b. The cognitive state is one of ambivalence.
   c. A common purpose of suicide is escape.
   d. Threats of suicide are rarely genuine expressions of intent.

6. Which of the following characterizes telephone crisis intervention efforts?
   a. Paraprofessionals are rarely used.
   b. Workers try to identify the client's stress and primary focal problems.
   c. Most people who commit suicide have previously called a suicide prevention hotline.
   d. Controlled evaluations show suicide hotlines are highly effective.

7. Mental health professionals are optimistic that suicide prevention is possible
   a. because they assume that a wish to live coexists with a wish to die.
   b. despite the fact that very few suicidal individuals give hints of their self-destructive intentions.
   c. despite the knowledge that suicidal individuals are determined to die.
   d. because suicide is such a rare event.

8. The main difference between crisis intervention and suicide prevention centers is that
   a. crisis intervention centers do not deal with suicidal people.
   b. crisis intervention stresses the need to educate the whole community.
   c. suicide prevention centers do not deal with distressed individuals.
   d. suicide prevention centers are available around the clock through telephone hotlines.

9. Community suicide prevention programs might include
   a. suggestions that negative feelings be kept tightly controlled.
   b. classroom discussions in which students are assured that another person's suicide is not their fault.
   c. media portrayals that dramatize the suicides of celebrities.
   d. discussions of the right to commit suicide.

10. Which of the following statements regarding health professionals and the law is *accurate*?
    a. Therapists have a responsibility to prevent suicide if they anticipate it.
    b. Lawsuits cannot be brought against a psychologist who fails to treat a person who threatens to commit suicide.
    c. "Living wills" are not recognized as valid in any state in the United States.
    d. The Constitution specifically states that professionals must save people's lives, even if the person wants to die.

APPLICATION MULTIPLE–CHOICE QUESTIONS

1. Dr. Ortman is interviewing the friends and family of a college student who committed suicide. She is also analyzing the student's suicide note and diary. Dr. Ortman is engaged in
   a. a form of treatment called "crisis intervention."
   b. a psychological autopsy.
   c. an assessment called "anomic evaluation."
   d. a medical autopsy.

2. Rita committed suicide when she was very drunk. Research suggests that the alcohol
   a. produced an intensified depression that caused the suicide.
   b. counteracted her previous angry emotional state.
   c. made her thinking constricted and rigid.
   d. allowed her to see the future more clearly.

3. A psychologist who made use of Durkheim's explanation for suicide would stress the
   a. early childhood experiences that led to anger turned inward.
   b. genetics of neurotransmitter imbalance.
   c. social factors that influence individuals.
   d. attention-seeking nature of suicide.

4. Karen leaves this suicide note: "Life is too hard for a weak person like me. The struggle is pointless; there is no escape from my pain. Goodbye." This note illustrates a(n) ____________________ suicide.
   a. egoistic
   b. altruistic
   c. psychotic
   d. dyadic

5. Dr. Wilton says, "The suicide rate for children under fourteen is rapidly decreasing, but it is increasing for those aged fourteen to twenty-five. Suicide is second only to automobile accidents as a cause of death among teens. Girls are three times as likely as boys to attempt it." What part of Dr. Wilton's statement is *inaccurate*?
   a. It is inaccurate to say that suicide is decreasing among those under fourteen.
   b. It is inaccurate to say that suicide is increasing among those fourteen to twenty-five.
   c. It is inaccurate to say that suicide is the second leading cause of death among teens.
   d. It is inaccurate to say that girls are more likely to attempt suicide.

6. Which adolescent is *most* likely to attempt suicide?
   a. George, whose parents are wealthy
   b. Paula, whose parents are alcoholics
   c. Jonathan, who is depressed during the summertime
   d. Nathan, who shows little hostility or anger

7. After a television news episode showing dramatic scenes of a tenth grader's suicide is broadcast, a second tenth grader at the same school kills herself. This kind of suicide is
   a. much more common than the news media have suggested.
   b. called an altruistic suicide.
   c. especially unfortunate because such depictions influence well-adjusted teens to kill themselves.
   d. called a copycat suicide.

8. Which of the following examples is most consistent with the results of Seiden's research on college suicide at the University of California at Berkeley?
   a. A graduate student with poor grades committed suicide.
   b. An undergraduate with below-average grades committed suicide during final examinations.
   c. A foreign student, younger than the average student, committed suicide.
   d. A freshman, male, science major committed suicide at home.

9. Marlene attempted suicide but was rescued by her husband. She refuses treatment. Her husband and psychiatrist agree that
   a. the danger is past.
   b. her attempt wasn't serious.
   c. Marlene was just feigning.
   d. she should be involuntarily hospitalized.

10. A psychologist is on the phone with a person who is considering suicide. The psychologist asks, "What methods have you thought about using to kill yourself?" and "When do you plan to do this?" What is the psychologist doing?
    a. a psychological autopsy
    b. writing a behavioral contract
    c. eliminating a copycat suicide
    d. assessing lethality

ANSWER KEY: KEY TERMS REVIEW

1. anomic suicide (372)
2. psychological autopsy (366)
3. altruistic suicide (372)
4. egoistic suicide (372)
5. suicidal ideation (365)
6. suicide (364)
7. lethality (381)

ANSWER KEY: FACTUAL MULTIPLE–CHOICE QUESTIONS

1. a. Psychological autopsies rely on suicide notes, which provide important information into the thinking and emotions of the person before he or she took his or her life.
   *b. The purpose of the psychological autopsy is to understand the causes for suicide so that prevention of future suicides is possible. (p. 366)
   c. A psychological autopsy is done after a death has occurred; it is too late for treatment.
   d. Suicide notes are provided by less than one-third of people who commit suicide; psychological autopsies are difficult because of the lack of firsthand information.

2. a. Although the figure of 30,000 cases per year is an underestimate, it is highly *unlikely* that the true incidence is forty times greater.
   b. Women are three times as likely as men to attempt suicide.
   c. The suicide rate among teens and young adults has risen dramatically.
   *d. The completed suicide rate is three times greater among men, although women are three times as likely to attempt suicide. (p. 367)

3. *a. Among ethnic groups, American Indians have the highest suicide rate in the United States; among adolescents, 26 per 100,000 take their own lives compared with 14 per 100,000 in the general population. (p. 369)
   b. Countries where the Catholic Church is influential have among the lowest suicide rates because the Catholic Church considers suicide a sin.
   c. Suicide is more likely when a person is divorced or single.
   d. In times of warfare and natural disaster, suicide rates drop.

4. a. Anomic suicide occurs when a dramatic event overwhelms the person's capacity to cope.
   b. Altruistic suicide occurs when the person is concerned with the group's greater good (for example, a suicide in protest of injustice).
   c. *Existential suicide* is a made-up term, not one defined by Durkheim.
   *d. Egoistic suicide occurs in social isolates, people who are not integrated into the cultural fabric. (p. 372)

5. *a. 5HIAA is a metabolite of the neurotransmitter serotonin, and it is abnormally low in people who commit suicide, even those who are not depressed. (p. 373)
   b. Phenylalanine is an amino acid unrelated to suicide.
   c. Thorazine is the brand name of a chemical used to treat schizophrenia.
   d. Dopamine is a neurotransmitter; too much dopamine activity is associated with schizophrenia.

6. a. Suicide attempters are likely to have a past history of psychological disturbance.
   *b. Suicide attempts tend to take place in the home. (p. 376)
   c. Recent polls indicate that 6 percent of teens admit to a suicide attempt; probably between 8 and 9 percent of teens engage in self-harmful behavior.
   d. Winter is the most typical time for adolescents to make suicide attempts.

7. *a. Suicidal adolescents frequently experience traumatic events prior to their suicide and live in unstable, chaotic families that can provide minimal support. (p. 377)
   b. Most adolescents are not really sure they want to die.
   c. Adolescents with economically stressed families are at higher risk.
   d. Firearms and hanging, highly lethal methods, are rarely used in *attempts*.

8. a. Black females have a relatively low suicide rate.
   b. Elderly black males have a relatively low suicide rate.
   *c. First-generation Asian Americans have a high rate of suicide, perhaps because of their cultural dislocation. (p. 381)
   d. White males have a suicide rate lower than that of Asian Americans.

9. a. An example of a verbal clue might be, "Everyone would be happier if I just shot myself."
   b. Lethality is determined by a person's plan to take his or her life and his or her access to the means of doing it.
   c. Learned helplessness has more to do with believing that one has no control over the consequences of one's actions.
   *d. Making a will is a physical action; therefore it is a behavioral clue. (p. 381)

10. a. Unfortunately, callers who were included in such evaluation studies saw no more benefit from calling the center than from discussing the problem with friends.
   *b. Only 2 percent of suicidal individuals use suicide prevention hotlines; about 95 percent of those who call once never call again. (pp. 385–386)
   c. No clear difference in community suicide rates has been found; those with hotlines can have higher, lower, and similar rates of suicide compared with communities not having hotlines.
   d. Because there is no way to trace callers, we do not know how many actually commit suicide.

ANSWER KEY: CONCEPTUAL MULTIPLE-CHOICE QUESTIONS

1. a. When people are in the depths of a severe depression, their motor behavior is so retarded and their thinking so impaired, that they are at low risk for suicide.
   *b. Negative expectations—or hopelessness—seem to be even more predictive of suicide than depression is. (p. 370)
   c. People contemplating suicide often have a reduced sense of self-worth.
   d. Cognitive slippage is a characteristic of schizophrenia and is unrelated to suicide.

2. a. Although Durkheim is interested in economic conditions, Freud never discusses social supports.
   b. Freud stresses unconscious conflicts, not genetics.
   *c. Freud sees suicide as a self-destructive act that originates in rage at another person; Durkheim emphasizes social conditions, including economic ones. (pp. 372–373)
   d. Freud's theory of suicide emphasizes the *thanatos* (death instinct) rather than the *libido* (sexual, id instinct).

3. a. Language and literature majors are more prone to suicide than others.
   b. Black students were not found to be at high risk.
   c. Most suicides take place at campus residences.
   *d. High-achieving undergraduates were among the most likely suicide victims; suicide is more prevalent at large universities than at small colleges. (p. 379)

4. a. Suicidal behavior peaks at the beginning of semesters, not at final examination time.
   *b. Suicide risk is high for the strongest students because they appear to have unrealistically high standards of performance. (p. 379)
   c. Women may be more inclined to commit suicide because of role confusion.
   d. Foreign students may be more inclined to commit suicide because of shame and fear of letting down their parents.

5. a. Pessimism about the future and belief that nothing can be done may predispose a person to suicide.
   b. Most individuals have dual motivations—to live and to die.
   c. The goal is to escape a perceived intolerable situation.
   *d. Verbal communication, indirect threats, and behavioral clues are all signs that predict suicide and should be treated seriously. (p. 381)

6. a. Paraprofessionals are frequently used in suicide hotlines.
   *b. Problem identification is critical before intervention can be made. (p. 384)
   c. It's estimated that 2% of suicides have contacted a hotline before committing suicide.
   d. Controlled studies are not available, since hotlines are anonymous.

7. *a. Mental health professionals operate under the assumption that most (if not all) people who are suicidal also have a desire to live. (pp. 382, 389)
   b. Most suicidal people leave clues to their intentions, although some are rather subtle.
   c. Mental health professionals do *not* believe that suicidal people have shut the door on living.
   d. Suicide is all too common.

8. a. Suicide is certainly a crisis and is a part of crisis intervention work.
   b. Crisis intervention focuses on direct care for the suicidal person rather than on community education.
   c. Suicide prevention centers take telephone calls from people in acute distress.
   *d. Suicide prevention centers have paraprofessionals who take telephone calls twenty-four hours per day; crisis intervention involves direct care after the person presents himself or herself to the counseling center. (pp. 382–384)

9. a. Interventions provide survivors with the opportunity to express strong negative feelings; bottling them up would be seen as impairing recovery.
   *b. In one program described in the text, children were reassured that their teacher's decision to commit suicide was not their fault; children need to have unnecessary guilt removed. (p. 386)
   c. Media portrayals that dramatize the suicides of celebrities or others may foster copycat suicides.
   d. It would not be appropriate for students to consider suicide a personal right under the circumstances of a tragedy in the school.

10. *a. Although laws are not clear on all points, therapists have an ethical duty to preserve life when they can. (p. 389)
   b. Therapists can be sued for refusing to offer life-protective treatment.
   c. "Living wills" are recognized as valid in fifteen states.
   d. The Constitution implies that people can refuse treatment that will save their lives (as in cases when those who believe in faith healing refuse medical treatment).

ANSWER KEY: APPLICATION MULTIPLE–CHOICE QUESTIONS

1. a. Crisis intervention involves assisting a person who may be contemplating suicide.
   *b. A psychological autopsy involves looking at material about the suicide victim to help us understand the person's motives. (p. 366)
   c. *Anomic evaluation* is a made-up term.
   d. Although medical autopsies are performed on suicide victims, they do not involve interviewing friends or family or analyzing suicide notes.

2. a. Alcohol typically does not intensify depression; it may actually relieve it partially and provide the person with energy enough to commit suicide.
   b. There is no reason to believe that alcohol will counteract anger.
   *c. Researchers believe alcohol foreshortens one's thinking (alcohol myopia), reducing the suicidal person's capacity to think of alternative solutions to problems. (p. 371)
   d. If anything, alcohol intoxication prevents one from seeing the future clearly.

3. a. Durkheim was a sociologist, not a psychodynamic thinker.
   b. Durkheim was a sociologist, not a physiological psychologist.
   *c. Durkheim was a sociologist; his interests included social integration, economic change, and individuals' responses to these factors. (pp. 371–372)
   d. Attention seeking might be a behavioral conceptualization of suicidal behavior; Durkheim was not a behaviorist.

4. *a. Edwin Shneidman's research on suicide notes illustrates that an egoistic suicide stems from inner torment that produces a sense of defeat. (p. 374; Focus On)
   b. Durkheim's altruistic suicide concept is applied to cases in which death is seen as a means of achieving a greater good for the group.
   c. There is no such category as "psychotic suicide"; if one existed, we would expect more scattered or paranoid thinking than is found in Karen's note.
   d. Shneidman's concept of dyadic suicide involves self-destruction out of anger or frustration with another person.

5. *a. The suicide rate has been increasing in the preteenage population. (p. 375)
   b. The suicide rate among those aged fifteen to twenty-four has tripled in the past thirty years.
   c. Automobile accidents are the leading cause of death; suicide is second.
   d. Girls are more likely to attempt suicide, although boys are more likely to be successful.

6. a. Children whose parents are in financial stress are more likely to commit suicide than those whose parents are well-off.
   *b. Suicide among teens is higher when their parents suffer from alcohol or other chemical dependencies. (p. 377)
   c. Suicide among teens tends to be most common during the winter months.
   d. Hostility and aggressiveness are strongly associated with suicide.

7. a. Copycat suicides are far less common than the media indicate.
   b. In altruistic suicide, one kills oneself for the group's greater good, such as *kamikaze* pilots did in World War II.
   c. Depictions of suicide do not seem to influence well-adjusted adolescents; they *do* have an impact on those with suicidal tendencies.
   *d. Copycat suicides are more likely to occur when media portrayals of suicide influence those with suicidal tendencies to take their own lives. (p. 378)

8. *a. Seiden found that graduate students who were doing poorly were a high-risk group for suicide. (p. 379)
   b. When undergraduates were superb students, the risk of suicide increased.
   c. Foreign students were at high risk, but older students were far more likely to commit suicide than younger ones.
   d. Older students were more likely to commit suicide; literature and language majors were more likely to do so than science majors.

9. a. She may be in great danger.
   b. Any attempted suicide is serious.
   c. Marlene's attempt may have been a cry for help, but that does not mean she was feigning.
   *d. She should be involuntarily hospitalized. (p. 382)

10. a. A psychological autopsy occurs after suicide is completed; this person is very much alive.
   b. A behavioral contract involves a written agreement that the person who is suicidal will not try to take their life, will rid themselves of the means to committing suicide, and will seek counseling.
   c. To eliminate copycat suicides we would need to change how the media disseminate information about suicides in the community.
   *d. Questions about suicidal plans and the means to carry them out are ways of assessing the chances a person will take his or her own life—lethality. (p. 381)

CHAPTER 13
Schizophrenia: Diagnosis and Symptoms

LEARNING OBJECTIVES

1. Discuss the history of the diagnostic category known as schizophrenia and the current DSM-IV criteria. (pp. 393–395)
2. Describe the symptoms of schizophrenia, including positive and negative symptoms, delusions, and perceptual distortions. (pp. 396–399; Focus On)
3. Describe the problems of communication and thought disturbance seen in schizophrenia, including loosening of associations and neologisms. (pp. 399–402)
4. Describe the motoric disturbances and negative symptoms seen in schizophrenia. (pp. 402–403)
5. Differentiate between the various subtypes of schizophrenia, including the paranoid, disorganized, catatonic, undifferentiated, and residual types of schizophrenia. (pp. 403–406)
6. Describe the psychotic disorders once considered schizophrenia including delusional disorder, brief psychotic disorder and schizophreniform disorder, and differentiate them from schizophrenia. Differentiate delusional disorder from paranoid schizophrenia. Describe shared psychotic disorder and schizoaffective disorder. (pp. 406–407; Focus On)
7. Describe the three phases of schizophrenia. (p. 408)
8. Discuss research on the long-term outcome of schizophrenia, including studies of schizophrenia in developing and developed countries. (pp. 408–411)

CHAPTER OUTLINE

1. **Schizophrenia: Diagnosis and symptoms** (pp. 393–394) Schizophrenia is a group of disorders characterized by cognitive distortions, personality disintegration, affective disturbances, and social withdrawal. It receives a great deal of attention because it is so disabling, the prevalence rate is 1 percent (and therefore millions of people are affected), and its symptoms and causes are diverse. The lifetime prevalence for schizophrenia is higher among African Americans and lower among Hispanic Americans than among the general population.

2. **History of the diagnostic category** (pp. 394–395) Emil Kraepelin first named the disorder *dementia praecox* (meaning "early insanity"), defining it as an early occurring, incurable organic disorder involving progressive mental deterioration. Eugen Bleuler objected to this, arguing that the disorder did not necessarily occur early in life. Bleuler proposed that four A's defined the disorder: autism (self-focus), associations (unconnected ideas), affect (inappropriate emotions), and ambivalence (uncertainty over actions). He also suggested that schizophrenia was caused by a combination of genetic and environmental factors with different possibilities for recovery of functioning. In early editions of the diagnostic manual, schizophrenia was broadly defined, using Bleuler's four A's. With the DSM-III, DSM-III-R, and DSM-IV, the definition became quite

restrictive. The current category in DSM-IV has aspects of both DSM-III and DSM-III-R. A diagnosis of schizophrenia should be given only if delusions, hallucinations, or disturbed thinking and emotional expression have impaired functioning for at least six months at some point in the person's life and for at least one month currently. Organic causes and affective disorders must be ruled out.

3. **The symptoms of schizophrenia: Positive symptoms** (pp. 396–402; Focus On) There appear to be three types of symptoms in schizophrenia: psychoticism (*hallucinations* and *delusions*) and disorganization, which are considered *positive symptoms;* and *flat affect* and other forms of social withdrawal, which are considered *negative symptoms*. People with schizophrenia often report delusions—false beliefs—that can take many forms. Unlike other people, individuals with schizophrenia reach delusional conclusions on the basis of little information; they can, however, be trained to challenge their delusions. Hallucinations are sensory perceptions not attributable to environmental stimuli. Hallucinations are not *pathognomonic* (distinctive) to schizophrenia. Auditory hallucinations are most common. Some believe that auditory hallucinations may stem from subvocal speech, and are phenomena people with schizophrenia can cope with in a variety of ways. During times when symptoms are prominent, hallucinations and delusions are so strong that they are treated as real; in other situations, people with schizophrenia can ward them off.

   Schizophrenic individuals have difficulty concentrating and communicating. One symptom is called *loosening of associations*, or cognitive slippage. Thoughts shift from topic to topic, and communication can be vague or overly concrete. *Neologisms*, made-up words using combinations of common words, are another classic symptom of schizophrenia, but this symptom occurs rarely. People with schizophrenia also show odd movements or postures. Maintaining an unusual body position is characteristic of catatonic schizophrenia.

4. **The symptoms of schizophrenia: Negative symptoms** (pp. 402–403) Negative symptoms are associated with poor prognosis and may be associated with structural abnormalities in the brain. Some symptoms are part of the disorder itself (primary symptoms), while others are the result of medication or hospitalization (secondary symptoms). Examples of negative symptoms are an inability to feel pleasure, take action, make meaningful speech, and express emotions where strong reactions are expected.

5. **Types of schizophrenia** (pp. 403–405; Focus On) *Paranoid schizophrenia* is the most common form of schizophrenia and is characterized by delusions or hallucinations, usually involving persecution or grandiosity. It is possible to differentiate this disorder from *delusional disorder* because delusional disorder involves less bizarre beliefs and is free from other dysfunctional behaviors. *Disorganized schizophrenia* features severe regression to a childish state without delusions. Behavior and speech tend to be bizarre. *Catatonic schizophrenia* is divided into an excited form marked by hyperactivity and a withdrawn form in which immobility and waxy flexibility are seen. Often patients swing from one state to the other. *Undifferentiated schizophrenia* is a form marked by a mix of symptoms; *residual schizophrenics* are those people whose symptoms are in remission.

6. **Psychotic disorders once considered schizophrenia, and other psychotic disorders** (pp. 406–407) In DSM-IV, the term *schizophrenia* is reserved for psychotic episodes lasting six months or more. *Brief psychotic disorder* is diagnosed when symptoms have lasted less than one month; the disorder in which symptoms last between one and six months is called *schizophreniform disorder*. DSM-IV recommends these disorders be "provisional." About two-thirds of those diagnosed with schizophreniform disorder will later be diagnosed with schizophrenia or schizoaffective disorder. Other psychotic disorders include shared psychotic disorder, in which a person who has a close relationship with a delusional person accepts those beliefs, and schizoaffective disorder, a combination of mood disorder and psychotic symptoms that last at least two weeks.

7. **The course of schizophrenia** (pp. 408–411; Critical Thinking) Most people with schizophrenia show poor premorbid personality before the onset of the disorder. The typical course of schizophrenia consists of three phases. The *prodromal phase* includes social withdrawal and peculiar speech or actions. In the *active phase,* symptoms are in full evidence, and by the *residual phase,* symptoms are no longer prominent. International studies show that return to work and reduction in symptoms is more common in developing countries than in the United States, the former Soviet Union, or Western Europe. This may be due to misdiagnosis rather than true recovery.

   It is unclear what the long-term outcome of schizophrenia tends to be. In one study, 78 percent of schizophrenics suffered a relapse; in another, long-term prognosis was favorable in half of the cases. Differences in outcome may be due to criteria used to define schizophrenia. Most individuals with schizophrenia recover enough to lead relatively productive lives.

KEY TERMS REVIEW

1. A group of disorders characterized by severe impairment of cognitive processes, personality disintegration, and social withdrawal is collectively called ________________.

2. A schizophrenic disorder in which the individual regresses to a childlike state but does not exhibit delusions is called ________________.

3. A schizophrenic disorder characterized by persistent and systematized delusions is called ________________.

4. A schizophrenic disorder characterized by extreme excitement or extreme withdrawal is called ________________.

5. A schizophrenic disorder characterized by a mix of symptoms that do not clearly fit any other type of the disorder is called ________________.

6. A disorder characterized by persistent but nonbizarre delusions not accompanied by any other unusual behaviors is called ________________.

7. False beliefs that are firmly held despite disconfirming evidence is called ________________.

8. A category of schizophrenic disorder reserved for individuals who manifested symptoms in the past but who now no longer show prominent signs of the disorder is called ________________.

9. Sensory perceptions not directly attributable to environmental stimuli are ________________.

10. Continual shifting between topics without meaningful connections is called ________________.

11. New words that are typically formed by combining words in common usage are called ________________.

12. A psychotic disorder that lasts no longer than one month is called ________________.

13. A psychotic disorder that lasts between one month and six months is called ________________.

14. Symptoms that are specific or distinctive to a disorder are called ________________.

15. The negative symptom in which little or no emotion is shown in situations where strong reactions are expected is called ________________.

16. Symptoms that are present during the active phase of schizophrenia and include hallucinations, delusions, and disorganized speech are called _____________.

17. The process of thinking, perceiving, judging, and recognizing is called _____________.

18. In schizophrenia, symptoms associated with poor prognosis—including flat affect, anhedonia, apathy, and avolition—are called _____________.

FACTUAL MULTIPLE-CHOICE QUESTIONS

1. The lifetime prevalence for schizophrenia is
   a. lower for African Americans than it is for the general population.
   b. much higher among males than females.
   c. roughly 10 percent.
   d. roughly 1 percent.

2. He called the disorder *dementia praecox* and thought that it was an organic problem with no possibility for recovery. Who is being described?
   a. Emil Kraepelin
   b. Sigmund Freud
   c. Eugen Bleuler
   d. David Rosenhan

3. According to the DSM-IV criteria, schizophrenia is diagnosed when
   a. the disorder has lasted at least two months at some point in the person's history.
   b. symptoms cause subjective distress but not necessarily functional impairment.
   c. marked disturbances of thinking, affect, or speech have led to a deterioration in functioning.
   d. organic causes have produced psychotic symptoms for more than one year.

4. Flat affect, anhedonia, and apathy are all symptoms of schizophrenia that are considered
   a. good signs of recovery.
   b. negative symptoms.
   c. behavioral symptoms.
   d. forms of delusions.

5. A false belief that others are plotting to embarrass or harm you is called a
   a. delusion of persecution.
   b. delusion of grandeur.
   c. psychomotor disturbance.
   d. neologism.

6. A schizophrenic who engages in neologisms is
   a. failing to display emotions that are appropriate for a situation.
   b. making up words that only he or she understands.
   c. standing in awkward postures but allowing others to move him or her like a mannequin.
   d. unable to concentrate and organize incoming information.

7. A person with schizophrenia begins a response with appropriate comments but then becomes incoherent and mentions things that are unrelated. This shifting from topic to topic is called
   a. anhedonia
   b. delusions of reference
   c. loosening of associations
   d. lack of insight

8. When the sole symptom is a delusion that does not affect functioning in other spheres of a person's life, the best diagnosis is
   a. paranoid schizophrenia.
   b. brief psychotic disorder.
   c. delusional disorder.
   d. paranoid schizophreniform disorder.

9. The active phase of schizophrenia
   a. follows the residual phase.
   b. includes symptoms at their early stages of development.
   c. continues throughout the schizophrenic's life.
   d. follows the prodromal phase.

10. International research seems to show that recovery from schizophrenia is
   a. more rapid in developed countries such as the United States.
   b. more rapid in developing countries such as India.
   c. virtually impossible no matter where it occurs.
   d. more dependent on good diet than on good therapy.

CONCEPTUAL MULTIPLE-CHOICE QUESTIONS

1. Which of the following symptoms is considered central to schizophrenia?
   a. Changing from one personality style to another
   b. Severely impaired thinking and social withdrawal
   c. Compulsive rituals and extreme anxiety
   d. An inability to feel loyalty toward others

2. Unchangeable false beliefs are to ______________________ as perceptions in the absence of stimuli are to ______________________.
   a. paranoid schizophrenia; catatonic schizophrenia
   b. delusions; hallucinations
   c. hallucinations; loosening of associations
   d. loosening of associations; hallucinations

3. People with schizophrenia have problems with attention. What problems, exactly?
   a. They crave the attention of others but withdraw from social attention.
   b. They focus their attention so narrowly that they are unaware of other people.
   c. They choose to focus their attention on fantasy instead of reality.
   d. They find it difficult to concentrate and organize incoming information.

4. Which statement about individuals diagnosed with schizophrenia is *accurate*?
   a. They tend to be unaware or only moderately aware of their symptoms.
   b. They tend to be very aware of their loose associations even while they have them.
   c. They are most aware of their symptoms when they are in the active phase of the disorder.
   d. Schizophrenia is the only disorder in which people who have symptoms are unaware that they are experiencing them.

5. Which form of schizophrenia is associated with poor prognosis and must be diagnosed with care because the symptoms may develop in response to medication and institutionalization?
   a. Schizophrenia with negative symptoms
   b. Paranoid schizophrenia
   c. Schizophrenia with positive symptoms
   d. Capgras's syndrome

6. ______________________ schizophrenia is the most common form of the disorder and is characterized by illogical and contradictory delusions.
   a. Paranoid
   b. Catatonic
   c. Disorganized
   d. Undifferentiated

7. In what kind of schizophrenia do patients stand in awkward positions for hours at a time?
   a. Paranoid
   b. Catatonic
   c. Disorganized
   d. Undifferentiated

8. Which of the following is a criterion for diagnosing residual schizophrenia?
   a. The presence of auditory or visual hallucinations
   b. Early onset of the disorder and extremely bizarre speech
   c. The presence of many severe schizophrenic symptoms at the same time
   d. The absence of prominent symptoms after an episode of full-blown schizophrenia

9. In what way is schizophreniform disorder different from schizophrenia?
   a. It involves thought disturbances that the patient can control; in schizophrenia, there is no control.
   b. It begins at an early age; in schizophrenia, the onset is in middle age.
   c. It involves no thought disturbances; in schizophrenia, thought disturbances are critical symptoms.
   d. It has not lasted six months or more; in schizophrenia, psychosis must have lasted at least that long.

10. Long-term outcome studies of schizophrenia indicate that
    a. Emil Kraepelin was wrong: in many cases, people recover.
    b. Eugen Bleuler was wrong: treatment rarely produces recovery.
    c. Sigmund Freud was right: unconscious conflicts continue throughout life.
    d. Emil Kraepelin was right: schizophrenia is a progressive illness.

APPLICATION MULTIPLE–CHOICE QUESTIONS

1. "In my opinion, there are a variety of disorders that we lump together under 'schizophrenia.' They have different causes that may include environmental factors, and different chances of recovery." These remarks best reflect the beliefs of
   a. Philippe Pinel.
   b. Eugen Bleuler.
   c. Emil Kraepelin.
   d. Dorothea Dix.

2. Kristin, a schizophrenic patient, believes that all events revolve around her. Whatever anyone says, it is about her. All news broadcasts contain hidden messages for her. Kristin's thinking illustrates
   a. a delusion of persecution.
   b. a delusion of grandeur.
   c. Capgras's syndrome.
   d. a delusion of reference.

3. Dr. Bodie says, "Although other disorders show delusions, hallucinations are pathognomonic to schizophrenia. Sometimes hallucinations accompany and are related to the delusions." What portion of this statement is *inaccurate*?
   a. It is inaccurate to say that delusions occur in disorders other than schizophrenia.
   b. It is inaccurate to say that hallucinations are pathognomonic to schizophrenia.
   c. It is inaccurate to say that hallucinations sometimes accompany delusions.
   d. It is inaccurate to say that hallucinations sometimes are related to delusions.

4. Justin was diagnosed with schizophrenia. He shows little emotional expression and has no motivation. He seems unable to feel pleasure. Justin's form of schizophrenia
   a. involves positive symptoms.
   b. is usually considered disorganized schizophrenia.
   c. usually has a very good prognosis.
   d. involves negative symptoms.

5. Dr. Ortlieb says, "In schizophrenia, the person has no control over his or her symptoms. These symptoms can involve the production of unique words called neologisms, an absence of emotion called flat affect, or false beliefs called delusions." What part of Dr. Ortlieb's statement is *incorrect*?
   a. The idea that schizophrenics have no control over their symptoms
   b. The idea that unique words are called neologisms
   c. The idea that schizophrenics do not show emotion
   d. The idea that false beliefs are called delusions

6. Jonathan has shown thought disturbances since he was eight years old. He is now twenty-seven and still acts in bizarre and silly ways. When most people would laugh, he cries. He shows no consistent delusions. Jonathan would most likely receive a diagnosis of
   a. schizophreniform disorder.
   b. catatonic schizophrenia.
   c. undifferentiated schizophrenia.
   d. disorganized schizophrenia.

7. When Tina is totally withdrawn, she shows waxy flexibility. When she is out of that state, she is extremely active and hypertalkative. Tina would most likely receive a diagnosis of ______________________ schizophrenia.
   a. paranoid
   b. catatonic
   c. undifferentiated
   d. residual

8. Barney believes that his office phone is monitored and that his boss is trying to poison the air in his office. Other than these unfounded suspicions, Barney shows no thought disturbance or functioning problems. Barney would most likely receive a diagnosis of
   a. paranoid schizophrenia.
   b. undifferentiated schizophrenia.
   c. brief psychotic disorder.
   d. delusional disorder.

9. Chuck responds to his father's death with a two-week psychotic episode during which he hears voices, is delusional, and shows bizarre affect. What diagnosis should Chuck receive?
   a. paranoid schizophrenia
   b. catatonic schizophrenia
   c. brief psychotic disorder
   d. prodromal schizophrenia

10. Dr. Jenkins says, "More than one-half of schizophrenics show moderate to complete recovery, although recovery rates differ depending on whether the country is developed or developing. Developing countries have very poor recovery rates." What part of Dr. Jenkins's statement is *inaccurate*?
   a. It is inaccurate to say that one-half of schizophrenics recover.
   b. It is inaccurate to say that recovery can be complete for any schizophrenic.
   c. It is inaccurate to say that the type of country affects recovery.
   d. It is inaccurate to say that developing countries have very poor recovery rates.

ANSWER KEY: KEY TERMS REVIEW

1. schizophrenia (393)
2. disorganized schizophrenia (403)
3. paranoid schizophrenia (403)
4. catatonic schizophrenia (404)
5. undifferentiated schizophrenia (405)
6. delusional disorder (403)
7. delusions (396)
8. residual schizophrenia (405)
9. hallucinations (398)
10. loosening of associations (401)
11. neologisms (402)
12. brief psychotic disorder (406)
13. schizophreniform disorder (406)
14. pathognomonic (398)
15. flat affect (396)
16. positive symptoms (396)
17. cognition (393)
18. negative symptoms (396)

ANSWER KEY: FACTUAL MULTIPLE–CHOICE QUESTIONS

1. a. The lifetime prevalence for African Americans is about 2 percent, twice that for the general population.
   b. Schizophrenia affects males and females equally.
   c. The lifetime prevalence is about 1 percent.
   *d. The lifetime prevalence of schizophrenia in the United States is about 1 percent. (p. 393)

2. *a. Emil Kraepelin used the term *dementia praecox* to describe what we now call schizophrenia; he saw the illness as organic and irreversible. (p. 394)
   b. Sigmund Freud had little to say about schizophrenia; most of his work was on neurotic conditions.
   c. Eugen Bleuler objected to Kraepelin's view that schizophrenia was a single entity without possibility of recovery.
   d. David Rosenhan is a modern psychologist who, in a famous study done in 1973, tested psychiatry's ability to detect psychosis.

3. a. The disorder must have lasted six months at some point in the person's life.
   b. Diagnosis requires a deterioration from previous levels of functioning and does not mention subjective distress.
   *c. Schizophrenia is diagnosed when there is marked cognitive and affective disturbance that leads to a deterioration in functioning from previous levels. (p. 395)
   d. Schizophrenia is ruled out if there are organic causes, and the duration of symptoms is six months, not one year.

4. a. These signs are called negative symptoms and are associated with poor prognosis.
   *b. Negative symptoms include flat affect (little emotional expression), anhedonia (inability to experience pleasure), apathy, alogia (lack of meaningful speech), and avolition (inability to take action). (p. 396)
   c. Flat affect is a symptom of emotional disturbance, as is anhedonia.
   d. None of these are forms of mistaken beliefs; delusions are positive symptoms.

5. *a. Delusions of persecution involve suspicions that others will harm or humiliate you. (p. 396)
   b. Delusions of grandeur involve a belief in self-importance (such as, "I am the king of the world").
   c. Psychomotor disturbances involve wild activity or extreme immobility.
   d. A neologism is a made-up word, not a false belief.

6. a. Failure to display emotions appropriate for a situation is an example of a negative symptom.
   *b. Neologisms are new words formed by combining words in common usage. (p. 402)
   c. Standing in awkward postures is typical of a catatonic schizophrenic.
   d. Difficulty with attention is a separate symptom of schizophrenia.

7. a. Anhedonia is a negative symptom meaning an inability to experience pleasure.
   b. Delusions of reference are mistaken beliefs that all events revolve around the person with the delusion.
   *c. Loosening of associations (also called cognitive slippage) is the cognitive symptom of shifting from topic to topic and therefore speaking in an incoherent way. (p. 401)
   d. Lack of insight is the inability of psychotic people to know that their thinking is bizarre.

8. a. In paranoid schizophrenia, delusions and other thought disturbances affect a wide range of functioning; there is a deterioration in functioning in all the schizophrenias.
   b. Brief psychotic disorder is diagnosed if symptoms last one month or less.
   *c. The term *delusional disorder* is reserved for highly compartmentalized delusions that do not have a broad effect on functioning. (p. 406; Focus On)
   d. There is no such subtype.

9. a. The active phase follows the prodromal phase.
   b. During the active phase, symptoms are at their peak.
   c. Schizophrenia includes three phases; the active phase may not last very long or may occur intermittently over a lifetime.
   *d. The three phases are the prodromal, the active, and the residual. (p. 408)

10. a. Recovery was slower in developed countries such as the United States and the former Soviet Union.
    *b. Recovery, including return to employment, was quicker in developing countries. (p. 410; Critical Thinking)
    c. Many studies indicate that moderation or elimination of symptoms is likely in one-half of cases.
    d. If diet were important, we would expect better recovery in developed countries than in developing ones, where food may be scarce.

ANSWER KEY: CONCEPTUAL MULTIPLE–CHOICE QUESTIONS

1. a. Changes in personality style are associated with dissociative identity disorder, not schizophrenia.
   *b. Schizophrenia is fundamentally a disorder of impaired cognitive processes and social withdrawal. (p. 393)
   c. Compulsive rituals are associated with obsessive-compulsive disorder, a nonpsychotic anxiety disorder.
   d. An inability to feel loyalty is a sign of antisocial personality disorder.

2. a. Although paranoid schizophrenia is characterized by false beliefs, catatonic schizophrenia involves motor disturbances, not hallucinations.
*b. False beliefs are delusions; false sensory perceptions are hallucinations. (pp. 396, 398)
c. False sensory perceptions are hallucinations, not delusions.
d. Loose associations involve incoherent thoughts, not consistent ones that defy evidence (delusions).

3. a. People with schizophrenia are often socially withdrawn; they do not seek attention from others.
b. They have the opposite problem—they cannot focus their attention narrowly.
c. While people with schizophrenia have trouble distinguishing fantasy and reality, it is untrue that the problem of attention is a choice they make.
*d. People with schizophrenia are easily distracted, and their ability to organize incoming information is severely impaired. (p. 401)

4. *a. A World Health Organization study found that lack of insight (not being aware of one's symptoms) was the most common symptom of schizophrenic people; more than 57 percent were either unaware or moderately unaware. (p. 399)
b. The opposite is true: most schizophrenic people are unaware of their symptoms.
c. Awareness of symptoms is more likely when people are in the residual phase of schizophrenia, when others can tell or show them how they behaved during the active phase.
d. Lack of insight is not pathognomonic for schizophrenia; it occurs in other disorders.

5. *a. Schizophrenia with negative symptoms (apathy, remaining mute, showing little emotion) is associated with poor prognosis, but these symptoms may be brought on by medication or institutionalization. (p. 403)
b. Paranoid schizophrenia is marked by positive symptoms and does not necessarily warrant a poor prognosis.
c. Schizophrenia with positive symptoms (delusions and hallucinations) has a more promising prognosis than the disorder with negative symptoms.
d. Capgras's syndrome is a delusion (positive symptom) in which people think there are doubles for oneself and others.

6. *a. The hallmark of paranoid schizophrenia is delusions; it is the most common subtype of schizophrenia. (p. 403)
b. Catatonic schizophrenia is characterized by psychomotor disturbances.
c. Disorganized schizophrenia features very regressive behavior without delusions.
d. Undifferentiated schizophrenia has no particular symptom picture. It may include delusions, but it is not the most common subtype.

7. a. Paranoid schizophrenia features consistent delusions.
*b. Psychomotor disturbances such as extreme activity and complete immobility are the fundamental signs of catatonic schizophrenia. (p. 404)
c. Disorganized schizophrenia is marked by extremely bizarre and childish behavior from an early age.
d. Undifferentiated schizophrenia is the label given when no particular symptom stands out.

8. a. Auditory or visual hallucinations are found in a variety of schizophrenic subtypes.
b. Early onset and bizarre behavior are signs of disorganized schizophrenia.
c. When many symptoms are simultaneously present, the diagnosis is usually undifferentiated schizophrenia.
*d. Residual schizophrenia is the diagnosis given to schizophrenics when they are in remission. (p. 405)

9. a. Schizophrenic patients report being able to control or modify their symptoms.
   b. Schizophrenia does not usually begin in middle age; age of onset does not differentiate these disorders.
   c. There are thought disturbances in schizophreniform disorder.
   *d. Duration is the only accurate means of differentiating these disorders. (p. 407)

10. *a. Conservative estimates indicate that one-half of schizophrenics will show moderate or complete recovery by the end of their lives. (p. 409)
   b. Long-term outcomes are fairly positive for one-half or more of cases.
   c. Although Freud assumed that unconscious conflicts occur throughout life, this is unrelated to the research finding that in one-half of cases, schizophrenic symptoms improve or disappear.
   d. This was Kraepelin's position, but research rejects this idea.

ANSWER KEY: APPLICATION MULTIPLE–CHOICE QUESTIONS

1. a. Philippe Pinel's contributions were made around the turn of the nineteenth century, almost 100 years before writings on schizophrenia began.
   *b. Bleuler disputed Kraepelin's view that *dementia praecox* was a unitary organic illness; he argued that a range of symptoms developed from a range of causes. (p. 394)
   c. Emil Kraepelin took the opposite position to this statement.
   d. Dorothea Dix established state mental hospitals in the United States; she was not a theorist about schizophrenia.

2. a. A delusion of persecution would involve threats of harm or humiliation.
   b. Delusions of grandeur involve a belief in one's special status or ability ("I can see through walls").
   c. Capgras's syndrome is a delusion that oneself and others have been replaced by identical doubles.
   *d. Delusions of reference involve beliefs that external events have personal meaning ("When police sirens are sounded, they are signaling me"). (p. 396)

3. a. It is accurate to say that delusions occur in disorders other than schizophrenia. For instance, delusional disorder's sole characteristic is delusions.
   *b. Hallucinations are not pathognomonic (distinctive and specific) to schizophrenia; people with other psychotic conditions hear voices or see things that are not there. (p. 398)
   c. Hallucinations sometimes accompany delusions, as when people who believe they are guilty of some terrible sin hear voices condemning them to hell.
   d. Hallucinations sometimes relate to delusions (see c).

4. a. Positive symptoms include activity such as bizarre gestures, as well as delusions, hallucinations, and disorganized thought.
   b. Disorganized schizophrenia is characterized by bizarre actions, fragmented thinking, and emotional expression that can include silly smiles or giggles.
   c. Schizophrenia involving an absence of emotion and motivation involves negative symptoms; these are associated with poor prognosis.
   *d. Negative symptoms such as the ones Justin shows are associated with poor prognosis. (p. 402)

5. *a. Schizophrenic patients report that they can take actions to reduce their symptoms. (p. 399)
   b. *Neologism* is the term for the made-up words that schizophrenics use in their disturbed speech.
   c. Flat affect, an absence of emotional expression, is an important symptom of schizophrenia.
   d. False beliefs that are unswayed by evidence are called delusions.

6. a. Schizophreniform disorder is diagnosed when symptoms last less than six months.
   b. Catatonic schizophrenia is characterized by psychomotor disturbances, which Jonathan does not display.
   c. In undifferentiated schizophrenia, symptoms are more diffuse than Jonathan's and are not so regressive.
   *d. Disorganized schizophrenia involves bizarre symptoms that have an early onset, as in Jonathan's case. (p. 403)

7. a. Paranoid schizophrenia is characterized by delusions.
   *b. Catatonic schizophrenia involves the psychomotor disturbances and social withdrawal seen in Tina's case. (pp. 404–405)
   c. Undifferentiated schizophrenia does not involve such bizarre behaviors as are described in Tina's case.
   d. Residual schizophrenia is diagnosed when a person has had an episode of full-blown schizophrenia and now shows some symptoms but not prominently enough to get another diagnosis.

8. a. In paranoid schizophrenia, delusions are part of a more general cognitive impairment that leads to deteriorated functioning.
   b. In undifferentiated schizophrenia, delusions are not predominant.
   c. Brief psychotic disorder is an acute condition that impairs functioning; it lasts less than one month.
   *d. In delusional disorder, paranoid ideas are highly organized, but no other thought disturbance is seen. (p. 406; Focus On)

9. a. Paranoid schizophrenia is diagnosed only after symptoms have lasted for six months or more.
   b. Catatonic schizophrenia is diagnosed after symptoms of psychomotor disturbance have lasted for six months or more.
   *c. Brief psychotic disorder is diagnosed in cases like Chuck's, where symptoms of thought disturbance last less than one month. (p. 406)
   d. Prodromal schizophrenia is not an official label in DSM-IV.

10. a. Long-term outcomes show that one-half of schizophrenic patients make moderate or complete recoveries.
   b. Some schizophrenics make complete recoveries.
   c. Recovery seems to be more rapid in developing countries than in developed ones such as the United States.
   *d. Although misdiagnosis may be the reason, higher recovery rates have been found in developing countries (Nigeria and India) than in developed countries (the United States and Great Britain). (p. 410; Critical Thinking)

CHAPTER 14
Schizophrenia: Etiology and Treatment

LEARNING OBJECTIVES

1. Discuss the utility in combining hereditary and environmental influences to understand the origins of schizophrenia. Discuss problems with interpreting genetic studies on schizophrenia. (pp. 414–416)
2. Describe the results of research using blood relatives and twins to investigate the genetics of schizophrenia. Evaluate the methodological problems of these types of research. (pp. 416–418)
3. Describe the results of adoption studies as well as those with high-risk populations. Evaluate the methodological problems of these types of research. (pp. 418–423)
4. Describe the biochemical theories of schizophrenia, including the dopamine hypothesis of schizophrenia and research results that strengthen and weaken this hypothesis. (pp. 423–425)
5. Describe the neurological impairments, cognitive, and information-processing deficits believed to be associated with schizophrenia. Evaluate the usefulness of a neurological explanation of schizophrenia. (pp. 425–428)
6. Discuss the role of stress in the development of schizophrenic symptoms. Describe the family environment theories of schizophrenia and the methodological problems with this research. (pp. 428–430)
7. Describe the importance of expressed emotion in schizophrenia. (pp. 430–431)
8. Discuss the social class and cross-cultural aspects of schizophrenia. (pp. 431–434)
9. Describe and evaluate the diathesis-stress model of schizophrenia. (p. 434)
10. Discuss the use of antipsychotic medications in the treatment of schizophrenia and the problems in using these drugs in treatment. Discuss changes in patients' rights to refuse medication. (pp. 434–437, 440; Focus On, Critical Thinking)
11. Describe the psychosocial therapies including institutional approaches, cognitive-behavioral therapy, Integrated Psychological Therapy, and interventions targeted at relapse prevention by reducing expressed emotion. Discuss the effectiveness of these treatments. (pp. 437–442)

CHAPTER OUTLINE

1. **Etiology of schizophrenia** (p. 414) The causes of schizophrenia may involve genetic, physiological, psychological, and environmental factors. Therapies include neuroleptics (antipsychotic medication) and psychotherapy, but relapse rates remain too high. Researchers disagree on the impact of social and genetic factors in the cause and development of this disorder.

2. **Heredity and schizophrenia: Problems in interpreting genetic studies, studies involving blood relatives** (pp. 415–416) The highest probability of selecting a schizophrenic from the general population would be reached by finding an individual with an identical twin who has the disorder. However, genetic studies are limited by the variety of subtypes of the disorder, as well as by sampling and definitional problems.

   We might assume that the closer the blood relationship between a person and a diagnosed schizophrenic, the higher the probability of the disorder in that person. However, relatedness and risk are not always linked because of problems in defining *schizophrenia,* in reliably diagnosing individuals, and in biased selection and analysis. Furthermore, such studies confound genetics and environment. The child of a person with schizophrenia has a 12- to 13-percent chance of developing the disorder; the risk in the general population is about 1 percent.

3. **Heredity and schizophrenia: Twin studies and adoption studies** (pp. 416–420) Since their genes are identical, we would assume that there would be stronger *concordance rates* among MZ twins than among DZ twins (who share about 50 percent of their genes) if schizophrenia is genetically transmitted. Concordance rates are usually two to four times higher in MZ twins than in DZ twins, but method problems, including definitions along the schizophrenia spectrum, account for a wide range in these findings. Clearly, there is a genetic influence in this disorder.

   Adoption studies screen out the effects of family environment. Heston (1966) found that five of forty-seven at-risk children (adoptees having schizophrenic birth mothers) later became schizophrenics themselves, but none of the control adoptees did. However, many at-risk children also became creative, successful adults. Other adoption studies also support the idea that heredity plays a major role in the transmission of schizophrenia. Kety et al. (1994) found that, among adoptees who developed schizophrenia, the disorder tended to exist in the relatives of the biological parents but not those of the adoptive parents.

4. **Heredity and schizophrenia: Studies of high-risk populations** (pp. 420–423) High-risk studies are developmental comparisons between children with schizophrenic parents and those with nonschizophrenic parents. Results of Mednick et al.'s research show that children who became sick had mothers with more severe schizophrenic symptoms who had experienced complications giving birth. They were also more disruptive as children and had a slower autonomic recovery rate. Israeli *prospective* studies indicate that schizophrenia has only developed among high-risk children. Social withdrawal was the characteristic most related to risk of developing the disorder. However, none of the high-risk children receiving adequate parenting developed schizophrenia or a schizophrenia-like disorder.

   Although high-risk population studies are a promising line of research, they have no control groups with other forms of psychopathology, generalizations may be difficult, and relevant variables and appropriate definitions of disorder may be missing.

5. **Physiological factors in schizophrenia** (pp. 423–428) After previous dead ends, the idea that a chemical imbalance exists in schizophrenics shows promise. The effects of phenothiazine drugs, L-dopa, and amphetamines support the *dopamine hypothesis,* which suggests that dopamine activity in certain areas of the brain is excessive in people with schizophrenia. However, some patients do not respond to phenothiazines or L-dopa in ways predicted by this biochemical theory. This could be due to there being varieties of schizophrenia. Other drugs, such as Clozapine, implicate the neurotransmitter serotonin.

Research supports the view that, especially in schizophrenics who show such negative symptoms as flat affect, there are neurological abnormalities, including cerebral atrophy and low cerebral glucose metabolism in the frontal lobes. These differences are seen in identical twins who are discordant for the disorder. People with schizophrenia show poorer sustained attention and eye movement coordination than nonschizophrenics, differences that are considered cognitive markers. Nuechterlein and his colleagues suggest that some neurological factors in schizophrenia predate the disorder and are unchanged during a psychotic episode, some are present beforehand but are worsened during the disorder, and some are short-term indicators that are the result of the disorder. However, even stable neurological abnormalities are not specific to schizophrenia, and some treatment effects run counter to prediction.

6. **Environmental factors in schizophrenia: Family influences** (pp. 428–430) Environmental factors act as stressors and thereby help produce psychopathology. Stress may induce hallucinations and trigger relapse. The family is an important source of stress. Psychodynamic theory focused on the personality of the *schizophrenogenic* mother, whereas family systems theory stresses the *double-bind theory* of communication patterns. Research on family influence has been hampered both by observations after the child has been diagnosed and by the lack of control groups.

7. **Environmental factors in schizophrenia: Expressed emotion** (pp. 430–431) Expressed emotion (EE)—highly critical, hostile, and overinvolved parenting—is related to increased relapse among schizophrenics, especially those who have stopped taking medication. However, as with other environmental factors, it is not clear whether these problems are the effect of schizophrenia or its cause; neither does EE appear to be pathognomonic for the disorder.

8. **Environmental factors in schizophrenia: Effect of social class, cross-cultural comparisons** (pp. 431–434) Schizophrenia is more common in the lower social classes than in the upper ones. Theories attribute this to the stress of poverty (breeder hypothesis) or downward drift theory (the loss in income occurring because the disorder makes earning a good living difficult). Research evidence can support both positions.

   Symptoms of schizophrenia in various countries studied appear to reflect cultural beliefs specific to the culture. Racial differences exist within the United States: African Americans are seen as exhibiting more severe, angry, and antisocial symptoms than do whites. Misdiagnosis based on race may be one explanation.

9. **The diathesis-stress model of schizophrenia** (p. 434) Lacking evidence for a single cause of schizophrenia, the growing consensus is that schizophrenia develops out of a genetic or acquired predisposition coupled with a stressful environment. The vulnerability may include impaired information processing, overreactivity, and poor social skills. The stressors may include an overstimulating environment where EE is present. Overreactions produce added stressors that build up until the symptoms of schizophrenia are triggered. Such a model implies that intervention should involve medication, individual coping skills, and family support.

10. **The treatment of schizophrenia** (pp. 434–442; Focus On, Critical Thinking) Antipsychotic medication *(neuroleptics)* is the principal means of treating schizophrenia today. A new drug, Clozapine, may be effective in cases not previously helped by neuroleptics. Although effective in many cases, medications can produce neurological conditions, including *tardive dyskinesia*, a disorder of involuntary movements for which there is no cure. Other side effects have led to legal action to provide patients with the right to refuse such medical treatment. Clinicians often misinterpret or ignore the symptoms of drug side effects. The need for maintenance dosages for schizophrenics is currently in question. But even when people with schizophrenia are recovering they face discrimination in the workplace.

    Psychosocial therapy is now often paired with drug treatment. Patients reported deriving most help from practical advice therapists give; they value the therapist's friendship. In inpatient settings, *milieu therapy* and social learning treatment have been shown to be more effective than traditional treatment. Milieu therapy allows patients to take more responsibility for decision making. In social learning, the client is taught social skills so that interactions are not avoided. Cognitive approaches have been useful in reducing delusions and hallucinations. *Integrated Psychological Therapy (IPT)* teaches patients to use information appropriately, respond to social cues, make conversation, and interact appropriately.

Intervention to reduce expressed emotion in families has also proven useful in reducing relapse rates. Families are given information about the disorder and taught ways to alter communication patterns. Schizophrenic patients can also be taught to respond to their parents' emotions more appropriately. Combining various treatments gives hope for even more successful therapy for schizophrenia in the future.

KEY TERMS REVIEW

1. The suggestion that schizophrenia results from an excess of dopamine activity at certain brain synapses is called the ____________________.

2. The suggestion that schizophrenia develops in an individual because, as a child, that person continually received contradictory messages from parents is called the ____________________.

3. A theoretical model postulating that inherited or acquired vulnerability and the effect of environmental stressors combine to produce schizophrenic episodes is called the ____________________.

4. Antipsychotic medications that can produce symptoms that mimic neurological disorders are called ____________________.

5. The likelihood that both members of a twin pair will exhibit the same disorder is called the ____________________.

6. A therapy program in which the hospital environment operates as a community, and patients have decision-making responsibilities is called ____________________.

7. An adjective describing a parent who is simultaneously or alternately cold and overprotecting, rejecting and dominating, and who may produce schizophrenia is ____________________.

8. A study that is performed before the symptoms of an illness have been identified to see how the disorder develops over time is called a(n)____________________.

9. A type of negative communication pattern found in some families with schizophrenic members, which involves hypercritical and overprotective parenting, is called ____________________.

10. Disorders that are considered to be genetically related to schizophrenia are part of the ____________________.

FACTUAL MULTIPLE-CHOICE QUESTIONS

1. The likelihood that two members of a twin pair will both develop a disorder is called the
   a. proband index.
   b. vulnerability index.
   c. concordance rate.
   d. MZ or DZ rate.

2. Heston's (1966) research examining the rate of schizophrenia among adopted children born to schizophrenic parents found
   a. no difference between the rate of the disorder in the control and at-risk groups.
   b. no cases of the disorder among control children.
   c. that 100 percent of the at-risk children developed the disorder.
   d. that at-risk children tended to be duller and less spontaneous than the controls.

3. Because phenothiazines reduce schizophrenic symptoms and amphetamine overdoses can mimic schizophrenic symptoms, it is believed that the neurotransmitter ________________ is involved in schizophrenia.
   a. L-dopa
   b. 5HIAA
   c. dopamine
   d. acetylcholine

4. People with negative-symptom schizophrenia (those who show flat affect and lack of drive) are believed to be at risk for
   a. abnormally low levels of dopamine.
   b. tardive dyskinesia.
   c. neurological abnormalities such as cerebral atrophy.
   d. high levels of expressed emotion in the family environment.

5. The theory that schizophrenia develops out of family environments in which there are contradictory messages and in which no responses go unpunished is called the
   a. double-bind communication theory.
   b. diathesis-stress model.
   c. breeder hypothesis.
   d. schizophrenogenic mother theory.

6. The most common flaws with earlier research on the families of schizophrenics were
   a. too few subjects and too narrow a definition of schizophrenia.
   b. analysis of interactions after one family member was diagnosed and a lack of control groups.
   c. a lack of control groups and overreliance on MZ and DZ twins.
   d. too few subjects and the use of a developmental method.

7. When the parents of schizophrenics engage in heated criticism and become overinvolved in the lives of their children, they engage in
   a. double-bind communications.
   b. social skill training.
   c. expressed emotion.
   d. tardive dyskinesia.

8. When a person's financial status goes down after a person is diagnosed with schizophrenia, a ________________ explanation of the relationship between the two is supported.
   a. schizophrenogenic
   b. biochemical
   c. stressful life events
   d. downward drift

9. Evidence from international research indicates that schizophrenia
   a. shows the same symptoms in every culture in the world.
   b. shows different symptoms depending on the culture in which it occurs.
   c. occurs with widely varying frequency, depending on the culture in which it occurs.
   d. has a slower onset in less-developed nations.

10. Which side effect is a well-established problem with antipsychotic medication?
    a. The development of phobias
    b. Paranoid delusions
    c. Expressed emotion
    d. Tardive dyskinesia

CONCEPTUAL MULTIPLE–CHOICE QUESTIONS

1. Because ____________________ studies of schizophrenics often use chronically ill patients and adopt very narrow definitions of the disorder, evidence of ____________________ may be inaccurate.
   a. sociological; the inheritance of the disorder
   b. genetic; the inheritance of the disorder
   c. psychoanalytic; the unconscious conflicts in the disorder
   d. genetic; cross-cultural differences in the disorder

2. Research on the relationship between the risk of developing schizophrenia and the degree of blood relatedness indicates
   a. completely inconsistent results.
   b. that schizophrenia is clearly a genetically caused disorder.
   c. that social class and stressors are more important than genetic factors.
   d. the closer the blood relationship to a person with schizophrenia the higher the risk of the disorder

3. Why is it impossible to demonstrate the inheritance of schizophrenia on the basis of blood relative studies?
   a. There are many different blood groups.
   b. There are many different kinds of schizophrenia.
   c. There are no probands in a blood relative study.
   d. There are environmental factors that are uncontrolled.

4. The value of a high-risk population study of schizophrenia over an adoption study is that it
   a. separates the effects of genetic factors from those of the environment.
   b. includes a control group.
   c. allows for the use of concordance rates.
   d. allows the investigator to see how the disorder develops.

5. Mednick et al.'s research indicates that high-risk children who develop schizophrenia are
   a. more likely to be identical twins than fraternal twins.
   b. extremely aggressive and slower to habituate to certain stimuli.
   c. extremely intelligent and had less severely disordered mothers.
   d. all identified as "sick" as young children.

6. High-risk population research studies on schizophrenia
   a. show reasonably strong evidence that heredity is involved in schizophrenia.
   b. show that 80 to 90 percent of diagnosed schizophrenics have a schizophrenic parent.
   c. indicate that family environment plays no meaningful role in the development of symptoms.
   d. have failed to show that heredity plays a major role in schizophrenia.

7. Which of the following is a reason to be cautious in using the results of high-risk population research studies to conclude that schizophrenia is biologically caused?
   a. There is no significant difference in the rate of schizophrenia in high-risk versus control subjects.
   b. Such studies rarely examine such nongenetic factors as pregnancy and birth complications.
   c. Most people diagnosed with schizophrenia do not have a schizophrenic parent.
   d. "High-risk" is defined in terms of dopamine sensitivity, and other neurotransmitters may be involved in the disorder.

8. According to the diathesis-stress model,
   a. the vulnerability to schizophrenia can be inherited or acquired.
   b. all people have about the same vulnerability to the disorder.
   c. once the disorder begins, stressful life events play no role.
   d. the presence of social supports has no effect on the outcome of a schizophrenic episode.

9. Kingdon and Turkington (1991) found that they could train schizophrenic patients in such a way as to reduce their delusions, need for hospitalization, and medication. What did the training involve?
   a. Patients were allowed to make decisions about their lives on the hospital ward.
   b. Patients were taught to analyze and give reasonable explanations for their symptoms.
   c. Patients were taught to respond to their parents with "expressed emotion."
   d. Patients were given practical advice and told to get in touch with their feelings.

10. What is the effect of reducing expressed emotion in the families of schizophrenic individuals?
    a. the need for medication is increased
    b. relapse rates are reduced
    c. other affective disorders take the place of schizophrenic symptoms
    d. communication skills are weakened

APPLICATION MULTIPLE–CHOICE QUESTIONS

1. Don and Ron are identical twins. Tim and Harry are fraternal twins. Don and Tim are both diagnosed as schizophrenics. According to the results of most research studies on twins,
   a. Ron has a greater chance of being schizophrenic than Harry.
   b. Ron and Harry have equal chances of being schizophrenic.
   c. Harry has a greater chance of being schizophrenic than Ron.
   d. there is little chance that either Harry or Ron will have schizophrenia.

2. A psychologist investigating the genetics of schizophrenia is *most* likely to find a high concordance rate for the disorder if
   a. she uses a broad definition of schizophrenia.
   b. the subjects are fraternal twins, rather than identical twins.
   c. she uses a narrow definition of schizophrenia.
   d. the subjects are distant relatives.

3. Dr. Arensky says, "Adoption studies such as Heston's (1966) show that few or none of the control-group children develop schizophrenia, and that those in the high-risk condition either develop the disorder or are socially dysfunctional. However, environmental factors play a major causal role." What idea here is *inaccurate*?
   a. It is inaccurate to say that the controls were free of the disorder.
   b. It is inaccurate to say that the high-risk children were more prone to the disorder.
   c. It is inaccurate to say that high-risk children always develop a form of psychopathology.
   d. It is inaccurate to say that environmental factors play a major causal role.

4. Based on the prospective, high-risk population research done in Israel on children with schizophrenic mothers, what policy might the government adopt?
   a. Refuse to allow children of schizophrenic mothers to live in a kibbutz.
   b. Ensure that children of schizophrenic mothers be given antidepressant medication.
   c. Provide therapy to children in school who seem overly involved in relationships.
   d. Make sure that children of schizophrenic mothers receive adequate parenting.

5. Brenda is diagnosed with schizophrenia. She has trouble sustaining her attention and processes visual information incorrectly. These characteristics exist before, during, and after her schizophrenic episodes. According to Nuechterlein, Brenda's behavior illustrates
   a. stable cognitive markers for the disorder.
   b. episode indicators of schizophrenia.
   c. signs of structural neurological abnormalities.
   d. signs of dopamine deficiency.

6. Marvin is diagnosed with schizophrenia. His mother is overprotective, rejecting, cold, and dominating. According to psychodynamic thinkers, Marvin's mother
   a. became this way in response to his disorder.
   b. could be considered schizophrenogenic.
   c. is probably an antisocial personality.
   d. is responding to castration anxieties.

7. Dr. Earl says, "The problem with these studies is that there were no control groups and the family's interactions were studied *after* a family member was diagnosed with schizophrenia." What kind of study is Dr. Earl discussing?
   a. Recent high-risk population studies
   b. Recent studies examining expressed emotion and relapse
   c. Earlier studies of double-bind communications
   d. Kraepelin's early twin studies

8. Cindy says, "I don't think that poverty causes schizophrenia; I think being so dysfunctional makes schizophrenics poor." Cindy's ideas illustrate the
   a. downward drift hypothesis.
   b. diathesis-stress model of schizophrenia.
   c. schizophrenogenic theory.
   d. breeder hypothesis.

9. An elderly schizophrenic patient who has been taking phenothiazines for twenty years shows involuntary thrusting of her tongue, lip smacking, and jerking movements of the neck. What is wrong with this patient?
   a. She has cerebral atrophy as a result of negative symptom schizophrenia.
   b. She has symptoms of the disorder that are still not controlled through medication.
   c. She has developed Parkinson's disease because of her medication.
   d. She has developed tardive dyskinesia because of her medication.

10. Harold has been diagnosed with schizophrenia and is currently in treatment. His counselor teaches him to recognize and respond to social cues. He also learns to retrieve appropriate information so he can make conversation with others. What kind of treatment is Harold receiving?
    a. Integrated Psychological Therapy (IPT)
    b. Milieu therapy
    c. Traditional institutional care
    d. Intervention to reduce expressed emotion

ANSWER KEY: KEY TERMS REVIEW

1. dopamine hypothesis (423)
2. double-bind theory (429)
3. diathesis-stress model (434)
4. neuroleptics (414)
5. concordance rate (415)
6. milieu therapy (438)
7. schizophrenogenic (429)
8. prospective study (421)
9. expressed emotion (430)
10. schizophrenia spectrum (417)

ANSWER KEY: FACTUAL MULTIPLE–CHOICE QUESTIONS

1. a. The proband is the index case, the person who has the disorder.
   b. *Vulnerability index* is a made-up term.
   *c. When all the co-twins in a twin study have the disorder, the concordance rate is 100 percent; when none of the co-twins has the disorder, the rate is 0 percent. (p. 415)
   d. MZ and DZ are terms for types of twins (monozygotic and dizygotic), and neither represents a likelihood of developing a disorder.

2. a. There was a considerable difference in the rate of schizophrenia between at-risk and control children.
   *b. None of the control-group children developed schizophrenia, compared with five of forty-seven in the at-risk group. (p. 418; Table 14.2)
   c. More than forty of forty-seven at-risk children did not develop the disorder.
   d. The at-risk children who were free of schizophrenia were highly successful adults and were unusually creative.

3. a. L-dopa is a drug used to treat Parkinson's disease because it is used by the body to manufacture dopamine.
   b. 5HIAA is a metabolite of the neurotransmitter serotonin and is involved in affective disorders.
   *c. Dopamine activity has been found to be excessive in certain areas of the brains of schizophrenics, and it is reduced by phenothiazines and increased by amphetamines. (p. 423)
   d. Acetylcholine is a neurotransmitter, but it is not implicated in schizophrenia.

4. a. Abnormally high levels of dopamine activity are a general finding in schizophrenia.
   b. Tardive dyskinesia is a serious side effect of heavy phenothiazine use.
   *c. Cerebral atrophy, ventricular enlargement (caused by the shrinkage of cerebral tissue), and low glucose metabolism are associated with negative-symptom schizophrenia. (p. 425)
   d. Expressed emotion is not correlated with negative-symptom schizophrenia.

5. *a. Double-bind communications involve contradictory messages that punish the child; the outcome is believed by some to be schizophrenia. (p. 429)
   b. The diathesis-stress model involves a predisposition to a disorder and environmental stresses that trigger symptoms.
   c. The breeder hypothesis is the idea that the stress of poverty induces schizophrenic symptoms.
   d. Schizophrenogenic mothers are central to psychoanalytic theory.

6. a. One of the problems with earlier research was that the definition of the disorder was too broad.
   *b. Both of these problems characterized earlier work and made its results suspect. (pp. 429–430)
   c. MZ and DZ twins were never used in family studies.
   d. One of the problems with earlier research was the failure to use a developmental method.

7. a. Double-bind communications involve contradictory messages but do not necessarily involve heated criticism.
   b. Social skill training is something professionals do when they teach clients to speak and act assertively.
   *c. Expressed emotion is defined in terms of overinvolvement and excessive criticism of family members and is associated with increased risk of relapse among schizophrenic people. (p. 430)
   d. Tardive dyskinesia is a neurological problem brought on by chronic, heavy use of antipsychotic medications.

8. a. Genetic explanations are supported by high-risk population, twin, or adoption studies.
   b. Biochemical explanations are supported by neurotransmitter imbalances or drug effects.
   c. Schizophrenogenic mothers are believed by psychoanalysts to generate schizophrenia by acting toward their children in a cold and domineering manner.
   *d. Downward drift suggests that poverty is the effect of schizophrenia; people cannot work well and so become poorer. (p. 431)

9. a. Research shows that symptoms are influenced by cultural values and concerns.
   *b. Symptoms differ among cultures; for example, Japanese schizophrenics are more passive than Italian schizophrenics. (p. 433)
   c. The incidence of schizophrenia is very stable across cultures (about 10%).
   d. If anything, abrupt onset is more common in less-developed nations.

10. a. There is no evidence that antipsychotic medication produces phobias.
   b. Antipsychotic medication reduces paranoid thinking.
   c. Expressed emotion is a family factor that seems to increase the chances of relapse in people with schizophrenia.
   *d. Tardive dyskinesia, involuntary tongue thrusting and lip smacking, is a sometimes irreversible side effect of antipsychotic medication. (pp. 437, 440; Critical Thinking)

ANSWER KEY: CONCEPTUAL MULTIPLE–CHOICE QUESTIONS

1. a. Sociological research would not reveal anything about the inheritance of the disorder.
   *b. Chronically ill subjects probably have a higher genetic component than other subjects; broad definitions of *schizophrenia* increase the chances of concordance and would inflate estimates of genetic contribution. (p. 415)
   c. Psychoanalytic research rarely uses schizophrenics, and the use of chronically ill patients is even rarer.
   d. Genetic research would not reveal anything about cross-cultural differences.

2. a. Results are not inconsistent: children run a 12- to 13-percent risk whereas for nieces or nephews the risk is about 2 to 3 percent.
   b. Because environmental influences are strong in family studies, such a statement is inaccurate.
   c. Family studies have not controlled for the effects of social class or other environmental effects.
   *d. The closer the blood relationship to a person with schizophrenia the higher the odds of developing schizophrenia. (p. 416)

3. a. Although there are different blood groups, blood-relative studies are interested only in the similarity of genes in the people being researched.
   b. Although there are different kinds of schizophrenia, this is not a problem specific to blood-relative research.
   c. There must be a proband, a person with the disorder in question, in any genetic research study.
   *d. Because people are raised by their family members, it is always impossible to separate the effects of genetics from those environmental effects (such as learning) in this type of research. (p. 416)

4. a. High-risk children are raised by their biological parents, so such a separation is not possible.
   b. Control groups are a part of both research designs, so this does not represent a specific advantage of high-risk population studies.
   c. Concordance rates are used in any study that compares a proband and someone else; they are used in twin, adoption, and other genetic research designs.
   *d. High-risk population studies begin observations before the onset of symptoms in the members of the high-risk populations; such studies have the advantage of being developmental or prospective studies. (p. 420)

5. a. High-risk population research does not involve twins of any kind.
   *b. Mednick et al. found that children who developed schizophrenia were aggressive, disruptive, slow to habituate, and had mothers who were more severely disturbed and who had had pregnancy complications. (p. 421)
   c. No difference in intelligence was reported, and the mothers were more disturbed.
   d. Many of the high-risk children did not develop the disorder.

6. *a. High-risk population studies show that children who receive inadequate parenting have a greater likelihood of developing the disorder; this is evidence that genetics is only a partial cause. (p. 421)
   b. The reverse is true: Only 10 to 20 percent of those with a schizophrenic parent develop the disorder.
   c. Inadequate parenting, a form of stress, plays a major role, as can be seen in the Israeli studies comparing children who developed the disorder and those who did not.
   d. Because more children in high-risk groups develop the disorder, genetic factors must play an important role.

7. a. High-risk population studies consistently find more cases of schizophrenia among those who are high-risk than among controls.
   b. Such studies do examine nongenetic biological factors; Mednick's work, for instance, found that high-risk children who develop schizophrenia have mothers who experienced pregnancy and birth complications.
   *c. The majority of people with schizophrenia do not have a schizophrenic parent, so whatever genetic vulnerability there is is less than that seen in high-risk population studies. (p. 423)
   d. "High-risk" is defined by having a mother who was diagnosed with schizophrenia; it has nothing to do with dopamine sensitivity.

8. *a. The diathesis-stress model involves the predisposition to be vulnerable; this can be inherited or acquired at an early age. (p. 434)
   b. Differences in vulnerability account for the very different rates of the disorder in different segments of the population.
   c. Stress is a part of the entire course of schizophrenia, from onset to recovery.
   d. Social supports appear to be an important way of preventing the predisposition from producing symptoms.

9. a. When patients are given responsibility for hospital ward government, it is called milieu therapy. Kingdon and Turkington used a cognitive approach.
*b. Kingdon and Turkington used a cognitive approach in which delusions and other symptoms were analyzed and given nonstigmatizing explanations. (p. 439)
c. Interventions interested in expressed emotion strive to reduce it; less expressed emotion reduces the relapse rate of people with schizophrenia.
d. Practical advice and getting in touch with one's feelings were two of the factors that schizophrenic individuals found useful in psychosocial therapy, not cognitive therapy.

10. a. Such training may actually reduce the need for medication since it improves the chances of staying symptom-free.
*b. Reducing expressed emotion in the family has been found to be a better way to reduce risk of relapse than medication alone. (p. 442)
c. There is no evidence that reducing expressed emotion has any negative effects.
d. These interventions improve communication skills.

ANSWER KEY: APPLICATION MULTIPLE–CHOICE QUESTIONS

1. *a. Identical twins have a higher concordance rate than fraternal twins because all of their genes are the same. (p. 416)
b. Because there is one-half the similarity of genes in fraternal twins, compared to identical twins, there should be a reduced likelihood for Harry.
c. Being a fraternal twin, Harry's likelihood is lower.
d. It is true that schizophrenia is rare, but as Meehl points out, an identical twin has about a 50 percent chance of developing the disorder if the other twin is so diagnosed.

2. *a. Broad definitions of schizophrenia increase the chances that both people being compared have the disorder, thereby inflating estimates of schizophrenia's heritability. (p. 417)
b. Since fraternals share only 50 percent of their genes (compared to 100 percent for identicals), using them would reduce concordance rates.
c. A narrow definition would exclude people who otherwise might be considered as sharing the disorder (being concordant).
d. The more distant the relatives, the fewer the genes in common.

3. a. This is accurate because past research reports that control-group children have a 0-percent chance of developing the disorder.
b. At-risk children are more likely to develop schizophrenia, so this is accurate.
*c. This is inaccurate because the at-risk children who did not develop schizophrenia (about half the cases) turned out to be creative and successful. (pp. 418–419)
d. Environmental factors, as in the Israeli kibbutz study, play a major role in the development of schizophrenia.

4. a. There was no significant difference in the likelihood of developing schizophrenia between high-risk children raised in a kibbutz or in a suburban town.
b. Although somewhat more high-risk children showed affective disorders than did controls, the overwhelming majority showed good adjustment.
c. The characteristic most associated with the development of schizophrenia was social withdrawal, not overinvolvement in relationships.
*d. None of the high-risk children who received adequate parenting developed schizophrenia; the results of the study point to the importance of both genetics and family nurturing. (pp. 422–423)

5. *a. Nuechterlein suggests that cognitive markers for schizophrenia must be present before, during, and after psychotic episodes; information processing problems like the ones Brenda shows are classic cognitive markers for the disorder. (p. 426)
   b. If a schizophrenic symptom only occurs during an episode, Nuechterlein considers it an episode indicator, not a true cognitive marker.
   c. Cognitive markers do not involve neurological abnormalities; an example of structural problems are enlarged ventricles.
   d. If anything, schizophrenia is characterized by excessive dopamine activity.

6. a. Psychoanalysts call this woman schizophreno*genic;* the suffix *genic* means "causing."
   *b. The schizophrenogenic mother was thought by analysts to be cold and intrusive, rejecting and dominating. (p. 429)
   c. Antisocial personality in parents is not associated with a likelihood of schizophrenia.
   d. Psychoanalysts attribute castration anxieties to men, not to mothers.

7. a. High-risk population studies involve observations of people before the diagnosis is made.
   b. Recent research on expressed emotion has included control groups.
   *c. Early double-bind communication studies did not look for similar patterns in nonschizophrenic families or investigate whether the patterns were the result of having a schizophrenic child rather than the cause. (p. 430)
   d. Kraepelin did no twin research.

8. *a. In downward drift theory, the fact that schizophrenics cannot be gainfully employed is the explanation for the correlation between low social class and the disorder. (p. 431)
   b. Diathesis-stress theory states only that a combination of predisposition and environmental stress produces the disorder; it says nothing about social class.
   c. Schizophrenogenic theory stresses the role of a dominating and rejecting mother; it says nothing about social class.
   d. If Cindy believed that the stress of poverty causes the disorder, this would be the best answer.

9. a. The negative symptoms of schizophrenia are flat affect and passivity.
   b. Although, in rare cases, lip smacking may be a psychotic behavior, it is far more commonly seen in tardive dyskinesia.
   c. The symptoms of Parkinson's disease are a shuffling gait and flat affect; medication can produce only similar symptoms, not the disease itself.
   *d. These are the classic signs of tardive dyskinesia, which is most likely in elderly individuals who have taken neuroleptic medications for some years. (p. 437; Critical Thinking)

10. *a. Integrated Psychological Therapy (IPT) has four components: cognitive differentiation, social perception (including responding to social cues), verbal communication, and social skills. (p. 441)
   b. Milieu therapy is an inpatient treatment in which patients are given responsibility for decision making.
   c. Traditional institutional care involves medication and "warehousing" patients.
   d. Interventions to reduce expressed emotion focus on the communication patterns and problem-solving abilities of family members who must deal with a schizophrenic.

CHAPTER 15
Cognitive Disorders

LEARNING OBJECTIVES

1. Define cognitive disorders and discuss their possible causes. Compare the prevalence rate for different population groups. List the DSM-IV categories of cognitive disorders and differentiate these disorders from other disorders involving cognitive problems that are not part of the cognitive disorders group. (pp. 445–447)
2. Describe the methods for assessing brain damage and the problem of linking functional loss to a specific brain location. (pp. 447–450)
3. Describe the dimensions by which brain damage is categorized. (pp. 450; Table 15.1)
4. Describe how cognitive disorders are categorized by cause and the problems in diagnosing cognitive disorders. (pp. 450–451)
5. Describe and differentiate dementia and delirium and discuss the possible causes of these disorders. (pp. 451–454; Focus On)
6. Describe the amnestic disorders and differentiate them from dementia and delirium. (p. 454)
7. List and differentiate the types of head injuries, their symptoms and aftereffects. (pp. 455–456)
8. Describe the health conditions that accompany old age, including the nature and effects of strokes and multi-infarct dementia. (pp. 456–458)
9. Discuss the extent and reasons for memory loss in older people. Discuss the characteristics of Alzheimer's disease, brain abnormalities, and what is known about its cause. (pp. 458–461; Critical Thinking)
10. Describe and differentiate among the following: Parkinson's disease, AIDS-related dementia, neurosyphilis (general paresis), encephalitis, meningitis, Huntington's chorea, cerebral tumors, and epilepsy. (pp. 461–466)
11. Describe methods of treating cognitive disorders, including medication and cognitive and behavioral approaches. (pp. 466–468)
12. Discuss the need for environmental interventions and methods of supporting the caregivers of individuals with cognitive disorders. (p. 468)
13. Discuss the class of disorders known as mental retardation, including different forms of retardation, how mental retardation is diagnosed, the four levels of retardation, and the predisposing factors associated with mental retardation. (pp. 468–471)
14. Explain the causes of mental retardation, including how environmental factors and nongenetic biogenic factors may be involved. (pp. 472–475)
15. Describe and discuss early intervention and employment programs and living arrangements for people with mental retardation. (pp. 475–476)

CHAPTER OUTLINE

1. **Cognitive disorders and the assessment of brain damage** (pp. 445–449) *Cognitive disorders* are those that affect thinking, memory, consciousness, and perception and that are due to brain damage. These behavioral disturbances are affected by social and psychological factors such as coping ability and stress. DSM-IV differentiates delirium, dementia, amnestic disorders, and other cognitive disorders. Overall prevalence of cognitive disorders is about 1 percent, with people over seventy-five years old having twenty-two times the rate of such disorders as those between eighteen and thirty-four. There is no gender difference, but African Americans have higher rates of severe cognitive disorders than whites or Hispanic Americans.

   Brain damage can be assessed through neuropsychological testing and neurological tests. The first uses behavioral responses from the patient on memory or manual dexterity tasks. The second directly monitors the brain through *electroencephalography (EEG), computerized axial tomography (CAT) scans, positron emission tomography (PET),* and *magnetic resonance imaging (MRI).* Each has its strengths and weaknesses.

2. **Localization and the dimensions of brain damage** (pp. 449–450) Neurological techniques can locate brain damage; however, there is extensive overlapping of functions in the brain. Localization is also complicated by *diaschisis,* where lesions in one area disrupt other intact areas, and by recovery of function after damage. Recovery can occur because of redundancy or plasticity in the brain. Brain damage ranges from mild to severe, and can be distinguished as endogenous or exogenous, diffuse or specific, acute or chronic.

3. **Diagnostic problems** (pp. 450–451) People without brain damage can be misdiagnosed as having a cognitive disorder. This is particularly likely for those suffering from severe depression or schizophrenia. The elderly are also vulnerable to misdiagnosis. Many older persons who function well score in the brain-damaged range on neuropsychological tests. The opposite is also true: Those with brain damage are misdiagnosed as having a psychological disorder. For this reason, follow-up testing at regular intervals is often recommended.

4. **Types of cognitive disorders: Dementia, delirium, and amnestic disorders** (pp. 451–454; Focus On) Within each of the types of cognitive disorders, clinicians categorize according to their cause, such as psychoactive substance-induced or general medical condition. The most prominent features of *dementia* are memory impairment; language disturbance *(aphasia)* and impairments in motor activities *(apraxia)* and misidentification of faces or objects *(agnosia);* and poor planning. These impairments hinder social and occupational life. The onset of dementia is usually gradual and is often caused by general medical conditions (especially Alzheimer's disease), substance abuse, or combinations of the two.

   Delirium involves impairments in consciousness (disorientation, incoherent speech, perceptual distortions), and it usually develops rapidly. *Amnestic disorders* entail an inability to retain new information or recall old information, or both, and may be caused by thiamine deficiency. While the three conditions have overlapping symptoms, dementias are usually accompanied by language problems such as aphasia and come on gradually (as opposed to delirium). Memory loss is the primary symptom of amnestic disorders.

5. **Etiology of cognitive disorders: Brain trauma** (pp. 454–456) *Brain trauma*—a physical wound to the brain—is one cause of cognitive disorders. Head injuries include *concussions,* when blood vessels are damaged by a blow to the head; *contusions,* when blood vessels rupture because of the brain's impact against the skull; and *lacerations,* when tissue is torn or pierced by an object penetrating the skull. More than eight million Americans suffer head injuries each year, and 20 percent of these result in serious head trauma. Personality changes as well as cognitive and motor impairments are common. Only one-third of closed-head injury patients return to gainful employment after traditional rehabilitation. New treatments for head-injury survivors, including cognitive retraining and coping skill training, hold promise.

6. **Aging and disorders associated with aging** (pp. 456–458; Critical Thinking) The aging population of the United States is growing.

   Stroke, the third major cause of death in the United States, is a common cognitive disorder in the elderly. Strokes (*cerebrovascular accidents*) occur when blood flow to an area of the brain is cut off, causing the death of that tissue (infarction). Common effects of stroke include loss of language function (various forms of aphasia), paralysis, and death in 50 to 60 percent of cases. At least 25 percent of stroke victims develop major depression. Causes of stroke include bursting of blood vessels and narrowing or blockage of blood vessels owing to the buildup of fatty material on interior walls. A series of small strokes is known as *multi-infarct dementia*; it is characterized by uneven deterioration of intellectual abilities, including memory loss.

   Memory loss in the elderly may be due to brain cell deterioration, multi-infarct dementia, and the normal aging process. Another cause is intoxication from prescribed medication. To assess age-related cognitive deficits, the individual's performance can be compared with general population norms, age-group norms, norms based on similarity in status or education, and the person's previous functioning.

7. **Alzheimer's disease** (pp. 458–461) *Alzheimer's disease*, involving atrophy of cortical tissue, leads to memory loss, irritability, and withdrawal. Death usually occurs within five years; Alzheimer's is the fourth leading cause of death in the United States. The likelihood of developing Alzheimer's increases with age, affecting 5 to 10 percent of those over sixty-five but 20 percent of those over eighty. Autopsies show neurofibrillary tangles and senile plaques in the brains of people with the disease. Alzheimer's cause is unknown, but heredity may play a role in some subtypes; infection, head injury, exposure to aluminum, and reduced neurotransmitter levels may be related to others.

8. **Other diseases and infections of the brain** (pp. 461–464) *Parkinson's disease* has the following symptoms: muscle tremors; a stiff, shuffling gait; and an expressionless face. The disorder is associated with insufficient dopamine levels.

   The majority of AIDS patients also suffer from dementia. It is not clear whether the AIDS virus affects the brain, AIDS-related infections cause neuropsychological problems, or depression and anxiety about having AIDS cause cognitive symptoms.

   Neurosyphilis (*general paresis*) is brain damage caused by the delayed effect of a syphilis infection. It occurs in about 10 percent of syphilis cases. Symptoms include memory impairment, delusions, paralysis, and eventual death.

   Encephalitis (sleeping sickness) is a viral infection of the brain that produces long periods of sleep followed by agitation and seizures.

   Meningitis, an inflammation of the membrane around the brain, can be caused by bacteria, viruses, or fungi, and has a wide range of effects and potential residual disturbances.

   Huntington's chorea is a genetically transmitted disorder that first shows in early middle age. Symptoms begin with twitches and progress to uncontrollable jerking movements, irritability, and confusion. Death comes within thirteen to sixteen years after onset. A gene has been identified that causes the disorder. It is frequently misdiagnosed as schizophrenia.

9. **Cerebral tumors** (p. 464) A tumor is a mass of abnormal tissue. Fast-growing tumors in the brain produce severe mental symptoms such as diminished attention, drowsiness, dementia, and mood changes. Removal of tumors can result in dramatic improvement of functioning.

10. **Epilepsy** (pp. 464–466) *Epilepsy* is a symptom, not a disorder. It involves brief periods of altered consciousness, often accompanied by seizures. About 2.5 million children and adults in the United States have epilepsy or some other seizure disorder. The most common neurological problem, epilepsy is often diagnosed during childhood. Causes are genetic as well as environmental. Although epilepsy cannot be cured, it can be controlled with medication.

    Tonic-clonic seizures (*grand mal*) are most dramatic and include an aura (a signal before seizures), tonic-clonic convulsions, and a coma (exhaustion) after the seizures are over. Causes ranging from tumors to illness to stress can account for epilepsy. Heredity may not be a necessary condition for onset; no personality type is associated with epilepsy.

11. **Etiology of cognitive disorders: Psychoactive substances** (p. 466) Substances can cause cognitive disorders by having effects on the nervous system. The most common substances involved include alcohol, amphetamines, cocaine, hallucinogens, and opiates.

12. **Treatment considerations** (pp. 466–468) Treatment approaches include medical strategies such as surgery and medication, and psychological efforts such as skills training, cognitive preparation, and psychotherapy.

    How family and friends can assist those with cognitive disorders is an important issue. Some suggestions are preserving a sense of control, maintaining interpersonal contacts that do not overwhelm, engaging in pleasant diversions, providing tasks that increase self-worth, and ensuring that caregivers obtain social support for themselves.

13. **Mental retardation** (pp. 468–476) Mental retardation is not technically a DSM–IV cognitive disorder, although cognitive abilities are affected. Until recently, people with *mental retardation* were considered incapable of benefiting from schooling and were institutionalized. It is estimated that about 75 percent of people with mental retardation, if given appropriate training, can be completely self-supporting. About 7 million people in the United States have mental retardation based on IQ scores below 70 and deficiencies in adaptive behavior. IQ scores are particularly problematic with Hispanic and African Americans. While some argue that genetics explain lower IQ scores among African Americans, others point to the disadvantages African Americans face, cultural biases in the IQ tests, and psychological maladjustments such as low self-esteem. The DSM-IV uses levels of retardation based on Wechsler IQ scores to categorize mental retardation into four types: Mild (IQ 50–55 to 70); Moderate (IQ 35–40 to 50–55); Severe (IQ 20–25 to 35–40); and Profound (IQ 0 to 20–25). The American Association on Mental Retardation uses the individual's need for support as a way of subdividing retardation, but uses an IQ score cutoff of 75, not 70.

    Environmental factors such as poor nutrition and substandard school or home environments are associated with retardation. Genetics may account for the low end of intelligence where appearance and health are normal. Genetic abnormalities result in severe forms of retardation such as *Fragile X Syndrome* or *Down syndrome,* whose characteristics include short stature, slanted eyes, and protruding tongue. There is an association between increasing age of the mother and higher risk of having a Down syndrome baby. Down syndrome stems from having an extra chromosome (trisomy 21), something that can be identified during pregnancy through amniocentesis.

    Retardation can be caused by environmental mishaps before birth (prenatal), during birth (perinatal), or after birth (postnatal). Important prenatal causes are infections during pregnancy and *fetal alcohol syndrome,* which causes small body and brain size and may cause retardation and hyperactivity. Important perinatal factors are prematurity, low birth weight, and trauma. Postnatal causes, which seem to be on the rise, include head injury sustained in auto accidents or in child abuse.

    Programs such as Head Start have had positive long-term results. High-risk children in such programs show improved school performance compared to control children, and families are positively influenced as well. People with mental handicaps can achieve more than was once imagined. More and more people with mental retardation are living in the "least restrictive environment." Nontraditional group living arrangements can be helpful if they teach living skills.

KEY TERMS REVIEW

1. A sudden stoppage of blood flow to a portion of the brain that leads to a loss of brain function is called a(n) ____________________ or ____________________.

2. The syndrome characterized by a continuous decline in intellectual ability and judgment and that often includes language problems and has a gradual onset is called ____________________.

3. Disorders involving impairments of thinking, memory, perception, or consciousness caused by brain damage are called ________________.

4. The progressively worsening cognitive disorder characterized by muscle tremors, stiff and shuffling gait, lack of facial expression, and social withdrawal is called ________________.

5. The cognitive disorder in which there is reduced ability to attend to stimuli, difficulty in shifting attention, and disorganized thinking, and which usually has a sudden onset, is called ________________.

6. The cognitive disorder that involves atrophy of the brain and leads to marked deterioration in memory and emotional functioning is called ________________.

7. Any disorder that is characterized by intermittent and brief periods of altered consciousness and is often accompanied by seizures is called ________________.

8. The death of brain tissue resulting from a decrease in blood supply to that tissue is called a(n) ________________.

9. A physical wound or injury to the brain is called a(n) ________________.

10. Cognitive disorders in which the primary symptom is an inability to learn new information or a failure to retain old information are called ________________.

11. The cognitive disorder characterized by uneven deterioration of intellectual abilities (dementia) that results from a number of cerebral infarctions is called ________________.

12. A neurological test that uses x-rays and computer technology to assess brain damage is called ________________.

13. A neurological test for the assessment of brain damage that measures the electrical activity of the brain is called a(n) ________________.

14. The technique that uses radio waves and a magnetic field to produce an image of the brain and to assess brain functioning is called ________________.

15. The technique for assessing brain damage that involves the injection of radioactive glucose and the monitoring of glucose metabolism is called ________________.

16. A process in which a lesion in a specific area of the brain disrupts other intact areas is called ________________.

17. The procedure in which fluid is taken from a pregnant woman's fetal sac is called ________________.

18. A group of congenital physical and mental defects related to a pregnant woman's consumption of alcohol is ________________.

19. A condition in which mental retardation and other birth defects is caused by an extra chromosome (trisomy 21) is ________________.

20. A disorder in which there is significant subaverage general intellectual functioning before the age of 18 and deficits in adaptive behavior, is ________________.

21. A cognitive disorder caused by viral infection that produces symptoms of lethargy, fever, delirium, and long periods of stupor and sleep is ____________________.

22. A rare degenerative disease characterized by involuntary twitching movements and eventual dementia is ____________________.

23. A medical condition in which there is inflammation of the membrane that surrounds the brain and spinal cord is ____________________.

24. A procedure used to assess brain damage in which radioactive gas is inhaled and then a gamma ray camera tracks the gas, and thus flow of blood through the brain, is ____________________.

25. A mass of abnormal tissue growing in the brain is a ____________________.

FACTUAL MULTIPLE–CHOICE QUESTIONS

1. A person showing behavioral disturbances that are caused by brain damage is considered to have a ____________________ disorder.
   a. cognitive
   b. general medical
   c. delirium
   d. psychotic

2. Treatment for cognitive disorders
   a. is always medical, never psychological.
   b. is always psychological, never medical.
   c. is often a combination of medical and psychological.
   d. is never psychological if the brain damage is irreversible.

3. When brain damage leads to permanent and irreversible loss of function, the disorder is considered
   a. chronic.
   b. diffuse.
   c. acute.
   d. endogenous.

4. Dementia is characterized by
   a. the inability to either comprehend or produce speech.
   b. fever, disorganized thinking, and an inability to concentrate on a particular stimulus.
   c. rapid onset and rapid recovery.
   d. slow-onset impairment of memory and judgment that interferes with functioning.

5. Difficulty in forming words and an inability to retain their meanings are central problems in
   a. aphasia.
   b. delirium.
   c. Parkinson's disease.
   d. strokes that affect the right side of the brain.

6. Young adults who survive severe head injuries typically
   a. make full recoveries.
   b. completely recover their mental functioning, but continue to have emotional disturbances.
   c. have continuing mental and emotional disturbances that make return to full employment unlikely.
   d. have continuing physical problems, but rarely emotional disturbances.

7. This organic mental disorder represents the third major cause of death in the United States. It can occur when blood vessels burst or when blocked blood flow causes brain tissue to die. What is this disorder?
   a. Aphasia
   b. Stroke (cerebrovascular accident)
   c. Senile dementia
   d. Alzheimer's disease

8. Which statement about Alzheimer's disease is *accurate*?
   a. Alzheimer's is usually caused by people taking too many prescription medications.
   b. Memory loss is the last symptom to appear in the disorder.
   c. Although a disabling disorder, Alzheimer's does not lead to early death.
   d. Alzheimer's accounts for almost 80 percent of dementia in older persons.

9. Which of the following is associated with Parkinson's disease?
   a. Stiff, shuffling walk
   b. Onset in adolescence
   c. Atrophy of large portions of the brain as a result of aging
   d. Excessive emotionality

10. Which statement concerning epilepsy is *accurate*?
   a. It is the third leading cause of death in the United States.
   b. It is most frequently diagnosed during childhood.
   c. It can be caused only by a genetic defect.
   d. It is an organic mental disorder that affects the limbic system.

CONCEPTUAL MULTIPLE–CHOICE QUESTIONS

1. Neuropsychological testing relies on
   a. electroencephalographs.
   b. CAT scans.
   c. radioactive chemicals.
   d. assessments of cognitive and behavioral functioning, such as memory and manual dexterity.

2. Plasticity is one explanation of why it is difficult to identify specific areas of the brain and their function. *Plasticity* refers to the fact that
   a. undeveloped portions of the brain can take up the functions of damaged portions.
   b. lesions in one area of the brain can disrupt function in distant, undamaged areas.
   c. no two brains are identical.
   d. one hemisphere of the brain controls behavior on the opposite side of the body.

3. Why is it important to know that dementia can be caused by factors other than aging?
   a. Because it makes psychotherapy unnecessary
   b. Because other causative problems can be corrected
   c. Because nearly 50 percent of the elderly are demented
   d. Because it used to be thought of as a functional disorder

4. When the primary symptoms are an inability to learn new information or recall past events and the probable cause is a thiamine deficiency, the diagnosis should be
   a. delirium caused by substance use.
   b. amnestic disorder.
   c. dementia caused by nutrition deficit.
   d. aphasia.

5. When portions of the brain are torn or pierced, survivors may have very serious symptoms, including intellectual impairment and personality changes. The cause is a
   a. concussion.
   b. form of epilepsy.
   c. brain laceration.
   d. cerebral tumor.

6. What one symptom is found in Alzheimer's disease, senile dementia, and multi-infarct dementia?
   a. Brain trauma
   b. Brief periods of unconsciousness
   c. Restlessness and irritability followed by excessive sleep
   d. Memory loss

7. What do encephalitis, meningitis, and neurosyphilis have in common?
   a. They are all associated with aging.
   b. They are all caused by viral or bacterial infections.
   c. They are all incurable and caused by genetic factors.
   d. They are all effectively treated with the neurotransmitter L-dopa.

8. Which of the following has occurred in the field of mental retardation in the past twenty-five years?
   a. The number of people with mental retardation who reside in public institutions has increased.
   b. There has been increased contact between people with mental retardation and the general population.
   c. Forms of mental retardation that were once believed to be treatable are now known to be hopeless.
   d. Research has shown that there is only one cause of mental retardation.

9. Based on DSM-IV criteria, a diagnosis of mental retardation requires
   a. IQ below 70, deficiencies in adaptive behavior, and onset before age eighteen.
   b. IQ below 50, inability to speak, and signs that the cause is biological.
   c. IQ below 100, inability to succeed in a school environment, and low self-esteem.
   d. IQ below 70, deficiencies in adaptive behavior, and onset after age eighteen.

10. Family and friends who are caregivers for people with irreversible cognitive disorders are advised to
    a. prevent the patient from taking on tasks unless they can be completed perfectly.
    b. prevent the patient from making personal decisions.
    c. maintain social contacts that are brief and without pressure.
    d. keep their anxieties and concerns private, and refrain from using outside help.

APPLICATION MULTIPLE–CHOICE QUESTIONS

1. Based on epidemiological research, which person has the highest likelihood of having a severe form of cognitive disorder?
   a. A white male teenager
   b. An African American woman who is seventy-six years old
   c. A middle-aged Hispanic American man
   d. An African American male who is twenty-six years old

2. Dr. Elsberg says, "My patient has experienced specific brain damage in the frontal and parietal lobes of the right hemisphere. We can expect that she will experience motor impairments and, if the injury is of an acute nature, there is a chance the damage is reversible." What is *inaccurate* about Dr. Elsberg's statement?
   a. It is inaccurate to say that right frontal damage leads to motor impairment.
   b. It is inaccurate to say that right parietal damage leads to motor impairment.
   c. It is inaccurate to say that acute injuries are reversible.
   d. Nothing Dr. Elsberg said is inaccurate.

3. John was not wearing his seat belt, and his head struck the windshield when he was in a car accident. He was dazed and had a headache for several days after the accident, but soon he recovered completely. John's problem would most likely be diagnosed as a
   a. cerebrovascular accident.
   b. cerebral infarction.
   c. laceration.
   d. concussion.

4. Mrs. Lee is a seventy-year-old woman whose children brought her to the doctor because she suddenly lost the ability to speak, was confused and had memory loss, and could not move the right side of her body. The doctors disagreed over Mrs. Lee's diagnosis. Dr. Chin believes that Mrs. Lee has a somatoform disorder, but Dr. Lau thinks that Mrs. Lee has a cognitive disorder. You are called in to give an opinion. What would you say?
   a. Agree with Dr. Chin that Mrs. Lee has a somatoform disorder, most probably conversion disorder.
   b. Agree with Dr. Lau that Mrs. Lee has a cognitive disorder.
   c. Disagree with both Drs. Lau and Chin, because Mrs. Lee shows signs of a dissociative disorder, most likely dissociative amnesia.
   d. Disagree with both Drs. Lau and Chin, because Mrs. Lee is showing signs of Korsakoff's syndrome.

5. An autopsy was done after George died. His memory problems were discovered to be the result of severe cortical atrophy; and, at a microscopic level, neurofibrillary tangles and senile plaques were discovered. These findings indicate that George suffered from
   a. Alzheimer's disease.
   b. multi-infarct dementia.
   c. Huntington's chorea.
   d. a stroke.

6. Larry has AIDS. He has trouble remembering where he has put things, and occasionally is frightened when he cannot concentrate or keep track of simple conversations. Larry's behavior illustrates
   a. early signs of delirium, a rare symptom in AIDS.
   b. Parkinson's disease, a common result of AIDS.
   c. dementia, a common symptom of AIDS.
   d. multi-infarct dementia, a rare symptom in AIDS.

7. Roger shows increasing muscle tremors, a shuffling walk, and an expressionless face. He also has delusions that people are poisoning him, and he is frequently depressed. Which of Roger's symptoms are *uncommon* in cases of Parkinson's disease?
   a. The delusions of persecution
   b. The expressionless face
   c. The muscle tremors
   d. The shuffling walk

8. A doctor says, "It is caused by bacterial, viral, or sometimes fungal infectious agents that attack and inflame the membrane surrounding the brain and spinal cord." What is the doctor describing?
   a. Neurosyphilis (general paresis)
   b. Meningitis
   c. Cerebral tumor
   d. Cerebrovascular accident (stroke)

9. Greg says, "There are more than seven million people in the United States with mental retardation. They have IQs less than 80, and most are able to support themselves. That is why there has been a big drop in the number of such people in public institutions." What part of Greg's statement is *incorrect*?
   a. It is inaccurate to say that there are more than seven million people with retardation.
   b. It is inaccurate to say that retardation involves IQs under 80.
   c. It is inaccurate to say that people with retardation can be self-supporting.
   d. It is inaccurate to say that there has been a drop in the number of people with retardation in public institutions.

10. A United States public health official is asked, "What is the predisposing factor most often involved with mental retardation?" Her answer should be:
   a. "In the largest percentage of cases we cannot clearly identify the cause."
   b. "Two causes account for most cases: head injury and lead poisoning."
   c. "Malnutrition and infections are the causes in the largest percentage of cases."
   d. "Psychological disorders such as depression and ADHD are the main reasons."

ANSWER KEY: KEY TERMS REVIEW

1. cerebrovascular accident; stroke (456)
2. dementia (452)
3. cognitive disorders (445)
4. Parkinson's disease (461)
5. delirium (453)
6. Alzheimer's disease (458)
7. epilepsy (464)
8. cerebral infarction (457)
9. brain trauma (455)
10. amnestic disorders (454)
11. multi-infarct dementia (458)
12. computerized axial tomography (CAT) scan (447)
13. electroencephalograph (EEG) (447)
14. magnetic resonance imaging (MRI) (448)
15. positron emission tomography (PET) scan (448)
16. diaschisis (450)
17. amniocentesis (474)
18. fetal alcohol syndrome (FAS) (475)
19. Down syndrome (472)
20. mental retardation (470)
21. encephalitis (462)
22. Huntington's chorea (463)
23. meningitis (463)
24. cerebral blood flow measurement (447)
25. cerebral tumor (464)

ANSWER KEY: FACTUAL MULTIPLE–CHOICE QUESTIONS

1. *a. Cognitive disorders are ones that are caused by either temporary or permanent brain damage and that affect memory, behavior, and affect in a way that significantly impairs functioning. (p. 445)
   b. General medical conditions do not necessarily affect thinking or other psychological functions.
   c. Delirium is a form of cognitive disorder in which symptoms involving disorientation, disruptions of the sleep-wake cycle, and other effects have a rapid onset.
   d. Psychotic disorders are ones in which delusions, hallucinations, and other breaks with reality are common symptoms; they do not need to involve brain damage.

2. a. Social skills training and other psychological treatments are useful in the treatment of many cognitive disorders.
   b. Such medical procedures as surgery and medication can be very effective in treating many cognitive disorders.
   *c. Medical treatments are often helpful for controlling symptoms; psychological treatments can help patients master their emotions and relearn functional behaviors. (p. 447)
   d. When brain damage is irreversible, social skills and other rehabilitative treatments that are psychological are often the only treatments available.

3. *a. *Chronic* means a continuing problem. (p. 450)
   b. *Diffuse* means that damage occurs in a broad region of the brain.
   c. *Acute* is the opposite of chronic; it means temporary.
   d. *Endogenous* means that damage is caused from within.

4. a. An inability to comprehend or produce speech is a definition of aphasia.
   b. Disorganized thinking and lack of concentration are characteristics of delirium.
   c. Rapid onset and recovery are characteristics of delirium.
   *d. Dementia is a cognitive deterioration in memory and judgment that makes living difficult; it usually has a gradual onset. (p. 442)

5. *a. Aphasia involves the loss of the ability to speak or to comprehend speech. (p. 453; Focus On)
   b. Delirium occurs when thinking is disorganized and attention and concentration cannot be maintained.
   c. Parkinson's disease affects motor control, not language.
   d. Strokes that affect the right hemisphere are less likely to produce language impairment (aphasia) than those that affect the left.

6. a. Full recoveries from severe head injury are fairly rare.
   b. Continuing problems of memory loss, inattention, and speech are common in severe head injury.
   *c. In the majority of cases, recovery includes a combination of problems that make gainful employment quite difficult. (p. 456)
   d. Those who recover from severe head injury often show irritability and depression, although they are unaware of it.

7. a. Aphasia is impairment of language comprehension or production; it is a symptom, not a disorder.
   *b. Stroke is the third major cause of death (400,000 or more cases annually) and is defined as tissue death (infarction) caused by insufficient blood flow. (p. 456)
   c. Senile dementia is caused by the aging process.
   d. Alzheimer's disease is caused by a general atrophy of brain tissue and is unrelated to a sudden shutoff of blood.

8. a. Excessive medication is a reason for misdiagnosing cognitive disorders, but Alzheimer's is not caused by medication.
   b. Memory loss is the first symptom to appear.
   c. Alzheimer's involves a prolonged deterioration that leads to death in an average of five years.
   *d. Alzheimer's accounts for about 80 percent of older people with dementias. (p. 458)

9. *a. Together with muscle tremors and an expressionless face, a stiff, shuffling gait is a fundamental sign of Parkinson's disease. (p. 461)
   b. Parkinson's disease rarely develops until a person is in his or her forties or fifties.
   c. Atrophy of large brain areas as a result of aging is associated with senile dementia.
   d. Lack of emotional expression is a symptom of Parkinson's disease.

10. a. The third leading cause of death is stroke.
    *b. Epilepsy is usually diagnosed early in life. (p. 465)
    c. Although there may be a genetic component in the cause of epilepsy, environmental factors such as drug use and head injury can cause the disorder as well.
    d. Epilepsy is not a disorder, but a symptom that involves uncontrolled electrical activity in many portions of the brain.

ANSWER KEY: CONCEPTUAL MULTIPLE-CHOICE QUESTIONS

1. a. Electroencephalographs record brain activity and are neurological tests.
   b. CAT scans are computer-composite pictures of the brain using x-rays; they are neurological tests.
   c. Radioactive chemicals are used in blood flow and positron emission tomography, both of which are neurological tests.
   *d. Neuropsychological tests such as the Halstead-Reitan use measurements of memory, cognitive flexibility, and manual dexterity to determine organic damage. (p. 447)

2. *a. Plasticity is the brain's ability to use undeveloped portions as substitutes for damaged areas; children born without an entire hemisphere can have the remaining hemisphere perform functions usually found in the missing one. (p. 450)
   b. When damage in one portion of the brain disrupts functioning in other, intact portions, the phenomenon is called diaschisis.
   c. While it is true that no two brains are the same, this is unrelated to plasticity.
   d. That one hemisphere controls specific functions underscores structure-function specificity, the opposite of plasticity.

3. a. Dementia and most of the other organic mental syndromes produce emotional problems that can be helped through psychotherapy.
   *b. Not much can be done to treat aging, but brain tumors, for example, can be surgically removed. (p. 452)
   c. Probably less than 15 percent of the elderly are demented.
   d. Dementia has always been seen as an organic symptom.

4. a. Delirium involves disorganized thinking rather than failure to learn or recall; it is not associated with a thiamine deficiency.
   *b. Amnestic cognitive disorder involves memory and learning problems and little else; Wernicke's encephalopathy, which is probably caused by thiamine deficiency, is the most common form of amnestic disorder. (p. 454)
   c. Dementia is not caused by nutrition deficit: the leading causes are Alzheimer's disease, stroke, and hydrocephalus. Dementias have other symptoms besides amnesia—delusions, hallucinations, and speech problems.
   d. Aphasias are speech impairments involving either the comprehension or expression of words and their meanings.

5. a. Aphasia is impairment of language comprehension or production.
   b. Epilepsy involves uncontrolled electrical activity in the brain.
   *c. A laceration is defined as a cut or tear caused by an external object, such as a bullet. (p. 455)
   d. Tumors are abnormal masses of tissue.

6. a. Brain traumas are sudden-onset causes and rarely produce dementias.
   b. Brief periods of unconsciousness are characteristics of petit mal epilepsy and concussions, not dementias.
   c. Restlessness and irritability followed by excessive sleep are prominent symptoms in encephalitis, not dementias.
   *d. All three are forms of dementia, and the chief symptom of dementia is memory loss. (p. 458)

7. a. The disorders associated with aging are stroke, Alzheimer's disease, and senile dementia.
   *b. All three are caused by infectious agents that produce damage to the brain or its surrounding membranes. (pp. 462–463)
   c. None of these disorders has a genetic link.
   d. Parkinson's disease is treated with L-dopa, since that disorder is associated with reduced amounts of dopamine.

8. a. Fewer and fewer people with mental retardation are in institutions.
   *b. Between 1967 and 1984, the number of institutionalized people with mental retardation was reduced by one-half; it is now understood that mentally retarded people should have opportunities to live and work in integrated settings. (p. 496)
   c. The reverse is true: There is greater hope for people once thought to be untreatable.
   d. There are many causes for mental retardation, from poverty to genetic abnormalities to head injury.

9. *a. These are the three criteria for diagnosing mental retardation, according to DSM-IV. (p. 496)
   b. Most people with mental retardation have IQs between 50 and 70, can speak, and experienced causes that are environmental.
   c. IQ must be below 70.
   d. DSM-IV requires onset before age eighteen; poor intellectual functioning that begins after eighteen is considered a dementia.

10. a. If tasks must be performed to perfection, patients with cognitive disorders lose confidence and give up trying.
    b. Allowing patients to have control in their lives increases their cognitive functioning and prolongs the quality of their lives.
    *c. Social contacts that are brief and do not overwhelm the patient counteract the social withdrawal that often occurs in cognitive disorders. (p. 468)
    d. Caregivers can become overwhelmed, emotionally drained, and physically ill; they need to vent their emotions and make use of such resources as self-help groups.

ANSWER KEY: APPLICATION MULTIPLE–CHOICE QUESTIONS

1. a. Teenagers and people up to the age of thirty-four have twenty-two times less likelihood of having a cognitive disorder as a person over seventy-five.
   *b. The likelihood is much greater for cognitive disorder among those over seventy-five, and African Americans have a higher rate of severe disorders than whites or Hispanic Americans; there is no gender difference. (pp. 446–447)
   c. Hispanic Americans have no greater likelihood of cognitive disorders than whites and a lower rate of severe disorders than African Americans; the older population has the highest prevalence of cognitive disorders.
   d. Although African Americans have a higher rate of severe cognitive disorders than whites or Hispanic Americans, twenty-six is too young to be at high risk.

2. a. Brain damage that is specific and in the right frontal area is associated with motor impairments.
   b. Brain damage that is specific and in the right parietal area is associated with motor impairments.
   c. The definition of *acute* is a nonpermanent condition; although recovery from central nervous system damage is difficult, acute conditions are relatively temporary.
   *d. Since right frontal and right parietal damage that is specific to those areas is associated with motor impairment (in fact, damage to any right hemisphere lobe is associated with motor problems), and acute disorders are ones that are temporary, nothing the doctor said is inaccurate. (p. 450; Table 15.1)

3. a. A cerebrovascular accident (stroke) is caused by internal problems such as atherosclerosis, not external ones like a car accident.
   b. A cerebral infarction occurs when tissue dies because, for example, the blood supply for that area was cut off.
   c. Such minor problems and rapid recovery would not be likely in a laceration, in which areas of the brain are cut or ripped.
   *d. A concussion causes relatively minor problems and usually leads to a full recovery. (p. 455)

4. a. Her age and the rapid onset would suggest that Mrs. Lee may have a vascular disease and has perhaps suffered a stroke.
   *b. Agree with Dr. Lau that Mrs. Lee has a cognitive disorder. (p. 445)
   c. Dissociative amnesia would not cause paralysis. The symptoms suggest a real physical problem.
   d. No mention is made of alcohol use by Mrs. Lee.

5. *a. Alzheimer's disease causes memory loss and is diagnosed at autopsy by atrophy of the cerebral cortex and the presence of neurofibrillary tangles (abnormal fibers that are tangles of brain filaments) and senile plaques (patches of degenerated nerve endings). (p. 460)
   b. Multi-infarct dementia is associated with a series of small strokes, not cerebral atrophy.
   c. Huntington's chorea is a genetically caused degenerative disorder but is unassociated with tangles or plaques.
   d. A stroke involves the death of tissue owing to blood and oxygen deficit, not cortical atrophy, tangles, or plaques.

6. a. Memory loss is associated with dementia, not delirium.
   b. Parkinson's disease cannot be acquired from AIDS and does not involve memory loss.
   *c. Memory loss is a key symptom of dementia, a problem that occurs frequently in people with AIDS. (p. 461)
   d. Multi-infarct dementia is caused by a series of small strokes, not by AIDS.

7. *a. Delusions of persecution are more commonly found in Alzheimer's disease or Huntington's chorea than in Parkinson's disease. (p. 461)
   b. An expressionless face is a symptom of Parkinson's disease.
   c. Muscle tremors are a fundamental symptom of Parkinson's disease.
   d. A stiff, shuffling walk is a central feature of Parkinson's disease.

8. a. Neurosyphilis is caused by an infection, but damage is done to the cerebral cortex, not the membrane around the brain.
   *b. Meningitis is an infection of the meninges (membrane around the brain and spinal cord) that can be caused by viruses, bacteria, or sometimes fungi. (p. 463)
   c. Cerebral tumors are abnormal masses that are not due to infections.
   d. Cerebrovascular accidents (strokes) occur when brain tissue dies because of a blood vessel rupturing or because of a blockage in blood flow through a blood vessel.

9. a. Approximately seven million people in the United States have IQs under 70 and are potentially retarded.
   *b. IQ must be below 70 for a person to be considered to have mental retardation; adaptive deficiencies and onset before eighteen are also required. (p. 470)
   c. Most people with mild mental retardation (the majority of those diagnosed with retardation) can be self-supporting.
   d. There has been a dramatic decline in the number of people with mental retardation who reside in institutions.

10. *a. According to DSM-IV, in 30 to 40 percent of cases, there is no clear causal factor, so "we don't know" is the best answer to the question. (p. 473)
   b. Head trauma and lead poisoning are associated with about 5 percent of cases.
   c. Malnutrition and infections are associated with less than 10 percent of cases.
   d. There is no association between depression and ADHD and mental retardation.

CHAPTER 16
Disorders of Childhood and Adolescence

LEARNING OBJECTIVES

1. Describe the characteristics of pervasive developmental disorders and identify the prevalence of behavior problems in children and adolescents. (pp. 480–481)
2. Indicate the prevalence of autistic disorder and describe the main impairments it entails. Describe diagnostic difficulties and research findings related to autism. Discuss the relation autistic disorder has to retardation and splinter skills. (pp. 481–484)
3. Differentiate between autism and Rett's disorder, childhood disintegrative disorder, Asperger's disorder, and pervasive developmental disorder not otherwise specified. (p. 484)
4. Discuss the etiology of autistic disorder, including psychodynamic, family, genetic, central nervous system impairment, and biochemical theories. (pp. 485–487)
5. Describe the prognosis and treatment for children with pervasive developmental disorders. Discuss drug therapy and behavior modification for these children. (pp. 487–488)
6. Discuss the problems with the diagnosis and classification of other developmental disorders. (pp. 488–489)
7. Describe the symptoms, prevalence, course, and etiology of the following: learning disorders, expressive language disorder, phonetic disorder, and stuttering. (p. 490)
8. Describe the symptoms, etiology, and treatment of the attention deficit/hyperactive disorders. Discuss the difficulty involved in making an ADHD diagnosis accurately. (pp. 489–495; Focus On).
9. Define and differentiate oppositional defiant disorder and conduct disorder and discuss the prevalence, etiology, and treatment of conduct disorders. (pp. 494–498)
10. Contrast the anxiety-related disorders of childhood, including separation anxiety disorder and school phobia. Discuss how they can be treated. (pp. 498–500; Focus On)
11. Describe the prevalence, symptoms, and treatment of childhood depression. (pp. 500–501)
12. Describe the symptoms, etiology, and treatment of chronic and transient tic disorders, including Tourette's syndrome. (pp. 501–504)
13. Discuss the various elimination disorders, including enuresis and encopresis. (pp. 504–505)
14. Describe the prevalence, symptoms, and subtypes of anorexia nervosa. Compare and contrast the symptoms of anorexia nervosa, bulimia nervosa, and binge eating disorder. (pp. 505–509)
15. Discuss the etiology of eating disorders. Evaluate the degree to which society creates eating disorders. Compare the attitudes toward weight of white and African-American females. Describe the treatment of eating disorders. (pp. 509–514; Critical Thinking)

CHAPTER OUTLINE

1. **Disorders of childhood and adolescence and mental retardation** (p. 480) About 20 percent of children and 40 percent of adolescents in the United States have a serious behavioral or emotional problem, costing more than $1.5 billion in treatment annually. Less than half of these children and adolescents receive treatment.

2. **Pervasive developmental disorders** (pp. 480–488) *Pervasive developmental disorders* are severe disturbances affecting language, social relations, and emotions, distortions that would be abnormal at any developmental stage. Prevalence of autistic disorder is about four to seven cases per 10,000 children; the other three pervasive developmental disorders occur at a rate of about twenty-two in 10,000.

   Autistic disorder was first described by Leo Kanner in 1943 and is characterized by an unusual lack of interest in others as well as by communication problems and bizarre, repetitive movements. Autistic children interact with others as though people were unimportant objects. Half do not speak; the other half often show *echolalia*—echoing whatever was just said—or pronoun reversal (where "you" is said instead of "I"). Most autistic children are mentally retarded, although *splinter skills* (special abilities) are found, most dramatically in *autistic savants*. Misdiagnosis as mental retardation only or as a different disorder or condition is common. Research shows that autistic children are less able than matched children to identify human characteristics. They seem not to have a theory of mind; they are unable to appreciate that others think.

   A new set of pervasive developmental disorders that do not meet the criteria for autistic disorders are *pervasive developmental disorder not otherwise specified, Rett's disorder, childhood disintegrative disorder*, and *Asperger's disorder*. Because they are new, little research on the causes of them is available.

   One early theory about the cause of autistic disorder was a psychodynamic view that parent-child interactions produce withdrawal. Current knowledge gives no justification for this idea. Most research points to a biological cause: Studies show high concordance ratios for MZ twins (36 percent), central nervous system impairment, and elevated serotonin and dopamine levels. The prognosis for children with pervasive developmental disorders is mixed. Those with severe retardation have worse outcomes, and those with greater verbal skills have more favorable outcomes. Treatment has involved intensive behavior modification, which has been effective in eliminating echolalia and self-stimulation while increasing verbal and social behaviors. Medications such as haloperidol and fenfluramine have produced mixed results.

3. **Other developmental disorders** (pp. 488–489) The definition of less severe childhood disorders often depends on the tolerance of the referring agent. Developmental problems are reported in normal as well as clinical populations. Cultural norms also influence what behaviors are considered problems. Diagnosis using the DSM-IV involves counting symptoms, but judgment is necessary in deciding if symptoms such as "often easily distracted" exist. Some disorders that focus on impairments are learning disorders, expressive language disorder, phonetic disorder, stuttering, encopresis, and enuresis.

4. **Attention deficit/hyperactive disorders and disruptive behavior disorders** (pp. 489–498) *Attention deficit/hyperactive disorder (ADHD)* is characterized by attention problems and may involve heightened motor activity. There are three types: predominantly hyperactive-impulsive, predominantly inattentive, and combined (showing both hyperactivity and inattentiveness). ADHD is a relatively common disorder, far more common in boys than in girls. In some cases, ADHD children continue to have antisocial or psychiatric problems as adults; those with attention problems but not hyperactivity have better outcomes. Research on specific brain impairments causing ADHD has produced conflicting findings. Food additives and sugar are not significant factors. Family variables seem related to ADHD, but it is not clear whether genetics or environment are at work.

Children with ADHD are typically treated with stimulant medication, but there is considerable controversy about the overmedication of children and the poorly supervised prescription of drugs. Self-instructional procedures, modeling, and parent training programs have been as effective as drug therapy.

Oppositional defiant disorder is characterized by negativistic and hostile behavior, but without serious violations of others' rights. DSM-IV criteria include "significant impairment in social and academic functioning," a raising of the threshold for diagnosis.

Conduct disorder involves a persistent pattern of antisocial behavior in which others' rights are violated. It is relatively common, particularly in boys, and can be subtyped according to age of onset (prior to age ten and after age ten). Oppositional defiant disorder often precedes conduct disorder and is coexistent with ADHD. Violence is quite likely among these children. Prognosis is poor, particularly if there is sexual aggression. Theories of cause include psychodynamic ideas concerning underlying anxiety, genetic factors, and inadequate parental behavior. Cognitive behavioral treatment that combines social skills and parent management training holds the most promise for treating conduct disorder.

5. **Anxiety disorders** (pp. 498–500) *Separation anxiety disorder* is marked by excessive anxiety when the child is separated from parents or home. Somatic symptoms are prominent. This and other childhood anxiety disorders are probably caused by an interaction between the child's temperament (very early personality style) and the home environment that parents establish. School phobia is one result of such anxiety, but that may be a separate syndrome. The causes of separation anxiety disorder may include overdependence on the mother (psychodynamic) and parental reinforcement of avoidance fears (learning). Prognosis is better when separation anxiety disorder is treated in childhood rather than in adolescence.

6. **Childhood depression** (pp. 500–501) Childhood depression is not listed under childhood disorders in the DSM-IV, but depression can occur in children as early as infancy. Prevalence of childhood depression ranges from 2 percent to 7 percent among children and adolescents. Depression in adolescence is common, particularly among girls. The symptoms are much the same as in adults; treatment requires support and cognitive and social skill training.

7. **Tic disorders** (pp. 501–504) *Tics* are involuntary, repetitive movements or vocalizations. Many children have a single, transient tic such as eye blinking. Others have one or multiple tics for a year or longer—chronic tic disorder. *Tourette's syndrome* is a puzzling disorder in which childhood tics evolve into grunting and barking, and finally *coprolalia* (the compulsion to shout obscenities). Stress appears to be a factor in causing these disorders, although multiple tics and Tourette's syndrome appear to be transmitted in families, and may be related to obsessive-compulsive disorder or ADHD. Treatment can involve haloperidol, which acts on dopamine receptors.

8. **Elimination disorders** (pp. 504–505) Enuresis (voluntary or involuntary bedwetting in inappropriate places) and encopresis (voluntary or involuntary defecation in inappropriate places) may have biological and psychological origins. Treatment may include medication and behavior modification procedures.

9. **Eating disorders** (pp. 505–514) Eating problems are becoming more prevalent among young people in the United States. In *anorexia nervosa*, a disorder found almost exclusively in women, fear of weight gain leads to self-starvation or eating and purging, with such consequences as low blood pressure and heart disease. The mortality rate is about 10 percent. About 75 percent show a distorted body image. The criteria for *bulimia nervosa* include eating large quantities of high-caloric foods at least twice weekly for three months, feeling a loss of control over eating, and following eating with self-induced vomiting, purging, or fasting. Much more prevalent than anorexia, bulimia is unrelated to an individual's weight. Binges tend to be related to negative emotions. Although *binge eating disorder* is similar to bulimia nervosa, the binge eating is not followed by vomiting, excessive exercise, or fasting.

The social desirability of thinness in women in western culture plays a major role in causing eating disorders. Such disorders are rare in Asia. African Americans also seem able to ignore the white media messages equating thinness with beauty. African-American women are more likely than white American women to be satisfied with their body shape and to feel that beauty stems from personality rather than thinness. White women in their twenties have especially high standards of thinness. In addition, those with these disorders tend to suffer from poor self-esteem, depression, and perceived lack of control. Initial treatment for anorexia focuses on weight gain (by feeding tube, contingent reinforcement for weight gain, or both). Cognitive-behavioral and family therapy sessions are common after weight gain, but relapse and continued obsession with weight are common. Bulimia has been successfully treated with psychotherapy, cognitive-behavioral treatment, and antidepressant medications.

KEY TERMS REVIEW

1. Disorders of childhood and adolescence that involve persistent patterns of antisocial behavior that violate the rights of others are called ____________________.

2. Repetitive, involuntary movements or vocalizations are called ____________________.

3. An eating disorder in which the person is intensely fearful of becoming obese and engages in either self-starvation or purging after eating is called ____________________.

4. A childhood disorder characterized by excessive anxiety concerning separation from parents and home is called ____________________.

5. A childhood disorder characterized by multiple motor and verbal tics that develop into a compulsion to shout obscenities is called ____________________.

6. A severe childhood disorder characterized by early onset, an extreme lack of interest in interpersonal relationships, and impairment in verbal and nonverbal communication is called ____________________.

7. An eating disorder characterized by the consumption of large quantities of food, usually followed by self-induced vomiting, is called ____________________.

8. A disorder of childhood and adolescence characterized by short attention span, impulsiveness, constant activity, and lack of self-control is called ____________________.

9. Severe disorders of childhood that affect language, social relationships, attention, and affect, and that include autistic disorder, are called ____________________.

10. A childhood disorder characterized by negativistic, argumentative, and hostile behavior that impairs social or academic functioning but does not usually involve serious violations of others' rights is called ____________________.

11. Disorders with onset in childhood that are characterized by involuntary and repetitive movements or vocalizations that last less than one year are called ____________________.

12. The childhood disorder characterized by involuntary, repetitive movements or vocalizations that last longer than one year is called ____________________.

13. An elimination disorder in which the child defecates into his or her clothes or bed is called ____________________.

14. An eating disorder similar to bulimia, but without compensatory behaviors such as vomiting, excessive exercise, or fasting is ________________.

15. An elimination disorder in which a child voids urine into his or her her clothes or bed is called ________________.

FACTUAL MULTIPLE–CHOICE QUESTIONS

1. Pervasive developmental disorders are childhood disorders that
   a. are quite common, with four to five cases per 100 births.
   b. are presently considered forms of schizophrenia.
   c. usually have their onset after age ten.
   d. involve behavior that is abnormal for any developmental stage.

2. In the majority of cases, autistic children are
   a. autistic savants.
   b. mentally retarded.
   c. able to speak like normal children.
   d. overly attached to their parents.

3. Treatment of children with pervasive developmental disorders
   a. usually includes psychodynamic approaches.
   b. involves humanistic and family systems approaches.
   c. is, in general, very difficult.
   d. has excellent long-term outcomes.

4. Heightened motor activity, impulsiveness, and school problems because of distractibility are all symptoms of
   a. attention-deficit/hyperactive disorder (ADHD).
   b. school phobia.
   c. conduct disorder.
   d. pervasive developmental disorder not otherwise specified.

5. The type of drug most often prescribed for attention deficit/hyperactive disorder is
   a. the tranquilizer haloperidol.
   b. the antimanic drug lithium carbonate.
   c. a stimulant.
   d. an antidepressant.

6. Which type of treatment has been most effective with adolescents with conduct disorders?
   a. Tranquilizers and central nervous stimulants
   b. Psychotherapy and incarceration
   c. Negative practice and relaxation skills
   d. Cognitive social skills and parent training

7. An individual who displays uncontrollable head-jerking and facial grimacing, and who shouts obscenities in public places would most likely be diagnosed with
   a. schizophrenia.
   b. obsessive-compulsive disorder.
   c. Korsakoff's psychosis.
   d. Tourette's disorder with coprolalia.

8. Anorexia nervosa patients
   a. rarely think about food.
   b. experience intense hunger pangs.
   c. rarely think about their body shape.
   d. know when they have reached their ideal weight.

9. Which disorder is characterized by argumentativeness and negativistic and hostile behavior?
   a. Conduct disorder
   b. Antisocial personality disorder
   c. Oppositional defiant disorder
   d. Attention deficit/hyperactive disorder

10. All of the following are disorders of childhood and adolescence *except*
    a. expressive language disorder.
    b. learning disorder.
    c. oppositional defiant disorder.
    d. dysthymic disorder.

CONCEPTUAL MULTIPLE–CHOICE QUESTIONS

1. Diagnosis of autism is deceptively difficult because
   a. symptoms are not noticeable until age six or later.
   b. most of the symptoms of autism are internalized and not observable.
   c. symptoms can vary widely among such children.
   d. parents are unwilling to accept that something is wrong with the child.

2. Parents have described their autistic children as being "embarrassingly honest," and "not really knowing what a joke is." These characteristics are interpreted as supporting the idea that autistic children
   a. view the world much more seriously than normal children.
   b. live in an inner world filled with auditory hallucinations and delusions.
   c. lack a "theory of mind" and so are unable to understand that others think.
   d. have brain damage in the left temporal lobe that causes language problems.

3. What do Rett's disorder and Asperger's disorder have in common?
   a. They are pervasive developmental disorders other than autistic disorder.
   b. Children with these disorders fail to develop any language skills.
   c. They are both successfully treated with antipsychotic medications.
   d. They are forms of anxiety disorder that have been eliminated from the list of DSM-IV childhood disorders.

4. Which statement about the causes of autism is *most accurate*?
   a. Recent research strengthens the belief that there is an underlying cause for all its forms.
   b. The only research on genetic influence was weak methodologically and showed no difference in concordance rates for MZ and DZ twins.
   c. Nearly all autistic children have abnormally low levels of serotonin, a pathognomonic sign for the disorder.
   d. Organic causes are likely, although research findings are inconsistent.

5. Some clinical psychologists are quite upset with the childhood and adolescent section of DSM-IV. Why?
   a. Because significant categories of disorders, such as tic disorders and eating disorders, have been eliminated
   b. Because conduct disorders have been separated from pervasive developmental disorders
   c. Because bothersome childhood behaviors that may be normal are now considered disorders
   d. Because all subjective judgments have been taken out of the diagnostic criteria

6. Which disorder does not belong with the others?
   a. Separation anxiety disorder
   b. Oppositional defiant disorder
   c. Conduct disorder
   d. Attention deficit/hyperactive disorder

7. Psychodynamic theory suggests that conduct disorder is caused by ____________________, whereas learning theory suggests it is caused by ____________________.
   a. underlying anxiety and emotional deprivation; central nervous system damage
   b. conflict over sexuality; parental reinforcement
   c. double-bind communication patterns; inconsistent discipline
   d. underlying anxiety and emotional deprivation; inconsistent discipline

8. It is much more likely in children from broken homes and is particularly apparent in adolescent girls. It is associated with low self-esteem and self-blame. What is being described?
   a. Childhood depression
   b. Tic disorders
   c. Separation anxiety disorder
   d. Conduct disorders

9. What behaviors differentiate anorexia nervosa from bulimia nervosa?
   a. Only anorexics are afraid of gaining weight.
   b. Only bulimics occasionally binge and purge.
   c. Only anorexics look like skeletons.
   d. Only bulimics tend to be women.

10. Dewayne, aged nine, was depressed. His doctor would probably prescribe
    a. antidepressant medication.
    b. no treatment because Dewayne is too young.
    c. further observation until the real problem surfaced.
    d. behavioral or cognitive therapy to prevent worsening of the condition.

APPLICATION MULTIPLE–CHOICE QUESTIONS

1. Warren is mentally retarded and autistic, yet he can calculate, in his head, the square root of any number and give the answer to three decimal points. This remarkable feat illustrates
   a. the autistic's superior ability to empathize.
   b. the term *echolalia*.
   c. the attention deficit that is found in autistics.
   d. the abilities of rare cases of autistic savants.

2. An autistic child is in an inpatient treatment facility. What form of therapy is *most* likely to be offered?
   a. Central nervous system stimulants such as Ritalin
   b. Group therapy
   c. Self-instructional procedures and role playing
   d. Intensive behavior modification

3. Chuck was diagnosed with attention deficit *without* hyperactive disorder when he was seven years old. He has difficulty concentrating, so he does poorly in school. As an adolescent, he was frequently arrested for criminal activity. What aspect of Chuck's case is unusual?
   a. It is unusual for boys to have attention deficits.
   b. It is unusual for attention deficit to be diagnosed at seven.
   c. It is unusual for attention deficit children to have school difficulties.
   d. It is unusual for children without hyperactive disorder to become criminals.

4. A child is being treated with stimulant medication while his parents get parent training. This child probably has the disorder called
   a. attention deficit/hyperactive disorder.
   b. separation anxiety disorder.
   c. Tourette's syndrome.
   d. pervasive developmental disorder.

5. Terry is in outpatient treatment and is being taught relaxation skills and social skills so she is less dependent on her mother. What disorder is probably being treated?
   a. Rett's disorder
   b. Oppositional defiant disorder
   c. School phobia
   d. Bulimia

6. Nathan is eight years old and has had a repetitive, involuntary eye blink for seven months. What should the wise diagnostician say?
   a. Nathan has a chronic tic disorder.
   b. Nathan's tic disorder could be transient, chronic, or an early form of Tourette's syndrome.
   c. Nathan has no disorder at all.
   d. Nathan has an early form of Tourette's syndrome.

7. Cheryl, a high school student, sometimes eats in binges. Should she be diagnosed as having an eating disorder?
   a. No, a large minority of women in the United States binge.
   b. Yes, it is a pathognomonic sign of anorexia nervosa.
   c. No, eating disorders are diagnosed on the basis of preoccupations about weight, not behavior.
   d. Yes, it is a pathognomonic sign of bulimia.

8. Diane, of an average weight, loved to eat and would fix huge meals which she would devour in one sitting. She would then spend a long time in the bathroom, where she said she was "freshening up." In reality, she was vomiting. Diane did not gain or lose weight because she was
   a. bulimic.
   b. depressed.
   c. anorexic.
   d. always dieting.

9. Lawrence plans to give a speech to his abnormal psychology class about ADHD. Which of the following should Lawrence say *best* explains the causes of ADHD?
   a. Anatomical brain differences caused by minimal brain dysfunction.
   b. Allergic reactions caused by an oversensitivity to dietic factors, especially sugar sensitivity.
   c. ADHD is probably caused by multiple pathways.
   d. Reactions to lighting conditions, especially x-rays emitted from flourescent lights.

10. Lam, age eight, has severe anxiety attacks and depression. Lam refuses to go to school. A psychologist discussing the case of Lam would say that he suffers from
    a. internalizing disorders.
    b. externalizing disorders.
    c. behavioral disorders.
    d. undercontrolled disorders

ANSWER KEY: KEY TERMS REVIEW

1. conduct disorders (496)
2. tics (501)
3. anorexia nervosa (506)
4. separation anxiety disorder (499)
5. Tourette's syndrome (501)
6. autistic disorder (481)
7. bulimia nervosa (or bulimia) (507)
8. attention deficit/hyperactive disorder (ADHD) (490)
9. pervasive developmental disorders (480)
10. oppositional defiant disorder (ODD) (494)
11. transient tic disorders (501)
12. chronic tic disorder (501)
13. encopresis (505)
14. binge eating disorder (509)
15. enuresis (504)

ANSWER KEY: FACTUAL MULTIPLE–CHOICE QUESTIONS

1. a. The prevalence rate of autistic disorder is closer to four to seven per 10,000; the other pervasive developmental disorders are twenty-two per 10,000.
   b. Pervasive developmental disorders are sufficiently different from schizophrenia to warrant their own category.
   c. Pervasive developmental disorders are usually evident in the first several years of life.
   *d. Pervasive developmental disorders involve bizarre behaviors or severe deficits, such as an absence of language, that are abnormal at any developmental stage. (pp. 480–481)

2. a. Only about 10 percent of autistics show the savant phenomenon.
   *b. Up to 75 percent of autistic children have IQs below 70. (p. 482)
   c. One of the key symptoms of autism is lack of speech or its dysfunctional quality.
   d. Autistic children fail to show affection for anyone, even their parents.

3. a. Psychoanalytic thinking about pervasive developmental disorders is largely discredited.
   b. Humanistic approaches are both uncommon and unlikely to be successful.
   *c. Because there are such profound impairments, the treatment of children with these disorders has had limited success. (p. 488)
   d. In one study, even among high-functioning patients with good verbal skills, only six of twenty-two were competitively employed.

4. *a. ADHD is characterized by short attention span, high motor activity, impulsivity, and poor self-control. (p. 490)
   b. School phobia is a subcategory of separation anxiety disorder and does not include these symptoms.
   c. Conduct disorder overlaps somewhat with ADHD but is characterized by repeated violations of the rights of others.
   d. This disorder is diagnosed when a child acts in a bizarre fashion at an early age, but this behavior does not match the criteria for autism.

5. a. Haloperidol is not used with ADHD; it has been somewhat effective with autistic children.
   b. Mania is not a problem for ADHD children.
   *c. Stimulants are frequently prescribed for children with ADHD. (p. 493)
   d. Antidepressants are not typically used to treat ADHD.

6. a. Psychoactive drugs have not been successful in treating conduct disorders.
   b. These children are not motivated to use psychotherapy; incarceration does not effectively "treat" them.
   c. Negative practice—the repetition of a behavior until it becomes aversive—is useful in eliminating tics; anxiety is not a problem for those with conduct disorders.
   *d. Cognitive social skills programs and Patterson's parent training groups have shown both short- and long-term effectiveness. (p. 497)

7. a. Some forms of schizophrenia have somatic elements, but not of this type.
   b. Obsessive-compulsive disorder does not include such physical manifestations.
   c. Korsakoff's psychosis is related to chronic alcohol abuse.
   *d. These symptoms are characteristic of Tourette's disorder with coprolalia. (p. 501)

8. a. Anorexics often spend hours preparing and serving food that they never eat.
   *b. Anorexics experience intense hunger pangs. (p. 507)
   c. Anorexics have a distorted self-perception of body image and are obsessed with their body shape.
   d. Anorexics fail to recognize successful weight loss.

9. a. Conduct disorders are characterized by a persistent pattern of antisocial behaviors that violate the rights of others. It is a diagnosis reserved for children and adolescents, not adults.
   b. The diagnosis of APD is not given to individuals under the age of 18.
   *c. Individuals diagnosed with oppositional defiant disorder defy and refuse direction from authorities. (p. 494)
   d. The diagnosis of ADHD involves the presence of socially disruptive behavior such as attentional problems or hyperactivity.

10. a. Expressive language disorders affect 3 percent to 5 percent of children, and include impairment in speech, vocabulary, or word usage subaverage for the child's developmental age.
   b. Learning disorders include problems in reading, math, or writing below that expected for the individual's age, education, and intelligence level.
   c. Although a controversial diagnosis, individuals diagnosed with oppositional defiant disorder defy and refuse direction from authorities.
   *d. Dysthymic disorder is one of the affective (mood) disorders and is characterized by a mild, chronic depressed mood. (p. 333)

ANSWER KEY: CONCEPTUAL MULTIPLE–CHOICE QUESTIONS

1. a. Autistic symptoms are noticeable at a very early age, even in infancy.
   b. Almost all autistic behaviors, from echolalia to wild tantrums to spectacular feats of memory, are observable.
   *c. Symptoms can vary widely, particularly with regard to level of functioning and developmental delay. (p. 483)
   d. There is no reason to believe that parents of autistic children are dysfunctional.

2. a. There is no evidence that autistic children view the world more seriously; they do not seem to take notice of many things in the world, particularly people.
   b. Autistic children do not have auditory hallucinations or delusions.
   *c. Frith (1991) has suggested that autistic children lack a "theory of mind," and cannot appreciate the thoughts and beliefs of others. Lacking this level of cognitive empathy they do not understand the concepts of embarrassment, lying, or jokes. (p. 483)
   d. No single area of the brain has been found to correlate with autistic disorder or, more specifically, the autistic person's inability to feel embarrassment or tell a joke.

3. *a. Four new pervasive developmental disorders have been added to DSM-IV: Rett's disorder, Asperger's disorder, childhood disintegrative disorder, and pervasive developmental disorder not otherwise specified. (p. 484)
   b. Children with Asperger's disorder have major impairments but normal language.
   c. These disorders are too new for us to know what treatments are effective.
   d. The childhood anxiety disorders eliminated from DSM-IV are avoidant disorder and overanxious disorder.

4. a. Research shows a multitude of causal factors, so it is unlikely that a single cause exists.
   b. A very strong study found that 36 percent of MZ twins were concordant while 0 percent of DZ twins were concordant.
   c. There is no pathognomonic sign for autism; when serotonin levels are abnormal in the disorder, they are high.
   *d. Many central nervous system abnormalities have been found, but research results are inconsistent and inconclusive. (pp. 485–486)

5. a. Both tic and eating disorders remain in DSM-IV.
   b. Pervasive developmental disorders involve psychotic, thoroughly dysfunctional behaviors; conduct disorders involve neither psychosis nor interpersonal dysfunction. They deserve to be separated.
   *c. Temper tantrums, argumentativeness, and problems doing arithmetic are now included as disorders; many clinicians see this as wrongly characterizing ordinary childhood difficulties as psychopathological. (p. 488)
   d. There are many subjective decisions, such as deciding if "often does not finish tasks" is abnormal given the child's developmental level and cultural norms.

6. *a. Oppositional defiant disorder, ADHD, and conduct disorder are all problems with excessive, defiant behavior and have little to do with anxiety. (pp. 494–497)
   b. Oppositional defiant disorder, ADHD, and conduct disorder are all problems with excessive, defiant behavior.
   c. Oppositional defiant disorder, ADHD, and conduct disorder are all problems with excessive, defiant behavior.
   d. Oppositional defiant disorder, ADHD, and conduct disorder are all problems with excessive, defiant behavior.

7. a. Learning theory does not speculate on central nervous system damage.
   b. For this disorder, conflicts over sexuality are not important in the psychoanalytic explanation of cause.
   c. Double-bind communications are important in explaining schizophrenic disorder.
   *d. Psychoanalysts believe such children are neglected and have underlying anxiety; behaviorists think they have learned to be antisocial because their parents failed to control them. (p. 497)

8. *a. Childhood depression is much more common when there is a broken home than when the family is intact, it is more prominent in adolescent girls, and as with adults, it involves cognitive distortions of self-blame. (p. 500)
   b. Tic disorders are most common in childhood, not adolescence; they are unrelated to divorce.
   c. Separation anxiety disorder is much more common in childhood than adolescence.
   d. Conduct disorders are far more common in boys than girls and involve problems of blaming others.

9. a. Both anorexics and bulimics are afraid of gaining weight.
   b. One form of anorexia involves binging and purging.
   *c. Anorexics starve themselves and look that way; bulimia is unrelated to body size (most are of normal weight). (pp. 506–508)
   d. Both forms of eating disorder are more common in women.

10. a. Most of the research on medication has been conducted with adults, not children, and many medications that work for adults do not work for children.
   b. Dewayne needs help if the symptoms are to be prevented from worsening.
   c. Dewayne has a real problem with depression that needs treatment.
   *d. Behavioral or cognitive therapy would be recommended to prevent worsening of the condition.

ANSWER KEY: APPLICATION MULTIPLE–CHOICE QUESTIONS

1. a. Frith (1991) suggests that autistic individuals have no "theory of mind"—they are especially deficient at empathizing with others.
   b. Echolalia is the meaningless repetition of phrases spoken by others.
   c. Autistics do not have the attention deficits seen in children with ADHD.
   *d. Astounding memory and artistic feats performed by otherwise severely dysfunctional individuals characterize autistic savants, who are unusual or rare cases. (p. 482)

2. a. Stimulant medication is used for children with ADHD.
   b. Because they do not attend to others and one-half do not speak, group therapy would be useless.
   c. Self-instructional procedures and role playing are too advanced for autistics, many of whom do not speak.
   *d. Intensive behavior modification for learning language and attending to others has had modest success in treating children with autistic disorder. (p. 488)

3. a. Males outnumber females with ADHD by four or five to one.
   b. ADHD is often detected in the preschool or early elementary school years.
   c. Because of attention problems, most ADHD children have great difficulty completing academic work.
   *d. The prognosis for attention deficit without hyperactive disorder is quite good; criminal behavior is more likely if there is hyperactivity and sexual aggression. (p. 491)

4. *a. Stimulant medication and parent training are typically used to treat attention deficit/hyperactive disorder. (pp. 493–494)
   b. Separation anxiety disorder is best treated with psychotherapy; if any medication were used it would probably be antianxiety drugs.
   c. Tourette's is believed to be triggered by stimulant medication in some cases, so those drugs would not be used in its treatment.
   d. Pervasive developmental disorder has sometimes been treated with haloperidol and fenfluramine, neither of which are stimulants.

5. a. Rett's disorder is a pervasive developmental disorder in which there is marked deterioration of social and language skills after at least six months of normal development.
   b. Oppositional defiant disorder involves defying parental rules and being hostile, not overly dependent.
   *c. School phobia is considered a problem of anxiety and poor social skills, but behaviorists would treat the disorder with relaxation and social skill training. (pp. 499–500)
   d. Bulimia is not related to dependency on a parent.

6. a. Chronic tic disorder is not diagnosed until after the tic has continued for one year.
   *b. No one can tell whether a transient tic will go away by itself, become a chronic tic disorder, or develop into Tourette's syndrome; accurate "diagnosis" is possible only with hindsight. (p. 501)
   c. A repetitive eye blink that goes on for seven months is, at least, a transient tic disorder.
   d. An eye blink is very common; it is far too early to diagnose Tourette's syndrome.

7. *a. Approximately 35 percent of women report binging or overeating; a diagnosis of bulimia requires meeting other criteria. (p. 509)
   b. Binging is not a specific sign of anorexia; bulimics also purge after binging.
   c. Eating disorders are diagnosed on the basis of both preoccupations and observable behaviors.
   d. Binging and purging is a fundamental sign of bulimia, but also occurs in anorexia.

8. *a. Bulimia nervosa involves the consumption of large quantities of food, usually followed by self-induced vomiting. (p. 507)
   b. Depression is not the most salient feature reflected in the bingeing described in this case.
   c. Anorexics often binge/purge, but their weight is drastically below normal minimum.
   d. Bulimics are not always dieting, because they can use the binge/purge cycle to eat as much as they want without gaining.

9. a. CAT scans do not reveal anatomical brain differences between persons with ADHD and normal individuals.
   b. Sugar does not cause hyperactivity.
   *c. Research findings on the causes of ADHD show inconsistent and conflicting results, suggesting that ADHD may consist of several types, probably caused by multiple pathways. (p. 491)
   d. Lighting conditions have no effect on hyperactivity.

10. *a. Internalizing disorders are those psychological difficulties that are considered inner-directed, and show core symptoms associated with overcontrolled behaviors such as anxiety and depression. (p. 499)
    b. Externalizing disorders are behavioral disorders that create problems for others.
    c. Behavioral disorders is another term for externalizing disorders.
    d. Undercontrolled disorders is another term for externalizing disorders.

CHAPTER 17
Individual and Group Therapy

LEARNING OBJECTIVES

1. Discuss the various biological therapies, including electroconvulsive therapy (ECT) and psychosurgery, and their use and effectiveness in treating mental disorders. (pp. 517–519)
2. Define psychopharmacology. Describe and evaluate the use of antianxiety, antipsychotic, antidepressant, and antimanic medications. (pp. 519–524)
3. Define psychotherapy and describe its basic characteristics. Discuss why traditional psychotherapy may not be effective with individuals from non-Western cultures. (pp. 524–525; Focus On)
4. Describe the goals and techniques of psychoanalysis and post-Freudian psychoanalytic therapy. Evaluate the effectiveness of psychoanalytic therapy. (pp. 525–528)
5. Describe the therapies based on the humanistic/existential perspective, including person-centered therapy, existential analysis, and gestalt therapy. (pp. 528–529)
6. Describe the therapeutic techniques based on classical conditioning, including systematic desensitization, flooding and implosion, and aversive conditioning. (pp. 529–531)
7. Describe the therapeutic techniques based on operant conditioning, including token economies and punishment. (pp. 531–532)
8. Describe observational learning techniques and cognitive-behavioral therapies. (pp. 532–534)
9. Discuss the goal of behavioral medicine and describe the techniques used to promote lifestyle changes, including biofeedback. (pp. 534–535)
10. Discuss research on the effectiveness of individual psychotherapy. (pp. 535–538)
11. Describe the common components and types of group therapy; evaluate the effectiveness of group therapy. Describe the functions of marital and family therapy, and the different emphases of the communications and systems approaches. (pp. 538–545)
12. Evaluate the factors involved in choosing a therapist. (p. 539; Critical Thinking)
13. Discuss the movement toward systematic integration and eclecticism. (p. 545)
14. Discuss the changes in mental health service delivery caused by managed health care. (pp. 546–547)
15. Describe primary, secondary, and tertiary prevention and give examples of each. (pp. 547–550)

CHAPTER OUTLINE

1. **Biology-based treatment techniques** (pp. 517–524) Biological treatment techniques have been used to alter patients' psychological states since ancient times. In our time, *electroconvulsive therapy (ECT)* was first used in the 1930s on the assumption that seizures would eliminate schizophrenic behavior. ECT has been found to be useful in treating severe depression, but the reasons for this are unclear. There is considerable controversy over the use of ECT. *Psychosurgery*, particularly lesioning the frontal lobes, was once a common treatment for schizophrenia, but now it is used only as a last resort. Videolaserscopy now allows surgeons to make extremely small laser incisions, guided by a video camera.

   The most common biology-based treatments are *psychopharmacology* (drug therapy) approaches. Antianxiety drugs, including propanediols (meprobamate compounds) and benzodiazepines (Librium and Valium) reduce tension, probably by blocking neural transmission, but they can be addictive and produce withdrawal effects. Antipsychotic drugs are used to treat schizophrenia and other psychotic conditions. Their effectiveness, not due to placebo effects, is superior to that of several forms of psychotherapy. Side effects include Parkinson-like symptoms, dry mouth, and tardive dyskinesia. Antidepressants include *tricyclics*, *MAO inhibitors*, and *fluoxetine (Prozac)*, and are used to treat depression. Studies following assertions about Prozac's safety showed no credible link between the drug and increased suicidality. Lithium, the principal antimanic drug, is effective in the treatment of bipolar disorder.

   Psychopharmacological considerations determine which drug in which amount should be prescribed for which condition and patient. Drugs are generally more effective for active symptoms like hallucinations than passive symptoms like social withdrawal.

2. **Psychotherapy** (pp. 524–525; Focus On) *Psychotherapy* is defined as the systematic application of techniques derived from psychological theory for the purpose of aiding psychologically troubled people. There are wide differences in strategies, but most psychotherapies agree that treatment is an opportunity for relearning, for developing new emotionally important experiences, for establishing therapeutic relationships, and for achieving hoped-for goals. However, traditional psychotherapy mirrors mainstream Western culture, making it less effective for those from non-Western cultures. Mental health services have been adapted for multiethnic populations. Individual psychotherapy is usually subdivided into insight-oriented and action-oriented approaches.

3. **Insight-oriented approaches to individual psychotherapy** (pp. 525–529) *Psychoanalysis*, devised by Freud, stresses the resolution of unconscious conflicts through techniques such as free association and dream analysis, analysis of resistance, the transference relationship, and interpretation of events. Post-Freudian psychoanalysis is more flexible than traditional psychoanalysis, but still holds to the idea of symptom substitution if underlying factors are not analyzed and altered. Controlled research does not confirm the existence of symptom substitution.

   Humanistic-existential approaches stress the self and personal responsibility. Rogers's *person-centered therapy* emphasizes the relationship between therapist and client over any techniques. *Existential analysis* adheres to no single theory but takes a strongly philosophical approach, and Perls's *gestalt therapy* uses the person's here-and-now totality of experience to produce change. Because neither existential nor gestalt therapy has generated research, their effectiveness is hard to evaluate.

4. **Action-oriented approaches to individual psychotherapy: Classical conditioning techniques, operant conditioning techniques, observational learning techniques, and cognitive-behavioral therapy** (pp. 529–534) Classical conditioning principles guide the action-oriented therapies of *systematic desensitization*, *flooding* and *implosion*, and *aversive conditioning*. In systematic desensitization, relaxation is paired with anxiety-provoking scenes to reduce anxiety. In flooding, clients confront their fears in real situations, whereas in implosion, the confrontation occurs in imagination. In aversive conditioning, an undesirable behavior such as smoking is

paired with a noxious stimulus. This can be done in imagination in a procedure called covert sensitization.

Operant principles are at work in *token economies,* where desired behaviors are contingently reinforced with tokens that can be exchanged for privileges or other reinforcers. *Contingent punishment* may be used to suppress self-destructive behaviors, as in autistic disorder.

Modeling, based on observational learning theory, is effective in the treatment of phobias, delinquency, and other behavior problems. *Cognitive-behavioral therapies* focus on clients' thoughts as well as on their coping skills. Ellis's rational-emotive psychotherapy challenges the client's irrational beliefs; Beck's therapy is less confrontative, but uses similar themes to treat depression. Stress inoculation therapy is another form of cognitive-behavioral treatment. For certain depressions, cognitive therapy may be at least as effective as drug treatment.

5. **Behavioral medicine** (pp. 534–535) Behavioral medicine links the biological and behavioral sciences for the purpose of changing people's lifestyles to prevent illness. *Biofeedback therapy* and counseling to reduce Type A behavior patterns have been useful in this effort. Most techniques for changing lifestyles involve establishing priorities, avoiding stressful situations, taking personal time, setting up an exercise schedule, proper diet, developing social supports, and learning to relax.

6. **Evaluating individual psychotherapy** (pp. 535–538; Critical Thinking) There are debates over the appropriateness of insight versus action therapies. In 1952, Eysenck created controversy by claiming that psychotherapy was ineffective. More recent studies have been methodologically cleaner, but Persons (1991) points out that therapy outcome studies fail to match the conditions of actual practice of assessment and psychotherapy. Use of *meta-analysis* to identify treatment effect size shows that those getting therapy show far more improvement than those untreated. There are a range of factors including experience, therapeutic orientation, and demographic characteristics of the therapist that should go into choosing a therapist.

7. **Group, family, and marital therapy** (pp. 538–545; Focus On) *Group therapy* has economic and therapeutic advantages over individual psychotherapy. There are many different forms of group therapy, including encounter groups, self-help groups, transactional analysis groups, assertiveness training groups, and psychodrama. The purposes and techniques of groups differ widely, but some common features are the experience of feedback on real-life social interactions, the opportunity for modeling, and the reduction of isolation through social support. There are advantages and disadvantages to group treatment. Measuring outcome for group therapy is more difficult than for individual treatment.

   Family therapy is a kind of group therapy seeking to modify family relationships to foster greater harmony. It is based on the assumption that the problems of the "identified patient" are symptoms of family distress. Two kinds of family therapy are the communications approach and the systems approach.

   Marital therapy also focuses on communications and system roles; it is not designed to save marriages, but to clarify understanding and options. Research on the effectiveness of family and marital therapy have generally not used rigorous designs, so strong conclusions are premature.

8. **Systematic integration and eclecticism** (pp. 545–546) Most practicing clinicians see themselves as eclectics—using diverse approaches and techniques. While eclectism calls for openness it can also encourage the haphazard use of concepts. Practitioners prefer the term *integrative* to *eclectic.*

9. **Community psychology** (pp. 546–550) *Community psychology* takes into account the impact of environmental factors on mental health and encourages the use of community resources to eliminate the conditions that cause psychological problems. It seeks to promote well-being and prevent psychopathology.

   Reform in the delivery of mental health services is underway in the form of managed health care. Care is shifting to health maintenance organizations (HMOs), care is increasingly short-term, providers are more often those with master's degrees, and quality assurance is emphasized.

Other changes may allow psychologists with appropriate training to prescribe medications and provide treatment by following treatment manuals.

Preventing psychopathology is a key feature of community psychology. There are three types. *Primary prevention* seeks to lower the incidence of new cases. Examples include Project Head Start, Munoz and colleagues' attempts to prevent depression community-wide, and early intervention to prevent juvenile delinquency. *Secondary prevention* attempts to shorten the duration of disorders by detecting them early and providing effective treatment. There are problems in providing both primary and secondary prevention. *Tertiary prevention* aims to help the readjustment of individuals who have received hospital treatment.

KEY TERMS REVIEW

1. Brain surgery performed to correct a severe mental disorder is called ____________________.

2. A form of therapy that involves the simultaneous treatment of two or more clients is called ____________________.

3. The study of the effects of drugs on the mind and behavior is called ____________________.

4. A humanistic-existential approach to therapy that emphasizes the client's awareness of his or her total experience in the here-and-now is called ____________________.

5. A humanistic therapy emphasizing the kind of person the therapist should be in the therapeutic process, rather than the techniques that he or she should use, is called ____________________.

6. Group therapy that is characterized by an attempt to modify relationships within the family is called ____________________.

7. The systematic application of techniques based on psychological principles for the purpose of helping psychologically troubled individuals is called ____________________.

8. A therapeutic approach in which a patient receives information about autonomic functions and is rewarded for influencing them in a desirable direction is called ____________________.

9. An effort to lower the incidence of new cases of disorders by strengthening resources or eliminating conditions that threaten mental health is called ____________________.

10. The application of electric voltage to the brain to induce convulsions and reduce depression is called ____________________.

11. A therapeutic approach that is concerned with the person's existence and involvement in the world and focuses on a complex encounter with the therapist is called ____________________.

12. A behavioral technique aimed at extinguishing fear by having the client confront the real-life threat at full intensity is called ____________________.

13. A behavioral technique aimed at extinguishing fear by having the client *imagine* the threat at full intensity is called ____________________.

14. Antidepressant compounds that are believed to correct the balance of neurotransmitters in the brain and that can interact with certain foods to cause dangerous side effects are called ____________________.

15. The treatment aimed at helping couples understand and clarify their communications, roles, and expectations is called ____________________.

16. Antidepressant compounds that relieve symptoms of depression but have fewer side effects than MAO inhibitors are called ____________________.

17. An approach to mental health that focuses on environmental factors and encourages the use of community resources to eliminate conditions that produce psychological problems is called ____________________.

18. A psychoanalytic method during which the patient says whatever comes to mind without censorship is called ____________________.

19. A treatment program based on operant conditioning principles that rewards patients for appropriate behaviors with objects such as poker chips, which can be exchanged for desired activities, is called ____________________.

20. During psychoanalysis, the process in which the patient unconsciously interferes with treatment to prevent exposing repressed material is called ____________________.

21. A classical conditioning technique in which an undesirable behavior is paired with an unpleasant stimulus to suppress the undesirable behavior is called ____________________.

22. During psychotherapy, the process in which the patient re-enacts early conflicts with parents by applying them to the therapist is called ____________________.

23. Efforts to facilitate the readjustment of people who have been in hospital treatment for mental disorders is called ____________________.

24. Positive responses to a drug or other experimental condition that result from expectations or other psychological factors rather than the medication's physiological action are called the ____________________.

25. An effort to shorten the duration of mental disorders and reduce their impact through early detection and referral for treatment is called ____________________.

26. Antidepressant drugs affecting the reabsorption of serotonin are called ____________________.

FACTUAL MULTIPLE–CHOICE QUESTIONS

1. This treatment was first used in the 1930s in the mistaken belief that epileptic seizures and schizophrenia could not both occur in the same person. Now it is used to treat severe depression. What form of therapy is this?
   a. Prefrontal lobotomy
   b. Electroconvulsive therapy (ECT)
   c. Phenothiazine medication
   d. Lithium carbonate

2. ____________________ drugs are used to treat people who are extremely tense. However, they have the potential to be overused and for people to become psychologically dependent on them.
   a. Antidepressant
   b. Phenothiazine
   c. Antimanic
   d. Benzodiazepine

3. Symptoms like those of Parkinson's disease and the drug-induced disorder tardive dyskinesia are serious side effects of prolonged treatment with
   a. electroshock.
   b. psychosurgery.
   c. antipsychotic medication.
   d. antianxiety medication.

4. Having new, important emotional experiences and engaging in a therapeutic relationship are both components of
   a. basic methods of resisting stress.
   b. biology-based approaches to treatment.
   c. action-oriented therapies only.
   d. all forms of psychotherapy.

5. Psychoanalysts who ask their clients to say whatever comes to their minds are using the technique
   a. that uncovers the manifest content of dreams.
   b. called countertransference.
   c. that exaggerates feelings in the here-and-now.
   d. called free association.

6. When certain behaviors are rewarded with coinlike objects or tally marks that can later be exchanged for privileges or desired activities, the treatment being used is
   a. an insight-oriented form of psychotherapy.
   b. a form of behavior therapy based on classical conditioning.
   c. called a token economy.
   d. called implosion or flooding.

7. The process of observing an adaptive individual and imitating that person's behaviors is called
   a. latent learning.
   b. modeling.
   c. rational-emotive learning.
   d. covert sensitization.

8. In ____________________, the client's irrational beliefs are identified and aggressively contradicted by the therapist.
   a. Beck's cognitive therapy
   b. token economies
   c. behavioral medicine
   d. Ellis's rational-emotive therapy

9. The application of a range of therapy techniques to fit the needs of an individual client is called
   a. action-oriented psychotherapy.
   b. insight-oriented psychotherapy.
   c. eclecticism.
   d. systems-oriented therapy.

10. Managed health care will have all of the following characteristics *except*
    a. longer-term treatment to ensure that symptoms are fully dealt with.
    b. a reduction in demand for Ph.D.'s services because they are too costly.
    c. continual assessment of the cost and efficiency of treatments.
    d. care provided through health maintenance organizations (HMOs).

CONCEPTUAL MULTIPLE–CHOICE QUESTIONS

1. Which statement about drug treatment is *accurate*?
   a. In many cases, medication cures mental disorders because it can teach new ways of acting.
   b. Because antipsychotic drugs give people a "high," discharged patients almost always continue to take their medication.
   c. Antipsychotic medication is a principal reason why prolonged hospitalization is no longer needed in most cases.
   d. The greatest danger of drug treatment is that it may lead to permanent memory loss.

2. Efforts to make therapeutic services more culturally appropriate for Asian and Hispanic clients
   a. have not been shown to alter the utilization of these services.
   b. are illustrations of tertiary prevention.
   c. have increased service utilization and lowered dropout rates among minorities.
   d. have tended to dilute the value of the treatment that is provided.

3. In what way is post-Freudian psychoanalysis different from traditional psychoanalysis?
   a. It no longer believes that interpersonal relations are important.
   b. It increases the number of sessions and places more emphasis on past situations.
   c. It loosens up previously rigid therapeutic techniques.
   d. It no longer believes in the unconscious motivation of behavior.

4. Person–centered and gestalt therapies are based on the ____________________ orientation toward abnormal behavior.
   a. psychodynamc
   b. humanistic-existential
   c. cognitive-behavioral
   d. family systems

5. In existential analysis, the therapist
   a. confronts the client with his or her irrational beliefs.
   b. fosters an encounter in which both people genuinely share each other's experiences.
   c. interprets dreams in relation to current concerns.
   d. takes over the client's responsibility for making choices.

6. Which of the following therapeutic techniques is *both* a form of classical conditioning and a means of reducing anxiety?
   a. Systematic desensitization
   b. Aversive conditioning
   c. Token economy
   d. Antianxiety medication

7. Typically, the goal of aversive conditioning is to
   a. decrease the frequency of undesirable behaviors.
   b. teach more adaptive coping skills.
   c. decrease the client's anxiety level.
   d. increase the client's level of self-understanding.

8. Which statement about research on the effectiveness of psychotherapy is *accurate*?
   a. The best research indicates that people who receive therapy are no more improved than those who do not.
   b. In general, people who receive therapy show greater improvement than those who do not.
   c. Psychotherapy is too recent a phenomenon; there is insufficient research on its effectiveness.
   d. Regardless of the problem, insight-oriented psychotherapy is more effective than action-oriented psychotherapy.

9. What do transactional analysis and system-oriented family therapy have in common?
   a. They are both based on psychoanalytic principles.
   b. They are both forms of group therapy.
   c. They are both based on aversive conditioning principles.
   d. They have both been found to be only minimally effective.

10. Primary prevention efforts seek to
   a. facilitate the readjustment to the community of people who were hospitalized for psychiatric problems.
   b. provide treatment to severely disturbed people in ways that are culturally sensitive.
   c. reduce the duration and impact of disorders by detecting them at an early stage.
   d. reduce the incidence of disorders by using community resources to eliminate conditions that cause psychological problems.

APPLICATION MULTIPLE–CHOICE QUESTIONS

1. Dr. Miller says, "I can't believe a schizophrenic patient received this form of treatment in the 1990s! It has little therapeutic effect, and the posttreatment effects can include permanent intellectual impairment or even death. The patient should have been given major tranquilizers." What kind of treatment is Dr. Miller upset about?
   a. Electroconvulsive therapy (ECT)
   b. Aversive conditioning
   c. Milieu therapy
   d. Prefrontal lobotomy

2. Ralph is first treated with tricyclic medications, but when they do not alter his symptoms, he is given a selective serotonin reuptake inhibitor (SSRI), which proves to be very effective. Ralph probably suffers from which disorder?
   a. Generalized anxiety disorder
   b. Schizophrenia
   c. Depression
   d. Bipolar disorder

3. Vera tells her therapist about one of her dreams, in which she drives her car toward an evil-looking man, trying to kill him. Her therapist says, "The man represents your father. Unconsciously, you resent him." The therapist is
   a. interpreting the latent content of the dream.
   b. using person-centered therapy techniques.
   c. showing evidence of countertransference.
   d. using free association.

4. A therapist with an existential point of view would be most likely to say which of the following?
   a. "I am less concerned with the client's self-awareness than with the client's ability to cope with stress."
   b. "Unless the repressed conflicts of the past are uncovered and dealt with, any changes in behavior will only be temporary."
   c. "Everyone has a set of irrational beliefs that must be attacked and changed through cognitive restructuring."
   d. "Until people can accept the reality of death, they cannot grow and take personal responsibility for their lives."

5. Jim has a severe snake phobia. His therapist teaches him relaxation skills and then has him imagine, while remaining relaxed, situations that place him in increasing contact with snakes. This kind of therapy is called
   a. flooding.
   b. systematic desensitization.
   c. covert sensitization.
   d. modeling.

6. To treat Helen's cocaine addiction, her therapist instructs her to pair imagined scenes in which she is ready to use cocaine with images of her coughing, choking, and having a heart attack. What kind of therapy is this?
   a. Sadistic eclecticism
   b. Covert sensitization
   c. Observational learning
   d. Token economy

7. Bradley is an autistic boy who repeatedly bangs his head on the walls and floor. Reasoning, token economy programs, and drug treatment have not stopped the behavior. What would be the most sensible treatment to try next?
   a. Prefrontal lobotomy
   b. Electroconvulsive therapy (ECT)
   c. Operant punishment
   d. Insight-oriented psychotherapy

8. Which of the following is a critique that a research psychologist might reasonably have made of Eysenck's 1952 study of psychotherapy effectiveness?
   a. "Your statistics inflate the usefulness of psychotherapy."
   b. "You failed to include an untreated control group in your study."
   c. "It is inappropriate to compare people getting psychotherapy with those getting drug treatment."
   d. "The improvement criteria applied to the untreated patients were different from those used with the treated ones."

9. Dr. Adelson says, "Any attempt to treat a child individually is doomed to fail. Johnny may be the 'identified patient,' but his symptoms serve a greater function." What kind of therapist is Dr. Adelson?
   a. A family therapist
   b. An action-oriented psychoanalyst
   c. One who uses systematic eclecticism
   d. A humanistic-existential therapist

10. Dr. Tanaka says, "The problem with these prevention programs is that the early detection of disorders is often unreliable and even if it is accurately identified, deciding which treatment would be most effective for the individual is quite difficult." What form of prevention is Dr. Tanaka objecting to?
    a. primary
    b. secondary
    c. tertiary
    d. insight-oriented

ANSWER KEY: KEY TERMS REVIEW

1. psychosurgery (518)
2. group therapy (538)
3. psychopharmacology (519)
4. gestalt therapy (528)
5. person-centered therapy (also client-centered therapy) (528)

6. family therapy (542)
7. psychotherapy (524)
8. biofeedback therapy (534)
9. primary prevention (548)
10. electroconvulsive therapy (518)
11. existential analysis (528)
12. flooding (530)
13. implosion (530)
14. monoamine oxidase (MAO) inhibitors (522)
15. marital therapy (544)
16. tricyclics (522)
17. community psychology (546)
18. free association (525)
19. token economy (531)
20. resistance (526)
21. aversive conditioning (531)
22. transference (527)
23. tertiary prevention (549)
24. placebo effect (521)
25. secondary prevention (549)
26. selective serotonin reuptake inhibitors (522)

ANSWER KEY: FACTUAL MULTIPLE–CHOICE QUESTIONS

1. a. Prefrontal lobotomies were used to treat schizophrenia; no assumption about the operation and epileptic seizures was made.
   *b. Meduna incorrectly connected schizophrenia and epilepsy, but ECT is now used for severe depression when drug treatment has been unsuccessful. (p. 517)
   c. Phenothiazines are antipsychotic drugs used to treat schizophrenia.
   d. Lithium carbonate is used almost exclusively to treat bipolar disorders.

2. a. There is little or no potential for overuse with antidepressants.
   b. Phenothiazines do not pose a threat of overuse and are prescribed for psychotic conditions, not anxiety.
   c. Lithium carbonate is the chief antimanic drug; it does not produce overdependence.
   *d. Benzodiazepines such as Valium and Librium are antianxiety drugs that have serious potential for psychological dependence. (p. 519)

3. a. The main side effects of ECT are memory loss and confusion.
   b. Psychosurgery produces cognitive impairments; it cannot produce a drug-induced disorder.
   *c. Antipsychotic medications such as the phenothiazines, when used for long periods to treat psychotic conditions, may produce symptoms of Parkinson's disease and the syndrome called tardive dyskinesia. (p. 522)
   d. Antianxiety medications may produce physical and psychological dependence, but not these side effects.

4. a. Although these might not hurt one's chances of resisting stress, the components of stress resistance typically include preparation, ambiguity reduction, and social support.
   b. Biology-based treatment involves little, if any, therapeutic relationship.
   c. Action-oriented therapies value these components, but not as much as do insight-oriented approaches.
   *d. These are two of the common features of all forms of psychotherapy. (p. 524)

5. a. The manifest content of dreams is the information one remembers after awakening.
   b. Countertransference is a therapist blunder; it occurs when the therapist reacts personally and emotionally to the patient's transferential responses.
   c. Gestalt therapists are far more likely to have clients exaggerate their feelings so that they can be aware of the here-and-now experience.
   *d. Free association involves the simple, but not very easy, request to "say whatever comes to mind." (p. 525)

6. a. Insight-oriented approaches rely almost exclusively on speech as the mode of change.
   b. Classical conditioning involves the pairing of stimuli and a passive organism; when certain behaviors are rewarded, operant procedures are being used.
   *c. In token economies, coins, points, stamps, or other such devices are token reinforcers that are given contingent on appropriate behavior; they are traded in for valued activities or privileges. (pp. 531–532)
   d. In implosion, fearful situations are imagined; in flooding, they are experienced for real.

7. a. Latent learning is any learning that occurs but is invisible until there is an incentive to demonstrate it.
   *b. In modeling, learning occurs when another's behavior is observed and then copied. (p. 532)
   c. In rational-emotive learning (therapy), irrational beliefs are challenged and changed.
   d. Covert sensitization is a procedure in which aversive conditioning is done by imagining noxious scenes.

8. a. Beck's cognitive therapy explores the client's illogical thinking but does so without aggressively challenging it.
   b. In token economies, appropriate behaviors are rewarded; belief systems are not important.
   c. Behavioral medicine may examine beliefs, but far more emphasis is placed on healthy activities.
   *d. Ellis's rational-emotive therapy assumes that symptoms stem from irrational beliefs that must be aggressively attacked and changed. (p. 533)

9. a. Action-oriented psychotherapy tends to be based on behavioral principles.
   b. Insight-oriented therapies rely on emotional awareness to provide the impetus for change, regardless of the client.
   *c. Eclecticism selects the best methods from various theoretical perspectives and applies them to meet individual clients' needs. (p. 545)
   d. Systems-oriented therapy is strictly associated with family therapy.

10. *a. Managed care, in an effort to cut costs and be efficient, stresses short-term care; the goal is to get the client to function, not to be "cured." (p. 546)
   b. Managed care will use more master's degree professionals because their services cost less than Ph.D.'s and M.D.'s.
   c. To provide cost-effective care, managed care will require continual assessment of the cost, benefit, and efficiency of treatment.
   d. Mental health care is shifting away from fee-for-service toward the administration of care through health maintenance organizations (HMOs).

ANSWER KEY: CONCEPTUAL MULTIPLE–CHOICE QUESTIONS

1. a. One thing drugs cannot do is teach new behaviors; they provide no cure.
   b. Antipsychotic drugs do not produce a "high"; if anything, the problem is that patients stop taking their medication because they don't like the side effects.
   *c. Because they can suppress psychotic symptoms and help people think straight, antipsychotic drugs have helped shorten the hospital stays of most psychotic patients. (p. 522)
   d. Drugs rarely, if ever, impair memory; the danger of this is from ECT.

2. a. At least in one study, modifying services for severely disturbed Asian clients showed an increase in service utilization from 10 percent to 34 percent over three years.
   b. Tertiary prevention attempts to make the readjustment of former inpatient clients easier in the community. It does not alter how treatment is provided.
   *c. In one study, utilization of services by Asians increased from 10 percent to 34 percent by making treatment more culturally appropriate; dropout rates have also been reduced. (p. 526)
   d. There is no evidence that treatment quality is diluted when services are provided in culturally sensitive ways; in fact, it is likely that treatment quality is improved when, for instance, clients can communicate in their native language.

3. a. Post-Freudian analysis places greater emphasis on interpersonal relations.
   b. Post-Freudian analysis usually requires fewer sessions and places more emphasis on current concerns.
   *c. The formal rules of therapy that Freud set down have been relaxed and modified in modern psychoanalysis. (pp. 527–528)
   d. All psychoanalysts, both Freudian and ego autonomy theorists, assume that behavior is unconsciously motivated.

4. a. Psychoanalytic therapies emphasize the intrapsychic components of personality, not the holistic approach of these two.
   *b. Person-centered therapy and gestalt therapy emphasize the current feelings of people and treat them holistically. (pp. 528–529)
   c. Cognitive-behavioral therapies stress the irrational beliefs and coping skills of people; neither of these two do.
   d. Family therapy includes communications and systems approaches; client-centered and gestalt therapy do not.

5. a. Confronting a client's irrational beliefs is a feature of Ellis's rational-emotive therapy.
   *b. Existential therapists are philosophically oriented and encourage genuine encounters from which clients are expected to grow. (p. 528)
   c. The interpretation of dreams in relation to the here-and-now is important in gestalt therapy.
   d. Humanistic-existential thinking emphasizes the need for personal responsibility for choices; therapists would not take over that responsibility.

6. *a. Systematic desensitization is a classical conditioning method because it pairs two stimuli; it is almost always used to eliminate anxiety symptoms. (p. 529)
   b. Aversive conditioning is often based on classical conditioning principles but is used to remove undesirable behaviors, such as excessive drinking or smoking.
   c. Token economies are based on operant conditioning because the consequences of behavior are altered.
   d. Antianxiety medication is certainly used to treat anxiety, but it represents a biology-based therapy.

7. *a. In aversive conditioning, noxious stimuli are paired with undesirable behaviors such as smoking or drinking in an attempt to decrease their frequency. (p. 531)
   b. Token economies, modeling, and cognitive-behavioral approaches stress the learning of new coping skills.
   c. Aversive conditioning would tend to increase one's anxiety; just imagine what the pairing of alcohol and vomiting would do for your tension level!
   d. Self-understanding is a high priority in insight-oriented therapies.

8. a. Only Eysenck's research showed that treated people were no more improved than untreated people, and this study has several limitations.
   *b. Meta-analysis of hundreds of studies (for example, work by Smith and Glass) shows that people treated with psychotherapy show far greater improvement than those who are untreated. (p. 538)
   c. Psychotherapy research has been done for more than thirty years; the research literature is quite extensive.
   d. Significant differences in effectiveness between insight- and action-oriented therapies are the exception rather than the rule; in those exceptions, action-oriented methods are superior.

9. a. Transactional analysis has some elements of similarity to psychoanalysis, but systems-oriented family therapy does not.
   *b. In transactional analysis, people meet in groups to become aware of their game playing; family therapy, by its nature, is group therapy. (pp. 542–543; Focus On)
   c. Neither transactional analysis nor systems-oriented family therapy is based on learning principles.
   d. The text reports no information on their effectiveness.

10. a. Efforts to facilitate the readjustment of former inpatient clients is considered tertiary prevention.
   b. Prevention is not so much concerned with the way treatment is presented as with what comes before treatment.
   c. Secondary prevention is the attempt to reduce the duration or impact of disorders by "nipping them in the bud," detecting them early and making referral to treatment.
   *d. Primary prevention is defined as efforts to reduce the incidence of new cases of disorder by mobilizing community resources to eliminate those environmental conditions that cause psychological problems. (p. 548)

ANSWER KEY: APPLICATION MULTIPLE–CHOICE QUESTIONS

1. a. Electroconvulsive therapy is still used in the 1990s (although not with schizophrenics) and does not lead to death.
   b. Aversive conditioning is used in the 1990s and does not have permanent side effects.
   c. Milieu therapy is a treatment for schizophrenia that involves self-government; it has no physiological side effects.
   *d. Psychosurgery such as prefrontal lobotomy has disappeared as a treatment for schizophrenia because of its serious side effects and its inferiority to drug therapy. (p. 519)

2. a. Antianxiety drugs, not tricyclics, would be given to a person with GAD.
   b. Antipsychotic drugs, not tricyclics, would be given to a person with schizophrenia.
   *c. Tricyclics and SSRIs, such as Prozac, are both antidepressants. (p. 522)
   d. Lithium would be given to a person with bipolar disorder, although antidepressants might help during the depression phase.

3. *a. The latent content of dreams is the symbolic meaning that is disguised in our recollection (the manifest content); this therapist is being unusually active in the interpretation. (p. 526)
   b. Person-centered therapy places little emphasis on technique and even less on interpreting dreams.
   c. Countertransference occurs when the therapist's emotional life interferes with the therapeutic relationship.
   d. In free association, the patient says whatever comes to mind.

4. a. Existentialists emphasize self-understanding.
   b. Psychoanalysts, not existentialists, emphasize the uncovering of repressed material.
   c. Rational-emotive therapy, not existential therapy, emphasizes irrational beliefs.
   *d. Confronting the reality of death represents an existential crisis; existential analysts encourage genuine encounters with self and others. (p. 528)

5. a. In flooding, the feared stimulus is confronted in "real life."
   *b. Systematic desensitization has three stages: relaxation training, the development of an anxiety hierarchy, and the pairing of the images on the hierarchy with relaxation. (p. 529)
   c. In covert sensitization, disgusting scenes and undesirable behaviors are paired in the imagination.
   d. Modeling involves behavior change through the observation of people who demonstrate adequate behavior.

6. a. There is no such psychological procedure as *sadistic eclecticism*.
   *b. In covert sensitization, undesirable behaviors are paired in the imagination with disgusting scenes as a way of reducing the likelihood of the behaviors. (p. 531)
   c. In observational learning, new skills are acquired by imitating others.
   d. In a token economy, desirable behaviors are rewarded with tokens that can be exchanged for reinforcing activities.

7. a. Prefrontal lobotomy may reduce negative behaviors, but it has the potential side effects of permanent intellectual impairment or even death.
   b. ECT, a treatment for depression, is never used as punishment.
   *c. Lovaas has used contingent punishment with electric shock as a method of suppressing self-destructive behavior in autistic children. (p. 532)
   d. Insight-oriented psychotherapy assumes verbal skills, which are nonexistent in autistic children.

8. a. Eysenck's statistics underestimated the value of psychotherapy.
   b. Eysenck did compare treated people with untreated people.
   c. Drug therapy did not exist at the time of Eysenck's research.
   *d. A stiffer criterion for improvement was applied to treated people than to untreated ones. (p. 536)

9. *a. Family therapists argue that although children's symptoms frequently label only them as "identified patients," the whole family is hurting and in need of therapy. (p. 542)
   b. Action-oriented therapists tend to take a behavioral approach and may or may not include family members in treatment.
   c. Systematic eclectic therapists may include family therapy (if it seems appropriate), but no statements about "any attempt being doomed" would enter their vocabulary, since they tend to be flexible.
   d. Humanistic-existential therapists would focus on the subjective experience of an individual client.

10. a. Primary prevention seeks to reduce the incidence of new cases, rather than trying to identify problems early in their development.
    *b. Secondary prevention has been criticized for attempting to detect disorders early and refer for effective treatment, because diagnosis is unreliable and treatment decisions can be inappropriate for a particular patient. (p. 549)
    c. Tertiary prevention involves facilitating the integration of former inpatients into community life.
    d. *Insight* is a term associated with psychotherapy, not prevention.

CHAPTER 18
Legal and Ethical Issues in Abnormal Psychology

LEARNING OBJECTIVES

1. Describe the range of legal and ethical issues relevant to abnormal psychology. (pp. 553–555)
2. Define criminal commitment processes and discuss criminal law's position on free will. (pp. 556–557)
3. Discuss the rationale for the insanity defense and the legal precedents that have shaped the current standing of the insanity defense, including the M'Naghten Rule, the irresistible impulse test, the *Durham* standard, the American Law Institute (ALI) Model Penal Code, and diminished capacity. (pp. 557–560)
4. Discuss the arguments for and against the plea "guilty, but mentally ill," including Thomas Szasz's arguments against the insanity defense and involuntary commitment. (pp. 560–561)
5. Describe the criteria for finding a defendant competent to stand trial and the procedures involved in determining it, including due process. (pp. 561–564; Focus On)
6. Describe the concept of civil commitment and the criteria by which individuals are committed. Explain why the assessment of dangerousness is difficult. (pp. 564–566; 568–569; Focus On)
7. Explain the rationale for civil commitment, the procedures involved, and the protections that exist against its abuse. Outline the criticisms of civil commitment. (pp. 566–567)
8. Discuss the key legal rulings concerning the rights of mental patients, including the level of proof necessary for commitment *(Addington v. Texas)*, the least restrictive environment principle, and the right to treatment *(Wyatt v. Stickney*, *O'Connor v. Donaldson*, and *Youngberg v. Romeo)*. (pp. 566–569)
9. Discuss the legal rulings concerning the right to refuse treatment *(Rennie v. Klein* and *Rogers v. Okin)* and the arguments for and against this right. Define the term *least intrusive treatment*. (pp. 569–570)
10. Discuss the reasons for and the impact of the deinstitutionalization of mental patients. Evaluate the present living conditions of many ex–mental hospital patients and the prospects for mainstreaming and alternative community programs. (pp. 570–572)
11. Distinguish between the concepts of confidential and privileged communications. Discuss when therapists may disclose confidential information and where there are exemptions to privileged communications. (p. 572)
12. Describe the duty-to-warn principle, the legal rulings related to it (*Tarasoff v. Board of Regents of the University of California*), and the criticisms of the duty-to-warn principle. (pp. 573–575; Critical Thinking)

13. Identify the position of professional organizations on the issue of sexual intimacies between therapist and client. Discuss the research on the impact of therapists' sexual involvement with clients. (pp. 575–576)

14. Discuss how mental health professionals need to accommodate the changes in the ethnic profile of Americans. Describe the ethical guidelines for working with culturally different clients and the information in DSM-IV that deals with multicultural influences. (pp. 576–578)

CHAPTER OUTLINE

1. **Legal and ethical issues in abnormal psychology** (pp. 553–555) Behaviors ranging from murder to public profanity to therapists touching their clients all have legal and ethical implications. Mental health decisions involve legal issues when psychologists consider a client or defendant's claim of insanity, competence to stand trial, need for involuntary hospitalization, dangerousness to others, or rights as a patient. The *Tarasoff* case raises questions about therapists' responsibility to potential victims versus their obligation not to breach confidentiality. Ethical questions also relate to therapists' conduct with clients.

2. **Criminal commitment** (pp. 556–564; Focus On) Criminal law assumes individual actions are based on free will. *Criminal commitment*—the incarceration of an individual for having committed a crime—is the consequence of criminal acts. The *insanity defense* recognizes that individuals may not always be held accountable for their criminal actions. The Kenneth Bianchi case highlights the need for psychologists to be on guard against those faking mental illness. The *M'Naghten Rule* defines insanity as not knowing right from wrong. The *irresistible impulse test* says that insanity is also involved when a person could not control his or her actions. The *Durham standard* argues that insanity must be a product of mental disease. The *American Law Institute (ALI) code* (1962) combines earlier definitions. In some regions, the concept of diminished capacity has been added, allowing that a mental disease or defect may reduce a person's specific intent to commit a crime.

   After the successful insanity defense by John W. Hinckley, Jr., the man who attempted to assassinate President Ronald Reagan, the definition of insanity changed to the individual not understanding what he or she did. The plea of "guilty, but mentally ill" was developed as well by some states, to separate mental illness and criminal responsibility. Thomas Szasz argues against both the insanity defense and involuntary commitment as being contrary to individual liberty and responsibility.

   Competency to stand trial assesses the individual's mental state at the time of the trial. There are several criteria for competence. If individuals are found incompetent, they are committed, but only for finite periods (*Jackson v. Indiana*, 1972), thereby protecting *due process*.

3. **Civil commitment** (pp. 564–567; Focus On) Individuals can be hospitalized against their will, although this should be avoided if possible. The criteria for commitment include danger to self or others, inability to care for self, inability to make responsible decisions, and unmanageable level of panic. Assessment of *dangerousness* is very difficult because it is rare, is influenced by specific situations, is best predicted by evidence inadmissible by courts, and is ill-defined.

   Involuntary civil commitment occurs when a client does not consent to hospitalization and it follows procedures that include professional testimony, formal hearings, and set periods of treatment. Controversy exists over the helpfulness of committing people for treatment against their will.

4. **Rights of mental patients** (pp. 567–570) Mental patients can be committed only with a level of proof that is "clear and convincing" (*Addington v. Texas*, 1979). Treatment should be provided in the *least restrictive environment*, confining people to hospitals only when they cannot care for themselves in less structured settings. *Wyatt v. Stickney* (1972) established the concept of *right to treatment* and stipulated minimal living conditions for care. *O'Connor v. Donaldson* (1975) also affirmed the right to treatment, although there is debate about who defines "treatment."

Several cases have supported the patient's right to refuse treatment and to receive treatment that takes the least intrusive form possible.

5. **Deinstitutionalization** (pp. 570–572) *Deinstitutionalization* is a policy begun in the 1960s involving the discharge of patients from mental hospitals. Reasons for this movement include the belief that living in institutions is harmful, that *mainstreaming* (integrating) patients back into the community can be accomplished, and that insufficient public funds necessitate early discharge. Critics of deinstitutionalization point to the problem of "dumping" patients on city streets and to the related problem of homelessness. The lack of community resources for discharged patients is a primary reason for the problems with deinstitutionalization.

6. **The therapist-client relationship: Confidentiality and privileged communication** (pp. 572–575; Critical Thinking) Ethics prohibit therapists from divulging information given by clients, in much the same way that attorneys and doctors may not reveal information. However, there are a number of situations that call for breaking the ethical standard of *confidentiality*. A narrower legal concept is *privileged communication*, which prevents disclosure of information without the client's permission. There are at least five situations in which the therapist is obliged to disclose privileged communications. One of them is when a client is likely to carry out a threat to attack someone else. The *Tarasoff v. Board of Regents* case (1976) established the duty-to-warn principle. It is unclear whether this principle applies to clients who are infected with the AIDS virus. There are several criticisms of the duty-to-warn principle.

7. **Sexual relationships with clients** (pp. 575–576) Sexual misconduct by therapists is considered one of the most serious of all ethical violations and is condemned by virtually all professional organizations. Clients who become sexually involved with their therapists (almost always female clients with male therapists) are adversely affected. Professional organizations process ethical complaints against therapists who engage in misconduct.

8. **Cultural pluralism and the mental health profession** (pp. 576–578) The proportion of racial, cultural, and ethnic minorities in the population of the United States is increasing. Mental health professionals need to be aware of biases, have adequate training, and adjust their methods to provide culturally appropriate services. DSM-IV includes information on culture-specific symptom patterns; the American Psychological Association has published guidelines for professionals serving culturally diverse populations.

KEY TERMS REVIEW

1. The plea that defendants use if they have committed a crime but plead not guilty because of mental illness at the time of the crime is called the ____________________.

2. The shift of responsibility for the care of mental patients from large hospitals to agencies in local communities is called ____________________.

3. The form of involuntary protective confinement in which a person is judged to be dangerous to self or others, even though no crime has been committed, is called ____________________.

4. The definition of insanity stating that a defendant is not responsible if he or she lacked the will-power to control his or her behavior is called the ____________________.

5. The concept of judging whether a defendant's mental state at the time of trial is sufficient to enable the defendant to assist in his or her own defense is called ____________________.

6. The principle that patients should be placed in an environment that gives maximum freedom considering the person's capacities is called the ____________________.

7. The involuntarily committed mental patient's right to receive therapy to improve his or her emotional state is called the ____________________.

8. The assessment of an individual's potential to harm self or others is the assessment of ____________________.

9. The integration of mental patients back into the community as soon as possible after treatment is called ____________________.

10. The legal checks and balances that guarantee the right to a fair trial, to face accusers, and to present evidence (among other things) is called ____________________.

11. The legal principle that prevents clients' confidential communications with their therapists from being disclosed in court without their permission is called ____________________.

12. The incarceration of an individual on the basis of the commission of a crime is called ____________________.

13. The ethical standard that protects clients from the disclosure of information without their consent is called ____________________.

14. The test of legal insanity that combines both cognitive and motivational criteria is called the ____________________.

15. Commonly called the "duty-to-warn principle," the mental health professional's obligation to break confidentiality when a client poses a clear danger to another person is called the ____________________ ruling.

16. The test of legal insanity that asks whether the person was overcome by an irresistible impulse is called the ____________________ standard.

17. The test of legal insanity that asks whether the accused knew right from wrong at the time the crime was committed is called the ____________________ rule.

FACTUAL MULTIPLE–CHOICE QUESTIONS

1. As a result of the successful insanity defense by John W. Hinckley, Jr.,
   a. defendants claim insanity in more than 20 percent of criminal cases today.
   b. the insanity defense was abolished.
   c. some states adopted alternative pleas, such as "guilty, but mentally ill."
   d. the criteria for defining "dangerousness" were made more rigorous.

2. The *Jackson v. Indiana* ruling of 1972 protects committed patients in what way?
   a. It protects them from being committed indefinitely without review.
   b. It protects them from coercive or ineffective treatment.
   c. It protects them from inadequate living conditions.
   d. It assures that information about them will not be divulged by their therapists.

3. Which statement about dangerousness in mental patients is *most accurate?*
   a. Psychologists tend to underpredict dangerousness in patients.
   b. Dangerousness is rarely used as a criterion for civil commitment.
   c. Psychiatric patients are no more dangerous to others than is the population at large.
   d. Among mental patients, the legal determination of dangerousness has little impact on whether or not violence will occur.

4. Which statement about involuntary civil commitment proceedings is *accurate?*
   a. Judges have sole discretion to decide whether the person needs to be in treatment.
   b. The person being examined can speak on his or her own behalf and is represented by counsel.
   c. In some states, a family physician can commit a person.
   d. A jury always decides whether a person needs to be committed.

5. *Addington v. Texas* (1979) has had its greatest impact on
   a. deinstitutionalization.
   b. the ethics of divulging confidential client information.
   c. the insanity defense.
   d. the standards used to determine civil commitment.

6. The principle of ____________________ argues that patients should be confined to hospitals only when they are unable to care for themselves.
   a. deinstitutionalization
   b. most intrusive treatment
   c. least restrictive environment
   d. privileged communication

7. The right of patients to receive adequate care in a satisfactory living environment was based on rulings in which cases?
   a. *Wyatt v. Stickney* and *O'Connor v. Donaldson*
   b. *Tarasoff v. Board of Regents* and *Rouse v. Cameron*
   c. *Jackson v. Indiana* and *Tarasoff v. Board of Regents*
   d. *Rogers v. Okin* and *United States v. Hinckley*

8. According to a recent court ruling, who decides what constitutes "therapy"?
   a. Mental health professionals
   b. A jury
   c. The patient and his or her family
   d. No one; this has not been legally determined.

9. Research on sexual relationships between therapists and clients indicates that
   a. more than one-third of male therapists admit to having had sexual intercourse with clients.
   b. complaints to state licensing boards about sexual misconduct have dropped dramatically in recent years.
   c. while sexual involvement with therapists is rather common, it rarely has a harmful effect.
   d. sexual intimacy has adverse effects on nearly all clients.

10. What changes have occurred in the DSM-IV that relate to clinical work with individuals from culturally diverse backgrounds?
    a. It now points out the disorders that never or rarely occur in certain cultural groups.
    b. It now explains the genetic basis for disorders occurring in certain cultural groups.
    c. It now gives guidelines on how symptoms of disorders among cultural groups may vary.
    d. It now instructs clinicians how to treat clients from culturally diverse backgrounds so their behavior becomes more similar to those in the majority culture.

CONCEPTUAL MULTIPLE–CHOICE QUESTIONS

1. According to the M'Naghten Rule, defendants are insane if, at the time of
   a. their trial, they cannot assist in their own defense.
   b. the crime, they did not understand the wrongfulness of their actions.
   c. the crime, they were unable to control their actions.
   d. their trial, they are severely mentally ill.

2. When psychologists assess a defendant to determine his or her competency to stand trial, they are interested in the
   a. person's mental state at present.
   b. person's dangerousness.
   c. availability and effectiveness of treatment alternatives.
   d. person's mental state at the time of the crime.

3. Being unable to care for oneself, being a dangerous threat to someone else, or being in a severe state of panic are
   a. ways of defining dangerousness.
   b. reasons for declaring someone insane.
   c. reasons for being allowed to refuse treatment.
   d. reasons for involuntary commitment.

4. If, in the future, the use of ECT and psychosurgery to treat mildly disturbed patients is not permitted, this can be attributed to the
   a. principle of duty to warn.
   b. need for patients to be competent before being tried.
   c. concept of deinstitutionalization.
   d. principle of least intrusive treatment.

5. Which statement about deinstitutionalization is *accurate*?
   a. Despite thirty years of efforts to reduce the number of mental patients in hospitals, no decrease has occurred.
   b. The goal of deinstitutionalization was to eliminate the insanity defense.
   c. Generally speaking, deinstitutionalization has led to the successful reintegration of mental patients into their home communities.
   d. Deinstitutionalization has been very successful in reducing the number of patients in state mental hospitals.

6. Which problem is *most* directly related to deinstitutionalization?
   a. Therapists unethically engaging in sexual relations with their clients
   b. Large numbers of discharged patients becoming homeless
   c. A dramatic increase in the number of successful insanity defense cases
   d. Greater abuse and neglect of patients in mental hospitals

7. The need for trust and openness in psychotherapy is the reason for
   a. the principle of duty to warn.
   b. deinstitutionalization.
   c. confidentiality of client information.
   d. the principle of least restrictive environment.

8. The concept of privileged communication is
   a. a legal one, similar to the arrangement between husband and wife.
   b. an ethical one that involves no legal obligation.
   c. a recent "invention" stemming from the *Tarasoff v. Board of Regents* (1976) ruling.
   d. not as available to the therapist and client as it is to the attorney and client.

9. Which statement about privileged communication is *accurate*?
   a. It can be broken when the therapist feels it would be helpful for therapy.
   b. It is a legal concept and is held by the client, not the therapist.
   c. The only exemption from privileged communication occurs in criminal cases.
   d. It is defined as an ethical standard protecting clients from disclosure of information.

10. Acccording to the American Psychological Association's ethical principles involving the treatment of culturally different clients,
   a. therapy is forbidden if the therapist and client come from different cultural backgrounds.
   b. therapists should have adequate training in multicultural psychology.
   c. it is the client's responsibility to conform to the cultural expectations of the therapist.
   d. therapists should focus on the symptoms of disorders, not the cultural or environmental influences of clients from culturally diverse backgrounds.

APPLICATION MULTIPLE–CHOICE QUESTIONS

1. The Kenneth Bianchi (Hillside Strangler) case illustrates the issue of
   a. competency to stand trial.
   b. deinstitutionalization.
   c. faking insanity.
   d. privileged communication between therapist and client.

2. David T. is a defendant in a murder case. He claims that a mental disorder prevented him from acting in any way other than the way he did. David T.'s insanity defense is based on
   a. the principle of least restrictive treatment.
   b. the notion of irresistible impulse.
   c. the M'Naghten Rule.
   d. the principle of competency to stand trial.

3. George is being examined by a psychiatrist to see whether he can assist his attorney in his own defense. In what kind of legal hearing is George engaged?
   a. Competency to stand trial
   b. Involuntary civil commitment
   c. Waiver of privileged communication
   d. An insanity defense trial

4. Judge Wallace says, "Thanks to *Jackson v. Indiana*, people are protected against the abuse of endless incarceration when they have committed no crime." The judge is talking about
   a. a ruling restricting deinstitutionalization.
   b. the new "guilty, but mentally ill" plea.
   c. the principle of least restrictive treatment environment.
   d. a ruling restricting confinement based solely on the grounds of incompetency.

5. Dr. Roland says, "When people are so mentally ill that they cannot control their actions and may harm others, we cannot wait until they have become violent. We must treat them involuntarily." Dr. Roland's comments argue
   a. against the insanity defense.
   b. against deinstitutionalization.
   c. for the concept of duty to warn.
   d. for civil commitment.

6. Mr. Birch, an attorney, says, "If this person is going to be involuntarily committed, the judge needs to have 'clear and convincing evidence' that the person is mentally ill and potentially dangerous." Mr. Birch is using the ruling in
   a. *Tarasoff v. Board of Regents* (1976).
   b. *Addington v. Texas* (1979).
   c. *Wyatt v. Stickney* (1972).
   d. *United States v. Hinckley* (1982).

7. Dr. Poole, director of a state hospital, says, "Because of deinstitutionalization, we need to release patients quickly. Although treatment is not required after discharge, while they are here, they have the right to the treatment standards outlined in *Wyatt v. Stickney*." What part of Dr. Poole's statement is *inaccurate*?
   a. The idea that deinstitutionalization might lead to quick discharge.
   b. The idea that *Wyatt v. Stickney* is linked to patients' rights.
   c. The idea that the right to treatment ends when a person is discharged.
   d. Nothing in Dr. Poole's statement is inaccurate.

8. Dr. Luborsky says, "It has reduced the number of patients in state hospitals by more than 50 percent but has led to the criminalization of the mentally ill and has increased the problem of homelessness in the United States." Dr. Luborsky is commenting on
   a. deinstitutionalization.
   b. the insanity defense.
   c. the right to refuse treatment.
   d. the principle of duty to warn.

9. Dr. Judd's patient, Mike V., is threatening to blow up his father-in-law's store. Dr. Judd thinks the threat is legitimate. According to ________________, Dr. Judd must ________________.
   a. *Rogers v. Okin* (1979); not divulge this information to the police
   b. *Wyatt v. Stickney* (1972); have Mike V. committed
   c. *Tarasoff v. Board of Regents* (1976); warn Mike's father-in-law
   d. *Youngberg v. Romeo* (1982); have Mike V. arrested

10. Vanessa saw a male psychotherapist for seven months. Toward the end of that time the therapist engaged in sexual intercourse with her. Vanessa can expect
   a. to find that none of the professional organizations for therapists will condemn sexual intimacies in therapist-client relationships.
   b. to suffer emotionally from this experience.
   c. to learn, unfortunately, that there are no ways to file ethical complaints against the therapist.
   d. to feel more and more independent of her therapist as a result of this behavior.

ANSWER KEY: KEY TERMS REVIEW

1. insanity defense (557)
2. deinstitutionalization (570)
3. civil commitment (564)
4. irresistible impulse test (559)
5. competency to stand trial (561)
6. least restrictive environment (567)
7. right to treatment (567)
8. dangerousness (565)
9. mainstreaming (570)
10. due process (563)
11. privileged communication (572)
12. criminal commitment (556)
13. confidentiality (572)
14. American Law Institute (ALI) Model Penal Code (560)
15. *Tarasoff* ruling (573)
16. *Durham* standard (559)
17. M'Naghten Rule (559)

ANSWER KEY: FACTUAL MULTIPLE–CHOICE QUESTIONS

1. a. The insanity defense is used in less than 1 percent of criminal cases.
   b. The insanity defense still exists but in a somewhat more restricted form.
   *c. The furor after the verdict led to the American Bar and Medical associations' requests for changes in the law, to the Insanity Reform Act of 1984, and to several states developing new pleas. (p. 560)
   d. Dangerousness is an issue in civil commitment cases, not in the insanity defense.

2. *a. Because of this ruling, people who are committed because they are incompetent to stand trial cannot be confined indefinitely without review. (p. 563)
   b. Relevant right to treatment rulings include *Wyatt v. Stickney* and *O'Connor v. Donaldson.*
   c. The relevant ruling here is *Wyatt v. Stickney.*
   d. This ruling deals with indefinite confinement, not privileged communication.

3. a. The error that psychologists make is *over*predicting dangerousness.
   b. Dangerousness is the chief criterion for civil commitment.
   *c. Despite the popular myth, few psychotic patients are assaultive and psychotic patients have only slightly higher rates of violent behavior than the population at large. (p. 565)
   d. Just as with other people, violent behavior among those with mental disorders is the result of both personality and situational factors.

4. a. Expert witnesses, such as psychologists and psychiatrists, testify to provide their assessments of the person's need for treatment.
   *b. Civil commitment proceedings include due process; the person can speak on his or her own behalf and have legal counsel. (p. 566)
   c. No longer can one person determine that another person should be committed; the legal proceedings provide greater protection of civil rights now.
   d. In most cases, commitment is decided by a judge, not a jury.

5. a. Deinstitutionalization is most affected by rulings involving the least restrictive environment principle.
   b. *Addington* had nothing to do with confidentiality.
   c. *Addington* had nothing to do with the placement of mental patients.
   *d. *Addington* raised the level of proof in civil commitment cases to "clear and convincing evidence" (75-percent certainty). (p. 567)

6. a. Deinstitutionalization is a related, but much broader, idea that considers all the reasons for using community agencies rather than large institutions.
   b. The legal principle is *least* intrusive treatment.
   *c. To ensure civil liberties, the principle of least restrictive environment allows for hospitalization only as a last resort. (p. 567)
   d. The principle of privileged communication is confined to therapist-client relationships.

7. *a. The *Wyatt* ruling of Judge Frank Johnson set the standards for mental treatment in institutions; *O'Connor* supported the right-to-treatment principle. (pp. 567–568)
   b. *Tarasoff* dealt with duty to warn; *Rouse* did involve right to treatment.
   c. *Jackson* limited the duration of confinement for people found incompetent; *Tarasoff* dealt with duty to warn.
   d. *Rogers* dealt with the right to refuse treatment; *Hinckley* was the insanity defense case involving the man who shot President Ronald Reagan.

8. *a. The case is *Youngberg v. Romeo* (1982), and the decision was that mental health professionals should define "therapy." (p. 569)
   b. *Youngberg* ruled that professionals decide.
   c. *Youngberg* ruled that professionals decide.
   d. Although the law in this area is new, the *Youngberg* case does give guidance.

9. a In a survey of 1,000 psychologists, 5.5 percent of the males admitted to sexual intercourse with clients.
   b. Complaints have increased significantly.
   c. In a survey of clients sexually involved with therapists, 90 percent reported being negatively affected.
   *d. In a survey of clients sexually involved with therapists, 90 percent reported being negatively affected. (p. 576)

10. a. DSM-IV lists disorders that may be culturally specific, but does not point out those that are absent in certain cultures.
    b. The DSM-IV omits all discussion of cause, genetics or otherwise.
    *c. A new section in DSM-IV provides guidelines on how clinical presentation of disorders among cultural groups may vary. (p. 577)
    d. Rather than expecting clients to conform to the behavior of the majority culture, DSM-IV seeks to reduce clinicians' possible cultural bias.

ANSWER KEY: CONCEPTUAL MULTIPLE–CHOICE QUESTIONS

1. a. The ability to assist in one's own defense is a criterion for competency to stand trial, not for insanity.
   *b. The M'Naghten Rule is a cognitive test that defines insanity in terms of the inability to know right from wrong when the crime was committed. (p. 559)
   c. Irresistible impulse is the definition of insanity as an incapacity to control one's actions.
   d. The insanity defense pertains only to the person's mental state when the crime was committed.

2. *a. Competency to stand trial is based on the defendant's current ability to understand the proceedings and to assist in his or her own defense. (p. 561)
   b. Dangerousness is most closely related to civil commitment cases, not competency.
   c. The availability of treatment does not pertain to competency to stand trial.
   d. The person's mental state at the time of the crime influences the validity of an insanity defense.

3. a. Although presenting a threat to someone else is a part of "dangerousness," the rest of the information suggests the broader category of concern, the need for commitment.
   b. Insanity is defined as being unable to appreciate the wrongfulness of an act or being incapable of resisting an impulse.
   c. Reasons for refusing treatment have more to do with delusional thinking than with dangerousness or a state of panic.
   *d. Dangerousness, an inability to care for oneself, and an extreme attack of anxiety are reasons for committing people to treatment against their will. (p. 564)

4. a. Duty to warn defines a situation in which therapists must break confidentiality.
   b. Competency is unrelated to treatment issues.
   c. Deinstitutionalization is concerned with *where* treatment occurs, not so much with the matching of patients and therapy methods.
   *d. This principle suggests that ECT and surgery are more intrusive therapies than insight or behavioral therapies and thus should not be used with mildly disturbed patients. (p. 569)

5. a. Deinstitutionalization has reduced hospital populations by more than one-half.
   b. The goal of deinstitutionalization was to dramatically reduce the reliance on hospitals for treatment.
   c. The great failure of deinstitutionalization is that discharged patients, lacking community support, return to the hospital.
   *d. The state hospital population of the United States dropped by more than 50 percent, and the average daily number of committed patients decreased by 75 percent. (p. 570)

6. a. Deinstitutionalization is unrelated to therapist-client relationships.
   *b. In many cases, discharged patients have been "dumped" in urban areas, and have no homes or social supports. (p. 571)
   c. Deinstitutionalization is unrelated to criminal commitment.
   d. If anything, the reduced populations in mental hospitals have led to improvements in care.

7. a. The duty-to-warn principle puts greater emphasis on protecting victims than on assuring confidentiality; this reduces openness.
   b. Deinstitutionalization is unrelated to therapist-client relationships.
   *c. Confidentiality in therapy is necessary if clients are to believe that they can be open without fearing that they may be hurt. (p. 571)
   d. This principle considers only the location of treatment.

8. *a. Privileged communication between therapist and client is a legal concept. (p. 572)
   b. It is the wider concept of confidentiality that is an ethical concept unprotected by the law.
   c. *Tarasoff* defined when privileged communication must be breached.
   d. Therapists and clients have the same legal privilege as attorneys and their clients.

9. a. The privilege is in the hands of the client, not the therapist.
   *b. Privileged communication is a legal concept; the privilege is the client's and only the client can waive it. (p. 572)
   c. There are other exemptions for the privilege: civil cases, cases involving civil commitment, and cases in which the client is under sixteen and the victim of a crime or abuse.
   d. Confidentiality is an ethical standard that has broader reach than the legal concept of privileged communication.

10. a. As long as therapists are aware of cultural differences and provide appropriate treatment, there is nothing to prohibit cross-cultural treatment.
   *b. Psychologists are expected to be aware of cultural differences and their own biases, to be able to identify situations in which specific therapeutic strategies must be modified to be culturally sensitive, and to obtain sufficient training to do these things. (p. 577)
   c. Ethical principles place responsibility for adjusting to cultural differences on the therapist, not the client.
   d. DSM-IV has an appendix that presents culture-bound syndromes; the APA ethical guidelines require psychologists to adjust treatment to be culturally appropriate.

ANSWER KEY: APPLICATION MULTIPLE–CHOICE QUESTIONS

1. a. Bianchi's lawyers considered using the insanity defense.
   b. Bianchi was on trial for a series of murders; he was not a mental patient.
   *c. Until Martin Orne uncovered Bianchi's faking, it was believed that he was suffering from multiple personality (dissociative identity) disorder. (pp. 558–559)
   d. Bianchi was not in therapy, so there was no such issue.

2. a. Treatment becomes an issue only after a person is found incompetent or insane.
   *b. Irresistible impulse is one definition of insanity; it is based on an inability to conform to the law because of a mental disease or defect. (p. 559)
   c. The M'Naghten Rule is a cognitive definition of insanity based on the lack of appreciation that what one did was wrong.
   d. Competency is defined as mental capacity at the time of the trial, not at the time of the crime.

3. *a. Competency involves a defendant's capacity to understand the proceedings and to assist in his or her own defense. (p. 561)
   b. Such an assessment assumes that a crime was committed; in civil commitment, no crime is presumed.
   c. Waiver of privileged communication is not based on a person's ability to act in his or her own defense.
   d. Insanity is concerned with a defendant's mental state at the time of the crime, not at the time of the trial.

4. a. *Jackson* protected people against indefinite confinement; the ruling supports deinstitutionalization.
   b. *Jackson* (1972) occurred some ten years before the Hinckley case, which led to calls for more stringent definitions of insanity.
   c. *Jackson* dealt only with how long a person could be confined, not where.
   *d. The *Jackson* ruling held that those who were committed because they were not competent to stand trial could not be "forgotten" and must either stand trial or be committed for treatment. (p. 563)

5. a. The insanity defense is unrelated to treatment.
   b. Although these comments have relevance to deinstitutionalization, that concept is much broader and deals with the need for community-based treatment.
   c. Duty to warn involves therapist-client relationships, not criminal cases.
   *d. Civil commitment deals with confining people for treatment before they have committed any crime. (p. 564)

6. a. *Tarasoff* decided the therapist's role in protecting potential victims of his or her client.
   *b. *Addington* determined necessary levels of proof in commitment cases. (p. 567)
   c. *Wyatt* established the right to treatment and the conditions under which treatment should be offered.
   d. *Hinckley* dealt with the insanity defense.

7. a. Deinstitutionalization has led to earlier discharge.
   b. *Wyatt* was a major case supporting the patient's right to treatment.
   c. There is no court ruling that suggests hospitals must provide treatment after discharge.
   *d. Because a, b, and c are all correct, there is nothing inaccurate in Dr. Poole's comments. (pp. 567–570)

8. *a. Deinstitutionalization has led to a reduction in hospital populations, but discharged patients often do not receive support in urban communities and wind up homeless or in jail. (pp. 570–571)
   b. The insanity defense has nothing to do with state hospital populations.
   c. The right to refuse treatment may lead to more untreated mental patients, but it does not as clearly lead to homelessness.
   d. Duty to warn is related to therapist-client relationships, not to hospitalization.

9. a. *Rogers* is a case involving the right to refuse treatment.
   b. *Wyatt* is a case involving the right to adequate treatment.
   *c. *Tarasoff* is the case that established the principle of duty to warn; Dr. Judd would be negligent if she did not warn. (p. 573)
   d. *Youngberg* is a case involving the definition of "treatment" for commited patients.

10. a. Virtually every organization that represents psychotherapists condemns sexual intimacy between therapist and client as unethical, immoral, and antitherapeutic.
    *b. In a survey of 559 clients who became sexually intimate with their therapists, 90 percent were adversely affected, many showing symptoms similar to those of rape and battered-spouse syndrome. (p. 576)
    c. Most states and professional organizations have means for filing ethical complaints; civil suits charging malpractice are always a legal recourse.
    d. Rather than become more independent, many clients become more dependent on their therapist following sexual intimacy.